Our Children Can't Wait

The Urgency of Reinventing Education Policy in America

Edited by Joseph P. Bishop

Foreword by Becky Pringle

TEACHERS COLLEGE PRESS
TEACHERS COLLEGE | COLUMBIA UNIVERSITY
NEW YORK AND LONDON

Published by Teachers College Press,® 1234 Amsterdam Avenue, New York, NY 10027

Copyright © 2023 by Teachers College, Columbia University

All rights reserved. No part of this publication may be reproduced or transmitted in any form or by any means, electronic or mechanical, including photocopy, or any information storage and retrieval system, without permission from the publisher. For reprint permission and other subsidiary rights requests, please contact Teachers College Press, Rights Dept.: tcpressrights@tc.columbia.edu

Library of Congress Cataloging-in-Publication Data is available at loc.gov

ISBN 978-0-8077-6710-8 (paper)
ISBN 978-0-8077-6711-5 (hardcover)
ISBN 978-0-8077-8110-4 (ebook)

Printed on acid-free paper
Manufactured in the United States of America

Contents

Foreword   *Becky Pringle*   v

Acknowledgments   vii

1. **Our Children Can't Wait: The Urgency of Reinventing Education Policy in America**   1
   Joseph P. Bishop

2. **Grappling With America's History to Inform Our Future Policies**   11
   Arnold F. Fege and John H. Jackson

3. **Making Children a National Priority: Overcoming the Marginalization and Invisibility of Children**   23
   Bruce Lesley

4. **Whose Vision of Racial Equity?: Reinventing Education Policy in Post–Civil Rights America**   41
   Sonya Douglass and Anna Kushner

5. **Developing Policy for the Whole Child**   58
   Linda Darling-Hammond and Channa Mae Cook

6. **Starting in School: Education Policies to Dismantle Systemic Racism**   76
   Tyrone C. Howard

7. **Youths' Health and Learning Connection**   92
   Alexandra Mays and Rochelle Davis

8. **Air Pollution, Exposure to Contaminants, and Education Policy**   109
   Sara Grineski and Timothy Collins

9. **Promoting Equity and Justice Through Integrated Schools and Communities** 133
   Jennifer B. Ayscue and Erica Frankenberg

10. **Housing Strategies as Education Policy** 154
    Megan Gallagher

11. **Reimagining School Safety During and After the COVID-19 Pandemic: A Call for Policy Strategies to Address Racial and Social Justice** 174
    Heather M. Reynolds and Ron Avi Astor

12. **Toward Transformative Justice in School Finance** 194
    Oscar Jiménez-Castellanos, Danielle Farrie, and David M. Quinn

13. **Youth Wildin' in the (Re)Shaping of Policy: Toward a Critical Model of Racial Justice and Community Accountability** 212
    Justin A. Coles, Keisha L. Green, and Jamila Lyiscott

14. **Youth Incarceration and Education Policy** 232
    Angela James

15. **Students Experiencing Homelessness: A National Crisis** 251
    Matthew H. Morton, Earl J. Edwards, and Melissa Kull

16. **Bringing the Vision Together: How to Reach the Policies We Need** 269
    Joseph P. Bishop

About the Contributors 281

Index 285

Foreword

At the height of the coronavirus pandemic, I was elected to lead the 3-million-member National Education Association—our country's largest labor union. We represent teachers, support staff, nurses, counselors, higher-education faculty, retired educators, and college students who aspire to be educators.

Thanks to my 30-plus years as a middle school science teacher, and long before COVID-19, I was well acquainted with the creativity, determination, and commitment that our nation's public school educators display every day as they work to prepare our students for the future.

When school buildings closed, educators shifted into an even higher, more heroic gear. They stepped into the gaps—as they always have and they always will—making sure that our students had access to the technology they needed to learn, providing students and families with the food they needed to eat, and so much more. In states, districts, communities, and schools across this nation, public school educators continued to light the spark for growth, change, purpose, and progress. I was not surprised. Rather, I was more proud than ever to be an educator.

The herculean efforts of educators forced the nation to see the faces of students, most of whom are Black, Brown, Indigenous, and living in marginalized communities and for whom the pandemic exacerbated inequities that are steeped in racism, which has for decades formed barriers to learning for far too many of our pupils.

Led by UCLA researcher Dr. Joseph P. Bishop, the masterful compilation of experts who speak from the pages of *Our Children Can't Wait* present a comprehensive examination of the many policies—from public health, funding, housing, and segregation and more—that fuel those inequities, affecting the lives, limitations, expectations, and mental and emotional challenges, especially in the wake of the global coronavirus pandemic, that our students bring with them through our schoolhouse doors.

Most importantly, this book makes clear that policy changes are not the remedy. Rather, for sustainable change to occur, this nation must also change what it does *and* what it prioritizes. That is the only way that we will build the racial and social justice that form the cornerstones of education justice.

Our Children Can't Wait is the right book at the right time. It provides an unapologetically clear-eyed view at the way in which racism has shaped both our nation and its public school system, and supplies detailed roadmaps for navigating the way forward, toward a future in which every student—Black, White, Brown, Indigenous, and Asian Americans and Pacific Islanders, LGBTQ+ and differently abled—can step boldly into their brilliance. This book contains the wisdom that will help us to build a future in which *every student* means *every student*.

Together, we will reclaim public education as a common good, and then transform it into something it was never designed to be—a racially and socially just and equitable system that prepares every student, everyone, to succeed in a diverse and interdependent world.

As Frederick Douglass said in his 1889 speech titled "The Nation's Problem," "The duty of today is to meet the questions that confront us with intelligence and courage." Within *Our Children Can't Wait*, Dr. Bishop and the expert authors he has assembled honor Douglass's call to duty with the turn of every page.

—Becky Pringle, President, National Education Association

Acknowledgments

Edited volumes are the result of many people working together toward a common goal, and this book is no exception. I am truly grateful for the support of many generous people and organizations like the Stuart Foundation and National Education Association, especially my family and friends. Without the unconditional support of my wife, Kristin, and our boys, this book would have stayed just another idea during the pandemic. They were the inspiration behind the countless hours of brainstorming, writing, editing, emails, and phone calls required for completing a book.

The intellectual seeds for this book took shape based on an article I coauthored with Pedro Noguera on the ecology of educational equity supported by the Stuart Foundation and The California Endowment. Thank you to our sensational team at the Center for the Transformation of Schools at UCLA for the critical work we do together, especially the *Beyond the Schoolhouse* research team. Tyrone Howard, faculty director for the Center, believed in this book from the beginning and was a constant source of encouragement throughout the process.

Critical editorial support for the book was provided by the Teachers College Press team, especially Brian Ellerbeck, Caritza Berlioz, and John Bylander.

This book never would have been possible without the willingness of longtime and newfound colleagues, experts, and scholars who agreed to write chapters for *Our Children Can't Wait*. The book's readers will benefit from their deep expertise, passion, commitment, and belief in a more just world. I will always be grateful to this group of contributors who made this book a priority during a time of extraordinary stress, loss, and uncertainty.

CHAPTER 1

Our Children Can't Wait
The Urgency of Reinventing Education Policy in America

Joseph P. Bishop

And so, emancipation for the Negro was really freedom to hunger. It was freedom to the winds and rains of Heaven. It was freedom without food to eat or land to cultivate and, therefore, was freedom and famine at the same time. And when White Americans tell the Negro to "lift himself by his own bootstraps," they look over the legacy of slavery and segregation. I believe we ought to do all we can and seek to lift ourselves by our own bootstraps, but it's a cruel jest to say to a bootless man that he ought to lift himself by his own bootstraps. And many Negroes by the thousands and millions have been left bootless because of all of these years of oppression and as a result of a society that deliberately made his color a stigma and something worthless and degrading.

—Dr. Martin Luther King Jr., May 8, 1967, *NBC News* Interview

OUR CHILDREN CAN'T WAIT: AN OVERVIEW

In this edited volume, scholars challenge inequality as something inevitable in America's schools and society, focusing on new, broader social policy responses to address persistent disparities in academic outcomes apparent by race and income. We explore the perspectives of multiple experts on interrelated policies beyond schools that profoundly affect students, such as neighborhood conditions, public health, community resources, housing, air quality, school safety, and segregation. To be clear, the chapters ahead are not about making excuses but are carefully written to spur productive thinking to help change behaviors, priorities, and systems for practitioners and lawmakers alike. We assert that factors outside of schools are contributing to the growth of students experiencing homelessness and the incarceration for young people of color, both examples of what happens when policies ignore broken systems and poor conditions for learning and health. We help readers reconsider with some of the best minds in the country what education policy is, what it could be, who it's for, and who should be shaping policy more directly at all levels of government. Finally, we make a compelling moral and economic argument that the United States must invest in ecosystems of support for students of color across the nation. Without a more precise racial equity policy focus, too many jobs will continue to be left unfilled with an aging population and shifting economic landscape, requiring higher-level social or analytical skills, or both (Pew Research Center, 2016).

Professional organizations that serve lawmakers, staff of policymakers, educators, organizers, philanthropists, and students studying policy as a vehicle for justice and equity, the ideas and research in this book is waiting for you to be applied to your day-to-day work. This book was curated because I saw a major gap in how we conceptualize policy and policy processes (see Chapter 16) both in state houses and in research. Too often we separate policies into neat, tidy buckets that don't exist. *Our Children Can't Wait* attempts to tie issues, frameworks, and efforts together in ways we haven't seen done yet.

To explore fundamental ideas of the book further, we have assembled an extraordinary team of experts. For each chapter, scholars briefly describe the significance of an issue (e.g., health, funding, safety) and its relationship to educational outcomes for students of color, then cast a new vision for policies based on promising examples. Each chapter concludes with local, state, and federal examples for readers and lawmakers to consider. The final chapter aims to integrate ideas and recommendations across chapters and offer readers a framework for policy action that can be applied to multiple settings. The book is organized into two sections: Part I, the historical, political, and policy landscape and Part II, the path forward.

In Chapters 2, 3, and 4, authors set the stage for what readers and lawmakers must consider when rethinking the purpose and power of education policy. In Chapter 2, Arnold F. Fege and John H. Jackson help readers make sense of how Reconstruction after Emancipation and the ideals of education at the center of democracy must be considered as part of the policy landscape. Bruce Lesley in Chapter 3 explains how political views toward children have made children's rights and policies an uphill battle. Both chapters leave readers with driving values to navigate the remaining chapters. In Chapter 4, Sonya Douglass and Anna Kushner fast-forward to the present, describing the characteristics of the current social, political, and cultural landscape of a "post–civil rights America." Such a place in which new policies centered on justice must be considered to produce meaningful change in the lives of Black, Indigenous, and historically marginalized communities is explored. The authors also make a bold request for research that doesn't just flip the script on reducing inequality but rather aims to dismantle it altogether.

In Chapter 5, Linda Darling-Hammond and Channa Mae Cook establish the need for a new national compass for organizing policies, aligned to emerging sciences on human development and student learning to support the whole child in the wake of unprecedented challenges for young people. They show how policies can play an instrumental role in fostering stronger relationships among adults and students and to ensure student development—physical, psychological, cognitive, social, and emotional.

In Chapter 6, Tyrone C. Howard returns to the seminal importance of school-centered policies to address systemic racism. The author describes how goals around disrupting differences in academic outcomes by race and income can be achieved by focusing on three key areas: (1) mental-health support; (2) strategies that can create opportunities to learn; and (3) discipline practices and policies that highlight specific examples of policies that fall within these focus areas.

In Chapter 7, Alexandra Mays and Rochelle Davis pivot from the clear relationship between healthy schools and student learning to spotlighting promising policies focused on healthy living and learning environments. The authors make a convincing case that health and wellness must guide education policy at all levels of government. This includes more funding mechanisms in place to ensure states, school districts, and schools have the resources needed to effectively implement health-centered policies.

In Chapter 8, Sara Grineski and Timothy Collins illustrate how environmental conditions surrounding schools and families can play a profound role in shaping students' health and achievement. The authors explore the nexus between an environmental justice and education justice agenda, showing how policies, in particular school-siting laws, or where a school is located and maintained, can prevent pollutants from reaching young people.

In Chapter 9, Jennifer B. Ayscue and Erica Frankenberg explore how racially and economically segregated neighborhoods are solidifying a profoundly unequal playing field in which to support student and family health and learning. The authors then cast a new vision of integrated schools and communities with immense social benefits, centering on regional approaches, fueled by greater political participation and efforts across education, housing, and transportation.

In Chapter 10, Megan Gallagher describes the essentiality of a high-quality, stable housing environment for students to thrive, with partnerships and policies from the field that are beginning to make a dent in housing equity issues that prioritize basic needs and social footing for families. The author outlines that the bridge between housing and academic success can be achieved through greater alignment between the housing and education sectors that prioritize low-income families of color.

In Chapter 11, Heather M. Reynolds and Ron Avi Astor set an inspiring vision for school and community safety, explaining how we can begin to shift funding and support from policing, punishment, and surveillance to long-term investments in prevention and empowerment of schools and communities. Cities, school boards, and states, the authors argue, can better utilize school safety assessments, capacity building, integration of academic and social goals, and partnerships with community organizations to achieve healthier, safer conditions for young people, families, and caregivers.

In Chapter 12, Oscar Jiménez-Castellanos, Danielle Farrie, and David M. Quinn recognize how the current ways in which schools and communities are funded reinforce the dysfunction of the greater economic and social system. The authors outline a new way of thinking about finance systems through a transformative justice paradigm to uproot existing structural challenges that often have been ignored in how public funds are allocated—a path toward resource redistribution and community building.

In Chapter 13, Justin Coles, Keisha L. Green, and Jamila Lyiscott challenge old paradigms for policymaking, showing how policies can be crafted with and for young people, especially historically marginalized youth of color. The authors give examples of how a youth-organizing policy framework grounded in racial justice can be utilized to fundamentally change today's social, political, and economic landscape.

In Chapter 14, Angela James describes a justice system that is growing with young people of color who are more likely to be housing insecure, in the foster-care system, or neglected by other social investments and policies. The author speaks to the moral and economic costs of having the highest rate of youth incarceration in the world, highlighting new evidence for better serving young people who are incarcerated. James presents a new policy anatomy for consideration at the local, state, and federal level in a way that emphasizes prevention, strategic investments, and personalized responses for young people that removes them from isolated, harmful, and punitive settings.

In Chapter 15, Matthew H. Morton, Earl J. Edwards, and Melissa Kull bring to light an issue that has been overlooked for generations but has grown to the point of a national crisis: the 1.3 million young people in the nation's K–12 systems who experience homelessness. The authors describe the policy landscape for supporting young people who are housing insecure and detail a vision in which young people are identified early for services and in which schools are the hub of delivering support for more upstream approaches.

In Chapter 16, I conclude with a framework that ties the policy themes across chapters together to acknowledge the ecology of systemic racism in our society and a new way of constructing social policies for the benefit of student development, learning, and health. Ecosystems of care at the city, district, regional, state, and federal levels represent a promising path forward if we are serious about a policy agenda extending beyond schools to create mobility across generational, racial, and economic differences. I begin to outline a plan for reaching an untouched policy terrain.

These chapters intend to cause policy upheaval and discomfort for the current political terrain, challenging readers to reimagine a new frontier where courageous leadership is achievable in today's politically polarized world to focus on structural issues like housing, health, the environment and their relationship to education. We recognize that what we are proposing faces an uphill battle in school-board meetings, city government, statehouses, and the hall of Congress (Hess & Noguera, 2021).

Regardless, there is great hope that the ideas and examples presented in *Our Children Can't Wait* leave us with a sense of unfulfilled promise to dream and wonder about what could be possible in a more just America. What if our policies reflected love, care, and strategic investments in young people and families? The Schott Foundation for Public Education recently asked that exact question, looking across cities at policies through its Loving Cities Index from Oakland, CA, to Minneapolis, MN, to Jackson, MS, and Springfield, MA, to determine where more bold policies that prioritize many of the themes outlined in this book are needed to right our past failings (Schott Foundation for Public Education, 2020).

Each chapter is grounded in strong evidence of a new policy path that can only be strengthened by the moral urgency of this moment to support youth like Sean described below, who are capable but deserve more personalized focus and policy support. Readers are left to consider whether we will continue to waste great human potential and double-down on investments in the justice system or alternatively invest in positive, healthy neighborhoods and schools for young children and families across America. The clock is ticking. Our children and our country can't wait for the policies that have escaped the grasp of far too many generations.

JUST PASSING THROUGH:
SEAN'S STORY AS FUEL FOR NEW POLICIES

Sitting in a mustard-yellow classroom chair on the top floor of a drop-in center for unhoused youth, I look across the table at a young man in his early 20s. Sean, who identifies as Latino, is decked out in college football swag, new attire from the drop-in center. At night, he is on his own without family or loved ones, sometimes sleeping on the street, couch surfing, or moving from one location to another. We speak after his long morning commute by bus across Los Angeles County. Sean shares with me that he attended six different districts and countless schools before he stopped going to school. When he talks about his schooling history, he describes a system in which he felt overlooked and uncared for: "I felt like I was passing through."

Sean's "passing through" reflects structural challenges in our society, realities that have come to define life in America for many youths, especially young people of color. Schools have a clear responsibility to play in the equation to support students but cannot tackle inherited issues of inequality alone. But to a large degree, Black- and Brown-majority schools and communities have been left to fend for themselves. The pandemic has made this abundantly clear. One principal recently shared with me just how much schools have been asked to do in response to COVID, especially in her school that serves mostly Latinx students.

> The pandemic has highlighted what a school's role in society truly means. . . . Bottom line, it turned into an on-the-ground relief effort for our families. It turned into the place that our families went to in order to get news, in order to get resources, in order to get everything they needed to move forward. Everything.
>
> When our students started losing their housing, we were doing their housing applications for renters' relief. And when their parents lost their jobs, we were applying for new jobs for them. When family members passed away, we were trying to figure out how to help parents navigate through what it looked like to get a death certificate, to make arrangements, and to try and figure those things out and to get them started on a GoFundMe page.

This type of narrative is sorely lacking in policy discussions; it is one that places schools at the forefront of care and support for families, both in school and before and after the school bell rings. Often, the dominant policy response to supporting young people is what John Powell, a professor at UC Berkeley calls a "moat approach," in which lawmakers construct moats or artificial barriers around issues or ourselves. This approach is all too common for interrelated issues like stable housing, neighborhood segregation, and education opportunities. For example, moat approaches like in-school-centered policy approaches are very common in education policy, especially at the federal level, as evident with No Child Left Behind (NCLB), which passed after the 9/11 attacks in the early 2000s, and Race to the Top (RTTT), Obama's signature education strategy. Each has done little to change learning conditions or academic outcomes for the most disadvantaged students (Hussar et al., 2020). NCLB mandated state tests and accountability systems, and RTTT pushed states to develop higher standards and richer assessments, data systems to support instruction, great teachers and leaders, and a focus on supporting struggling schools. These were worthy pursuits, but each did little to acknowledge just how much conditions outside of schools can fundamentally alter life for young people by the time they reach the classroom. We expect young people to leave their challenges neatly outside the schoolhouse door.

This reality is true for other policy areas outside of education that often haven't been linked to an education agenda. This includes health services that can be made more readily available to families in schools and school systems, city transportation planning that prioritizes school routes, preventing student exposure to environmental pollutants, and affordable housing strategies that seek to dismantle heavily segregated, under-resourced neighborhoods. Each represents key investments to support greater mobility for families and to change the educational, social, and economic trajectory for future generations. Examples of how a new policy thinking is taking shape across the United States—one that takes a radically different approach—are explored more in this book.

Our Children Can't Wait presents a clear path forward for our country, by bridging scholarship, ideas, and original thinking on education policy as a vehicle for dismantling inequality, thereby setting a redemptive path forward for reckoning with race in America. Over 50 million students are served in K–12 nationally; 14,000 school districts and 130,000 schools can provide a powerful connection point for education services, health services, social services, job training, and even delivery of hot meals to so many families (Irwin et al., 2021). A different policy approach for lifting young people and families is backed up by significant evidence showing that a variety of "out-of-school" factors (e.g., prenatal influences; inadequate medical, dental, and vision care; food insecurity; environmental pollutants; family relations and stress; neighborhood conditions) are the strongest contributors by as much as two-thirds to the persistence of academic disparities among students (Berliner, 2009; Johnson, 2014). A broader conception of education policy that takes in-school (e.g., educator capacity, curriculum, funding, school climate) and out-of-school factors (neighborhood conditions, public health, safety, etc.) into consideration simultaneously, not as mutually exclusive approaches to building school systems anchored in racial equity and justice, has become a national necessity (Bishop & Noguera, 2019). The subsequent chapters not only provide the political, social, and historical context for rethinking policy but also draw linkages between out-of-school factors and the policies needed to radically change education outcomes for a new majority population.

A BEYOND-SCHOOLS APPROACH IN THE COVID LANDSCAPE

Default policy approaches have become especially inadequate during a global pandemic (COVID-19) that has taken the lives of more than 1,000,000 Americans, when the U.S. Surgeon General has warned of an unprecedented mental-health crisis for youth (U.S. Department of Health & Human Services, 2021), and an estimated 167,000 young people have lost a parent or caregiver because of the virus (Stolberg, 2021; Treglia et al., 2021). One school district leader described the reality, explaining just how much broader social inequities have bled into the experiences of students, staff, and families over the past several school years.

The pandemic has brought in all the inequities that exist in the system that supports students, the ecosystem that is surrounding student learning. We think of schools as places where the students come to the classroom, but the school is not alone. It's not a one isolated ecosystem; the school lives within the context of the community. So, all the factors that affect the health, economic crisis, any type of context of outcomes that happen in the community and especially to parents and families, employment—all of the social-economic factors that live with it outside the sphere of the school affect the school.

This narrative is reflected in social patterns across the country. Stark differences in unemployment and infection rates for people of color affected by COVID-19 have resurfaced enduring racial tensions and America's unequal playing field (Kuhfeld et al., 2020). Poverty rates are growing in states such as California, Hawaii, Nevada, and Rhode Island with spiking unemployment numbers because of COVID-19 (U.S. Bureau of Labor Statistics, 2020). Child poverty patterns remain stubbornly persistent, affecting 13 million young people (Annie E. Casey Foundation, 2020).

In our K–12 school system, one of two students, or over 30 million youth, are from low-income families (Southern Education Foundation, 2015). Student demographic patterns suggest that schools are becoming increasingly racially and ethnically diverse, reflecting changes in the broader population (Schaeffer, 2021). However, more public school students attend schools where at least half of their peers are the same race or ethnicity (Schaeffer, 2021), pointing to significant implications for the political and cultural landscape in which policy decisions take shape. Student homelessness is on the rise nationally by 15% over the last 3 years, totaling over 1.3 million students (National Center for Homeless Education, 2021). States like California have seen a 48% increase over the last decade in kindergarten to high school students experiencing homelessness, with 7 out of 10 unhoused students being Latinx (Bishop et al., 2020).

The next several chapters in the book set the stage for understanding how a legacy of slavery and discrimination in the United States have been cemented by largely harmful policies that have reinforced social and educational inequities. Authors challenge readers to consider deeper questions about who policies have been crafted for, or "policies for whom?," exploring the lack of policy focus on our youngest learners, and the sciences of learning and development provide the impetus for a new policy foundation. Understanding this foundational set of issues in the early chapters requires policymakers and educators to reflect on the origins of education policy in order to shape a new path forward in key places like school-board meetings, city councils, state legislatures, and in the halls of Congress.

REFERENCES

Annie E. Casey Foundation (2020). *Kids Count data profile 2020.* https://www.aecf.org/m/databook/2020KC_profile_US.pdf

Berliner, D. C. (2009). *Poverty and potential: Out-of-school factors and school success.* Education Policy Research Unit. https://nepc.colorado.edu/sites/default/files/PB-Berliner-NON-SCHOOL.pdf

Bishop, J. P., Camargo Gonzalez, L., & Rivera, E. (2020). *State of crisis: Dismantling student homelessness in California.* Center for the Transformation of Schools, School of Education & Information Studies, University of California, Los Angeles. https://secureservercdn.net/198.71.233.214/38e.a8b.myftpupload.com/wp-content/uploads/2020/10/cts-state-of-crisis-report.pdf

Bishop, J. P., & Noguera, P. A. (2019). The ecology of educational equity: Implications for policy. *Peabody Journal of Education, 94*(2), 122–141.

Hess, F. M., & Noguera, P. A. (2021). *A search for common ground: Conversations about the toughest questions in K-12 education.* Teachers College Press.

Hussar, B., Zhang, J., Hein, S., Wang, K., Roberts, A., Cui, J., Smith, M., Bullock Mann, F., Barmer, A., & Dilig, R. (2020). *The condition of education 2020* (NCES 2020-144). National Center for Education Statistics. https://nces.ed.gov/pubsearch/pubsinfo.asp?pubid=2020144

Irwin, V., Zhang, J., Wang, X., Hein, S., Wang, K., Roberts, A., York, C., Barmer, A., Bullock Mann, F., Dilig, R., & Parker, S. (2021). *Report on the condition of education 2021* (NCES 2021-144). National Center for Education Statistics. https://nces.ed.gov/pubsearch/pubsinfo.asp?pubid=2021144

Johnson, H. B. (2014). *The American dream and the power of wealth: Choosing schools and inheriting inequality in the land of opportunity.* Routledge.

Kuhfeld, M., Soland, J., Tarasawa, B., Johnson, A., Ruzek, E., & Liu, J. (2020). *Projecting the potential impacts of COVID-19 school closures on academic achievement* (EdWorkingPaper No. 20-226.). Annenberg Institute for School Reform at Brown University.

National Center for Homeless Education. (2021). *Student homelessness in America school years 2017–18 to 2019–20.* https://nche.ed.gov/wp-content/uploads/2021/12/Student-Homelessness-in-America-2021.pdf

Pew Research Center. (2016). *The state of American jobs.* Retrieved from https://www.pewresearch.org/social-trends/2016/10/06/1-changes-in-the-american-workplace/

Schaeffer, K. (2021). *U.S. public school students often go to schools where at least half of their peers are the same race or ethnicity.* Pew Research Center. https://www.pewresearch.org/fact-tank/2021/12/15/u-s-public-school-students-often-go-to-schools-where-at-least-half-of-their-peers-are-the-same-race-or-ethnicity/

Schott Foundation for Public Education. (2020). *Creating loving systems across communities to provide all students an opportunity to thrive.* http://schottfoundation.org/sites/default/files/loving-cities-2020.pdf

Southern Education Foundation. (2015). *A new majority: Low-income students now a majority in the nation's public schools.* Retrieved from http://www.southerneducation.org/getattachment/4ac62e27-5260-47a5-9d02-14896ec3a531/A-New-Majority-2015-Update-Low-Income-Students-Now.aspx

Stolberg, G. (2021, December 9). Children, coping with loss, are pandemic's "forgotten grievers." *New York Times.* https://www.nytimes.com/2021/12/09/us/politics/children-lost-parents-caregivers-covid-grief.html

Treglia, D., Cutuli, J. J., & Arasteh, K. (2021). *Hidden pain: Children who lost a parent or caregiver to COVID-19 and what the nation can do to help them.* COVID Collaborative. https://www.covidcollaborative.us/assets/uploads/img/HIDDEN-PAIN-FINAL.pdf

U.S. Bureau of Labor Statistics. (2020). *Economic news release. Table 1. Civilian labor force and unemployment by state and selected area, seasonally adjusted.* https://www.bls.gov/news.release/laus.t01.htm

U.S. Department of Health & Human Services. (2021, December 7). *U.S. surgeon general issues advisory on youth mental health crisis further exposed by COVID-19 pandemic* [Press release]. https://www.hhs.gov/about/news/2021/12/07/us-surgeon-general-issues-advisory-on-youth-mental-health-crisis-further-exposed-by-covid-19-pandemic.html

CHAPTER 2

Grappling With America's History to Inform Our Future Policies

Arnold F. Fege and John H. Jackson

> We deal here with the right of all our children, whatever their race, to an equal start in life and to an equal opportunity to reach their full potential as citizens. Those children who have been denied that right in the past deserve better than to see fences thrown up to deny them that right in the future.
>
> —*Milliken v. Bradley*, 418 U.S. 717, 783 (1974),
> Justice Thurgood Marshall in dissent

AMERICA'S HISTORIC PROBLEM

As described in Chapter 1 of this volume, America has had a troubled relationship with race since the country's beginnings. The central focus of this chapter is to inform—not to inflame—a clear path forward for learning from our past failings that reflect the myriad ways discrimination has shaped the lives of Black, Latinx, and Indigenous populations across generations.

At America's core is a nation born in hope for a thriving democracy with increased opportunity but also a nation that used instruments of violence and oppression over humanity to implement that vision. That oppression, as oppression often does, metastasized into systemic racism and inequities and spread through every organ of the nation (education, economy, health care, policing, etc.). This reality is so embedded in every facet of life in the United States that it is nearly impossible to point to a social vehicle of opportunity, including the education of millions of students, where policies have not either excluded people of color or reinforced fractured social structures and patterns of racism. This chapter touches upon the foundational policies that have determined the social, economic, and political landscape in our country, including slavery, defining citizenship for communities of color, and drawing connections to our history as a way of thinking about the true purpose of education policy as an instrument of justice and reconciliation.

The historical tensions defining the United States between citizenship, political voice for all, and what it means to be a full participant present an important context. Even before the United States had a constitution, the founders believed that the experiment called self-government depended on an educated public. As historian John Sharp Williams (1913) concluded, Thomas Jefferson's impact on American schools is pronounced because "democracy and education are interdependent."

All these idealistic aspirations were soon compromised by economic reality as the Constitution ratified in 1788 acquiesced to slavery as a fact of American life by agreeing to the three-fifths compromise, which stated that every five slaves would only count as three people for taxation and representation purposes. Several years later, the Naturalization Act of 1790, which linked citizenship to possessing White male status, became the law of the land. Narrow concepts of social policy, especially education policy, ignore the exclusion of Blacks and Indigenous communities that dates to our country's founding universal education efforts. According to Grimke (1968), the idea was that Black and Indigenous people belonged to races inferior to Whites. "In the dilemma associated with the social status of the two races," says historian Lawrence Cremin (1980):

> Education was deeply involved, in both the teaching proffered to blacks and Indians by the dominant white society and the teaching blacks and Indians conducted for and among themselves. If there were educational correlates of freedom that were central to the life of the young Republic, there were also correlates of oppression—the latter constituting a tragic contradiction in light of the society's professed values and its hopes of serving as a virtuous example to the world. (p. 219)

Despite the passage of the Fourteenth Amendment to the federal Constitution, which bestowed citizenship on all persons born or naturalized in the United States, Henry Steele Commager said, "In the end, whatever the unclarities, the prevailing assumption was clear: people could be educated to transcend the barriers of ethnicity and religion in order to become full-fledged members of the American community, but they could not be educated to transcend the barriers of race" (1970, pp. 147).

While many of the policies discussed were implemented centuries ago, today Black people make up more than 17% of the population, and all people of color combined make up 45% of the population, yet according to Robin DiAngelo (2017) at the time when her book *White Fragility* was published:

- The 10 richest Americans were White
- The U.S. Congress was 90% White
- 96% of U.S. governors were White

- News managers who decide which news is covered were 85% White
- 82% of teachers were White
- 84% of full-time college professors were White

These statistics are clear evidence that America has not achieved a system of equal opportunity to succeed regardless of race or ethnicity, especially in places of great influence. To the contrary, in the United States both qualitative and quantitative data clearly indicate that success and failure are too often influenced by race, and the aspiration of forming a "more perfect Union" recognized the weaknesses in the early founding of the government. As DiAngelo (2017) opines, the statistics represented "power and control by a racial group that is in the position to disseminate and protect its own self-image, worldview, and interests across an entire society" (p. 31). More importantly, we cannot ignore that the numbers are also representative of a dominance of resources and wealth. In the United States, over the last 30 years, the growth in incomes of the bottom 50% has been zero, whereas incomes of the top 1% have grown by 300% (DiAngelo, 2017, p. 60). You don't get these heavily slanted, racially identifiable outcomes without the preferential treatment, and head start, that Whiteness was given from America's early beginnings.

The public school, then, is at the center of "public building," defined as "a diverse array of citizens constantly joining together to decide on interests, the interests of the community as a whole" (Mathews, 2008). In fact, says Derek W. Black (2020), "public education may be the one institution that helps rebind the nation's wounds" (p. 12). Black further says "If those who care about public education concede the war over the fundamental concept of public education or make their war about something other than fundamental democratic values, they will wake up one day with nothing left to fight for. They may even wake up without a democracy" (p. 30).

It is unlikely that schools will change unless communities change, unless citizens become an effective public community by increasing their capacity to band together and act together, according to David Mathews of the Kettering Foundation. There is nothing inevitable about democratic education. This has been true since the post-Reconstruction period birthed the basic structures of the racial and economic relationships and the power struggles that play out in education today (Rooks, 2017).

AMERICA'S HISTORIC PROMISE

Before and after Reconstruction, before and after Jim Crow, before and after *Brown v. Board of Education*, before and after the Second Reconstruction embodied in the War on Poverty and ESEA (the Elementary and Secondary

Education Act), equal public education opportunity made some strides, but they have often been elusive, sporadic, and met with periods of strong backlash that usually led to policy setbacks.

An important part of the story of America highlights the power of common people coming together at critical moments in our history to reaffirm a vision of opportunity, democracy, and a better way of life for all generations to come. On America's universal arc are indeed the brutality waged against Native Americans, the slave trade, the Fugitive Slave Act law, the Jim Crow Laws of the 1950s and 1960s, and numerous incidents of tragic state-sponsored violence against people of color. Yet also on that moral arc are Harriet Tubman and those who established the underground railroad to free slaves, abolitionists, soldiers who fought for the Emancipation Proclamation, those who marched on Washington in 1963 to secure the Civil Rights and Voting Rights Acts, those establishing Sanctuary cities, and the hundreds of thousands of young and old peaceful protesters who are all committed to bending America's moral arc toward justice. These countless individuals represent America's promise of unparalleled opportunity and upward social and political mobility.

Our challenge is consistently harnessing the energy of those individuals and channeling that public will to concretize the social and economic policy levers needed to create a more equitable and just ecosystem for children to learn and families to thrive. Although the problem of structural racism has been braided in America's history and growth, this is not a problem that is insurmountable or unsolvable. There is nothing wrong with our nation that eliminating structural racism won't fix. We will likely always have individual cases of racial bias with us. Still, structural racism, which creates racially identifiable educational outcomes, can be weakened, unraveled, and become an outlier. We can achieve a time when our children are not able to predict the success or failure of a group of their peers by their race or ethnicity.

From the 1950s through the 1970s, we saw America begin to use the legal lever to tackle systemic racism and its disparities with the passage of *Brown v. Board of Education*, the Civil Rights Act, Voting Rights Act, fair housing laws, and so forth, and while none of these policies eliminated the disparities, it is indisputable that they helped address some disparities impacting Black children and families. Yet, to put it bluntly, 60 years of under-resourced and disjointed progress is insufficient to remedy over 150 years of oppression. We find ourselves at the intersection of America's historic problem and America's historic promise.

AMERICA'S PROGRESS MOMENT

Today, the dual pandemics of COVID-19 and structural racism experienced or witnessed by most offers one of those rare moments in time where, as a nation, we can boldly and courageously move into the next era and chapter of equity in public education. The dual pandemics also created a willingness among both public- and private-sector partners to engage their institutional capacity to reimagine their institutions and bring them in line with prevailing notions of equity, justice, and love to dismantle systems of inequity thoroughly.

Similar to the Reconstruction period of the 1860s following the Civil War, today most systems (education, political, economic, criminal justice, health, housing, etc.) that have undergirded systemic racism in the United States have been severely weakened by COVID and disrupted by those who are demanding change. Most would likely agree that these two events have dramatically cracked America's foundation. The choice before us is whether we do patchwork on our old system or seize the opportunity to build a stronger foundation.

Now is the ideal moment to construct a new imagination where opportunity and democracy have intentionally uncoupled from structural racism and brutal oppression and where the concept of belonging is explicitly uncoupled from Whiteness. We may find ourselves at one of the last moments to flatten the curve on structural racism. In the 2010 *Grutter v. Bollinger* decision, Supreme Court Justice Sandra Day O' Connor questioned the country's ability to effectively use the legal lever in 25 years to affirmatively address racial disparities. As such, we find ourselves at the point where activating the wealth that was endowed by the bodies and land of people of color provides the best path forward for building a better country for our children. Diversity without inclusion is an empty and hollow endeavor.

While this has been a difficult time in America's history, and the fractious environment has tested our democratic institutions, it has also made us aware of the importance of public schools as democratic institutions to parents, students, teachers, and local communities. Before COVID-19, not all school districts and communities had the same educational opportunities and resources, and so not everyone was affected by the virus equally. COVID-19 has dramatically exposed the inequities and gaps that were often ignored and neglected for many years, for many children, in many school districts, and for many families. This was more than a public education issue; it was an American issue, way beyond the capacity for the school to control.

Students of color, LGBTQ+ students, students from low-income backgrounds, students who are English learners, students with disabilities, students in the tribal nations, students in the territories, student in rural communities, and other vulnerable groups such as students experiencing homelessness, incarceration, hunger, abuse, trauma, and students in foster care, are less likely to have rigorous, engaging, and positive educational experiences than before the pandemic (Organization for Economic Cooperation and Development, 2020). And now we know that the many inequities that have accumulated over the decades are in full view: school closures, distance learning, instructional loss, hybrid models, mass shootings, mental-health needs, childcare, housing, food insecurity, and schools opening and closing fell heavily on these populations as well as on those in rural school districts and communities. It was said that we were in the same storm but not all in the same boats. This is borne out by a recent McKinsey & Company report that children who were learning remotely had learning losses, but the losses were greatest among vulnerable children, which widened the equity and opportunity gap even more (Dorn et al., 2020).

This time around, policymakers need to avoid the sideshows of the past: vouchers, private and for-profit charter schools, no-excuses education, competition, choice, high-stakes standardized testing, and student push-out tactics. On a policy level, these elements all represent subsets of the technical or "educentric" aspects of education, while often shifting attention away from the foundational human and relationship-building elements of education, including the health, social–emotional, and developmental needs of students and families.

Now, we must assess the conditions of our systems far more stringently than we assess our students. State and local systems impacting children and families must be assessed for built-in structural racism, discrimination, and inequities. Previously, we tested our students and blamed them if they failed, even though they were caught up in systems that almost assured failure. We ended up using standardized tests as a proxy for equity, but for kids in poverty there was no standardized funding or resources. We also had a system that focused on remediation and interventions after our students showed failure, mostly on standardized tests, but we abandoned a system that assured success before our children failed. It is time to recalibrate the technical side of education and merge it with social and emotional learning, trauma-informed services, developing strategies for instructional loss, and reimagining what an equitable education might look like—completely different from the current system. To be sure, the current system is effective at reproducing the existing social order, but that's not what families, student learners, and teachers need (Reville, 2014). It's not our teachers and parents who have failed—it's a system that is not designed to respond to the post-pandemic developmental and academic needs of our students, families, and community.

In 2018, as racism and hate narratives continued to dominate the national dialogue, the Schott Foundation for Public Education proffered the Loving Cities Index as a way for state and local decision-makers to better assess their systems. The Loving Cities Index aimed to reverse historical local policies and practices rooted in racism and bias and replace them with policies that create loving systems from birth. By providing a dashboard for cities, the index delivers the cross-sector supports (education, health, transportation, etc.) necessary for students to have an opportunity to learn and thrive (Schott Foundation, 2020).

To date, Schott has developed profiles for 20 cities, and none of the cities offered over 55% of the systemic supports needed for all children to thrive. This scoring system considered overall access to indicators as well as racial gaps in access. Schott's Loving Cities initiative challenges the notion that school-based reforms alone can provide students a fair and substantive opportunity to learn. Instead, we draw attention to the large and growing body of research that shows clear connections between economic and racial inequity, and gaps in access to housing, health care, and community.

Yet instead of boring directly to addressing inequities such as resources, teacher shortages, school climate, criminal justice, school support, community services, school discipline, and summer programs, too many policymakers often have taken the path of least resistance and avoided the arduous work of implementing equitable policies.

At a time when communities of color have gained access to local decision-makers about what is best for their children and are able to influence education and the resources to educate their children through local empowerment and strengthening local control, governors (primarily conservative) are finding ways to eradicate local power and diminish local equity voices through state intervention (Morel, 2018). State initiatives, such as district takeovers, book banning, curricula restrictions (framed as opposition to Critical Race Theory), and various other measures that limit local control, have never been about producing citizens of color with all the rights and powers that go along with citizenship, contends Domingo Morel (2018), but rather are proof, once again, that education cannot be separated from creating citizens. Community voice isn't just an abstraction. Parents, teachers, faith leaders, and other local stakeholders are at ground zero when it comes to truly understanding the educational needs of children in their communities and the challenges they face when it comes to receiving a quality education. Most importantly, they are not in the game to profit financially through contractual relationships with various outside vendors, for profit contractors and enterprises, or private entities.

In many cases, our pandemic experience with virtual instruction led to unraveling the old factory model. It certainly changed parents and families' relationships with their child's school. For the first time, parents were able to investigate the classroom virtually, rather than just to be spectators at meetings. It also served to begin revealing how teachers and parents use time, questioning the 180-day school year, or the 55-minute Carnegie Unit and coverage of classroom material. On that basis, relationships become as important as programs, the neighborhood as important to learning as what is inside the schools. In short, the factory model school of the 19th century is not designed to meet the educational, social, economic, and safety net needs of the 21st century, and it does not support those communities that often have difficulty accessing the schools in providing the services.

WHOLE SYSTEM, WHOLE CHILD

A new vision for the education of children must consider the whole child within the context of the ecosystems or communities in which they live. It takes a healthy living and learning environment to provide all students a fair and substantive opportunity to learn.

In this scenario, our public school becomes the connective tissue to the ecosystem. It is what holds all the other pieces together, but most importantly, it holds the democracy together and assures an adequate and equitable education and life skills for all our kids. It also builds on the human ecosystem, strengthening relationships between the home and school, between parents and teachers, between community and the common good. Therefore, it is important to break down the silos and build those relationships that connect, rather than isolate, the important child advocacy work that our professionals do each day. Yet schools alone cannot reverse the impact of deep poverty on children, families, and communities. We can no longer view education as simply the things that go on inside that building we call "school." We must broaden the focus of education to encompass the communities around the school building so that we do not cut the funding of categorical programs, and continue to create an environment where professionals are not identified by their program but by their collaborative relationship between each other and the public schools.

That is why *Brown v. Board of Education* is cited at the top of this chapter—a unanimous belief that integration in all its forms is essential for a diverse and inclusive society and public school system.

There is a growing realization that not only is the school the center of the community, but the community is the center of the school. As the community-school movement grows, the local public school system is often the only entity situated to meet the needs of students from families in deep poverty by providing meals as well as a safe place to be during the day. This is especially true of rural and smaller school districts and communities. Data tells us that the road to success is tougher for young people who are engaged with the foster-care system, are hungry, face school suspensions, need juvenile justice advocacy, lack secure housing and Internet access, have special education needs and language barriers, may be from low-income households, or have family members who are victims of the opioid epidemic. These young people need expanded school supports to succeed, supports that are often not thought of when planning college access programs, and for whom the current model and school architecture are not designed to tackle many issues outside of their control of the school building.

While the public school is still the center of the community and democracy, the work of the school is beyond the school building and beyond the school system. The whole policy and the whole system serve the academic and developmental needs of the whole child (Darling-Hammond & Harvey, 2018). The whole incorporates a human ecosystem and all its interlocking elements, both inside the school system and outside, both individual and community power and engagement. Without a defined plan to impact the system, educators will be caught in the middle of a factory model policy and system that is not compatible with a more individualized approach.

The Schott Foundation's Loving Cities approach of assessing the degree to which communities, through their systems, were showing love, care, capacity, and stability to all their children and families regardless of race or ethnicity provides a dashboard for districts to look at the whole system and whole child.

Researchers, such as the Harvard economist Raj Chetty, have made clear that the neighborhood and larger ecosystem in which a child grows up is perhaps the chief determinant of that child's social and economic mobility (Reeves & Krause, 2018). Of course, the quality of the school the child attends is another important variable, but so are the level of residential segregation, the neighborhood's social capital, the stability of that child's family, and the neighborhood's level of poverty.

An emerging field of practice centered on "place" (i.e., where a child grows up) has championed providing comprehensive services to neighborhoods to effectively combat poverty (Fontana, 2021). These services include high-quality education and cradle-to-career youth programming, physical- and mental-health support, workforce development, affordable housing, and community leadership. This is a time to plan with the community the systemic changes required to respond to the demographic changes hitting urban and rural public schools. To integrate via technology, face-to-face and through community organizations, a true community education model enables schools to respond to the needs of the "whole child" (Centers for Disease Control and Prevention, 2021).

So, this is a moment in time—a short moment, before the comforting chorus of "getting back to the old normal" gets too loud and powerful. If we can set clear expectations for our students, we can do the same for policymakers and our politicians at the state and federal levels. Bringing the country together, leading national conversations about race and policing and discipline and criminal justice reform, a diverse teaching profession, college affordability, empowered engagement of low-income and minority parents, student voice, advisory councils, a national commission on children and youth—whatever the vehicles, they should lead to a national plan that is specifically targeted at what Andre Perry (2020) calls "dismantling the sources of inequality" (p. 214). The fight to form a civic family that lives under a just, equitable, and loving roof will press on, concludes Perry. This is precisely why advocates of democracy have always placed a high value on education—and this education is not only formal schooling but public discussion, debate, controversy, transparency, ready availability of reliable information—this is what makes public education unique.

It is virtually impossible to provide Black and Brown children a fair opportunity to achieve their full potential without significantly addressing the broader systemic inequities. Their living inequities have become so drastic that it is impossible to systemically decouple them from their learning disparities. As data show, racial inequities in access to health care, affordable housing, and healthy food make as much (if not more in some cases) of an impact on Black, Brown, and Native students' educational outcomes than the education factors themselves. And yet while these inequities more pervasively impact students of color, they impact all students while undermining our democracy, economy, and humanity.

Educators might ask: How do we kickstart and support cities in closing the support deficits impacting children and families? Historically, when the nation has faced severe challenges with little prospect for recovery, policymakers have infused cash to jumpstart economic engines. Most recently, the CARES Act of 2020 sought to ameliorate economic fallout from the coronavirus pandemic. There was the American Recovery and Reinvestment Act of 2009, which aimed to remedy the fallout from the housing crisis. There was the Economic Growth and Tax Relief Reconciliation Act (EGTRRA) in June 2001. Following the September 11 terrorist attacks, Congress passed the Job Creation and Worker Assistance Act (JCWAA), signed into law in March 2002. While these are relatively recent examples, in the past 80 years, government officials have regularly infused cash into the economy to stave off financial hardship and alleviate American suffering. Eliminating systemic racism would be an economic stimulus on its own. Most recently, Congress passed the American Rescue Plan, which provided millions of dollars to state and local school districts for purposes of eliminating the racist and discriminatory policies still in existence and grounded in the past.

The United States has relied on similar fiscal packages for everything except the existential crisis that is structural racism. Even when the nation contemplated and passed specific measures to alleviate harm, those measures were never intended to help Black people, and often specifically excluded the Black community. This is work that must be financially stimulated at the federal level. Now is the time for lawmakers and voters to recognize the mutuality of interest which rests on the willingness of all involved to share enough with one another to accomplish what no one person can do alone, that the public interest is not only about one's individual needs but about the needs of all, that when partisanship gives way to what are community and common goods, we will create and prioritize to all on a fair and open basis to fund and provide them publicly.

Despite the obstacles and the struggles, we must keep hope that the country still believes that every child should receive a quality public education that prepares them for citizenship and the world of work and continues to serve as the great equalizer moving another generation of young people into the middle class, and that education is the critical key to expanding opportunity for all our students and families.

In his probing treatise *Where Do We Go From Here: Chaos or Community?*, Dr. Martin Luther King Jr. (1967/2010) puzzles over the nation's contradiction of democracy on one hand and its strange ambivalence on the question of racial justice on the other, reminding us: "Procrastination is still the thief of time. Life often leaves us standing bare, naked and dejected. Over the bleached bones and jumbled residues of numerous civilizations are written the pathetic words, 'Too late.' We are confronted with the fierce urgency of *now*, and urgent fact that tomorrow is today" (p. 202). In short, our most marginalized and vulnerable children can wait no longer. The urgency of this moment is clear, but bigger questions around who is driving a policy agenda and for whom the table is being set is explored further in the next chapter.

REFERENCES

Black, D. W. (2019). The fundamental right to education. *Notre Dame Law Review*, 94(3), 1059–1114.

Black, D. W. (2020). *Schoolhouse burning: Public education and the assault on American democracy*. Public Affairs.

Centers for Disease Control and Prevention. (2022). *Whole School, whole community, whole child (WSCC)*. Retrieved from https://www.cdc.gov/healthyschools/wscc/index.htm

Commager, H. S. (1973). *Documents of American history* (9th ed.). Appleton-Century-Crofts.

Cremin, L (1980). *American education: The national experience 1783–1876*. Harper Collins.

Darling-Hammond, L., & Cook-Harvey, C. M. (2018). *Educating the whole child: Improving school climate to support student success*. Learning Policy Institute.

DiAngelo, R. (2018). *White fragility: Why it's so hard for white people to talk about racism*. Beacon Press.

Dorn, E., Hancock, B., Sartakatsannis, J., & Viruleg, E. (2020). *COVID-19 and learning loss—disparities grow and students need help*. McKinsey & Company.

Fontana, D. (2021, August 8). America's hidden crisis of power and place. *Washington Post Magazine*. https://www.washingtonpost.com/magazine/2021/08/02/americas-hidden-crisis-power-place/

Grimke, F. (1968). *The nature and tendency of free institutions*. Harvard University Press.

King, M. L., Jr. (2010). *Where do we go from here: Chaos or community?* Beacon Press. (Original work published 1967)

Mathews, D. (2008). The public and the public schools. *Phi Delta Kappan, 89*(8), 560–564.

Morel, D. (2018). *Takeover: Race, education and American democracy.* Oxford University Press.

Organization for Economic Cooperation and Development (OECD). (2020). *The impact of COVID-19 on student equity and inclusion: Supporting vulnerable students during school closures.* https://www.oecd.org/coronavirus/policy-responses/the-impact-of-covid-19-on-student-equity-and-inclusion-supporting-vulnerable-students-during-school-closures-and-school-re-openings-d593b5c8/

Perry, A. M. (2020). *Know your price: Valuing Black lives and property in American cities.* Brookings Institution Press.

Reeves, R. V., & Krause, E. (2018, January 11). *Raj Chetty in 14 charts: Big findings on opportunity and mobility we should all know.* Brookings Institution. https://www.brookings.edu/blog/social-mobility-memos/2018/01/11/raj-chetty-in-14-charts-big-findings-on-opportunity-and-mobility-we-should-know/

Reville, S. P. (2014, April 24). How to create a new K–12 engine. *Education Week.* https://www.edweek.org/education-industry/opinion-how-to-create-a-new-k-12-engine/2014/04

Rooks, N. (2017). *Cutting school: Privatization, segregation, and the end of public education.* The New Press.

Schott Foundation for Public Education. (2020). *Creating loving systems across communities to provide all students an opportunity to thrive.* http://schottfoundation.org/sites/default/files/loving-cities-2020.pdf

Williams, J. S. (1913). *Thomas Jefferson: His permanent influence on American institutions.* AMS Press.

CHAPTER 3

Making Children a National Priority
Overcoming the Marginalization and Invisibility of Children

Bruce Lesley

INTRODUCTION

Our nation's children stand at a crossroads. Now, more than ever, we need to make investments in the next generation if we care about their *now* and their *future*. The role that education plays in the lives of children cannot be understated, whether before, during, or after the pandemic. Public education has always played that role for children, but it is also fundamental to our nation's success and our democracy as a whole. Over the history of our nation and more than any other issue of importance to children, education has always been front and center (Black, 2020).

Thus, educational issues and how to address them through policies and practices are the main foci of this book. Yet, for children to thrive and be successful, we must also confront the nonschool factors that affect children's well-being and school success, including race, gender, disability, child poverty, child health (including mental health), child hunger, child abuse, homelessness, trauma, and immigration status. On a daily basis, educators are engaging with and impacted by how public policies outside of schools influence the well-being and success of children both inside and outside of the classroom.

Even before the most recent global COVID pandemic and economic recession, too many children were not doing well. But the twin threats of the pandemic and the recession have negatively impacted every aspect of their lives. Hundreds of thousands of U.S. children have lost a parent or caregiver (Goodman et al., 2022), and millions have had their education, childcare, economic security, nutrition, child welfare, and housing negatively impacted (DeParle, 2020).

The health of children has also been negatively impacted, with many children experiencing COVID-related issues such as hospitalization, long COVID, and even death, in addition to compromised mental health, substance abuse, declines in childhood vaccination rates, and a lack of treatment for other health conditions (Lesley, 2020a). UNICEF (2020) referred to children as the "hidden victims of [the] COVID pandemic."

In a UNICEF report published before the pandemic, the United States was compared to other wealthy nations on dozens of child well-being measures, including child poverty and child mortality rates, and ranked 36th out of 38 countries—behind countries such as Romania, Slovakia, Greece, Poland, and Estonia (Gromada et al., 2020). This is due in part to the fact that the United States invests far less than other nations, as a share of Gross National Product (GNP), in children (Hoynes & Schanzenbach, 2018). Citing data from the Organization for Economic Cooperation and Development (OECD, 2019), Hoynes and Schanzenbach explain, "The United States is near the bottom of countries belonging to the OECD in 'family benefits public spending' as a share of GDP (third from the bottom, above only Mexico and Turkey), with a share less than half the OECD average" (p. 91). In sharp contrast, U.S. spending on the elderly is close to the OECD average (Hoynes & Schanzenbach, 2018).

Federal spending dedicated to children declined to just 7.64% of overall spending in 2020—an all-time low (First Focus on Children, 2021). In contrast, researchers at the Urban Institute estimate that 45% of the federal budget dedicated to retirement and health benefits for adults, 15 percent on defense, 8 percent on interest on the national debt, and 22 on all other federal programs. On a per capita basis, it is estimated that per capita spending on senior citizens was about 6 times higher than that for children in 2017 (Hahn et al., 2020).

The downward trend in children's funding and outcomes was particularly profound in recent years, as the Trump administration sought to impose significant cuts to children's programs in the federal budget. The federal share of spending on children during the Trump administration declined by nearly 25% between fiscal year 2016 and 2020. Compounding the harm, Trump's FY 2021 budget proposal sought $21 billion in cuts to children's programs, in large part by the Administration's proposal to eliminate or consolidate into block grants 59 children's programs, including several educational programs (First Focus on Children, 2020).

Recent investments in children through passage of the American Rescue Plan (ARP) Act in 2021 reversed that trend and spending as a share of the federal budget increased to 11.15% (see Figure 3.1 from First Focus on Children, 2021), but that increase is temporary because ARP was an emergency spending measure and much of it expired at the close of 2021.

The fact is that funding matters when it comes to improving the lives of children, including their public education (Baker, 2017; Lesley, 2010; Putnam, 2016). Research across an array of studies points to positive outcomes for children from increased education investments, such as reduced class size, improved teacher quality, and better education attainment and

Making Children a National Priority

Figure 3.1. First Focus on Children: Federal Total Spending: 2016-2021 on Children

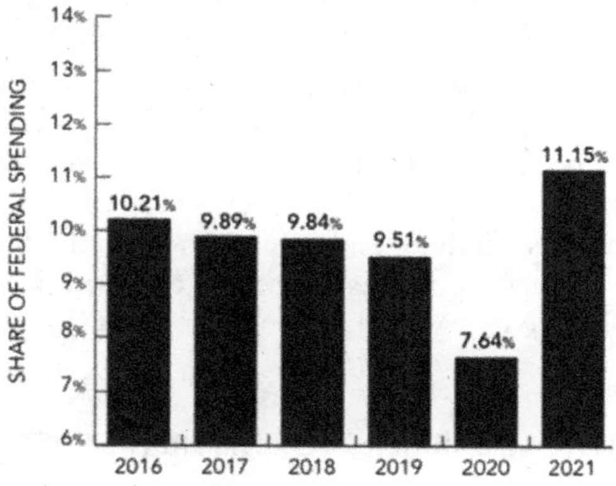

[Bar chart showing Share of Federal Spending by year:
- 2016: 10.21%
- 2017: 9.89%
- 2018: 9.84%
- 2019: 9.51%
- 2020: 7.64%
- 2021: 11.15%]

Source: First Focus on Children (2021).

outcomes (both high school graduation and college-going rates) (Equity & Excellence Commmission, 2013; Jackson & Mackevicius, 2021). We also know that investments in nonschool factors, such as expanding high-quality early childhood programs and health insurance coverage and reducing child poverty, child hunger, and child homelessness improves the full array of child well-being measures, including education (Currie, 2005; Duncan & Le Menestrel, 2019; McCoy-Roth et al., 2012). "Early interventions can improve cognitive as well as social–emotional skills. They promote schooling, reduce crime, foster workforce productivity, and reduce teenage pregnancy" (Heckman, 2013).

As previously mentioned, compounding the long-term trend toward divestment in children, the coronavirus global pandemic and economic recession have negatively impacted children—both in the United States and globally. As noted above, virtually every aspect of the lives of children has been negatively impacted by these dual challenges (Newkirk, 2020; OECD, 2020).

For children to thrive in all aspects of their lives, they need affirmative support *by* parents (e.g., fundamental human needs and love) and government (e.g., public schools, social services, and safety), but sometimes they also need protection *from* parents (e.g., child abuse and neglect and denying children access to needed care) and government (e.g., child detention, corporal punishment in schools, and rights restrictions such as censorship). To achieve these goals, there must also be an underlying understanding that children have fundamental rights (Todres & King, 2020). These rights are both affirmative (e.g., the right to an education, the right to health care, the right to shelter, etc.) and negative or defensive (e.g., protection from abuse, privacy rights, protection against restrictions on free speech, etc.).

That understanding is sadly lacking in the United States, as we are the only nation in the world that has failed to ratify the U.N. Convention on the Rights of the Child (Davidson, 2014; Mousin, 2019; Todres, 2014). Kids' issues are, in many ways, subordinated to the interests of adults in politics and society. Therefore, despite underlying sympathy and desire for children to be a priority in policymaking, as their success is fundamental to our nation's future, there remain significant barriers in the United States to do what is right by our nation's children. Kids are often shoved into the background or ignored, even when the policy is specific to children. Let's consider some of these barriers in two categories: (1) political and (2) societal.

POLITICAL BARRIERS TO CHILDREN'S SUCCESS

First, when it comes to children, too often policy and political debates focus on the adults rather than on the needs, concerns, and voices of children themselves. Children lack political clout for some obvious reasons, such as: (1) kids do not vote; (2) kids do not have political action committees (PACs); and (3) kids do not have active membership groups like the AARP for senior citizens that can demand attention and action. As a result, children often lack voice, agency, and self-determination in political and policy debates, even on those issues of significant importance to their lives. This occurs despite the fact that children have knowledge or insight due to "first-hand experience of the situation" and deserve to have their voices and needs heard, valued, and fully considered (Stafford et al., 2021). Unfortunately, adults often engage in "protectionism," which seeks to shield children from politics and policy discussions, and a perception that young people lack competence to engage.

This latter perception sidelines children and pushes them into the shadows. Consequently, when policymakers and the public are making decisions about government assistance and funding for children's programs, such as the Child Tax Credit (CTC) or Temporary Assistance for Needy Families (TANF), they often weigh conflicting factors such as empathy for children with concerns about "deservedness" with respect to parents. This can lead to resistance or outright opposition to funding children's programs by policymakers (Feldman et al., 2020).

In early 2022, for example, an estimated 3.7 million children were pushed into poverty because Congress allowed the fully refundable portion of the CTC that was included in the American Rescue Plan (ARP) Act to expire (Parolin et al., 2022). A key U.S. senator in the debate, Sen. Joe Manchin (D-WV), expressed opposition to the extension of the refundable portion of the CTC, which targets assistance to low-income families with children, because of an expressed stereotype that poor parents might take the CTC and "choose" not to work or "buy drugs" instead of caring for their children. Headlines read that the "poorest parents" were being cut out of the CTC, but it is children that will suffer the most (Scott & Siegel, 2021; Zeballos-Roig, 2022). The expiration of the CTC resulted in a $1,000–1,600 tax increase per child for most families in the country but up to $3,600 per child for the poorest families.

Furthermore, in school debates where the focus shifts to "parental rights" and cultural wars, the educational, health, and safety needs and privacy rights of children can be forgotten (e.g., academic success, social, emotional learning, equity, inclusion, teacher–student confidentiality, vaccination policies, extracurricular activities, etc.). When it comes to overall policy, a focus on parents can be detrimental to children in several ways. First, it cues perceptions of "deservedness" and other prejudices that people may have against low-income parents, parents of color, and immigrant parents rather than the needs of children. As noted earlier, stereotypes and prejudices against parents can lead to a decline in support for making investments in children.

Second, although there is a "parental rights" movement seeking to pass new laws asserting the overriding primacy of parents in decision-making with respect to the lives of children, parents have always been recognized as fundamental to the upbringing, education, and well-being of children. In *Troxel v. Granville*, the Supreme Court affirmed "the interest of parents in the care, custody, and control of their children" to be "perhaps the oldest of the fundamental liberty interests recognized by this Court." Unfortunately, new "parental rights" bills over-emphasize the power and control of parents, deemphasize and minimize the role of government, and eliminate or deem nonexistent the rights and voice of children and youth, even when it comes to their own well-being and future.

We should not need reminding that, tragically, there are some parents who are violent, criminal, unfit, and a danger to children. For example, a 2016 congressionally chartered Commission to Eliminate Child Abuse and Neglect Fatalities found:

> Every day, four to eight children in the United States die from abuse or neglect at the hands of their parents or caretakers. No one knows the exact number, and there has been little progress in preventing these tragic deaths. Most of the children who die are infants or toddlers. (p. 12)

Some of these bills explicitly state that parental rights "may not be limited or denied" short of an "action or decision that would end life," which could be both detrimental to the health and well-being of children and against the will of a child or adolescent. The language reopens grave concerns about the role some parents have played in decisions to impose female genital mutilation, conversion "therapy," rebirthing "therapy," certain types of involuntary institutionalization of children, seclusion and restraint, forced sterilization of children with disabilities, other harmful or detrimental "care," or the outright denial of health care and treatment by parents to their children (Kapnick, 2020; Martinez, 2020; Morales, 2021; Serena, 2018; Volokh, 2014; Wilson, 2016; Zadrozny, 2019). There is a clear and much-needed affirmative role for both government, including schools, and children in protecting the health, education, and safety of children that should not be minimized or eliminated.

Third, when the attention is centered almost exclusively on the debate between parental and governmental oversight of children, attention to the fundamental needs, concerns, and rights of children are often lost. Again, the voice of children and their needs and concerns should never be subjugated or ignored. The "best interests" of children are not a "bipolar struggle between parents and the State," according to Supreme Court Justice John Paul Stevens (*Troxel v. Granville*, Stevens dissent). He adds:

> There is at minimum a third individual, whose interests are implicated in every case to which the statute applies—the child.... [T]o the extent parents and families have fundamental liberty interests in preserving such intimate relationships, so, too, do children have these interests, and so, too, must their interests be balanced in the equation. (pp. 86, 88)[1]

Young learners can provide important insights into their concerns, interests, needs, and their hopes and dreams, but only if adults choose to pay attention to them (see Figure 3.2). The voices and the rights of children should not be ignored or dismissed by either parents or governmental entities (Dailey & Rosenbury, 2018). As Peleg (2021) writes, "Children's best interests must be a primary consideration, and this cannot be done without giving proper weight to children's own insights."

Furthermore, concerns about violence, abuse, injustice, and discrimination against children in families, schools, prisons, and institutions can best be eliminated if kids are heard, engaged and empowered by people with the authority to take action. The silencing or dismissal of the voices of children and youth and the harm they experience can protect the abusers rather than the children (Lesley, 2018).

Figure 3.2. Key Stakeholders Involved in Children's Rights

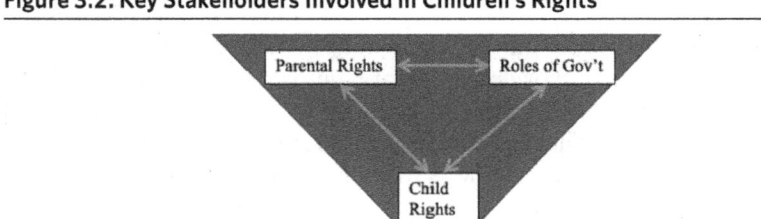

One example that illustrates the silencing of and harm done to youths, as mentioned, is the U.S. Women's Gymnastics team. In 2018, more than 150 young women came forward and told a judge about sexual abuse and molestation they had experienced in the program as far back as 1997 (Lynch, 2018). As Olympic medalist Aly Raisman (2018) explained in that courtroom:

> Abuse goes way beyond the moment, often haunting survivors for the rest of their lives, making it difficult to trust and impacting their relationships. . . . If over these many years, just one adult listened and had the courage and character to act, this tragedy could have been avoided.

In addition to needing their voices to be heard to protect kids, children depend on the parents, grandparents, other adults, and government officials to hear and affirmatively act to ensure their education, health, well-being, and safety needs are being fully addressed. In Chapter 2, Arnold Fege and John H. Jackson show how that interaction can greatly benefit children and schools.

The problem is that those engaged with and knowledgeable about the needs of children, such as teachers and childcare providers, often have their own political and policy needs and concerns that limit their advocacy focus on kids. As Myles (2015) points out, our policies shortchange both children and the "adults who most directly attend to children." Moreover, while parents and grandparents may demonstrate strong support for their *own* children (in-group), they are not necessarily supportive of helping *other* people's children (out-group), as Putnam (2016) demonstrated in *Our Kids: The American Dream in Crisis.* He points to a "widening socio-economic gap" and an individualist tradition in the United States that undermines support for helping poorer children and families.

In the case of older voters, they are strong advocates for programs of importance to themselves, such as Social Security and Medicare, but they express far weaker levels of support for children's issues like education, early childhood, and child health programs. In a 2014 poll conducted by American Viewpoint on behalf of First Focus Campaign for Children, 27% of grandparents cited senior issues as the most important concern for their vote for Congress compared to just 0.4% for children's issues. Therefore, grandparents ranked their own policy concerns over those of children by a gaping 70-to-1 margin (American Viewpoint, 2014).

Although mothers (16%) made children's issues the most important issue for their vote in that 2014 poll, fathers (0.7%) rarely made kids' policies their top priority. In total, twice as many parents and grandparents cited senior issues (14%) as the most important issue in their 2014 vote for Congress than cited children's issues (6%) (Huntington & Scott, 2015).

As a result, kids are often treated as an afterthought by lawmakers. Freeman (1997) explains in his book *The Moral Status of Children*:

> It is important that all those who formulate policy should be compelled to consider the impact their policies have on children. . . . All too rarely is consideration given to what policies formulated at the level of government, bureaucracy or local state level do to children. This is all the more the case where the immediate focus of the policy is not children. But even in children's legislation the unintended or indirect effects of changes are not given the critical attention they demand. But where the policy is not "headlined" children, immigration policy or housing policy for example, the impact on the lives of children is all too readily glossed over. (pp. 77–78)

Child advocates often refer to the invisibility of kids in public policy discussions.

Ingram et al. (2007) utilize the social construction framework to explain how lawmakers are motivated to target certain populations in both positive and negative terms and choose to distribute policy "benefits and burdens." They explain that children—referred to under the category of "dependents" in their model—are often viewed sympathetically but lack political power. They write:

> Lack of political power sharply curtails their receipt of benefits, which tend to be inadequate and limited by rules such as means-testing or by funding shortfalls. . . . Dependents lack the political power to effectively demand more. Benefits, when provided, tend to be heavy on rhetoric and low on financing. Policymakers must take care not to appear to be mean-spirited, but they prefer not to expend important resources on dependents unless necessary. (p. 103)

Confirming the social construction framework's theory, a report by the Committee for a Responsible Federal Budget (2018) finds that the federal budget process systematically disadvantages and shortchanges our nation's children. The following are findings of the analysis:

- *While much of spending on adults is mandatory, spending on children is disproportionately discretionary* and thus must be reviewed and renewed with other appropriations.
- *Spending on children is disproportionately temporary,* and it requires far more regular reauthorization and appropriation than programs for adults.
- *Spending on adults is rarely limited while spending on children is often capped,* constraining what can be spent for most major children's programs.
- *Most programs for children lack built-in growth,* leading spending on children to erode relative to spending on adults and relative to the economy.

- *Programs for children lack dedicated revenue* and, thus, lack the political advantage and protection of programs for seniors that enjoy this benefit.
- *Growing spending on adults is burdening younger generations* by driving up debt and, thus, reducing future income and increasing costs.

The shortchanging of children is a matter of political decision and indecision or inaction.

SOCIETAL BARRIERS TO CHILDREN'S SUCCESS

Although kids don't vote, don't have PACs, and aren't members of political advocacy groups, children don't have access to these political tools in other countries, either. And yet many of those countries make far greater investments in their kids than the United States does (Hoynes & Schanzenbach, 2018).

There are three additional and unique American political barriers that create challenges to creating sustaining political support for our nation's children. They are: (1) demographic change and the racial generation gap; (2) perceptions of "deservedness" and the parent bubble; and (3), once again, perceptions of children that lead to their marginalization and invisibility in American society.

First, as Pastor et al. (2017) have noted:

> America is in the midst of two dramatic demographic shifts: rising diversity, with the highest levels of diversity among our youngest, and rapid aging as the baby boomers head into retirement. . . . These twin forces—the browning and graying of America—are widening the demographic divergence between our youngest and oldest: a phenomenon known as the racial generation gap. (p. 1)

Over three-quarters (75.5%) of the elderly population in the United States is White non-Hispanic, which is in sharp contrast to children, among whom the majority (50.4%) are now kids of color (Aizer et al., 2022). Frey (2018) refers to this demographic disparity as the racial or cultural generation gap (see also Pastor et al., 2017, and Brownstein, 2012).

As our demographics have shifted, studies have shown that support for children's programs among the elderly, particularly if they are from different racial groups, has historically declined (Frey, 2018; Lesley, 2016; Pastor et al., 2017; Portuba, 1997). For example, Portuba (1996) finds:

> An increase in the fraction of a jurisdiction's population over the age of 65 tends to reduce per-child school spending, and that the effect is especially pronounced

when the elderly residents are from a different ethnic group than the school-age population. (p. 21)

Frey (2018) adds:

> It has been shown that those states with the largest gains in minority children, but mostly white seniors—including Texas, California, Florida, Georgia, North Carolina and Arizona—rank among the lowest third of states on a measure of child well-being that includes education, health and other areas in which state government programs can assist.

Other studies have found that White Americans are threatened by the concept that minority groups, largely driven by a younger, more diverse generation, may become the nation's majority (Brown et al., 2021. The United States will either choose to embrace its growing racial and ethnic diversity or become increasingly polarized with ongoing negative political and policy consequences for our nation's youngest citizens.

Furthermore, just as is the case with policymakers, children may be negatively impacted in society by what child advocates refer to as the "parent bubble." For those who value individualism, researchers find that their fundamental belief is that "hard work contributes to success" (Feldman et al., 2020). Individualists have stronger notions of "deservedness" and tend to demonstrate less compassion or empathy toward "able-bodied poor or unemployed working-age adults" seeking government assistance than they would toward children who are "typically not held accountable for their situation" (Feldman et al., 2020). In fact, a recent study found that an increased visibility of children improved both the salience and activation of prosocial values as well as financial support for prosocial causes and charity by the public (Wolf et al., 2022).

The field of political psychology tells us that one reason that children are forgotten by policymakers and the public in policy debates is that, in a complex, information-rich world, society's attention is often captured by people and issues that pose either an opportunity or a threat.

As Neuberg et al. (2020) explain:

> Groups stereotyped as generally low in power and status—children, elderly people, poor people—are thus especially likely to be invisible, whereas high status groups—middle-aged adults, rich people—are especially unlikely to be invisible. (p. 284)

In the case of child poverty, kids are likely viewed as low in status because they are *both* children and poor. Neel and Lassetter (2019) describe the status of children in this context as "goal irrelevant" (p. 637) because they pose neither a clear opportunity nor a threat to society (see Figure 3.3).

Figure 3.3. Relevance Appraisal Matrix

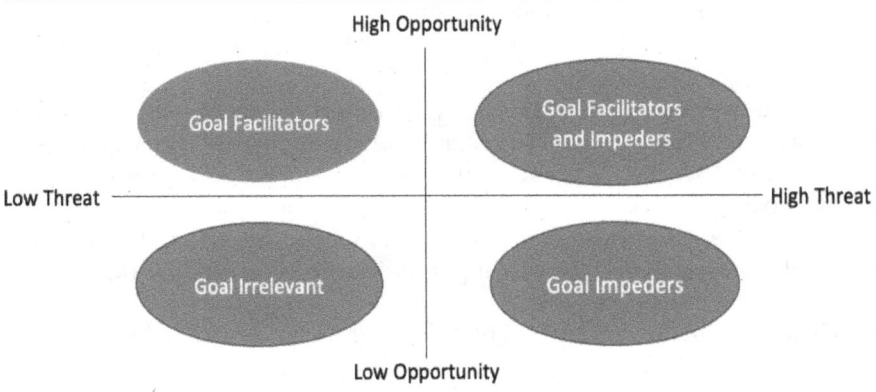

Source: Adapted from Figure 1 in "The Stigma of Perceived Irrelevance: An Affordance-Management Theory of Interpersonal Invisibility," by R. Neel and B. Lassetter, 2019, *Psychological Review, 126*(5), 634–659. Copyright © 2019 American Psychological Association. Used with permission.

Although invisibility or goal irrelevance may not elicit negative stereotypes or prejudices, it does lead to negative consequences, including "indifference" and "passive neglect" (Neel & Lasseter, 2019).

Others have argued there are outright negative stereotypes, prejudice, and oppression directed at children. Pierce and Allen first identified "childism" or prejudice against children in the 1970s and defined it as "the automatic presumption or superiority of any adult over any child; it results in the adult's needs, desires, hopes, and fears taking unquestioned precedence over those of the child" (Pierce & Allen, 1975, p. 15; see also Bruehl, 2009, and Myles, 2015). Miller refers to various forms of cruelty to children in parenting and educational practices as "poisonous pedagogy" (Miller, 1984).

Furthermore, in research into right-wing authoritarianism, there are some concerning linkages and measures related to child-rearing practices (MacWilliams, 2016). According to Hetherington et al. (2018):

> . . . in today's world, where culture-war issues dominate the political landscape, child-rearing priorities and party are now tightly intertwined, making the partisan divide so deep and intense that it has become all but intractable.

These types of viewpoints and behaviors tend to further marginalize and subjugate children. As such, children can be viewed as an out-group and socially separated, as has been witnessed in cases where neighborhood covenants, restaurants, airlines, and local government zoning policies often work to discriminate against, restrict, or further "invisiblize" kids in society.

The media also often reflects society by focusing on parents when it comes to issues related to families and "leaves children in the background," according to a report by FrameWorks (Hestres et al., 2021). The study finds:

> Media coverage in which children are invisible undermines collective concern about children themselves. In addition, people are more likely to apply judgments of deservingness to parents than children—to think that parents may not deserve support because they have, people think, made bad choices that have led to their situation. In these ways, parent-focused framing could potentially undercut support for policies that provide benefits to families. (p. 18)

There are many ways to overcome the obstacles associated with focusing policies on children, the central purpose of the next section.

OVERCOMING BARRIERS TO SUCCESS

To address their barriers, educators, parents, other child advocates, and young people themselves will need to pursue a number of pathways toward improving child well-being. First, although there is much to worry about when it comes to children, public opinion polling indicates that, when voters are asked, they do express strong support for children's policy issues. Although most pollsters do not include children as an option when asking voters what their top issues are (kids are, once again, treated as an afterthought), a May 2019 poll by survey company Seltzer & Co. prior to the Iowa presidential caucuses did include children in their questions and found that 80 percent identified "improving the health, education, and well-being of children" as a high priority for the next president to address. In fact, children were cited more often as a higher priority than any other issue in that poll (Shope & Herink, 2019).

The following paragraphs describe steps that can be taken to move beyond partisan gridlock and center the health and education of young people as a policy priority that cuts across party lines.

Political psychologists have found that "strong partisan identity was far more likely than strong ideology or commitment to a single issue to drive campaign activity" (Huddy et al., 2015, p. 10). There are recent examples that highlight how education policy and funding can be made a focus of political action. Chapter 2 of this book, for example, highlights how community schools have successfully brought kids to the center of some communities.

After years of budget cuts to education programs at the state level during the last decade, a grassroots movement, Red for Ed, was created. This movement created a social identity or common bond of supporters who were protective of public schools and children and demanded increased funding for public schools and student supports.

In April 2018, the Arizona Education Association estimated more than 70,000 people participated in Red for Ed events (Sandler & McCrory, 2018). Alicia Ehinger, a 1st-grade teacher at Alta Loma Elementary School in Peoria, was quoted by *Cronkite News* as saying she was excited and nervous about the march. "It's been an emotional roller coaster the last few days," she said. "We're doing this for our students. Arizona kids deserve so much more. . . . Every single child can be anything they want to be with the help of us" (Sandler & McCrory, 2018). Other Red for Ed marches occurred in states and local communities across the country and helped raise attention to education issues and funding shortfalls. Due to this increased activity and attention, state and local lawmakers responded by increasing funding for public schools in many locations across the country (Blanc, 2019).

Support for children has been shown to be high on other issues as well. For instance, a nationwide poll by Lake Research Partners in November 2020, which was in the field just before the last presidential election, found that children received strong support from Democrats, Independents, and Republicans on broad issues and on specific issue proposals. A majority of voters supported establishing a "best interests" standard to govern government policy decisions (81% vs. 13%), creating an independent Children's Commissioner (65% vs. 26%), committing to cut child poverty in half (70% vs. 20%), and covering all children with health insurance (85% vs. 12%). After describing a specific legislation proposal, the American Family Act, to expand and improve the Child Tax Credit and reduce child poverty by 40%, voters expressed support for the bill by a wide (71% vs. 18%) margin (Lesley, 2020b).

Consequently, there is strong but often latent sympathy and support for children in our society. This book outlines a number of policies and investments that would make enormous differences in the lives of our children. To overcome the various systemic barriers in our educational and political systems that prevent sustained support and investment in the next generation, things must change.

To achieve success both in and out of schools, we must be attentive to and devise ways to overcome key political and societal barriers, including making children visible to policymakers and in society. We must overcome the "parent bubble" and marginalization of children. We must help the media, the public, and government understand "every policy issue is a children's issue" and that there is a role that parents, government, *and* children play in addressing them.

To invoke the words of Gabriela Mistral, Chilean poet and Nobel Prize winner:

> Many things we need can wait. The child cannot. Now is the time his bones are being formed, his mind developed. To him, we cannot say tomorrow, his name is today.

We must make the best interests of every child a priority and focus of both government and society. And last, children and youth need adults to lean in and listen to the voices of children and be their advocates.

NOTE

1. For other examples of Supreme Court decisions recognizing fundamental rights and liberties of children, see Island Trees Sch. Dist. v. Pico (1982), 457 U.S. 853; Parham v. J. R. (1979), 442 U. S. 584, 600; Planned Parenthood of Central Mo. v. Danforth (1976), 428 U. S. 52, 74; Tinker v. Des Moines Independent Community School Dist. (1969), 393 U. S. 503, 506–507; In re Gault (1967), 387 U. S. 1, 13.

REFERENCES

Aizer, A., Hoynes, H., & Lleras-Muney, A. (2022). *Children and the U.S. social safety net: Balancing disincentives for adults and benefits for children* (Working Paper 29754). National Bureau of Economic Research.

American Viewpoint. (2014). *Poll for First Focus Campaign for children.* Unpublished.

Baker, B. D. (2017). *How money matters for schools* (School Finance Series). Learning Policy Institute. https://learningpolicyinstitute.org/sites/default/files/product-files/How_Money_Matters_REPORT.pdf

Black, D. W. (2020). *Schoolhouse burning: Public education and the assault on American Democracy.* Hachette Book Group.

Blanc, E. (2019). *Red state revolt: The teachers' strike-wave and working-class politics.* Verso.

Brown, X., Rucker, J. M., & Richeson, J. A. (2021). Political ideology moderates White Americans' reactions to racial demographic change. *Group Processes & Intergroup Relations, 25*(3), 642–660. https://doi.org/10.1177/13684302211052516

Brownstein, R. (2012, April 18). The gray and the brown: The generational mismatch. *Yahoo News.* https://news.yahoo.com/gray-brown-generational-mismatch-1500 41350.html

Bruehl, E. Y. (2009). Childism—Prejudice against children. *Contemporary Psychoanalysis, 45,* 251–265.

Commission to Eliminate Child Abuse and Neglect Fatalities. (2016). *Within our reach: A national strategy to eliminate child abuse and neglect fatalities.* U.S. Government Printing Office.

Committee for a Responsible Federal Budget. (2018). *Budgeting for the next generation: Does the budget process prioritize children?* https://www.crfb.org/papers/budgeting-next-generation-does-budget-process-prioritize-children

Currie, J. (2005). Health disparities and gaps in school readiness. *The Future of Children, 15*(1), 117–138.

Dailey, A. C., & Rosenbury, L. A. (2018). The new law of the child. *Yale Law Journal, 127*(6), 1448–1741. https://www.yalelawjournal.org/article/the-new-law-of-the-child

Davidson, H. (2014). Does the U.N. Convention on the Rights of the Child make a difference? *Michigan State International Law Review,* 22(2), 497–530.

DeParle, J. (2020, August 22). The coronavirus generation. *New York Times.* https://www.nytimes.com/2020/08/22/sunday-review/coronavirus-poverty-child-allowance.html

Duncan, G., & Le Menestrel, S. (Eds.). (2019). *A roadmap to reducing child poverty* (Consensus Study Report). The National Academies Press. https://nap.nationalacademies.org/catalog/25246/a-roadmap-to-reducing-child-poverty

Equity and Excellence Commission. (2013). *For each and every child: A strategy for education equity and excellence.* U.S. Department of Education, Office of Elementary and Secondary Education. https://oese.ed.gov/resources/oese-technical-assistance-centers/state-support-network/resources/every-child-strategy-education-equity-excellence/.

Feldman, S., Huddy, L., Wronski, J., & Lown, P. (2020). The interplay of empathy and individualism in support for social welfare programs. *Political Psychology,* 41(2), 343–362.

First Focus on Children. (2020). *Children's budget 2020.* https://firstfocus.org/resources/report/childrensbudget2020

First Focus on Children. (2021). *Children's budget 2021.* https://firstfocus.org/resources/report/childrens-budget-2021

Freeman, M. (1997). *The moral status of children.* Kluwer Law International.

Frey, W. H. (2018). *Diversity explosion: How new racial demographics are remaking America.* Brookings Institution Press.

Goodman, M. L., Kidman, R., & Theron, L. (2022, February 24). Integrative approach required to support children affected by COVID-19. *The Lancet: Child and Adolescent Health,* 6(4), 218–219. https://pubmed.ncbi.nlm.nih.gov/35219403/

Gromada, A., Rees, G., & Chzhen, Y. (2020). *Worlds of influence: Understanding what shapes child well-being in rich countries* (Innocenti Report Card, no. 16). UNICEF Office of Research.

Hahn, H., Lou, C., Isaacs, J. B., Lauderback, E., Daly, H., & Steurle, C. E. (2020). *Kids' share 2020: Report on federal expenditures on children through 2019 and future projections.* Urban Institute. https://www.urban.org/research/publication/kids-share-2020-report-federal-expenditures-children-through-2019-and-future-projections

Heckman, J. J. (2013). *Giving kids a fair chance.* The MIT Press.

Hestres, L. E., Rochman, A., Bosso, D., & Volmert, A. (2021). *How are children's issues portrayed in the news? A media content analysis.* FrameWorks.

Hetherington, M. J., Weiler, J., & Smith, A. E. (2018, November 29). How you think about raising children says a lot about your political views. *Vox.* https://www.vox.com/first-person/2018/11/29/18116789/trump-bolsonaro-right-wing-populism-voting-child-rearing

Hoynes, H. W., & Schanzenbach, D. W. (2018). Safety net investments in children. *Brookings Papers on Economic Activity, Spring 2018,* 89–150.

Huddy, L., Mason, L., & Aarøe, L. (2015). Expressive partisanship: Campaign involvement, political emotion, and partisan identity. *American Political Science Review,* 109(1), 1–17.

Huntington, C., & Scott, E. (2015). Children's health in a legal framework. *The Future of Children,* 25(1), 177–199.

Ingram, H., Schneider, A., & DeLeon, P. (2007). Social construction and policy design. In Paul A. Sabatier (Ed.), *Theories of the policy process* (2nd ed.). Routledge.

Jackson, C. K., & Mackevicius, C. (2021). *The distribution of school spending impacts* (Working Paper 28517). National Bureau of Economic Research.

Kapnick, I. (2020, November 20). 11th circuit splits with sister courts on gay-conversion bans. *Courthouse News Service*. https://www.courthousenews.com/11th-circuit-splits-with-sister-courts-on-gay-conversion-bans/

Lesley, B. A. (2010). *Money does matter! Investing in Texas children and our future*. The Equity Center. https://www.equitycenter.org/sites/default/files/2018-09/moneymatters.pdf

Lesley, B. (2016). *The racial generation gap and the future for our children*. First Focus on Children.

Lesley, B. (2018, April 1). *Protecting our kids: Why we need a commissioner for America's children*. Medium. https://medium.com/voices4kids/give-children-a-voice-in-our-democracy-891b768c840d

Lesley, B. (2020a, April 11). *COVID-19: How the health of children is at stake*. Medium. https://medium.com/voices4kids/covid-19-how-the-health-of-children-is-at-stake-98d53115d9ec

Lesley, B. (2020b, November 23). *Survey: The American people are unified in their support of children*. Medium. https://medium.com/voices4kids/survey-the-american-people-are-unified-in-support-of-children-461c15907a37

Lynch, L. (2018, January 19). "He could have been stopped in 1997": Survivor of Larry Nassar's alleged sex abuse says victims were ignored. *CBC Radio*. https://www.cbc.ca/radio/thecurrent/the-current-for-january-19-2018-1.4493695/he-could-have-been-stopped-in-1997-survivor-of-larry-nassar-s-alleged-sex-abuse-says-victims-were-ignored-1.4493702

MacWilliams, M. C. (2016, January 17). The one weird trait that predicts whether you are a Trump supporter. *POLITICO Magazine*. https://www.politico.com/magazine/story/2016/01/donald-trump-2016-authoritarian-213533/

Martinez, A. B. (2020, February 27). Female genital mutilation: The status of U.S. laws restricting the practice. *ACS In Brief*. https://www.acslaw.org/inbrief/female-genital-mutilation-the-status-of-u-s-laws-restricting-the-practice/

McCoy-Roth, M., Mackintosh, B. B., & Murphey, D. (2012). When the bough breaks: The effects of homelessness on young children. *Child Trends: Early Childhood Highlights*, *3*(1), 1–11.

Miller, A. (1984). *For your own good: Hidden cruelty in child-rearing and the roots of violence*. Farrar, Straus and Giroux.

Morales, C. (2021, April 25). $1 million in toxic bleach sold as "miracle" cure, officials say. *New York Times*. https://www.nytimes.com/2021/04/25/us/miracle-bleach-cure-covid-19.html

Mousin, C. A. (2019). Rights disappear when U.S. policy engages children as weapons of deterrence. *AMA Journal of Ethics*

Myles, A. (2015). *Casting light on childism: Recognizing, resisting, and transforming prejudice and oppression against children* [Doctoral dissertation, Widener University]. Widener University ProQuest Dissertations Publishing.

Neel, R., & Lassetter, B. (2019). The stigma of perceived irrelevance: An affordance-management theory of interpersonal invisibility. *Psychological Review*, *126*(5), 634–659.

Neuberg, S. L., Williams, K. E. G., Sng, O., Pick, C. M., Neel, R., Krems, J. A., & Pirlott, A. G. (2020). Toward capturing the functional and nuanced nature of social stereotypes: An affordance management approach. *Advances in Experimental Social Psychology, 62*, 245–304.

Newkirk, V. R., II (2020, March 24). The kids aren't all right. *The Atlantic.* https://www.theatlantic.com/health/archive/2020/03/what-coronavirus-will-do-kids/608608/

Organization for Economic Cooperation and Development (OECD). (2020, Aug. 11). Combatting COVID-19's effect on children. https://read.oecd-ilibrary.org/view/?ref=132_132643-m91j2scsyh&title=Combatting-COVID-19-s-effect-on-children&_ga=2.71476435.1721095950.1631924509-2014588205.1631924509

Organization for Economic Cooperation and Development (OECD). (2019). Family benefits public spending. https://data.oecd.org/socialexp/family-benefits-public-spending.htm

Parolin, Z., Collyer, S., & Curran, M. A. (2022). *December child tax credit payment kept 3.7 million children from poverty.* Center on Policy and Social Policy at Columbia University. https://www.povertycenter.columbia.edu/news-internal/monthly-poverty-december-2021

Pastor, M., Scoggins, J., & Treuhaft, S. (2017). *Bridging the racial generation gap is key to America's economic future.* PolicyLink and the University of Southern California Program for Environmental and Regional Equity (PERE).

Peleg, N. (2021, September 2). *In debates about opening schools, we're neglecting an important voice: our children's.* The Conversation. https://theconversation.com/in-debates-about-opening-schools-were-neglecting-an-important-voice-our-childrens-167179

Pierce, C. M., & Allen, G. B. (1975). Childism. *Psychiatric Annals, 5*(7), 266–270.

Portuba, J. M. (1997). Demographic structure and the political economy of public education. *Journal of Policy Analysis and Management, 16*(1), 48–66.

Portuba, J. M. (1996, July). *Demographic structure and the political economy of public education* (Working Paper 5677). National Bureau of Economic Research.

Putnam, R. D. (2016). *Our kids: The American Dream in crisis.* Simon & Schuster.

Raisman, A. (2018, January 20). Full text of Aly Raisman's statement. *New York Times.* https://www.nytimes.com/2018/01/20/sports/full-text-of-aly-raismans-statement.html

Sandler, G., & McCrory, C. (2018, April 26). Tens of thousands hit street to protect education funding in Red for Ed march to Capitol. *Cronkite News.* https://cronkitenews.azpbs.org/2018/04/26/red-for-ed/

Scott, R., & Siegel, B. (2021, December 20). Sen. Joe Manchin suggests Child Tax Credit payments would be used to buy drugs. *ABC News.* https://abcnews.go.com/Politics/sen-joe-manchin-suggests-child-tax-credit-payments/story?id=81865740

Serena, K. (2018, March 14). *The tragic tale of Candace Newmaker, the girl who died in a "rebirthing" treatment.* All That's Interesting. https://allthatsinteresting.com/candace-newmaker

Shope, L., & Herink, J. (2019, June 24). Poll shows voters' focus on issues affecting Iowa children. *Des Moines Register.* https://www.desmoinesregister.com/story

/opinion/columnists/2019/06/24/poll-shows-voters-focus-issues-affecting-iowa-children/1547231001/

Stafford, L., Harkin, J., Rolfe, A., Burton, J., & Morley, C. (2021). Why having a voice is important to children who are involved in family support services. *Child Abuse & Neglect, 115*, 104987. https://doi.org/10.1016/j.chiabu.2021.104987

Todres, J. (2014). A child rights framework for addressing trafficking of children. *Michigan State International Law Review, 22*(2), 557–594.

Todres, J., & King, S. M. (Eds.). (2020). *The Oxford handbook of children's rights law*. Oxford University Press.

Troxel v. Granville, 530 U.S. 57. (2000).

Troxel v. Granville, 530 U.S. 57 (2000) (Stevens, J., dissenting).

UNICEF. (2020, April 9). *Don't let children be the hidden victims of COVID-19 pandemic* [Statement]. UNICEF. https://www.unicef.org/press-releases/dont-let-children-be-hidden-victims-covid-19-pandemic

Volokh, E. (2014, Apr. 18). Sterilization of the "intellectually disabled." *Washington Post*. https://www.washingtonpost.com/news/volokh-conspiracy/wp/2014/04/18/sterilization-of-the-intellectually-disabled/

Wilson, J. (2016, Apr. 13). Letting them die: Parents refuse medical help for children in the name of Christ. *The Guardian*. https://www.theguardian.com/us-news/2016/apr/13/followers-of-christ-idaho-religious-sect-child-mortality-refusing-medical-help

Wolf, L. J., Thorne, S. R., Iosifyan, M., Foad, C., Taylor, S., Costin, V., Karremans, J. C., Haddock, G., & Maio, G. R. (2022). The salience of children increases adult prosocial values. *Social Psychological and Personality Science, 13*(1), 160–169.

Zadrozny, B. (2019, May 21). Parents are poisoning their children with bleach to 'cure' autism. These moms are trying to stop it. *NBC News*. https://www.nbcnews.com/tech/internet/moms-go-undercover-fight-fake-autism-cures-private-facebook-groups-n1007871

Zeballos-Roig, J. (2022, January 4). Joe Manchin digs in on cutting the poorest parents out of the Biden child tax credit as Build Back Better looks dead in the water. *Business Insider*. https://www.businessinsider.com/manchin-digs-in-biden-child-tax-credit-work-requirement-2022-1

CHAPTER 4

Whose Vision of Racial Equity?
Reinventing Education Policy in
Post–Civil Rights America

Sonya Douglass and Anna Kushner

INTRODUCTION

The themes raised by Arnold Fege, John Jackson, and Bruce Lesley in the previous chapters are still shaping today's most contested battles that center on race, education, and social policies. This chapter expands on those issues, exploring educational policies focused on racial equity in the post–Civil Rights Era and the role of education in a constitutional democracy (Allen, 2016). We use critical policy analysis (Horsford et al., 2019) as a framework to discuss the possibilities associated with racial equity efforts informed by the Black freedom struggle for equal education in service of an emancipatory vision of education. More specifically, we ask: (1) What assumptions and ideologies support education policies focused on diversity and integration and to what end? (2) How might schools and districts serve as levers for community empowerment, civic participation, and social change? We conclude with a discussion of how research, policy, and practice partnerships will be key to ensuring community voices are central to the education politics and policy change and that efforts to advance racial equity will be led by those whose perspectives are closest to the problem and, thus, best equipped to guide and assess the conceptualization of the solution, its appropriateness, and its effectiveness. The chapter also includes guiding questions for further consideration and discussion.

THE POLITICS OF RACE AND EQUITY: COMPETING VALUES IN EDUCATION

In the United States, education has long been considered "the great equalizer" (Mann, 1848/1957). Even then-president Donald Trump proclaimed that "education is the civil rights issue of our time" (Darville, 2017), echoing the sentiment of past presidents, including Barack Obama and George W. Bush. However, definitions of equality and fairness in the United States are mutating. Despite over 60 years of legislation intended to make the education system more just, discussions of race, racism, and even educational equity are becoming more controversial. School board meetings across the country are engaging in heated debates and sometimes violent confrontations over the teaching of critical race theory[1] and ideas viewed by some as "anti-American." Presently, there is a highly partisan movement seeking to ban conversations about systemic racism, the Pulitzer Prize–winning *1619 Project*,[2] and what some call "critical race theory" from public schools across the United States.

These controversial topics share one thing in common: they acknowledge the racist and racializing history of the United States, acknowledging the still-present impact of chattel slavery, segregation, and Jim Crow that affects the social and material lives of Americans to this day. Beginning in 2020, then-president Donald Trump strongly opposed this "anti-American propaganda," claiming that "if not removed, [it] will dissolve the civic bonds that tie us together. It will destroy our country" (Wise, 2020). In response, he began the "1776 Commission," designed to promote "patriotic education" and teach the promise of the founding documents that stated that "all men are created equal" instead of encouraging children to "hate America for the wrongs committed in the past." Although the federal government does not control the education curriculum taught in the United States, and the funding for the 1776 Commission was miniscule, this commission highlights the deeply entrenched ideologies that antiracist educators and lawmakers face.

The controversy over critical race theory is an issue at the nexus of race and education that reveals the deep-seated nature of systemic racism and discrimination that often manifests in educational policies and practices in the United States. As of November 2021, legislation banning the *New York Times' 1619 Project* and critical race theory has been proposed in over 22 states and signed into law in nine states, including Idaho, Oklahoma, Tennessee, Texas, Iowa, New Hampshire, South Carolina, Arizona, and North Dakota (Ray & Gibbons, 2021). One state's bill goes so far as to prohibit teaching any materials that promote the idea that "an individual should feel discomfort, guilt, anguish or any other form of psychological distress on account of the individual's race or sex." The central argument of the ban is that because it focuses on race, it is inherently racist. This (false) conceptualization of critical race theory has been generalized to include concepts valued and taught in the U.S. education system, including equity. In June 2021, one high school teacher and reporter for *The Federalist* spoke out condemning equity, stating:

> This is just one example of how critical race theory—or equity— treats everyone regardless of their color or race as mere avatars . . . It

sounds lovely—equity—but it is poison. Because equity is not about equality of opportunity, which is foundational to American political culture and economic strength. It is about equal outcomes, which is foundational to Marxist political ideology. (Ruiz, 2021)

In short, some politicians are seeking to rebrand educational equity as anti-American and anti-White, despite decades of popular and bipartisan support for equality-oriented education policy. This is somewhat ironic, considering how the concept of equity has evolved from a vision of redistribution in the 1960s to something closer to the equality of opportunity that this educator calls for. Educational equity is now routinely conceptualized as individual achievements, high test scores, and access to an education that will allow future laborers to contribute to the economy productively (Horsford, Scott, & Anderson, 2019).

The language of civil rights has been coopted by progressive education advocates "to emphasize individualistic aspirations through the expansion of choice and individual empowerment" (Hernández, 2016, p. 3; see also Scott, 2013a, 2013b). School choice is widely used as a mechanism to increase competition and subsequently improve the quality of education available to students. However, many schools, especially "No Excuses"–style charter schools, hyper-individualize students, and place the responsibility on them to close the achievement gap. This colorblind approach to education reform frames structural and political barriers to equity as "excuses" for minoritized students' "gaps" in achievement (Ellison & Iqtadar, 2020).

WHOSE VISION OF RACIAL EQUITY AND TO WHAT END?

Critical policy analysis (CPA) provides us with a viewpoint from which to see concerns about equity and a framework through which to interpret them. To understand the importance of CPA, it is useful to detail the underlying assumptions of traditional policy analysis. Traditional frameworks of policy analysis, based heavily in traditions of positivism, rationality, and functionalism largely assume that policymakers and implementors are rational actors and are primarily concerned with policy outcomes (Levinson et al., 2009; Nagel, 1984; Young & Diem, 2017). This conceptualization of policy focuses on inputs and outcomes, and often treats the process of implementation as a black box. Critical policy analysis, on the other hand, does not presume rationality; instead, it interrogates the politics, power structures, beliefs, and assumptions made in traditional policy analysis frameworks (Young & Diem, 2017). CPA draws from a variety of interrelated critical frameworks that help thinkers challenge assumptions in our day-to-day lives, like critical race theory, Black feminist theory, and neoliberalism.

Using critical policy analysis helps us answer the question, "Whose vision of racial equity?" is guiding our priorities in education.

Despite both the history of equality-oriented education policy and partisan calls to ban it, equity remains a central concern in education policy. Schools continue to be segregated and unsafe for Black students given the rise in hate crimes, police violence and brutality, and racially discriminatory policies and practices that create hostile environments and traumatic experiences in the very places where children and youth should feel safe and affirmed. Although some liberal and progressive school communities are advocating for more racially and socioeconomically diverse and integrated schools, these conceptions of diversity and integration leave something to be desired. Often, these reforms become explicitly tied to individual students' achievement; success and failure are personal and removed from a larger political and social context. When school promotes individual achievement over community well-being, schooling promotes individual students' social mobility rather than preparing citizens for collaborative, political engagement through schooling for democratic equality (Labaree, 1997). Inherently, this emphasis on schooling for social mobility seeks to expand on the capital that individual students have access to because of their education; a student's education is thought of as a private good that prepares the individual for economic success in the market as an adult.

This tension can be understood through the concept of neoliberalism. Neoliberalism is "a theory of political economic practices that proposes that human well-being can best be advanced by liberating individual entrepreneurial freedoms and skills" (Harvey, 2007). Notably, neoliberals advocate for the privatization of social goods and the retrenchment of the public sphere (Apple, 2010, 2018). As Lipman (2011) observed, diversity discourses are firmly embedded within a larger neoliberal project promoting the self-interest of individuals, and the benefits they will accrue from school diversity and integration. Conversations about diversity are often framed as "beneficial for all students," and not necessarily as a policy alternative with a social-justice orientation. Diversity projects may result in a "social justice for the advantaged' (Horsford, 2016) whereby the private desires of the dominant group hold greater value than the public good, undermining any meaningful efforts to address educational inequality" (Horsford, Scott, & Anderson, 2019, pp. 15). Desegregation efforts that fail to address and disrupt racial hierarchies will not create educational equity for students of color. In fact, they are likely to reinforce cultures of low expectations for Black students and serve as a useful distraction from holding educational leaders and policymakers accountable for adequate and equitable funding of schools in terms of resources, culturally relevant teachers who are endorsed by the communities they serve, and representation among leadership.

How did the United States go from "separate but equal" to "social justice for the advantaged?" Ironically, much of the top-down judicial and legislative push to increase equity and diversity in schools has had a neo-liberalizing effect. In the next section, we trace the history of equity policy in education from the 1950s to the present.

THE BLACK FREEDOM STRUGGLE FOR EQUAL EDUCATION

The goal of the *Brown* ruling, and other civil rights legislation was to bring about equality of opportunity, but it was not universally seen as a harbinger of positive change. As some previously all-White schools allowed Black students into their hallways and classrooms, many of the Black schools closed their doors for good. Often, Black teachers and principals were left without jobs (Horsford, 2011; Moody, 1971; Tillman, 2004), and Black students now attending majority-White schools were left without teachers who cared for them, let alone education leaders who shared a racial or cultural background (Horsford, 2011; Morris, 2008).

Regardless of its criticisms and shortcomings, the *Brown* ruling that ended state-sanctioned segregation was a major civil-rights victory, and it did not occur in isolation; the growing role of the federal government in the quest for educational equality set the stage for a new era of education policy. Over the next 10 years, the United States federal government would pass a variety of legislation to support the civil rights movement and the demand for Black people to be treated equally under the law. For example, the Elementary and Secondary School Act (ESEA) of 1965, which included language intended to bring about more equitable access to education by providing schools that served low-income students with more funding. Additionally, the Federal Civil Rights Act of 1964 withheld federal funding for any program that discriminated on the basis of race, color, national origin, or gender, which would eventually aid in the enforcement of the *Brown* decree by allowing the federal government to withhold funds from districts that discriminated against Black students (Minow, 2004).

It also required the U.S. Office of Education to publish a report describing the extent of racial segregation in U.S. schools and how adversely students of color were affected by existing segregation. This report, formally called *Equality of Educational Opportunity* but more widely known as the Coleman Report, highlighted the way Black students had fewer educational opportunities than White students and that a subsequent "gap in achievement" between White and non-White students existed, especially in the southern United States. This report was the foundation for all subsequent achievement gap discourse, which remains prevalent today. From this point on, equality in education would be defined as attaining similar achievement scores on standardized tests in order to close the "achievement gap," and policymakers would increasingly scrutinize and track the achievement of minoritized students, imbuing them with *badges of inferiority*—symbols of persistent underachievement that would continue to associate Black educational performance with deficiency and relegate Black learners to life at the bottom of Derrick Bell's metaphorical well (Bell, 1994; Horsford & Grosland, 2013).

FROM CIVIL RIGHTS TO HIGH-STAKES TESTING AND ACCOUNTABILITY

In 1983, the U.S. National Commission on Excellence in Education published *A Nation at Risk: the Imperative for Education Reform*, which broadcasted concerns of a "rising tide of mediocrity" that was causing the United States to fall behind on a global scale and pushed education policymakers to focus on "excellence" for all students (United States National Commission on Excellence in Education, 1983). This report sounded the alarm regarding dropping SAT scores and grades, not acknowledging that more marginalized students were being offered access to these benchmarks than previously recorded. This publication set the stage for the standards movement in education that has shaped policy ever since. Furthermore, *A Nation at Risk* posited that schools, not society, are responsible for students' low performance, creating an artificial separation between students' academic achievements and their lived experiences. This report shifted popular discourse about education from "equality" to "excellence," introduced the notion of accountability, and highlighted individual returns on education, setting the stage for hyperregulation and neoliberal reforms in the future (Mehta, 2015).

The accountability and standards movement formed in the 1980s continued to shape education policy in the 1990s and into the new millennium. The most notorious example of accountability came in the 2001 reauthorization of the ESEA—No Child Left Behind (NCLB). This reauthorization is in service of educational equality, and was intended to close "the achievement gap between high- and low-performing children, especially the achievement gaps between minority and nonminority students, and between disadvantaged children and their more advantaged peers" (NCLB, 2001, Sec. 1001 [3]) by enforcing adequate yearly progress (AYP) requirements to ensure that "all schools" and "all students" meet *the same* academic standards in reading and mathematics. Schools not making AYP were first given additional federal funds to spend on improving instruction, but, eventually, schools could be taken over if they were "underperforming." NCLB required schools and districts to disaggregate their data by "sub-groups" in six categories—race/

ethnicity, economic disadvantage, disability, limited English proficiency, migrant status, and gender.

Notably, this was the first time that schools had to publicly report out achievement data by race/ethnicity, forcing stakeholders to consider whether a school was serving all enrolled students. This further institutionalized the shift from equality to equity. Instead of an emphasis on equality, or "everyone getting the same," the policy of disaggregating data by race/ethnicity shifted the conversation to equity, or "everyone getting according to their need." However, policymakers did not take outside school factors, like resources and fairness of assessments, into consideration when determining goals. So-called "achievement gaps" persisted in schools failing to make adequate yearly progress, and schools began to intervene following the guidance of the law. These interventions had a neoliberalizing effect on schools, including introducing measures of school choice and contracting with vendors to provide additional services for students. If schools consistently failed to make AYP, they were threatened with closing or becoming charter schools.

The threat of not achieving test scores high enough to make AYP led to increased surveillance and hyperregulation in schools, especially those serving predominantly low-income students and students of color (Horsford, 2019). Fearing eventual closure, schools serving "under achieving" students became hyperregulated, increasing standardized testing, test preparation, core-content instruction, and the number of private partners and consultants coming into the school community to help "close the gaps" in student achievement. This increased effort to make students pass standardized assessments often came at the expense of humanizing educational experiences. Herein lies a paradox of the quest for educational equity: although increased testing, achievement monitoring, and test preparation were reforms intended to promote educational equity and close achievement gaps, these practices resulted in further marginalization of Black students and other students of color.

The popular fixation on "closing achievement gaps," even when intended to improve the outcomes of marginalized students, can reinforce marginalized students' enduring "badges of inferiority" (Bell, 1994; Horsford & Grosland, 2013). Furthermore, these efforts remained entirely separate from social or political context that would explain these gaps and did not include social reforms that might address inequality outside of the classroom. While No Child Left Behind monitored low-income students' achievement and held schools accountable for their progress, the law did not address students' holistic needs (Darling-Hammond & Cook-Harvey, 2018; Darling-Hammond & Cook, this volume) hunger, the growing number of students experiencing homelessness, or the rising levels of economic inequality across the United States (Bishop & Noguera, 2019; Gallagher et al., 2020; this volume; Edwards, Morton, & Kull, this volume). Nor did it address growing concerns with the relationship between the education and carceral systems (James, this volume).

Without adequate school funding (Jiménez-Castellanos, Farrie, & Quinn, this volume), physical (Davis & Mays, this volume), environmental (Grineski & Collins, this volume), and mental-health supports, responsive and affirming school-safety protocols, and discipline policies that do not perpetuate harm against students of color (and especially Black boys), monitoring academic achievement is insufficient (Howard, this volume; Astor & Reynolds, this volume). While schools receive additional funding to support "underachieving" students, this money was punitive and encouraged public/private partnerships rather than giving local education agencies and schools the resources they needed to serve their students. Finally, while choice policies were integrated into NCLB to allow for students to leave failing schools for higher-achieving ones, this legislative reform did not sufficiently address the racial and socioeconomic segregation that many researchers believe perpetuates students' unequal outcomes (Ayscue & Frankenberg, this volume). Put more concretely, fragmented approaches to education reform will not eradicate inequality; reform must be holistic and address the myriad social and economic factors that impact, and often undermine, efforts to improve academic outcomes (Bishop & Noguera, 2019). Race-centered policies must be the primary aim of any holistic approaches, the theme of the next section.

RACIAL EQUITY AND EDUCATION POLICY IN POST-CIVIL RIGHTS AMERICA

Since the spring of 2020, the quadruple pandemics of COVID-19, the resulting economic recession, climate change, and anti-Black violence in the form of police brutality and White terrorism have fueled a movement for racial equity across public and private sectors, systems, and institutions to once and for all right the wrongs of the nation's racist past and reimagine its future. Despite the centrality of equality and freedom to America as a constitutional democracy, the ironies and contradictions associated with these concepts in a nation that continues to struggle in its capacity and willingness to protect the rights of all its citizens has created especially wicked problems for educational leaders and policymakers responsible for advancing racial equity in schools. Commitments to equality, opportunity, and justice across race and class lines have now shifted toward a focus on antiracism and antiracist leadership absent a sufficient grounding in the essential nature of equality and freedom in a democracy and how these ideals must be cherished and upheld through the investment in an effective and coordinated system of education in the United States.

While we might invoke Mann's characterization of education as "the great equalizer of the conditions of men" or many presidents and almost every Education Secretary's claim that education is "the civil rights issue of our time," the role that schools and education play in American society are important to consider as we reflect on the past to develop a more effective path toward educational equality and freedom. That path forward should include the following key tenets:

1. There is value in examining the history of civil rights advocacy, education policy, and activism to contextualize how the fight for antiracism and racial equity are informed by the Black freedom struggle. In fact, the hotly debated and greatly misunderstood analytical framework, critical race theory, proves particularly useful here given its attention to the pervasive nature of racism in American life, the centering of people of color, and critical examinations of Whiteness, liberalism, and racial politics in determining which groups enjoy the rights and protections of citizenship and which groups do not.

Prior to the 1950s, the practice of separate-but-equal schooling was codified in law, until the *Brown v. Board* decision of 1954 would once and for all end the practice of Jim Crow segregation, made constitutional by *Plessy vs. Ferguson*'s (1896) doctrine of separate-but-equal. In their majority opinion, the Supreme Court determined that racial segregation did not violate the equal protection clause of the 14th Amendment if the facilities provided to different races were equal. In his majority opinion, Justice Henry Billings Brown argued, "If the civil and political rights of both races be equal one cannot be inferior to the other civilly or politically. If one race be inferior to the other socially [*sic*], the Constitution of the United States cannot put them upon the same plane."

It is essential for our democracy to dismantle policies and practices imbued with systemic and institutional racism by advocating for a more equitable distribution of opportunities and resources in ways that remedy the wrongs of the past in service of equality and freedom. Although "separate but equal" was the justification for having segregated schools for Black students, these schools were never provided with adequate funding or resources. Thus, one could argue that it was not simply the fact that separate was never equal but the audacity associated with establishing a social order that is segregated based on race, yet declaring the system fair, just, and colorblind in the eyes of the law.

Desegregating schools by making them more racially and socioeconomically diverse continues to be a popular reform goal among liberals and progressives in the public and private sectors.[3] Furthermore, school desegregation, despite *Brown II*'s "all deliberate speed" provision supported by individual and institutional acts of White resistance, drastically reconfigured the public sphere. While plans for achieving integration have varied by state, district, and lower-court rulings, the prevailing idea is that by encouraging diversity and championing individual choice, integration will occur (Yoon, 2017). In reality, rather than enrolling their children in schools that would promote racial integration, White families have pulled their children out of public schools with racially diverse populations that exceeded their idea of what was comfortable or appropriate in terms of racial composition, or would move to another neighborhood to avoid school assignments. In those cases, White families were often opting for private academies and taking their economic resources with them (Cashin, 2004; Horsford, 2019). Legal scholar and critical race theorist Derrick Bell famously reflected that *Brown vs. Board of Education* would have better served Black people if it had challenged the "equal" rather than the "separate" in separate but equal (Bell, 2004). Nearly 20 years before the *Brown* ruling, sociologist W.E.B. Du Bois shared similar sentiments; when discussing school segregation in 1935, he proclaimed that "Negro children need neither segregated schools nor mixed schools. What they need is education" (Du Bois, 1935).

2. Diversity serves as a race-neutral, colorblind policy solution that is more likely to gain support from Whites than redistributive funding policies but does not significantly contribute to the redistribution of resources inherent to equitable solutions.

What diversity means to those who seek it and what type of diversity people support, however, remains unclear (Bell & Hartmann 2007; Moore & Bell, 2011). Diversity is used in two common ways: it can be used to refer to the presence of racial minorities (Bell & Hartmann, 2007; Plaut et al., 2011; Unzueta & Binning, 2010), and it can be defined in broader ways that are colorblind and inclusive to White folks (Berrey, 2015; Plaut, et al., 2011; Unzueta & Binning, 2010). For example, when companies work to increase diversity, a common strategy for addressing the Equal Employment Opportunity Act, they often do so by recruiting racial minorities but also promote diversity in other ways, including ethnicity, gender, sexual orientation, and socioeconomic background. While hiring candidates from different backgrounds is important, this broad focus on diversity diverts from the policy power of the Equal Employment Opportunity Act, which was passed in 1972 to prevent discrimination against Black job applicants.

Advocates proclaim that attending diverse schools raises academic outcomes (as measured by test scores) for students of color (e.g., Card & Rothstein, 2007; Cook, 2018; Dee & Penner, 2017; Johnson & Nazaryan, 2019; Reardon et al., 2012). In most cases, however, such benefits are not discussed within the sociopolitical contexts that established separate and unequal access to high-quality teaching and learning opportunities and resources (Darling-Hammond, 2015). School diversity is also marketed as beneficial to

White students, who gain access to multicultural capital (Turner, 2018) from attending diverse schools (e.g., Ahmed, 2007; Roda & Wells, 2013; Warikoo, 2016).

CENTERING CRITICAL RESEARCH PERSPECTIVES TO REINVENT EDUCATION POLICY IN POST-CIVIL RIGHTS AMERICA

The value of critical race perspectives and approaches to studying the problem of inequality is that rather than simply "measuring inequality" or making "inequality discoveries," there is an opportunity to conduct research that centers and integrates the needs, concerns, interests, and priorities of people of color, in ways that go beyond how they experience inequality or the extent to which it has gotten better or worse, but rather what must be done to reduce it. This makes critical race theory and critical policy analysis useful tools when it comes to social change and action. By situating history, economics, policy, law, and politics as central to the analysis of contemporary education issues and solutions, CRT has been especially useful in elucidating and bringing attention to problems of race and racism. Yet there is a danger in taking up these frameworks without taking the time to study and really understand the propositions that are so integral to critical race theory. It is more than a list of tenets or phrases that are used to convey White power, privilege, or White supremacy. Rather, when foundational knowledge is missing (and must be acquired) among those individuals responsible for leading our nation's classrooms, schools, school districts, local and state boards of education, legislators, advocates, and allies, we find ourselves with an incomplete policy picture.

To be sure, racial awakenings have presented a window of opportunity whereby individuals who did not realize or want to know the true source of racial inequality have a greater glimpse into what those closest to the problems of inequality have been saying all along. Policymakers in search of equitable approaches and outcomes must take a hard look at the research evidence upon which they are creating and supporting policy (see Doucet, 2019; Tuck & Yang, 2014). When it comes to the use of research evidence and its potential impact on the transformation of the U.S. education system, there is no greater lever for change than providing policymakers, administrators, and systems-level leaders committed to racial equity with research evidence that is relevant, routine, and relational, and informed by the voices, experiences, and perspectives of people of color.

For example, the Black Education Research Collective (BERC) conducted a national survey and regional focus groups to better understand how Black parents, teachers, students, education, and community leaders understand how the COVID-19 pandemic and systemic racism have impacted the education of Black children. When asked about priorities as the nation recovers from the quadruple pandemics we are currently facing, respondents gave a variety of answers, including responsive curriculum, increasing the number of Black teachers in schools, mental-health services, and centering students' needs (Horsford et al., 2021). Notably absent was the "learning loss" that dominates reports that do not center the voices and standpoints of Black respondents and other respondents of color (e.g., Dorn et al., 2020; Engzell et al., 2021). This example highlights the different policy and reform priorities that arise depending on who identifies and answers research questions about educational equity. This logic extends to the role and voice young people have in evaluating their own educational experiences—see Green & Coles, this volume for a more detailed discussion of youth voice and educational equity.

Policymakers around the country are also beginning to respond to the call to ensure policy is informed, written, and evaluated by people of color. For example, in 2015, a school district in Brooklyn, New York, revised its middle school student assignment policy to create more racially and socioeconomically diverse schools. Instead of enforcing a new policy from the top down, district officials partnered with the community, circulated a survey, held a series of listening workshops, and developed a policy that reflected the desires and needs of community members. Policymakers made efforts to center the voices of community members of color; although they did not ask for respondents' demographic data in their survey, they weighted the responses from neighborhoods with larger populations of Black, Latinx, and Asian families when making policy recommendations. This shift resulted in the removal of all school screens for middle schools in the district (*D15 Diversity Plan*, 2018).

Racial reckonings in education in 2020–2021 among researchers and practitioners alike have drawn much-needed attention to the racially segregated nature of the research evidence and scholarship upon which school diversity and integration policies and their advocacy are based (Horsford, 2019, 2021). Future research must question scholarship that privileges White perspectives and voices on matters of race and ask: *Whose conceptions of diversity and integration are being advanced in this narrative? How does one's racial experience, identity, and understanding of what it means to be raced or experience racism inform their knowledge and interpretations of what is happening at the nexus of race and schooling? How might education research conducted by individuals who have never experienced racism be methodologically limited or flawed, and what are the implications of the limitations for the field's inability to address the issues of civil rights in education once and for all?*

While critical policy analysis makes explicit the ways in which race permeates the research conceptualization process and its implications for policy development, implementation, and analysis, many questions remain. *How might research evidence that centers the perspectives of people of color be used to inform an educational vision and agenda for racial equity? How will greater racial diversity and representation among education policymakers and leaders influence how research evidence is conceptualized, valued, and utilized? Whose research evidence will be trusted in terms of quality, methodology, rigor, and representativeness of the policy problems facing communities of color?*

By asking critical questions together, across research, practice, and policy communities, there is great promise in how research can be used to empower communities as they advocate for themselves. The movement for racial equity and justice can only be advanced by research focused on addressing racial and social inequalities, rather than measuring efficiency or effectiveness. Even in our framing of equity in education, equity becomes a lever for achieving the goals of efficiency or effectiveness rather than how schools and districts can serve as levers for racial equity and social change at a greater scale. Research evidence capturing this perspective is the type of work that must be supported, as it is foundational to any racial equity or social justice agenda in education or public policy. Such an agenda must move beyond inequality discoveries and reinvent education policy grounded in critical scholarship as the basis for systemic change and action.

NOTES

1. Critical race theory (CRT) is a set of academic concepts that emerged from legal theory in the 1970s that reinforce the idea that race is socially constructed, and racism is systematic and embedded in legal systems and policies across the United States (Delgado & Stefancic, 2013).

2. The 1619 Project began as a series of essays and media published in *The New York Times Magazine* in 2019. It seeks to "[illuminate] the legacy of slavery in the contemporary United States, and highlights the contributions of Black Americans to every aspect of American society" (https://1619education.org/about-1619-project).

3. See, for example, the Century Foundation's Bridges Collaborative (https://tcf.org/bridges-collaborative) which was founded to promote a national integration agenda and encourage integration-centered partnerships between schools and housing authorities, or even the Federal Department of Education's "Diversity & Opportunity" website (https://www.ed.gov/diversity-opportunity) that encourages diversity initiatives and promotes opportunities for funding that increase racial and socioeconomic diversity in schools.

REFERENCES

Ahmed, S. (2007). The language of diversity. *Ethnic and Racial Studies, 30*(2), 235–256.

Allen, D. (2016). *Education and equality*. University of Chicago Press.

Apple, M. W. (2010). On doing critical policy analysis. *Educational Policy, 33*(1) 276–287.

Apple, M. W. (2018). *The struggle for democracy in education: Lessons from social realities.* Routledge.

Bell, D. (2004). *Silent covenants:* Brown v. Board of Education *and the unfulfilled hopes for racial reform.* Oxford University Press.

Bell, D. (1994). *Faces at the bottom of the well: The permanence of racism.* Hachette UK.

Bell, J. M., & Hartmann, D. (2007). Diversity in everyday discourse: The cultural ambiguities and consequences of "happy talk." *American Sociological Review, 72*(6), 895–914.

Berrey, E. (2015). Making a civil rights claim for affirmative action: Bamn's legal mobilization and the legacy of race-conscious policies. *Du Bois Review: Social Science Research on Race, 12*(2), 375–405.

Bishop, J. P., & Noguera, P. A. (2019). The ecology of educational equity: Implications for policy. *Peabody Journal of Education, 94*(2), 122–141.

Brown v. Board of Education, 347 U.S. 483 (1954).

Card, D., & Rothstein, J. (2007). Racial segregation and the black-white test score gap. *Journal of Public Economics, 91*(11–12), 2158–2184.

Cashin, S. (2004). *The failures of integration: How race and class are undermining the American dream.* Public Affairs.

Cook, J. (2018). *Race-blind admissions, school segregation, and student outcomes: Evidence from race-blind magnet school lotteries.* Institute of Labor Economics.

D15 Diversity Plan. (2018). https://d15diversityplan.com/

Darling-Hammond, L., & Cook-Harvey, C. M. (2018). *Educating the whole child: Improving school climate to support student success.* Learning Policy Institute.

Darling-Hammond, L. (2015). *The flat world and education: How America's commitment to equity will determine our future.* Teachers College Press.

Darville, S. (2017, March 01). *Echoing Bush and Obama, Trump calls education "the civil rights issue of our time"—and asks for a school choice bill.* https://www.chalkbeat.org/2017/2/28/21102870/echoing-bush-and-obama-trump-calls-education-the-civil-rights-issue-of-our-time-and-asks-for-a-schoo

Dee, T. S., & Penner, E. K. (2017). The causal effects of cultural relevance: Evidence from an ethnic studies curriculum. *American Educational Research Journal, 54*(1), 127–166.

Delgado, R., & Stefancic, J. (2013). *Critical race theory: The cutting edge.* Temple University Press.

Dorn, E., Hancock. B., Sarakatsannis, J., and Viruleg, E. (2020). *COVID-19 and learning loss—disparities grow and students need help.* McKinsey & Co. https://www.mckinsey.com/industries/public-and-social-sector/our-insights/covid-19-and-learning-loss-disparities-grow-and-students-need-help

Doucet, F. (2019). *Centering the margins: (Re)defining useful research evidence through critical perspectives.* William T. Grant Foundation.

Du Bois, W. E. B. (1935). Does the Negro need separate schools? *Journal of Negro Education, 4*(3), 328–335. https://eportfolios.macaulay.cuny.edu/kafka18/files/2018/01/does-the-negro-need-seperate-schools.pdf

Elementary and Secondary Education Act, 20 U.S.C. § 70 (1965). https://uscode.house.gov/view.xhtml?path=/prelim@title20/chapter70&edition=prelim

Ellison, B. S., & Iqtadar, S. (2022). A qualitative research synthesis of the "No Excuses" charter school model. *Educational Policy, 36*(5), 915–941.

Engzell, P., Frey, A., & Verhagen, M. (2021). Learning loss due to school closures during the COVID-19 pandemic. *Proceedings of the National Academy of Sciences of the United States of America, 118*(7), 1–7.

Gallagher, M., Brennan, M., Oneto, A. D., & O'Brien, M. (2020). *Aligning housing and education.* Urban Institute. https://www.urban.org/sites/default/files/publication/102704/aligning-housing-and-education_0.pdf

Harvey, D. (2007). *A brief history of neoliberalism.* Oxford University Press.

Hernández, L. E. (2016). Complicating the rhetoric: How racial construction confounds market-based reformers' civil rights invocations. *Education Policy Analysis Archives, 24*(103).

Horsford, S. D. (2011). *Learning in a burning house: Educational inequality, ideology, and (dis) integration.* Teachers College Press.

Horsford, S.D. (2016). Social justice for the advantaged: Freedom from racial equality post-Milliken. *Teachers College Record, 118*(3), 1–18.

Horsford, S. D. (2019). School integration in the New Jim Crow: Opportunity or oxymoron? *Educational Policy, 33*(1), 257–275.

Horsford, S. D. (2021, March 17). Whose vision of racial equity will guide schools? *Education Week.* https://www.edweek.org/leadership/opinion-whose-vision-will-guide-racial-equity-in-schools/2021/03

Horsford, S. D., Cabral, L., Touloukian, C., Parks, S., Smith, P. A., McGhee, C., Qadir, F., Lester, D., & Jacobs, J. (2021). *Black education in the wake of COVID-19 and systemic racism: Toward a theory of change and action.* Black Education Research Collective, Teachers College, Columbia University. https://www.academia.edu/download/86018479/38986.pdf

Horsford, S. D., & Grosland, T. J. (2013). Badges of inferiority: The racialization of achievement in U.S. education. In M. Lynn & A. D. Dixson (Eds.), *Handbook of critical race theory in education* (pp. 153–166). Routledge.

Horsford, S. D., Scott, J. T., & Anderson, G. L. (2019). *The politics of education policy in an era of inequality: Possibilities for democratic schooling.* Routledge.

Johnson, R. C., & Nazaryan, A. (2019). *Children of the dream: Why school integration works.* Basic Books.

Labaree, D. F. (1997). Public goods, private goods: The American struggle over educational goals. *American Educational Research Journal, 34*(1), 39–81.

Lipman, P. (2011). *The new political economy of urban education: Neoliberalism, race, and the right to the city.* Routledge.

Levinson, B. A., Sutton, M., & Winstead, T. (2009). Education policy as a practice of power: Theoretical tools, ethnographic methods, democratic options. *Educational Policy, 23*(6), 767–795.

Mann, H. (1957). Twelfth annual report. In L. Cremin (Ed.), *The republic and the school: Horace Mann on the education of free men* (pp. 79–112). Teachers College. (Original work published 1848)

Mehta, J. (2015). Escaping the shadow: "A nation at risk" and its far-reaching influence. *American Educator, 39*(2), 20.

Minow, M. (2004). Surprising legacies of *Brown v. Board*. *Washington University Journal of Law and Policy, 16*.

Moody, C. D. (1971). *Black superintendents in public school districts: Trends and conditions*. Northwestern University Press.

Moore, W. L., & Bell, J. M. (2011). Maneuvers of whiteness: "Diversity" as a mechanism of retrenchment in the affirmative action discourse. *Critical Sociology, 37*(5), 597–613.

Morris, J. E. (2008). Research, ideology, and the Brown decision: Counter-narratives to the historical and contemporary representation of Black schooling. *Teachers College Record, 110*(4), 713–732.

Nagel, S. S. (1984). *Contemporary public policy analysis*. The University of Alabama Press.

National Commission on Excellence in Education. (1983). *A nation at risk: the imperative for educational reform*. National Commission on Excellence in Education.

No Child Left Behind Act of 2001, P.L. 107–110, 20 U.S.C. § 6319 (2002).

Plaut, V. C., Garnett, F. G., Buffardi, L. E., & Sanchez-Burks, J. (2011). "What about me?" Perceptions of exclusion and whites' reactions to multiculturalism. *Journal of Personality and Social Psychology, 101*(2), 337.

Plessy v. Ferguson, 163 U.S. 537, (1896).

Ray, R., & Gibbons, A. (2021). Why are states banning critical race theory? Brookings Institute.

Reardon, S. F., Grewal, E. T., Kalogrides, D., & Greenberg, E. (2012). Brown fades: The end of court-ordered school desegregation and the resegregation of American public schools. *Journal of Policy Analysis and Management, 31*(4), 876–904.

Roda, A., & Wells, A. S. (2013). School choice policies and racial segregation: Where white parents' good intentions, anxiety, and privilege collide. *American Journal of Education, 119*(2), 261–293.

Ruiz, M. (2021, June 12). Loudoun County anti-critical race theory rally: Teacher says "our student body suffers." *Fox News*. https://www.foxnews.com/politics/loudoun-county-anti-critical-race-theory-rally

Scott, J. T. (2013a). A Rosa Parks moment? School choice and the marketization of civil rights. *Critical Studies in Education, 54*(1), 5–18.

Scott, J. T. (2013b). School choice and the empowerment imperative. *Peabody Journal of Education, 88*(1), 60–73.

Tillman, L. C. (2004). (Un) intended consequences? The impact of the *Brown v. Board of Education* decision on the employment status of Black educators. *Education and Urban Society, 36*(3), 280–303.

Tuck, E., & Yang, K. W. (2014). R-words: Refusing research. In D. Paris & M. T. Winn (Eds.), *Humanizing research: Decolonizing qualitative inquiry with youth and communities* (pp. 223–247). Sage Publications.

Turner, E. O. (2018). Marketing diversity: Selling school districts in a racialized marketplace. *Journal of Education Policy, 33*(6), 793–817.

Unzueta, M. M., & Binning, K. R. (2010). Which racial groups are associated with diversity? *Cultural Diversity and Ethnic Minority Psychology, 16*(3), 443.

Warikoo, N. K. (2016). *The diversity bargain and other dilemmas of race, admissions, and meritocracy at elite universities*. University of Chicago Press.

Wise, A. (2020, September 17). Trump announces "Patriotic Education" commission, a largely political move. *NPR News*. https://www.npr.org/2020/09/17/91412

7266/trump-announces-patriotic-education-commission-a-largely-political-move

Yoon, Ee-Seul. (2017). Neoliberalizing race? Diverse youths' lived experiences of race in school choice. *Research in Education* 97(1), 76–94.

Young, M. D., & Diem, S. (2017). *Critical approaches to education policy analysis: Moving beyond tradition.* Springer.

Developing Policy for the Whole Child[1]

Linda Darling-Hammond and Channa Mae Cook

New knowledge about human development from neuroscience and education research demonstrates that effective learning for children depends on secure attachments; affirming relationships; rich, hands-on learning experiences; and explicit integration of social, emotional, and academic skills. A positive school environment supports students' growth across all the developmental pathways—physical, psychological, cognitive, social, and emotional—while reducing the stress and anxiety that can create biological impediments to learning. Such an environment enables a "whole child" approach to education that addresses the distinctive strengths, needs, and interests of students as they engage in learning.

Amid an ongoing COVID-19 pandemic, educators, students, and communities are grappling with unprecedented sources of continuous stress, including, in many communities, high rates of illness and death; heightened unemployment; food and housing insecurity; school closures and quarantines; and remote learning with inadequate access to technology for many. The degree of continuing trauma for children caused the American Academy of Pediatrics, American Academy of Child and Adolescent Psychiatry, and the Children's Hospital Association to jointly declare a National State of Emergency for Children's Mental Health in October 2021. Meanwhile, educators are experiencing burnout at alarming rates.

The disruptive nature of this pandemic underscores the need for schools to prioritize opportunities for students and educators to connect with one another, build relationships, and attend to the persistent mental-health challenges that accompany this stress and trauma. Schools that have pursued opportunities for both adult and student social–emotional learning (SEL) have been better equipped to address these challenges. New research from the Yale Center for Emotional Intelligence found that "educators whose schools or districts provided social and emotional support and SEL guidance to their staff reported fewer challenges implementing SEL during distance learning, less self-judgment and emotional exhaustion, and used SEL with their students more" (Zieher et al., 2021).

As a response to the ongoing adversity, this moment has also introduced many innovative funding and policy changes. A focus on social–emotional learning, mental-health supports, learning acceleration, robust expanded learning opportunities during summer and after school, and universal free school meals are just some of the emergent shifts in traditional schooling that may not have come to fruition under typical conditions. This shift in focus provides an on-ramp to a more comprehensive whole-child approach that can take hold if policymakers and district leaders build upon one-time investments to create the infrastructure needed to move away from the depersonalized factory model that has persisted for over a century to consider that new ways of schooling are needed, not just in response to COVID-19 but also in response to what we now know from science about how children learn and develop.

KEY LESSONS FROM THE SCIENCES OF LEARNING AND DEVELOPMENT

In recent years, a great deal has been learned about how biology and environment interact to support human learning and development. A summary of the research (Cantor et al., 2018; Osher et al., 2018) from neuroscience, developmental science, psychology, sociology, and the learning sciences points to the following six foundational principles about human learning and development:

1. The brain and development are malleable. The brain grows and changes throughout life in response to experiences and relationships. The nature of these experiences and relationships matters greatly for development.

Optimal brain development is shaped by warm, consistent relationships; empathetic back-and-forth communications; and modeling of productive behaviors. The brain's capacity develops most fully when children and youth feel emotionally and physically safe; when they feel connected, supported, engaged, and challenged; and when they have rich opportunities to learn, with materials and experiences that allow them to inquire into the world around them.

2. Variability in human development is the norm, not the exception. The pace and profile of each child's development is unique.

Because each child's experiences create a unique trajectory for growth, there are multiple pathways—and no one best pathway—to effective learning. Rather than assuming all children will respond to the same teaching approaches equally well, effective teachers personalize supports for different children, and effective schools avoid prescribing learning experiences around a mythical average. When schools try to fit all children to one pace and sequence, they miss the opportunity to reach each child, and they can cause children to adopt counter-productive views about themselves and their own learning potential, thus, undermining their progress.

3. Human relationships are the essential ingredient that catalyzes healthy development and learning.

Supportive, responsive relationships with caring adults are essential for healthy development and learning. Positive, stable relationships can buffer the potentially negative effects of even serious adversity. When adults have the awareness, empathy, and cultural competence to appreciate and understand children's experiences, needs, and communication, they can promote the development of positive attitudes and behaviors and build confidence to support learning.

4. Learning is social, emotional, and academic.

Emotions and social relationships affect learning. Positive relationships, including trust in the teacher, and positive emotions, such as interest and excitement, open the mind to learning. Negative emotions such as fear of failure, anxiety, and self-doubt reduce the capacity of the brain to process information and to learn. Learning is shaped both by intrapersonal awareness, including the ability to manage stress and direct energy in productive ways, and by interpersonal skills, including the ability to interact positively with others, resolve conflicts, and work in teams. These skills can be taught and fostered through SEL.

5. Children actively construct knowledge based on their experiences, relationships, and social contexts.

Students dynamically shape their own learning. Learners compare new information to what they already know to learn. This process works best when students engage in active, hands-on learning and when they can connect new knowledge to personally relevant topics and lived experiences. Effective teachers draw those connections, create engaging tasks, watch, and guide children's efforts, and offer constructive feedback with opportunities to practice and revise work. Teachers also provide opportunities for students to set goals and assess their own work and that of their peers so that they become increasingly self-aware, confident, and independent learners.

6. Adversity affects learning—and the way schools respond matters.

Each year in the United States, 46 million children are exposed to violence, crime, abuse, or psychological trauma, as well as homelessness and food insecurity. These adverse childhood experiences create toxic stress that affects attention, learning, and behavior. Poverty and racism, together and separately, make chronic stress and adversity more likely. In schools where students encounter implicit bias and punitive discipline tactics rather than support for handling adversity, their stress is magnified. Thus, it is critically important for schools to be sensitive to trauma and prepared to reduce, rather than exacerbate its effects.

BUILDING POSITIVE CLASSROOM AND SCHOOL ENVIRONMENTS THROUGH PRACTICE AND STRATEGIES

To support student achievement, attainment, and behavior, research suggests that schools should attend to the following four major domains:

1. Building a positive school climate in both classrooms and the school as a whole
2. Shaping positive student behaviors through social and emotional learning
3. Developing productive instructional strategies that support motivation, competence, and self-directed learning
4. Creating an integrated system of supports that address obstacles to learning, including the effects of trauma and adversity

Warm, caring, supportive student-teacher relationships, as well as other child–adult relationships, are linked to better school performance and engagement, greater social competence, and willingness to take on challenges (Osher et al., 2018). Students who are at higher levels of risk for poor outcomes can benefit especially from nurturing relationships with teachers and other adults, which can increase student learning and support their development and wellness (Roorda et al., 2011), especially when these relationships are culturally sensitive and responsive (Hammond, 2016). Students learn best when they can connect what happens in school to their cultural contexts and experiences, when their teachers are responsive to their strengths and needs, and when their environment is "identity safe" (Steele & Cohn-Vargas, 2013), reinforcing their value and belonging. This is especially important given the societal and school-based aggressions many children, especially those living under adverse conditions, experience.

Creating schools that support strong attachments and relationships. Personalizing the educational setting so that it constructs opportunities for stronger relationships among adults and students so that adults can respond more effectively to individual students' interests and needs, as well as their home and community contexts, is one of the most powerful levers to change the trajectories for children's lives.

For example, small schools or learning communities with personalizing structures—such as advisory systems in which advisors work with a small group of students over multiple years, teaching teams that share students, and opportunities for students to stay with the same teachers over 2 years or more (known as looping)—have been found to improve student achievement, attachment, attendance, attitudes toward school, behavior, motivation, and graduation rates (Bloom & Unterman, 2014; Darling-Hammond et al., 2006; Felner et al., 2007; Friedlaender et al., 2014).

These strategies allow educators to create a community within the school where caring is a product of individuals knowing each other in multiple ways. Teachers in such personalized settings report a heightened sense of efficacy, while parents report feeling more comfortable reaching out to the school for assistance.

Creating supportive classroom communities. Within these structures, teachers can develop an intentional community that ensures a sense of belonging and safety, with shared norms represented in all the school's activities. In addition, a culture of participation encourages student agency and leadership in the context of a culturally responsive curriculum that values diverse experiences and involvement in the community (Hamedani et al., 2015; Noguera et al., 2017).

Productive classrooms are organized around the promotion of student responsibility (LePage et al., 2005). This includes developing respectful relationships not only between teachers and students, but also among the students themselves, as students are taught to develop social competencies, such as making friends, managing conflict, and caring for others. Teachers take time to socialize students to their roles as community members. Teachers and students together create common norms for behavior in various situations, so that students can learn how to interact respectfully, take turns, voice their needs and concerns appropriately, and solve problems that may occur.

Developing community practices that strengthen relationships is critical. These practices for teachers may include classroom meetings, "check-ins" at the beginning of class about how students are doing, and routines for how to work in groups productively, engage in respectful discussions, or resolve conflicts. They may also include regular student–teacher conferences.

In collaborative communities, members feel personally connected to one another and committed to each other's growth and learning.

Building relational trust and family engagement. Relational trust among teachers, parents, and school leaders is another key resource that predicts the likelihood of gains in achievement and other student outcomes where instructional expertise is also present. Trust derives from an understanding of one another's efforts and goals, along with a sense of obligation toward each other, grounded in a common mission. As Bryk & Schneider put it: "Trust is the connective tissue that holds improving schools together" (Bryk & Schneider, 2002). Relational trust is fostered in stable school communities by skillful school leaders, who actively listen to concerns of all parties and avoid arbitrary actions, and who nurture authentic parent engagement, grounded in partnerships with families, to promote student growth.

Schools can nurture strong staff–parent relationships by building in time and supports for teachers and advisors to engage parents as partners with valued expertise. They can do this by planning teacher time for home visits, positive phone calls and text or email messages home, school meetings and student–teacher–parent conferences scheduled flexibly around parents' availability, and regular exchanges between home and school (Darling-Hammond et al., 2016; Osher & Osher, 2002). Students with involved parents have more self-confidence, feel school is more important, earn higher grades, and are more likely to attend college (Henderson & Mapp, 2002).

Enabling culturally competent classrooms. If students are to feel safe and have a sense of belonging, they must be understood and respected by their teachers. One aspect of this understanding derives from an appreciation of culture—that is, the shared cultural practices, norms, and belief systems that humans construct in a range of communities defined by family, religion, region, activities or interests, ethnic group membership, or other bonds. Each person belongs to multiple cultural communities that enact "repertoires of practice" (Gutierrez & Rogoff, 2003). At its root, culturally sensitive teaching must appreciate the complexity of individuals' multiple contexts for development, as these provide grist for instruction and insights for how to help students make connections among ideas.

The way students are treated in school—or in society outside of school—can exacerbate or ameliorate social-identity threat, which can affect students who are members of groups that have been evaluated negatively in society—for example, racial, ethnic, or linguistic minorities; students with disabilities; those from low-income families; or others (Tajfel & Turner, 1986). Social-identity threat can be triggered when people feel they are at risk of being stigmatized in a given situation by cultural representations that associate a social identity with undesirable characteristics. Such feelings of threat lead to significant stress, release of cortisol and adrenaline, symptoms of anxiety and depression, and, sometimes, challenging behavior that results from an attempt to protect one's identity from perceived attack (Major & Schmader, 2018).

Stereotype threat is a form of social-identity threat that is often activated in schools by implicit bias and low expectations for children of color, new English learners, and children from low-income families. When students believe they are or might be treated differently or unfairly, the marginalization and anxiety that ensue undermine academic performance. Stereotype threat can be mitigated in the classroom through teachers' use of affirmations that the student is seen as competent. Many dozens of studies have shown that when students receive such affirmations, performance on tests, grades, and other academic measures improve significantly in ways that are frequently maintained over time (Steele, 2011).

Teachers can convey affirming attitudes by exposing students to an intellectually demanding curriculum and supporting them in mastering it, conveying their confidence that students can learn; teaching students' strategies they can use to monitor and manage their own learning; encouraging students to excel; and building on the individual and cultural resources they bring to the school. Culturally responsive teaching uses "the cultural knowledge, prior experiences, frames of reference, and performance styles of ethnically diverse students to make learning encounters more relevant to and effective for them. It teaches *to and through* the strengths of these students" (Gay, 2000).

Shaping Positive Student Behaviors

Crafting school and classroom environments that support and encourage positive student behavior as well as learning requires recognizing that academic, social, and emotional learning are interconnected—and that both can be explicitly taught. University of Chicago researchers explain that because social and emotional skills are malleable, a "key task for educators becomes the intentional development of these skills, traits, strategies, and attitudes in conjunction with the development of content knowledge and academic skills" (Farrington et al., 2012, p. 5). This requires both explicit teaching of social and emotional skills and competencies, and the use of educative and restorative approaches to discipline.

Development of social, emotional, and academic competencies. Educators have long known that students' academic learning and social–emotional learning go hand in hand and that the development of prosocial mindsets, skills, and habits give students the capacity to persist through challenging work, collaborate with others, take risks while learning, think critically, and communicate effectively. Social, emotional, and other conditions of cognitive engagement influence the affective salience of instruction, how safe students feel, and how students focus their attention and make decisions (Osher & Kendziora, 2010). Furthermore, these factors affect how the nervous system responds and the degree to which students tap their cognitive and psychological resources.

The Collaborative for Academic, Social, and Emotional Learning (CASEL) defines social and emotional learning (SEL) as the process through which all young people and adults acquire and apply the knowledge, skills, and attitudes to develop healthy identities, manage emotions, and achieve personal and collective goals, feel and show empathy for others, establish and maintain supportive relationships, and make responsible and caring decisions (CASEL, n.d.).

Formal programs teaching SEL have shown considerable success. A meta-analysis of 213 studies of SEL programs representing more than 270,000 students from all kinds of school settings found that these students showed greater improvements than comparison students in their social and emotional skills; attitudes about themselves, others, and school; social and classroom behavior; and test scores and school grades, including an average 11 percentile point gain in achievement. They also experienced reductions in misbehavior and aggression, as well as in stress and depression (Durlak et al., 2011). These benefits have been found to endure and to serve as a protective factor (e.g., preventing conduct problems and drug use) on follow-up measures collected 6 months to 18 years later (Jones et al., 2015; Taylor et al., 2017).

Outcomes can also be enhanced when SEL is embedded throughout the school day and integrated into other subject matter (Jones & Bouffard, 2012). Greater integration allows for transfer of learning by capitalizing on teachable moments and opportunities to reinforce and practice skills throughout the school day.

Developing Educative and Restorative Approaches to Discipline

A developmentally appropriate approach to schoolwide discipline recognizes students' behaviors as demonstrations of a developmental need and as a set of skills that need to be taught and developed, not demanded. Explicit teaching of self-regulation, conflict resolution, and other skills creates a virtuous circle of responsible behavior.

Research finds that coercive discipline, in which teachers manage student behavior largely through punishments, inhibits the students' development of responsibility (Lewis, 2001), ultimately increasing misbehavior, as students increasingly abandon their own self-responsibility for their learning and behavior and develop resistance and opposition to school (Mayer, 1995), while exacerbating discriminatory treatment of students (Townsend, 2000). A punitive environment undermines learning by heightening anxiety and stress, placing extra demands on working memory and cognitive resources, which drains energy available to address classroom tasks (Pennington et al., 2016). Punishment and exclusion have harmful effects on students, particularly for many students of color and for students with disabilities, who are not only disproportionately removed from class and school but also are removed for longer terms (Mayer, 1995; Osher et al., 2010). The frequency of student suspensions is linked to academic declines and an increased likelihood of dropping out (Raffaele Mendez, 2003).

By contrast, in developmentally grounded schools, classroom management is approached as something that is done *with* students and not *to* them. An educative approach supports learning, as teachers' proactive and positive responses create a safe and empowering classroom environment through reinforcing and reminding language (including verbal and nonverbal cues); approaching students in a nonthreatening manner; presenting students with problem-solving options as a means of deescalating potentially explosive situations; and using nonpunitive, restorative consequences (Turnaround for Children, 2016). Students who learn in such supportive communities have higher levels of self-understanding, commitment, performance, and belongingness, and fewer discipline problems (Sergiovanni, 1994). These settings reduce the likelihood of disruptive behavior occurring in the first place.

Restorative justice is an approach to dealing with conflict by identifying or naming the wrongdoing, repairing the harm, and restoring relationships. Research suggests that restorative practices result in fewer and less racially disparate suspensions and expulsions, fewer disciplinary referrals, improved school climate, higher quality teacher–student relationships, and improved academic achievement across elementary and secondary classrooms (Fronius et al., 2016; Gregory et al., 2016).

Providing Supports for Student Motivation and Learning

Learning is a function both of teaching—what is taught and how it is taught—and student perceptions about the material being taught and about themselves as learners. Students' beliefs and attitudes have a powerful effect on their learning and achievement.

Four key mindsets have been identified as important for students' perseverance and academic success. They include:

1. Belief that one belongs at school.
2. Belief in the value of the work.
3. Belief that effort will lead to increased competence.
4. A sense of self-efficacy and the ability to succeed. (Farrington, 2013)

Shaping productive mindsets can set into motion a cascade of effects that accumulate over time, resulting in more positive school outcomes, such as increasing school affiliation and self-concept, leading to higher levels of academic engagement that becomes self-reinforcing (Yeager & Walton, 2011). The core principle that skills can always be developed is consistent with evidence that the brain is constantly growing and changing in response to experience. In practical terms, providing feedback focused on effort and process encourages students to adopt a growth mindset, whereas feedback that focuses on traits (e.g., "smarts") has negative consequences for student motivation and achievement (Mueller & Dweck, 1998).

Students will work harder to achieve understanding and will make greater progress when they are motivated to learn something. However, motivation is not just inherent in the individual; it can be developed by skillful teaching. Specific pedagogical moves that support students' developmental learning process and increase intrinsic motivation include

- choice of tasks;
- well-designed questions;
- use of multiple and varied representations of concepts;
- design of instructional conversations and "joint productive activity" (Tharp et al., 2000);
- encouragement for students to elaborate, question, and self-explain; and
- opportunities for students to collaborate with peers (Barron & Darling-Hammond, 2008; Bransford & Donovan, 2005).

In addition, assessments that represent learning in authentic ways and place value on growth rather than on scores earned at one discrete moment have been found to create higher motivation and higher levels of cognitive engagement (Blumenfeld et al., 1992). Assessments such as projects and portfolios also emphasize higher-order thinking and performance skills; collaboration and communication skills; and a host of cocognitive skills such as self-regulation, executive function, resilience, perseverance, and growth mindset (Darling-Hammond et al., 2002; Noguera et al., 2017).

Creating Multi-Tiered Systems of Support to Address Student Needs

A key aspect of creating a supportive environment is a shared developmental framework among all the adults in the school, coupled with procedures for ensuring that students receive additional help for social, emotional, or academic needs when they need them, without costly and elaborate labeling procedures standing in the way. Multi-tiered systems of support (MTSS) include multidisciplinary student support teams—on-site pupil services personnel (e.g., social workers, school psychologists, counselors, and nurses) who are skilled in culturally competent academic and behavioral assessment, care coordination, and family engagement with support teams.

While there can be many tiers of support, most systems include three tiers (Adelman & Taylor, 2008). The first tier is universal—everyone experiences it. Ideally, it uses teaching strategies grounded in universal designs for learning that are broadly successful with children who learn in different ways, as well as use of explicit social–emotional learning models and positive behavioral support strategies that are culturally and linguistically competent (Osher et al., 2016). Tier-2 services and supports address the needs of students who are at some elevated level of risk or who need some additional support in particular areas. The risk may be demonstrated by behavior (e.g., number of absences) or be due to having experienced a known risk factor (e.g., the loss of a parent.). These services may include academic supports, family outreach, counseling, and/or behavioral supports. Schools may operate counseling groups to support students who have experienced loss or violence, who are managing traumatic events, and who need mental-health supports. Tier-3 services involve intensive interventions for students who are at particularly high levels of risk or whose needs are not sufficiently met by tier-2 interventions. Tier-3 services might include wraparound services, one-on-one mental-health supports, and effective special education (Darling-Hammond et al., 2020).

Interventions, not students, are tiered, and supports can and should be provided in normative environments. Students receive services as needed for as long as needed but no longer. Providers should recognize that students have strengths in many areas, building upon student assets and not just focusing on deficits. Because tier-2 and -3 services demand more of students and families, it is particularly important that they be implemented in a child- and family-driven manner that is culturally competent. This can maximize engagement and minimize errors that occur when students, families, or teachers are not asked about their context and needs. Interventions should minimize removal from the normative classroom or extracurricular environments and learning. These supports often benefit from collaboration with local service agencies and community-based organizations with communication feedback loops to school-based staff. Key is that a whole-child approach is taken; students are dealt with in connected rather than fragmented ways; and care is personalized to the needs of individuals. Such an approach requires policies that are constructed to maximize student health, development, and learning, as described in the next section.

POLICY RECOMMENDATIONS

The growing knowledge base about learning and development suggests that our education system should focus on at least three major recommendations that support the well-being of young people:

Recommendation #1: Focus the System on Developmental Supports for Young People

States guide the focus of schools and professionals through the ways in which accountability systems are established, guidance is offered, and funding is provided. To ensure developmentally healthy school environments, states, districts, and schools can:

- Include measures of school climate, social–emotional support, and school exclusions in *accountability and improvement systems*, so that these are a focus of schools' attention and data are regularly available to guide continuous improvement.
- Adopt *standards* or other guidance for social, emotional, and cognitive learning that clarifies the kinds of competencies students should be helped to develop and the kinds of practices that can help them accomplish these goals.
- Replace zero-tolerance policies regarding school discipline with *discipline policies* focused on explicit teaching of social–emotional strategies and restorative discipline practices that support young people in learning key skills and developing responsibility for themselves and their community.
- Incorporate educator competencies regarding support for social, emotional, and cognitive development, and restorative practices into *licensing and accreditation requirements* for teachers, administrators, and counseling staff.
- Provide *funding* for school climate surveys, social–emotional learning and restorative-justice programs, and revamped licensing practices (including appropriate assessments) to support these reforms. As suggested later in the text, additional investments are needed for multitiered systems of support, integrated student services, extended learning, and professional learning for educators to enable school progress.

Recommendation #2: Design Schools to Provide Settings for Healthy Development

To provide school settings for healthy development within a productive policy environment, educators and policymakers can:

- Design schools for *strong, personalized relationships* so that students can be well-known and supported. For instance, create small schools or learning communities within schools, loop teachers with students for more than one year, create advisory systems, support teaching teams, and organize schools with longer grade spans. These examples strengthen relationships with students and improve student attendance, achievement, and attainment.
- Develop schoolwide norms and supports for *safe, culturally responsive classroom communities* that provide students with a sense of physical and psychological safety, affirmation, and belonging, as well as opportunities to learn social, emotional, and cognitive skills.
- Ensure that *integrated student supports* are available to support students' health, mental health, and social welfare through community school models or community partnerships, and parent-engagement and restorative-justice programs.
- Create *multitiered systems of support (MTSS)*, beginning with universal designs for learning and personalized teaching, continuing through more intensive academic and nonacademic supports, to ensure that students can receive the right kind of assistance when needed, without labeling or delays.
- Provide *extended learning time* to ensure that students do not fall behind, including skillful tutoring and academic supports, such as Reading Recovery; summer programs to avoid summer learning loss; and support for homework, mentoring, and enrichment.
- Design *outreach to families* as part of the core approach to education, including home visits and flexibly scheduled student–teacher–parent conferences to learn from parents about their children; outreach to involve families in school activities; and regular communication through positive phone calls home, emails, and text messages.

Recommendation #3: Ensure Educator Learning for Developmentally Supportive Education

To help educators learn how to redesign schools and develop practices that support a positive school climate, the state, counties, districts, schools, and educator preparation programs can:

- Invest in *educator wellness* through strong preparation and mentoring that improve efficacy and reduce stress, mindfulness and stress management training, social–emotional learning programs that benefit both adults and children, and supportive administration.

- Design *pre-service preparation programs* for both teachers and administrators that provide a strong foundation in child and adolescent development and learning; knowledge of how to create engaging, effective instruction that is culturally responsive; skills for implementing social–emotional learning and restorative-justice programs; and an understanding of how to work with families and community organizations to create a shared developmentally supportive approach. It is also recommended to include supervised clinical experiences in schools that model how to create (and for administrators, how to design and foster) a positive, developmentally supportive school climate for all students.
- Offer widely available *in-service development* that helps educators continually build on and refine student-centered practices; learn to use data about school climate and a wide range of student outcomes to undertake continuous improvement; problem-solve around the needs of individual children; and engage in schoolwide initiatives in collegial teams and professional learning communities.
- Invest in educator *recruitment and retention,* including forgivable loans and service scholarships that support strong preparation, high-retention pathways into the profession—such as residencies—that diversify the educator workforce, high-quality mentoring for beginners, and collegial environments for practice. A strong, stable, diverse, well-prepared teaching and leadership workforce is perhaps the most important ingredient for a positive school climate that supports effective whole-child education.

The emerging sciences of learning and development makes it clear that a whole-child approach to education, which begins with a positive school climate that affirms and supports all students, is essential to support academic achievement as well as healthy development. Research and the wisdom of practice offer significant insights for policymakers and educators about how to develop such environments. The challenge ahead is to assemble the whole village—schools, health-care organizations, youth and family serving agencies, state and local governments, philanthropists, and families—to work together to ensure that every young person receives the benefit of how to best support their healthy path to a productive future.

NOTE

1. This chapter draws on L. Darling-Hammond and Channa Cook-Harvey, *Educating the Whole Child: Improving School Climate to Support Student Success.* Learning Policy Institute, 2018.

REFERENCES

Adelman, H. S., & Taylor, L. (2008). School-wide approaches to addressing barriers to learning and teaching. In B. Doll & J. Cummings (Eds.), *Transforming school mental health services: Population-based approaches to promoting the competency and wellness of children.* Corwin Press.

Barron, B., & Darling-Hammond, L. (2008). How can we teach for meaningful learning? In L. Darling-Hammond, B. Barron, P.D. Pearson, A.H. Schoenfeld, E. K. Stage, T. D. Zimmerman, G. N. Cervetti, & J. L. Tilson (Eds.), *Powerful learning: What we know about teaching for understanding.* Jossey-Bass.

Bloom, H. S., & Unterman, R. (2014). Can small high schools of choice improve educational prospects for disadvantaged students? *Journal of Policy Analysis and Management, 33*(2), 290–319.

Blumenfeld, P. C., Puro, P., & Mergendoller, J. (1992). Translating motivation into thoughtfulness. In H. H. Marshall (Ed.), *Redefining student learning* (pp. 207–241). Ablex Publishing Corporation.

Bransford, J. D., & Donovan, M. S. (2005). Scientific inquiry and how people learn. In National Research Council, *How students learn: History, mathematics, and science in the classroom* (pp. 397–420). National Academies Press.

Bryk, A. & Schneider, B. (2002). *Trust in schools: A core resource for improvement.* Russell Sage Foundation.

Cantor, P., Osher, D., Berg, J., Steyer, L., & Rose, T. (2018). Malleability, plasticity, and individuality: How children learn and develop in context. *Applied Developmental Science, 23*(4), 307–337. doi: 10.1080/10888691.2017.1398649

Collaborative for Academic, Social, and Emotional Learning. (n.d.). *Fundamentals of SEL.* https://casel.org/fundamentals-of-sel

Darling-Hammond, L., Ancess, J., & Ort, S. W. (2002). Reinventing high school: Outcomes of the coalition campus schools project. *American Educational Research Journal, 39*(3), 639–673.

Darling-Hammond, L. , & Cook-Harvey, C. (2018). *Educating the whole child: Improving school climate to support student success.* Learning Policy Institute.

Darling-Hammond, L., Flook, L., Cook-Harvey, C., Barron, B., & Osher, D. (2020) Implications for educational practice of the science of learning and development, *Applied Developmental Science, 24*(2), 97–140. https://doi.org/10.1080/10888691.2018.1537791

Darling-Hammond, L., Ramos-Beban, N., Altamirano, R. P., & Hyler, M. E. (2016). *Be the change: Reinventing school for student success.* Teachers College Press.

Darling-Hammond, L., Ross, P., & Milliken, M. (2006). High school size, organization, and content: What matters for student success? *Brookings Papers on Education Policy, 2006/2007* (9), 163–203.

Durlak, J. A., Weissberg, R. P., Dymnicki, A. B., Taylor, R. D., & Schellinger, K. B. (2011). The impact of enhancing students' social and emotional learning: A meta-analysis of school-based universal interventions. *Child Development, 82*(1), 405–432.

Farrington, C. (2013). *Academic mindsets as a critical component of deeper learning.* University of Chicago Consortium on Chicago School Research.

Farrington, C. A., Roderick, M., Allensworth, E., Nagaoka, J., Keyes, T. S., Johnson, D. W., & Beechum, N. O. (2012). *Teaching adolescents to become learners: The role of noncognitive factors in shaping school performance: A critical literature review*. University of Chicago Consortium on Chicago School Research.

Felner, R. D., Seitsinger, A. M., Brand, S., Burns, A., & Bolton, N. (2007). Creating small learning communities: Lessons from the project on high-performing learning communities about "what works" in creating productive, developmentally enhancing, learning contexts. *Educational Psychologist, 42*(4), 209–221.

Friedlaender, D., Burns, D., Lewis-Charp, H., Cook-Harvey, C. M., Zheng, X., & Darling-Hammond, L. (2014). *Student-centered schools: Closing the opportunity gap*. Stanford Center for Opportunity Policy in Education.

Fronius, T., Persson, H., Guckenburg, S., Hurley, N., Petrosino, A. (2016). *Restorative justice in U.S. schools: A research review*. WestEd

Gay, G. (2000). *Culturally responsive teaching: Theory, research, and practice*. Teachers College Press.

Gregory, A., Clawson, K., Davis, A., & Gerewitz, J. (2016). The promise of restorative practices to transform teacher-student relationships and achieve equity in school discipline. *Journal of Educational and Psychological Consultation, 26*(4), 325–353.

Gutierrez, K., & Rogoff, B. (2003). Cultural ways of learning: Individual traits or repertoires of practice. *Educational Researcher, 32*(5), 19–25.

Hamedani, M. G., Zheng, X., Darling-Hammond, L., Andree, A., & Quinn, B. (2015). *Social emotional learning in high school: How three urban high schools engage, educate, and empower youth*. Stanford Center for Opportunity Policy in Education.

Hammond, Z. (2016). *Culturally responsive teaching and the brain: Promoting authentic engagement and rigor among culturally and linguistically diverse students*. Corwin Press.

Henderson, A. T., & Mapp, K. L. (2002). *A new wave of evidence: The impact of school, family, and community connections on student achievement*. National Center for Family & Community Connections with Schools.

Jones, D. J., Greenberg, M. T., & Crowley, D. M. (2015). Early social-emotional functioning and public health: The relationship between kindergarten social competence and future wellness. *American Journal of Public Health, 105*(11), 2283–2290.

Jones, S. M., & Bouffard, M. B. (2012). Social and emotional learning in schools: From programs to strategies. *Social Policy Report, 26*(4), 1–33.

LePage, P., Darling-Hammond, L., & Akar, H. (2005). Classroom management. In L. Darling- Hammond & J. Bransford (Eds.), *Preparing teachers for a changing world: What teachers should learn and be able to do* (pp. 327–357). Wiley.

Lewis, R. (2001). Classroom discipline and student responsibility: The students' view. *Teaching and Teacher Education, 17*(3), 307–319.

Major, B., & Schmader, T. (2018). Stigma, social identity threat, and health. In B. Major, J. F. Dovidio, & B. G. Link (Eds.), *The Oxford handbook of stigma, discrimination, and health* (pp. 85–103). Oxford University Press.

Mayer, G. R. (1995). Preventing antisocial behavior in the schools. *Journal of Applied Behavior Analysis, 28*, 467–478.

Mueller, C. M., & Dweck, C. S. (1998). Praise for intelligence can undermine children's motivation and performance. *Journal of Personality and Social Psychology, 75*(1), 33–52.

Noguera, P., Darling-Hammond, L., & Friedlaender, D. (2017). Equal opportunity for deeper learning. In R. Heller, R. Wolfe, & A. Steinberg (Eds.), *Rethinking readiness: Deeper learning for college, work, and life*. Harvard Education Press.

Osher, D., Bear, G., Sprague, J., & Doyle, W. (2010). How we can improve school discipline. *Educational Researcher, 39*(1), 48–58.

Osher, D., Cantor, P., Berg, J., Steyer, L., & Rose, T. (2018). Drivers of human development: How relationships and context shape learning and development. *Applied Developmental Science, 24*(1), 6–36.

Osher, D., & Kendziora, K. (2010). Building conditions for learning and healthy adolescent development: Strategic approaches. In B. Doll, W. Pfohl, & J. Yoon (Eds.), *Handbook of youth prevention science*. Routledge.

Osher, D., Kidron, Y., DeCandia, C. J., Kendziora, K., & Weissberg, R. P. (2016). Interventions to promote safe and supportive school climate. In K. R. Wentzel & G. B. Ramani (Eds.), *Handbook of social influences in school contexts*. Routledge.

Osher, T. W., & Osher, D. (2002). The paradigm shift to true collaboration with families. *Journal of Child and Family Studies, 11*(1), 47–60.

Pennington, C. R., Heim, D., Levy, A. R., & Larkin, D. T. (2016). Twenty years of stereotype threat research: A review of psychological mediators. *PLoS ONE, 11*(1), e0146487.

Raffaele Mendez, L. M. (2003). Predictors of suspension and negative school outcomes: A longitudinal investigation. In J. Wal & D. J. Losen (Eds.), *Deconstructing the school-to-prison pipeline* (pp. 17–34). Jossey-Bass.

Roorda, D. L., Koomen, H. M., Spilt, J. L., & Oort, F. J. (2011). The influence of affective teacher–student relationships on students' school engagement and achievement: A meta-analytic approach. *Review of Educational Research, 81*(4), 493–529.

Sergiovanni, T. J. (1994). *Building community in schools*. Jossey-Bass.

Steele, C. M. (2011). *Whistling Vivaldi: How stereotypes affect us and what we can do*. W.W. Norton & Company.

Steele, D. M., & Cohn-Vargas, B. (2013). *Identity safe classrooms: Places to belong and learn*. Corwin Press.

Tajfel, H., & Turner, J. C. (1986). The social identity theory of intergroup behavior. In S. Worchel & W. G. Austin (Eds.), *Psychology of intergroup relations* (pp. 7–24). Nelson-Hall.

Taylor, R. D., Oberle, E., Durlak, J. A., & Weissberg, R. P. (2017). Promoting positive youth development through school-based social and emotional learning interventions: A meta-analysis of follow-up effects. *Child Development, 88*(4), 1156–1171.

Tharp, R. G., Estrada, P., Dalton, S., & Yamaguchi, L. A. (2000). *Teaching transformed: achieving excellence, fairness, inclusion, and harmony*. Westview Press.

Townsend, B. (2000). The disproportionate discipline of African American learners: Reducing school suspensions and expulsion. *Exceptional Children, 66*, 381–392.

Turnaround for Children. (2016). *Classroom and behavior management (CBM) unit overview*. Author.

Yeager, D. S., & Walton, G. M. (2011). Social-psychological interventions in education: They're not magic. *Review of Educational Research*, *81*(2), 267–301.

Zieher, A. K., Cipriano, C., Meyer, J. L., & Strambler, M. J. (2021). Educators' implementation and use of social and emotional learning early in the COVID-19 pandemic. *School Psychology*, *36*(5), 388–397. doi.apa.org/fulltext/2021-89954-007.html

CHAPTER 6

Starting in School
Education Policies to Dismantle Systemic Racism

Tyrone C. Howard

The need to reinvent public policy in the United States is predicated on a willingness to significantly rethink how schools support all students and place an intentional focus on those who are most vulnerable—more pointedly, young people of color. Before we start the work of transforming learning experiences in schools in a number of ways, there needs to be a larger discussion and analysis of the role that systemic racism plays in the educational experiences of students of color (Givens, 2021; Lynn & Dixson, 2022). School districts across the country must be willing to explicitly name and examine how students of color, specifically those from low-income backgrounds, language learners, students with special needs, students experiencing homelessness, and those in foster care have been among the most underserved and marginalized students in schools (Howard, 2020; Milner, 2020). And policies centered on schools, or in-school policies, must reflect a radical rethink about the distribution of resources, interventions, and ideologies with an asset-based approach, and greater degrees of family/community engagement.

The salience of systemic racism creates a more intense set of realities that put certain students at a considerable disadvantage when it comes to educational equity. Education cannot improve wholesale until those who have been most affected by cumulative disadvantage have equity-minded policies that are dedicated to improving their educational experiences and outcomes (Johnson et al., 2021; Noguera et al., 2019). Thus, efforts to rethink educational policy cannot rely on a one-size-fits-all approach that has typically guided many educational efforts.

This book has been direct and unapologetic in its focus on how we think beyond schools to address deep-seated inequities and structural racism that have been present in U.S. society for centuries but are often on full display in schools. Unfortunately, many students' experiences and outcomes are profoundly shaped by zip code, socioeconomic status, skin color, parental education status, and mental health. This chapter will provide a brief overview of three in-schools policies and practices that represent an important step in disrupting several of the chronic realities that harm students of color in today's education systems: (1) Equitable conditions and opportunities to learn; (2) Mental health supports; and (3) Addressing school discipline policies. The chapter will also offer practical considerations for educators and lawmakers that can provide a window into reimagined possibilities for informing future policies and eradicating racial disparities at the local, state, and federal levels.

SCHOOLS THAT REFLECT AMERICA'S HISTORY

Since its inception over 4 centuries ago, schools have been viewed as institutions dedicated to providing students with knowledge, skills, dispositions, and values dedicated to enlightenment and opportunity (Spring, 2016). The earliest iterations of school were steeped in a hypocrisy that was endemic to U.S. life, law, and culture: the promise of education as a proverbial equalizer, yet denying countless students equitable educational opportunities (Elliot, 2021; Kozol, 2012). The idea that opportunity was to be provided to "all" while certain populations, namely Indigenous individuals, enslaved Africans, women, and Whites who did not own property, were denied educational opportunities is not lost in the current education moment. Fast-forward to the 21st century; an analysis of educational opportunities would reveal that racial, socioeconomic, and gender inequities persist when it comes to educational access (Sensoy & DiAngelo, 2017).

U.S. schools, like all other institutions, have been challenged to actualize the idea of full inclusion and equity in a democratic society. Racism has been a primary explanation of that reality. Despite noted progress, many institutions, schools being primary among them, continue to struggle to become beacons of implanting and sustaining racial equity and justice. From underfunded and racially segregated schools to racially based busing programs, educational tracking, opportunity gaps, and disproportionate school discipline affecting students of color, racism remains a reality in U.S. schools (Howard, 2020; Milner, 2020). As school issues remain a challenge, out-of-school factors are just as challenging for many students of color (Noguera et al., 2019). Hence, issues tied to poverty, access to vital support services, environmental hazards, and homelessness become far too common, and a greater coordinated effort between local, state, and federal supports is desperately needed. It is in these areas where we find youth of color are most harmed, and educational prospects are severely compromised.

This chapter highlights the necessity of tackling in-school and out-of-school conditions simultaneously as more students are impacted by the negative effects of poverty and systemic racism. Policies that allocate appropriate resources for students, teachers, instructional aides, sufficient technology supports, and smaller class sizes are all informed by responsive and thoughtful policies to improve classroom conditions. Moreover, policies that are mindful of the current circumstances that students face in the COVID moment would ensure that adequate mental-health supports, behavioral and learning specialists, are a staple at all schools, especially educational settings with high-need populations.

CREATING CONDITIONS AND OPPORTUNITIES TO LEARN FOR VULNERABLE STUDENT POPULATIONS

Many of the risk factors that challenge learning occur long before students enter school, which can begin to explain the chronic underperformance of America's most vulnerable student populations (Lewis-McCoy, 2014). To enhance opportunities to learn for minoritized students who are often the most vulnerable, educational policies must place an intentional focus on the multiple social determinants of health and well-being that disproportionately affect youth of color in this country. This includes environmental hazards, disinvestment in public infrastructure, safe drinking water, and access to quality medical services, all structural obstacles for many communities of color. Policies must recognize and understand that the social determinants of health, particularly those that lead to toxic stress, can effectively be informed by cross-collaborative, transparent, and communicative efforts between the education, social-welfare, mental-health, public-policy, medical, environmental, and legal fields—domains that are integral to helping families thrive (Wolf et al., 2007).

UCLA's Center for the Transformation of Schools' *Beyond the Schoolhouse: Digging Deeper: COVID-19 & Reopening Schools for Black Students in Los Angeles* revealed that the physical, social, emotional, and psychological state of Black families has been profoundly impacted by structural racism, apparent in economic, housing, health, and social patterns, especially in education systems, significantly affecting students' opportunities to learn.

Planning to address the social determinants of health is essential to the goal of reimagining schools, enhancing student learning, and reinventing public policy engagement through a race-conscious lens (Bishop & Noguera, 2019). This type of comprehensive approach also lays the foundation for shared responsibility across systems and communities when families engage with educational supports, social-service agencies, state and county departments, and community-based organizations. Recognizing that there are currently support efforts across municipalities can create opportunities to align existing prevention plans across the states and counties.

The Los Angeles County of Mental Health and UCLA Public Partnership for Wellbeing offers a collection of resources, supports, and opportunities to frontline workers, school staff, and care professionals, designed to help them acquire the knowledge, skills, and dispositions of working with youth in the COVID era. Policies that would incentivize those systems working together and learning in professional learning communities are vital in developing greater cross-system understanding and collaboration. Thus, the collaborations can advance holistic approaches to student development, health, and learning. Creating opportunities to learn must involve not only critical partnerships but also in-school policies like those highlighted in this chapter that extend beyond ensuring the qualifications and training of educators.

Students' preparedness and readiness are vital to learning. To that end, when many youths of color enter schools combatting a myriad of social ills rooted in structural inequality and limited opportunities, new ways of thinking about and creating policy must be adhered to in a thoughtful and responsive manner. The development of policies and systems where there is additional funding to disrupt the effects of Adverse Childhood Experiences (ACEs), which disproportionately harm youth of color, health disparities, and where environmental problems are greatest would be a more direct way to improve opportunities to learn and improve outcomes.

There are additional policy considerations that have an important influence on in-school learning. The presence of School Resource Officers has been shown to have a different influence on students of color compared to their White peers (Haro, 2020). During the George Floyd uprising of 2020, a group of Black students and concerned community members across Los Angeles pushed for a reduction of school resource officers in schools and for an increase in greater mental-health support on campuses. Subsequently, the Los Angeles Unified School District board voted to cut $25 million from the $70 million school police budget in response to calls from dozens of community groups to divest from law enforcement and the ways in which kids are pushed out of school and into the criminal legal system. The school board policy then decided to reallocate the $25 million into a Black student-achievement plan to improve school experiences and outcomes for Black students. Such policy shifts are monumental and can have an important influence on students' experiences in schools.

While the focus here has been on policy considerations that can improve learning outcomes, it is important to note that policy and legislative acts can also undermine school quality. As discussed in Chapter 5, one need look no further than the uproar around critical race theory being taught in K–12 schools. Critical race theory, which has its roots in legal scholarship, is an academic framework that examines the nexus of the legal system in the United States and the role that race, and racism, plays in it. As of January 2022, 29 states have introduced bills or taken other steps that would restrict teaching critical race theory or limit how teachers can discuss racism and sexism, according to an *Education Week* analysis. Thirteen states have enacted these bans, either through legislation or other avenues. Putting restrictions on the manner in which teachers can or cannot talk about issues tied to race and racism is startling—when so many chapters of the history of the United States are rooted in the quest for racial justice. While scholars have highlighted how for many students the introduction of concepts, theories, issues, and histories of people of color are beneficial for students of color (Banks, 2021), such mandates are concertized in schools across the country.

Additional policies that research shows have a notable influence on students are universal Pre-K (Nash et al., 2021; Wechsler et al., 2016), class size (Blatchford et al., 2011), and teacher quality (Darling Hammond, 2010). States across the nation have varying intervention on how they address these areas that require a much deeper analysis than the space allowed for this work. Nonetheless, placing an equity spotlight that investigates how learning, and opportunities to learn (Milner, 2020), are informed by these policies is essential, as we move toward evidence-based approaches to support our most vulnerable student populations.

SUPPORTING MENTAL HEALTH

The year 2020 will go down unequivocally as one of the most monumental, historical, and trying years in U.S. history, and one that will be in the history books for decades to come. Along with the direct health impact of the COVID-19 virus—which has claimed the lives of millions of people worldwide and over one million Americans—the nation has endured isolation, exasperation, anxiety, a profound economic downturn, and great uncertainty about the future. All of this has been compounded by racist violence and ethnic hostility, political turmoil, and even armed insurrection in the nation's capital at the start of 2021. We are all, understandably, tired, frustrated, and outright fearful. While the pandemic impacted all groups, communities of color were hit hardest by the pandemic (Horsford et al., 2021). A multitude of challenges lie before us, and much of this work lies in the nation's schools, and the hope, promise, and possibility that can come from schools in this trying moment in our nation's history. Educators can and must play an important role in helping keep students' mental health a top priority and in helping them make meaning of what we have all witnessed and experienced over the last year (Dalton et al., 2020).

Mental-health issues have not been as major of a part of the school landscape as this moment demands, but to address the academic disparities that have only gotten worse for Black, Brown, and low-income students, rethinking policies that mandate minimum levels of mental-health supports is necessary now (Darling-Hammond et al., 2020). This moment feels different because it is different. The massive loss of life in a short span of time, the subsequent economic fallout, and the accompanying racial strife and political climate have created a confluence of circumstances that many adults are seeking to understand; these realities are having a monumental impact on millions of students across the country (Journell, 2021). And unfortunately, many teachers are left to fend for themselves when it comes to the social, emotional, and mental well-being of students. While billions of public dollars are flowing into schools for COVID support (Griffith, 2021), the actual use, implementation, and oversight and accountability that these resources are tied to its intended purposes—to help address patterns spurred by the pandemic—remains elusive. Furthermore, it is important to remember that these are one-time dollars; hence, while many districts may have an influx of social workers, psychologists, and counselors for the 2021–2022 academic year, the sustainability of these positions and supports are going to be minimal at best.

Keeping in mind the current dearth of supports by way of counseling to students, consider that the American School Counselor Association recommends that schools have a 250-to-1 ratio of students to counselors, and that school counselors spend at least 80% of their time working directly with or indirectly for students. Unfortunately, many schools have survived for years with ratios two-to-three times higher than this rate. Across all U.S. schools, the average student-to-school-counselor ratio is 464 to 1, with states such as Arizona (905-to-1), Michigan (741-to-1), Illinois (686-to-1), California (663-to-1), and Minnesota (659-to-1) having excessively high ratios that cannot adequately provide students the access to skilled adults for academic and social emotional supports. Students of color are most likely to be in districts with higher than recommended student-to-teacher ratios. Students who have complex sets of social and emotional needs are not going to adequately be served with such significant rates of noncompliance of student-to-counselor ratio. Equity-minded policy must rethink ways to permanently invest funding at the federal, state, and local levels to guarantee counselors are trained to work with students academically but also to understand how mental health can shape academic performance.

Hence, a policy recommendation that could be implemented would be mandating that counties and states ensure all schools be equipped with at least one mental-health specialist, one school psychologist, and one social worker. Some states are becoming more explicit in mental-health support at the classroom and school level. In Florida, the state board of education voted to require every Florida public school to provide students in grades 6–12 with at least 5 hours of mental-health instruction. The board specified both the number of hours and the general content of the instruction. The instruction must include awareness of signs and symptoms; process for getting or seeking help for oneself or others; awareness of resources; and what to do or say to peers struggling with mental-health disorders. Helping students to talk about and identify mental-health needs is an important first step, but not having access to culturally responsive mental-health practitioners can render this knowledge and awareness moot; resources must accompany awareness.

In New York, The Mental Health Association (MHANYS), an affiliate of Mental Health America, advocated for and helped to pass important legislation, and implemented the first law in the nation requiring schools to teach students about mental health (Jones, 2018). As a nonprofit advocacy organization, MHANYS shares important advocacy strategies that may be helpful to other states wishing to pursue similar legislative solutions to enhance mental-health literacy among youth nationally. A post-legislative strategy that was used to implement New York's mental health–education law was also discussed. Other states are providing students time to deal with mental-health challenges. Consider that students in Illinois will be able to take up to five excused mental health days starting in January of 2022 because of a bill signed into law by Gov. J. B. Pritzker. Hence, students who decide to take a mental-health day will not be required to provide their school with a doctor's note and will be able to make up any work that was missed on their day off. When you consider a report from the Center for Disease Control and Prevention found that between March and May of last year hospitals across the country saw a 24% increase in the number of mental health–emergency visits by kids ages 5 to 11 and a 31% increase for kids 12 to 17, it is clear that permanent mental-health supports for students are warranted immediately.

Moreover, special provisions can and should be made to ensure that high-need schools are allotted ongoing funding that would be exclusively dedicated to mental-health supports and social service specialists. Historically, high-need schools have served a greater number of students of color than middle or elementary schools making the nexus between race and mental health increasingly vital. Race-conscious policies can help to address the dissonance between mental-health concerns and seeking care for many communities of color.

Consider that Native American children have traditionally reported the highest depression rates of any racial group, and the suicide death rate for those between the ages of 15 and 19 is more than double that of their White peers (Quirk, 2020). African Americans are less likely to seek mental-health supports despite having high levels of depression (Dalencour et al., 2017), and Latinx children and adolescents are at significant risk for mental-health problems, and, in many cases, at greater risk than White children—such problems often tied to psychological stresses associated with immigration and acculturation (National Survey on Drug Use and Health, 2016). Hence there is an obvious need to dedicate culturally responsive mental-health supports in schools and communities where students of color are most likely to live and learn.

Many states and counties have significant dollars housed in departments of mental health that do not find their ways into schools to assist practitioners in real time as students grapple with depression, anxiety, bipolar disorders, and other mental-health challenges. Moreover, the fact that the majority of teachers are not trained to understand and adequately address mental-health matters only underscores this challenge. Local policymakers can be strategic about available resources to policymakers to create strategies and intervention informed by young people so they can help identify what type of academic, social, and emotional support they need to succeed. The greater focus on prevention of behavior and mental-health supports, the better. Policies that would incentivize matching dollars or block grants for districts and counties that prioritize mental-health supports would be strongly encouraged.

It might also be prudent to have local and statewide agencies establish common strategies and models for supporting school districts as they work to create engaging and personalized learning experiences for marginalized student populations. More recently, many districts have adopted community school models where there are wraparound services located at the school site that could include but not be limited to mental-health supports, after-school programming, legal assistance and supports, and medical and dental supports. From an academic perspective, universal screening strategies to frequently monitor and adjust instruction, particularly in core subjects, coupled with social–emotional support could be mandatory for all students.

To provide more concrete examples of how the Community Schools model has included integrated health services, which are informed by district, city, county, or statewide policy efforts, consider the following. At the urging of board recommendation from the New York Department of Education, the Fannie Lou Hamer Freedom High School (FLHS) in New York City created a comprehensive health service (including a specialized teen clinic) through a partnership with the Children's Aid Society Bronx Family Center. FLHS partnered with the Helen Keller Institute to offer free vision screenings, and eyeglasses were made available to any student who needed them, while a health educator and a full-time social worker provided support during the school day. An extended learning program focuses on youth development, health supports including culinary arts and a student government engaging with local officials. Children's Aid Community Schools have worked hand in hand with educators to elevate education by combining the best practices of a public school with services tailored to address the complex challenges children face.

Similar models were created in other cities based on policy interventions. Cincinnati Public Schools (CPS) has an especially strong policy infrastructure, with a 2009 community learning center established to meet students out-of-school needs. A CPS Board of Education policy states that all district school buildings will serve as community learning centers. The Board also developed written guidelines for the establishment of partnerships. The goal of community learning centers is to support student achievement while revitalizing neighborhoods and maximizing the community's return on its investment in public schools. A full-time resource coordinator who knows the specific needs of the school, its families, and the community are key to the success of a community learning center. The resource coordinator recruits partnerships and develops supports to meet the individual needs of students to impact school success and reflect community interests.

ADDRESSING SCHOOL DISCIPLINE POLICIES

One of the key policies that schools must revisit are issues tied to school discipline. For decades, many schools across the country have operated under a zero-tolerance policy in responding to student behavior. The genesis of zero-tolerance policies dates to the late 1990s and early 2000s when school shootings emerged across the country. The idea, while well-intended, has resulted in deleterious results for disproportionate numbers of Black and Indigenous students (Losen & Martinez, 2020; Morris & Perry, 2016). Far too many policies have continued, including the problem of over-policing and surveillance of students.

For example, districts that have adopted policies or have education codes that have amorphous categories such as "willful defiance," "insubordination," or "disrespect" as reasons for suspending students have highly subjective interpretations to teachers that may not have cultural acuity to today's diverse student populations. Moreover, policies that allow the suspension of preschool-age students have also contributed to racially disproportionate punishment rates. Policies that did not collect data along racial/ethnic and gender lines also have contributed to the inability to understand how race and punishment have become all too familiar in schools across the country.

Policymakers should replace punitive discipline approaches with more culturally sustaining interventions that serve a clear educational purpose. Hence, the goal should be for lawmakers to call for nonpunitive and restorative strategies—alternatives that teach understanding harm and healing, enhance social and emotional learning, and help students recognize hurt caused to others (Ginwright, 2016). Policymakers should consider supporting a range of alternatives, including trauma-informed practices, implicit bias training, restorative, and culturally responsive practices that emphasize remedying root causes. A focus on the educational purpose should also encourage those using suspensions to reduce their duration. The success of alternative approaches frequently entails training to help teachers to improve classroom management skills in ways that are aligned with these responses. Administrators must also be provided with the training and support they need to implement discipline reforms with integrity and to improve equity in resources and outcomes. It would also be beneficial for states to establish policies that require all districts to have discipline taskforces with the

Department of Education to support counties and districts in reducing exclusionary discipline, sharpen data systems, and put additional resources into mental-health supports (Wood, Harris, & Howard, 2018).

As schools across the country have grappled with the way discipline among students would be handled, students of color in particular have felt the deleterious effects of current policies. As schools have moved away from the zero-tolerance mantra, many have adopted the amorphous categories of willful defiance and insubordination as catch-all categories to discipline students, which have incredibly high levels of subjectivity. From a policy standpoint, districts need to radically rethink the nature of discipline considering the growing data during the COVID era that highlights the levels of depression, anxiety, and stress that many students and teachers are under, which can result in mislabeling and harsh disciplinary referrals (Losen & Martinez, 2020).

Responsive policies that are concerned with school discipline need to be replete with accompanying mental-health supports. Second, districts need to engage in robust reexamination of education codes and categories for school suspensions and expulsions. Many of these areas are antiquated and have not been examined for decades. To that end, creating policies that make data transparent around school and district suspensions and expulsions, incident types, repeat students, year-to-year data comparisons, and referring teachers can help to build a deeper understanding of holistic supports for students whose deeper life challenges are the real challenge and not the behaviors that result in suspension.

The following are policy recommendations that need to be considered to help implement nonpunitive and restorative strategies:

- *Eliminate or radically rethink in-school suspensions.* In most states and districts, there are two primary categories of school suspension: in-school and out-of-school (also called out-of-house) suspensions. In an in-school suspension, the students are typically placed in another classroom or location, office, or space to work independently in a group with other students who were similarly suspended or identified as difficult, behaviorally challenged, or insubordinate. Little learning typically takes place in these spaces. Usually an uncredentialed staff member "watches" these students, and little instruction or behavioral support or counseling takes place. Out-of-school suspensions temporarily bar a child from the school grounds, usually meaning they remain at home. School suspensions can occur for mandatory reasons, such as distributing drugs, bringing a firearm or weapon to campus, and fighting; however, they can occur for small innocuous actions as well. In many instances, in-school suspensions occur under highly subjective categories such as students being disrespectful, insubordination, or being willfully defiant. Revised policies would eliminate these practices and prevent schools from claiming that their out-of-school suspensions have dramatically decreased while not acknowledging that in-school suspensions have soared.

- *Review what is suspendible behavior.* In many districts and states, there is wide variation in what is viewed as a suspension-level behavior; and there are typically high levels of subjectivity involved in various infractions across and within schools and districts. It is common for a district to have guidelines for suspension-level behavior that do not consider the age and developmentally appropriateness of a student. For example, it is developmentally appropriate for a student in early childhood education to turn around in their seat and talk with their peers, ask teachers questions in a particular manner, fidget, move, talk continuously, talk to others during instruction, and other age-appropriate behaviors. However, there are a number of districts that have created policies that do not attend to what should be viewed as developmentally appropriate behavior based on age. All districts should be required to have suspension criteria based on grade-level expectations and cultural considerations. Teachers should be required to engage in ongoing training around child development, culturally informed behaviors, and practices.
- *Review ADA policies and suspensions.* Schools receive money for the attendance of each student per day (Average Daily Attendance). For many districts, when a student receives an out-of-school suspension, their daily attendance monies are reduced for each day beyond the first day of the suspension. For example, if a student is suspended Monday for 2 days, the school receives attendance monies for Monday but not for Tuesday and Wednesday. This is irrespective of whether the student was in attendance for 5 minutes or 5 hours. Thus, many schools will implement an out-of-school suspension for the day of the infraction and have the student return the following day to ensure that attendance monies are not lost. It would be important that policies consider that attendance monies be restricted for both the day of the suspension as well as subsequent days. An alternative course is a funding formula based on the proportion of the day the student was in the classroom or with a school counselor. Otherwise, schools receive monies for services and support that they are not actually providing.
- *Revisit policies of policing presence.* In many districts, counties, and states, the presence of police officers or school resource officers is larger than the number of counselors, therapists, or social workers. The persistent police presence in schools must be reconsidered in the current moment. As schools seek to move toward more

healing and restorative practices, excessive funding on police and punishment needs to be reevaluated. Moreover, studies have shown that schools with higher numbers of Black and Brown students are more likely to have police presence on campus (Nance, 2013). As schools seek to decrease suspensions, equity-centered policies such as drastically reducing or eliminating police presence in schools needs to be seriously considered.

- *Eliminate out-of-school suspensions.* Require student suspensions to automatically be in-school suspensions rather than out-of-school suspensions unless it is determined that the student poses a danger to people or property or causes a disruption of the educational process. Education code in Washington, DC, works toward eliminating out-of-school suspensions. D.C. Code § 38-236.04 reads, "Beginning in school year 2019–2020 for students in K-5, and school year 2020–2021 for students in 6–8, no student may be subject to an out-of-school suspension or disciplinary unenrollment . . . that the student has willfully caused, attempted to cause, or threatened to cause bodily injury or emotional distress to another person, including behavior that happens off school grounds. Beginning in school year 2020–2021, no student in grades 9 through 12, except a student over 18 years of age at a school where more than ½ of the students are over 18 years of age, may be subject to an out-of-school suspension or disciplinary unenrollment for: violating dress code rules; willful defiance; or behavior off school grounds."
- *Set forth guidelines* to assist school districts with developing, reviewing, and revising student discipline and school-safety policies. Require that parents/caregivers, students, and school district personnel be involved in the development of district student discipline policies, and that the policies be reviewed annually by a district's committee on personnel policies. Explore School-Wide Positive Behavioral Interventions and Supports (SWPBIS) as an alternative to suspensions and to reduce school discipline referrals.
- Require local school districts to provide certain *classroom management training* to school personnel. Frequently teachers' inability to address students' behavior leads to student exclusion from classrooms and subsequent suspensions. School master plans must make provision for pre-service and ongoing grade-appropriate classroom management training for teachers, principals, and other appropriate school personnel regarding positive behavioral supports and reinforcement, conflict resolution, mediation, cultural competence, restorative practices, guidance and discipline, and adolescent development.
- Address the need to create *safe and supportive learning environments* where positive behaviors are taught and reinforced.

Gives schools the tools they need to align their efforts to reduce suspensions and expulsions with other essential initiatives necessary to create safe and supportive school environments.

LOOKING FORWARD

Today's educators continue to find themselves confronting complex, enduring layers that make it difficult to effectively teach in the current moment. At the core is the enormous question: How can we ensure all students can learn and be socially and emotionally well, by successfully combating the effects of chronic disparities, histories of racism, and accumulative disadvantages? These disparities and disadvantages often appear unrelenting and historical in nature, and as such are incredibly daunting for educators to address.

In the past, educators and education researchers have zoomed in on a certain set of topics as they relate to improving academic disparities for all students, and especially for low-income and racially diverse students. The topics that tend to get discussed, dissected, and debated as we aim to improve school experiences and outcomes for students of color are school choice, charter schools, teacher preparation, parent engagement, early childhood education, and curricular and instructional approaches. At this moment, our policies need to be bolder, more creative, race conscious, and have explicit accountability mechanisms.

What is not as prevalent in these current policy discussions is the persistent impact of various toxic stressors, cumulative disadvantage, social determinants of health, the persistence of racism, and cultural considerations. Namely, stressors such as trauma, anxiety, abuse, neglect, discrimination, racism, and depression remain in schools across the nation—all of which have only been intensified by COVID-19 and the current racial and political climate. These toxic stressors are not typically referenced when describing why certain students do not thrive in school. These stressors do, however, have an enormous impact on students' cognitive and social–emotional well-being—*and* their ability to learn in school. A nuanced manner of understanding the complexities of policy and practice with a commitment to justice, political, and economic opportunity is what schools must tap into. Centering race conscious approaches in public policy considerations also means unpacking structural racism and unpacking how they have long plagued BIPOC communities.

The structure of exclusion by way of school funding, access to housing and home loans, opportunities for employment, and denial of pathways to political and economic opportunity are contemporary forms of institutional racism in today's schools. The historical way people of color and low-income individuals have not only been denied access to equitable medical care but at times unknowingly experimented on are also examples. Others would point to the disproportionate number of people of color involved in the U.S. penal system as another example of institutional structures that treat people of color in a fundamentally different way than their White peers (Alexander, 2010). Within the context of schools, institutional racism could be the manner in which school funding disproportionately affects children of color; lack of access to AP and honors classrooms; less access to highly qualified teachers, counselors, and nurses; and constant placement in overcrowded classrooms all represent institutional disadvantages that plague students of color far more than their White counterparts. This work requires a willingness to tackle current and historical issues in an honest and discussion-driven manner that helps students make explicit connections from historical/social/political realities to their personal lives. Our aim is to make clear that school transformation is elusive, *unless* education policy is anchored in race-conscious knowledge, human sensibilities, and applicable strategies that are steeped in knowing students' current realities, our nation's historical indifference and hostility toward people and communities of color, and the real possibility of schools to be seen as sites of hope, care, support, and transformation.

REFERENCES

Alexander, M. (2010). *The new Jim Crow*. The New Press.

Banks, J. A. (2021). *Transforming multicultural education, policy, and practice*. Teachers College Press.

Bishop, J. P., & Noguera, P. A. (2019). The ecology of educational equity: Implications for policy. *Peabody Journal of Education, 94*(2), 122–141.

Blatchford, P., Bassett, P., & Brown, P. (2011). Examining the effect of class size on classroom engagement and teacher-pupil interaction: Differences in relation to prior pupil attainment and primary vs. secondary schools. *Learning and Instruction, 21*, 715–730.

Census Bureau. *U.S. census bureau. 2011–2015 American community survey 5-year estimates*. 2015. Retrieved from https://www2.census.gov/programs-surveys/acs/tech_docs/table_shells/2015/S1502.xlsx

Dalencour M., Wong, E. C., Tang, L., Dixon, E., Wells, K., & Miranda, J. (2017). The role of faith-based organizations in the depression care of African Americans and Hispanics in Los Angeles. *Psychiatric Services, 68*(4), 368–374.

Dalton, L., Rapa, E., & Stein, A., 2020. Protecting the psychological health of children through effective communication about COVID-19. *Lancet Child Adolescent Health, 4*(5), 346–347. https://doi.org/10.1016/S2352-4642(20)30097-3.

Darling Hammond, L. (2010). *The flat world and education. How America's commitment to equity will determine our future*. Teachers College Press.

Darling-Hammond, L., Schachner, A., & Edgerton, A. K. (with Badrinarayan, A., Cardichon, J., Cookson, P. W., Jr., Griffith, M., Klevan, S., Maier, A., Martinez, M., Melnick, H., Truong, N., Wójcikiewicz, S.). (2020). *Restarting and reinventing school: Learning in the time of COVID and beyond*. Learning Policy Institute.

Elliot, A. (2021). *Invisible child. Poverty, survival, and hope in an American city*. Random House.

Ginwright, S. (2016). *Hope and healing in urban education*. New York: Routledge.

Givens, J.R. (2021). *Fugitive pedagogy, Carter G. Woodson, and the art of Black teaching*. Cambridge, MA: Harvard University Press.

Griffith, M. (2021). *An unparalleled investment in U.S. public education: Analysis of the American Rescue Plan Act of 2021*. Learning Policy Institute. https://learningpolicyinstitute.org/blog/covid-analysis-american-rescue-plan-act-2021.

Haro, B. (2020). *Unveiling the everyday school pushout factors of Latina students at Dolores Huerta High School: Social control, school discipline, and gender violence* [Unpublished dissertation]. University of California, Los Angeles, Los Angeles, CA.

Horsford, S. D., Cabral, L., Touloukian, C., Parks, S., Smith, P. A., McGhee, C., Qadir, F., Lester, D., & Jacobs, J. (2021). *Black education in the wake of COVID-19 and systemic racism: Toward a theory of change and action*. Black Education Research Collective, Teachers College, Columbia University.

Howard, T. C. (2020). *Why race and culture matter in schools: Closing the achievement gap in America's classrooms* (2nd. ed). Teachers College Press.

Johnson, Jr., S. L., Bishop, J. P., Howard, T. C., James, A., Rivera, E., & Noguera, P.A. (2021). *Beyond the schoolhouse, digging deeper: COVID-19 & reopening schools for black students in Los Angeles*. Center for the Transformation of Schools, School of Education & Information Studies, University of California, Los Angeles.

Jones, S. (2018, August 16). Schools are required to teach mental-health lessons this fall in two states. And that's a first. *Education Week*. https://www.edweek.org/teaching-learning/schools-are-required-to-teach-mental-health-lessons-this-fall-in-two-states-and-thats-a-first/2018/08

Journell, W. (2021). *Post-pandemic social studies: How COVID-19 has changed the work and how we teach*. Teachers College Press.

Kozol, J. (2012). *Savage inequalities: Children in America's schools*. Crown.

Lewis-McCoy, R. L. (2014). *Inequality in the promised land. Race, resources and suburban schooling*. Stanford University Press.

Losen, D. J., & Martinez, P. (2020). *Lost opportunities: How disparate school discipline continues to drive differences in the opportunity to learn*. Learning Policy Institute and Center for Civil Rights Remedies at the Civil Rights Project, UCLA.

Lynn, M., & Dixson, A. D. (2022). *Handbook of critical race theory in education* (2nd ed.). Routledge.

Milner, H.R. (2020). *Start where you are but don't stay there* (2nd ed). Harvard Education Press.

Morris, E. W., & Perry, B. L. (2016). The punishment gap: School suspension and racial disparities in achievement. *Social Problems*, 63(1), 68–86. https://doi.org/10.1093/socpro/spv026

Nance, J. P. (2013). Students, security, and race. *Emory Law Journal*, 63(1) .http://scholarship.law.ufl.edu/facultypub/372

Nash, K. T., Glover, C. P., & Polson, B. (2021) *Toward culturally sustaining teaching. Early childhood educators honor children with practices for equity and change*. Routledge.

National Survey on Drug Use and Health. (2016). https://www.samhsa.gov/samhsa-data-outcomes-quality/major-data-collections/ reports-detailed-tables-2015-NSDUH

Noguera, P., Bishop, J. Howard, T & Johnson, S. (2019). *Beyond the schoolhouse: Overcoming challenges & expanding opportunities for Black youth in Los Angeles County*. Center for the Transformation of Schools, Black Male Institute, Graduate School of Education & Information Studies, University of California, Los Angeles.

Quirk, A. (2020, July 28). *Mental health support for students of color during and after the coronavirus pandemic*. Center for American Progress. https://www.americanprogress.org/article/mental-health-support-students-color-coronavirus-pandemic/

Sensoy, Ö., & DiAngelo, R. (2017). *Is everyone really equal*. (2nd ed). Teachers College Press.

Spring, J. (2016). *Deculturalization and the struggle for equality: A brief history of the education of dominated cultures in the United States (Sociocultural, Political, and Historical Studies in Education)* (8th ed.). Routledge.

Wechsler, M., Melnick, H., Maier, A., & Bishop, J. (2016). *The building blocks of high-quality early childhood education programs* (policy brief). Learning Policy Institute.

Wolf, S. H., Johnson, R. E., Phillips, R. L., & Philipsen M. (2007). Giving everyone the health of the educated: An examination of whether social change would save more lives than medicine. *American Journal of Public Health*, 97(4). https://doi.org/10.2105%2FAJPH.2005.084848

Wood, J. L., Harris F., III, & Howard, T. C. (2018). *Get out! Black male suspensions in California public schools*. Community College Equity Assessment Lab and the UCLA Black Male Institute.

CHAPTER 7

Youths' Health and Learning Connection

Alexandra Mays and Rochelle Davis

Fundamental to supporting the success of all children is prioritizing the critical connection between student and family health and learning. Until this is accomplished, any efforts to address the opportunity gap will be compromised. While COVID-19 has increased student and staff health and wellness needs, including mental-health issues, these are not new problems. According to data collected prior to COVID-19, more than 40% of school-aged children and adolescents have at least one chronic health condition, such as asthma, obesity, other physical conditions, and behavior/learning problems (National Survey of Children's Health, 2018). Students with unmanaged physical- and mental-health issues are more likely to fall behind in school and lose opportunities for learning. Many of the health issues that affect learning disproportionately impact Black and Hispanic students, signaling health disparities as a catalyst of the opportunity gap.

While the health and learning connection is well-documented and understood, many policies and practices at the national, state, and district level make it challenging for schools to integrate emerging best practices for supporting student health—and, thus, their learning—into the daily routine of school. Even though there is widespread support for student health and healthy school environments, and though many state policies and practices take this into account, these policies are fragmented and are not yet integrated to best support the whole child (Solomon et al., 2018). The COVID-19 pandemic has demonstrated the importance of schools as community anchors that children and families rely on for much more than an education. The pandemic, and calls for racial justice, have also exposed the vast inequities our educational and health systems are built on—in terms of health disparities that disproportionately affect communities of color and the unequal educational resources, schools and communities must meet the immediate needs brought on by the pandemic.

This is a pivotal moment in our nation's history. Amidst massive and simultaneous failings, we must rise to the challenge of rebuilding the infrastructure designed to support our children's educational and health needs. A positive learning environment that ensures all individuals can take advantage of healthy and high-quality relationships, experiences, and environments is critical for transformative learning and development.

One reason for this is the profound impact still being felt of No Child Left Behind's (NCLB) single-minded focus on academic outcomes. NCLB led states to build education accountability systems that did not incorporate key nonacademic measures that contribute to learning, such as school climate, student engagement, or chronic absenteeism rates. When these factors are not measured, they are discounted as nonessential, making it more difficult for schools to make the case for them and making it impossible to fund them.

Other policies and practice barriers magnify the problem. School systems that have decided to prioritize improved student-health services, for instance, struggle with funding because of what is known as the "wrong pocket problem," where schools are forced to bear the cost of policies promoting mental and physical health because systems are not in place to share the burden appropriately across sectors. Fortunately, with greater understanding of the myriad factors that impact student learning, and changes in education and health policy, including the federal Every Student Succeeds Act (ESSA), there are important opportunities to address these barriers and increase access to positive school environments for students across the country. To ensure all students and staff can learn and work in a healthy school environment, it is critical to advance changes at the federal, state, and local levels that integrate health and wellness into education policy and practice rather than creating separate policies for school health that only further the silos that currently exist.

This chapter will highlight these opportunities and underscore the importance of ensuring that education policy and practice reflect the science of learning and development by fully integrating best practices for supporting student health and healthy school environments.

THE IMPACT OF STUDENT HEALTH ON LEARNING

Ignoring health issues, or regarding them as outside the scope of educational priorities, can undermine efforts to improve academic performance. Addressing the dual challenges of poor health and poor academic performance in underserved communities will give all children—regardless of ethnic or economic background—better opportunities for health and education.

Across the country, chronic and acute physical and mental health issues disproportionately impact low-income children and children of color. These health-related issues may include the following:

- Asthma: Compared to White children, asthma prevalence is higher in children who are Hispanic (1.3 times), Black (1.6 times), and American Indian/Alaska Native (1.3 times) (National Center for Health Statistics, 2018).
- Oral health: Children aged 5 to 19 years from low-income families are twice as likely (25%) to have cavities than children from higher-income households (11%) (Dye et al., 2012).
- Mental health: Over 25% of American Indian or Alaskan Native youth, 11.8% of Black youth, and 8.9% of Hispanic youth reported attempting suicide in 2019, compared to only 7.9% of White youth. Black youth, especially Black boys, and younger Black youth, have demonstrated rapid increases in suicide attempts and suicide deaths over the past decade (Lindsey et al., 2019).
- Obesity/food insecurity: 40% of Black children and 39% of Hispanic children are overweight or obese compared with 26% of White children (Child & Adolescent Health Measurement Initiative, n.d.). In addition, the proportion of households where children had "very low food security," is between three and four times as high in African American or Hispanic households as it is in White households (Coleman-Jensen et al., 2014).

If these health issues are left untreated or undermanaged, they can adversely affect children's attendance, their ability to see, hear, and pay attention in the classroom, and their chances of graduating from high school. For example, asthma accounts for one-third of all days of missed instruction (Millard et al., 2009). Mental-health problems can also significantly impact student learning and can affect a student's energy level, concentration, dependability, mental ability, and optimism, thus, hindering performance. Research suggests that depression is associated with lower grade point averages, and that cooccurring depression and anxiety can increase this association. Depression has also been linked to dropping out of school (Eisenberg et al., 2009). These consequences are not only limited to students' school years. Absences and poor performance can curtail students' potential through high school and into adulthood (Sum et al., 2009).

In addition, schools in underserved communities, particularly those serving students of color, often maintain less healthy settings for learning, with poorer air quality, less access to physical activity, higher exposure to environmental toxins, fewer health services, inadequate facilities, and less access to healthy foods and safe drinking water during the school day (Grineski & Collins, 2018). Schools in low-income communities are less likely to have parks, playgrounds, or green spaces for outdoor play (Bates et al., 2018). More than half of public schools do not have a full-time school nurse or counselor on staff, and only 13% of the nation's students have access to services through a school-based health center (Love et al., 2019; Willgerodt et al., 2018). Addressing these disparities in school conditions and student health could help close opportunity gaps.

The Whole School, Whole Community, Whole Child model (WSCC) from the Centers for Disease Control and Prevention and ASCD provides a helpful framework for understanding what it means to create a school environment that achieves this. WSCC highlights the components every school should have to ensure the health, safety, and well-being of their students, staff, and environment (Division of Population Health, National Center for Chronic Disease Prevention and Health Promotion, 2022). The WSCC model defines 10 important areas of a healthy school: health education; physical education and activity; nutrition environment and services; health services; counseling, psychological, and social services; social and emotional climate; physical environment; employee wellness; family engagement; and community involvement (see Figure 7.1). WSCC also underscores the need for alignment and integration across the education, public health, and school health sectors to ensure all children thrive and emphasizes the role of the families, caregivers, and community in supporting the school, the connections between health and academic achievement, and the importance of evidence-based school policies and practices.

EXISTING EDUCATION POLICIES THAT INTEGRATE STUDENTS' HEALTH

While there is significant work to be done to ensure health is prioritized in schools across the country, there are a number of existing federal policies that establish a foundation upon which this work can be built.

Federal Policies

The Every Student Succeeds Act

The Every Student Succeeds Act (ESSA), the first major overhaul of our national education law since 2001, recognizes the vital role that health plays in education. It also transferred significant authority from the federal government to states. This means that states have an opportunity to develop strategies and plans for implementing ESSA in ways that support student health and wellness (Every Student Succeeds Act , 2015). While it is ultimately up to states to determine how to leverage the opportunities ESSA presents to support student health, the law represents a paradigm shift in promoting equitable access to a high-quality education that supports student health. The following are examples of how ESSA recognizes the role health plays in education.

Figure 7.1. The Key Components of a Healthy School Environment as Defined by WSCC

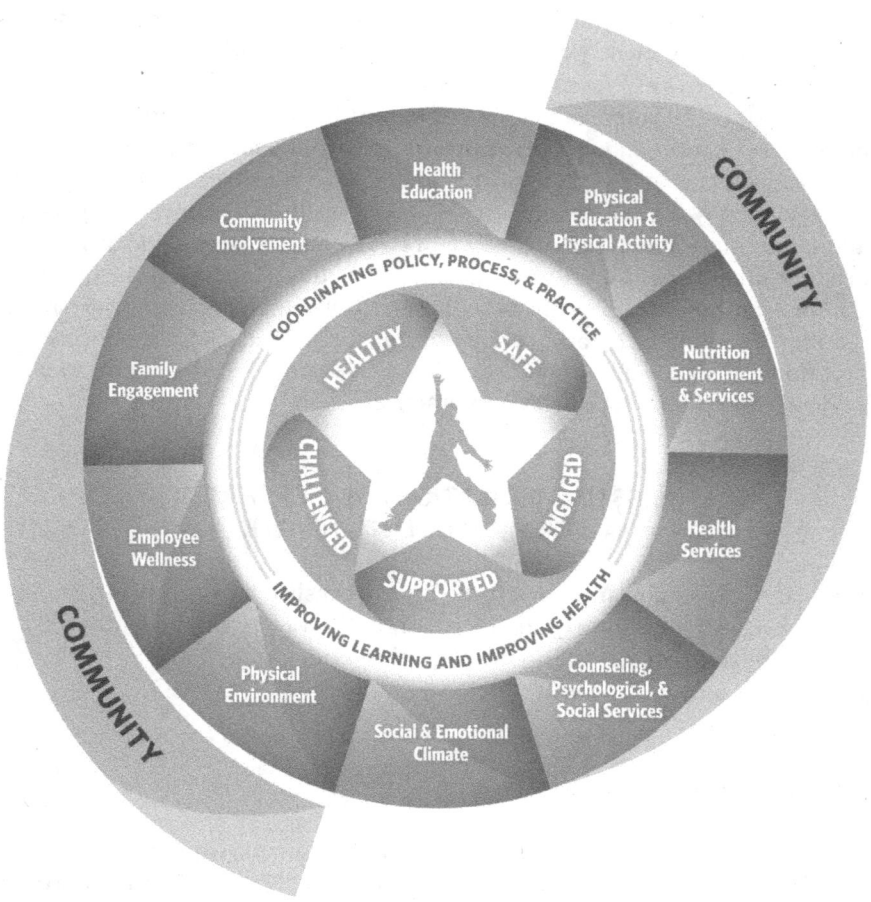

Indicator of School Quality or Student Success. Along with measures of academic achievement (student performance on state assessments in English language arts and mathematics, which may include growth in proficiency), graduation rates, and English language proficiency, ESSA requires states to include at least one indicator of school quality or student success (SQSS) in their state accountability system. All indicators must provide valid, reliable, and comparable information within each state's accountability system.

States then use school performance on these indicators to identify schools for either comprehensive support and improvement or targeted support and improvement. Districts with such schools can use data from statewide indicators to inform the needs assessments and school improvement plans required under ESSA. States can also select additional indicators to use as part of their broader continuous school improvement efforts across all schools, regardless of identification status.

The inclusion of SQSS measures in state accountability systems presents an important opportunity to elevate the connection between health and learning. Examples of SQSS indicators states have included measures of chronic absenteeism (commonly defined as missing 10% or more of the school year for any reason), school climate, suspension rates, and physical education/activity.

Student Support and Academic Enrichment Grants program (Title IV-A). This program provides designated funding states and districts can use to promote student health, increase access to well-rounded education, and improve the use of technology. The total funding is authorized at $1.6 billion, and ESSA stipulates that each state will receive an allocation based on the Title I funding formula. Any school district that receives more than $30,000 through this program must conduct a needs assessment and use the funding to address the needs identified. Funding from Title IV-A can then be used to address those needs. This flexible funding plays a key role in enabling school districts to support the health and wellness connection and has proven especially critical during COVID-19.

Elementary and Secondary Emergency Education Relief (ESSER) Fund

In 2020 and 2021, Congress passed three stimulus bills that provided over $190 billion for K–12 schools in one-time funds through ESSER. This included over $120 billion for K–12 schools through the American Rescue Plan Act of 2021. The funding to SEAs and LEAs represents a historic opportunity to support learning conditions and address inequities in education. While there is a wide range of needs to address with ESSER funds, the three stimulus bills and supporting guidance from the U.S. Department of Education highlighted student and staff health as eligible and important uses of the funds.

In addition, the one-time nature of these funds made them an excellent fit for potential investments that build the capacity of state education agencies and local education agencies to support student health so that they are well equipped to continue this work after ESSER funds are spent. This includes leveraging federal ESSER funds to strengthen programs that generate sustainable sources of funding, such as Medicaid, for school health programs and services.

In addition to federal education policy and funding opportunities, there are also opportunities within health-care policy, such as Medicaid, to support the health and learning connection.

School Medicaid

Since 1988, Medicaid has reimbursed states for certain medically necessary services provided in a school-based setting to children with an Individualized Education Programs (IEP) or Individualized Family Services Plan (IFSP) and in other limited situations, providing billions of dollars of federal funding to support school health services. Medicaid spending on school health services represents less than 1% of total federal Medicaid program costs. Yet, it represents a significant source of revenue for schools, making Medicaid the third-largest funding stream for K–12 public schools (MACPAC, 2018).

In 2014, the Centers for Medicare and Medicaid Services (CMS) clarified that Medicaid can pay for health and mental health services delivered in schools to Medicaid-enrolled students without an IEP or IFSP (Centers for Medicare and Medicaid Services, 2018). States can now permit school districts to receive Medicaid reimbursement for Medicaid-eligible services provided to all Medicaid-enrolled students in school-based settings (not just services included in a student's IEP). However, to advance this opportunity, states need to make a series of updates to policy and practice, including potentially amending their state Medicaid plan.[1] This change creates tremendous potential for school districts to use Medicaid funds to support and enhance health- and behavioral-health services offered in schools and access sustainable funding to advance efforts to support student health.

A NEW VISION FOR EDUCATION POLICY AND PRACTICE THAT RECOGNIZES THE HEALTH AND LEARNING CONNECTION

For decades, states, school districts, and schools across the country have focused efforts on measuring student achievement and school quality through academic data and assessments. However, the COVID-19 pandemic offered states a pause to reassess both the inadequacies of relying solely on academic data to characterize and represent educational outcomes.

By incorporating new, more holistic data, education leaders can better understand a true baseline of where students are and their ongoing progress, at the individual and aggregate levels. This data can also allow states, districts, and schools to target interventions to improve equity between student subgroups and provide a more sensitive and nuanced picture of student challenges and capabilities beyond their acquisition of content.

To achieve this vision, education policy and practice must embrace the following components:

- education accountability and improvement systems include health-and-wellness measures
- school staff training and supports include a focus on health
- health data to inform decision-making
- sustainable funding is available to support school health
- cross-sector partnerships
- engagement of families and youth

Education Accountability and Improvement Systems Include Health-and-Wellness Measures

Including health-and-wellness indicators connected to learning in education and state accountability systems, state and local report cards and school improvement planning, can explicitly validate the importance of these issues and require that districts and schools address identified needs. Possible measures that could be integrated include the following:

Chronic absenteeism. Chronic absenteeism is most commonly defined as missing 10% or more of school days for any reason: excused, unexcused, or suspension. Chronic absenteeism is a proven early warning sign of academic risk and school dropout. While the causes of chronic absenteeism are multifold, research shows that student health and a school's health and wellness environment are key factors that can contribute to a student being chronically absent.

Chronic absenteeism impacts students in all parts of the country and is prevalent among all races, but significant disparities exist. Compared to their White peers, American Indian and Pacific Islander students are over 50% more likely to lose 3 weeks of school or more, Black students are 40% more likely, and Latinx students are 17% more likely to miss extended school time (U.S. Department of Education, 2019).

Including chronic absenteeism data in education accountability systems is a key strategy for accomplishing this and helping states and communities better understand the underlying causes of chronic absenteeism and intervene accordingly.

School climate. Over the last 3 decades, a growing body of research attests to the importance of school climate, as it directly impacts telling indicators of success such as increased teacher retention, lower dropout rates, decreased incidences of violence, and higher student achievement (Thapa et al., 2013). Students who experience positive learning environments that are safe, supportive, and engaging are more likely to improve academically, participate more fully in the classroom, and develop skills that will help them be successful in school and in life.

Research also supports the fact that there is a racial school-climate gap: Black and Latinx students often report that their schools' climates are less positive than their White and Asian counterparts (Voight, 2013). This is supported by the fact that Black students are more likely to be referred to law enforcement or subjected to school-related arrests (U.S. Department of Education, Office for Civil Rights, 2019).

School climate is best measured through surveys that recognize student, parents, and school personnel voice. Research demonstrates that utilizing a climate survey tool recognizes the unique nature of each school's history, strengths, and needs and goals, and provides benchmarks as well as a road map for school-improvement efforts. A comprehensive school-climate survey tool can measure the percentage of students who report attending school with a positive school climate; percentage of students who report that discipline policies are applied fairly and equitably to all students; and the percentage of students who report that teachers and other adults have high expectations for them.

School Staff Trainings and Supports Include a Focus on Health

Professional-development programs provide an excellent opportunity to ensure that teachers and staff understand how to integrate health and wellness into their interactions with students, but such programs vary widely from state to state in the way that they address student health issues. As the adults who spend the most waking hours with children during the week, it is important that all school personnel are equipped to look out for the health and safety of their students.

School staff need preparation—both pre- and in-service—and resources to understand how they can address student-health issues and promote a healthier school environment. This means making sure that school staff learn the best practices for supporting student health at school as a part of their training. It means supporting teachers and principals in the workforce with ongoing professional development. Health and wellness preparation also gives school staff the skills to identify student health needs and to connect students with appropriate school resources and school leaders the skills to shape school-wide environments that promote health, and, in turn, improve academic outcomes.

In addition to supporting professional development for teachers and staff, it is important to support workplace wellness. Positive working environments are important for teacher retention and teacher productivity. There is a direct link between the well-being of teachers and the educational outcomes of their students. According to a report from Pennsylvania State University and the Robert Wood Johnson Foundation, "elementary school teachers who have greater stress and show more symptoms of depression create classroom environments that are less conducive to learning, which leads to poor academic performance among students." Effects of teacher stress range from lower scores on math tests to more behavior problems and lower levels of social adjustment and student engagement. High stress and poor working environments lead many teachers out of the profession. Turnover is most likely to occur in poorly performing schools. This contributes to a long-term destabilization of low-income neighborhood schools. This cycle deepens existing inequities in the school system.

This work is more critical than ever following COVID-19 and the immense stress the pandemic and resulting school-building closures placed on school staff. Ensuring school staff feel safe and supported in the school environment is key to ensuring their success in the workplace and retaining school staff.

Ensuring Health Data Is Available to Inform Decision-Making

Ensuring states, school districts, and schools have access to health data to inform decision-making can help ensure health and wellness are prioritized and that school staff understand the health-and-wellness issues impacting their school community. For example, health data can be integrated into school-level needs assessments and school improvement planning to ensure programming and resources are directed at students with health issues that can impact their ability to learn. In addition, health data can guide efforts to connect students and their families with wraparound services and supports, including access to meals, health care, and housing.

While there are many sources of existing health data that can be leveraged to inform decision-making (e.g., local public-health data, school health-provider records, meal-participation-rates data is not always integrated into decision-making tools (Solomon et al., 2018).[2] In addition, data-sharing barriers often exist that limit the ability of schools and healthcare providers to share individual data that can ultimately help support the success of students. Establishing cross-agency data-sharing agreements and memoranda of understanding to support the sharing of this data and integration into both education and health care accountability systems is needed to advance the health and learning connection.

Sustainable Funding Is Available to Support School Health

Schools and school districts must have access to the funding needed to support school health. To accomplish this, there must be significant change in the way schools are funded—at every level of government in a way that accounts for the impact of poverty and structural racism. In its final report released in 2013, the Department of Education's Equity and Excellence Commission issued a clear and powerful charge: Efforts to improve our school system "must start with equity"—particularly equity of resources. To achieve this goal, the commission instructed all levels of government to improve or redesign methods of school funding to adopt truly equitable funding systems.

Studies have found that there can be no equity when school districts in wealthier areas and those that serve mainly White student populations receive thousands more per student (from state and local funding) than districts in low-income areas and those that serve mostly students of color. Education policy needs to think beyond simply "equal" funding: Students in poverty and from historically underinvested communities need more funding than those in wealthier communities. Weighted student funding—which differentiates school budgeting based on the demographics that each school serves—can fund quality programs that have the greatest impact on the student population.

A key component of equitably distributing school funding is ensuring resources for school health and wellness are integrated within school-funding formulas. This could include designating funding to hire school health professionals and doing so in a way that ensures school districts serving higher-need communities receive additional resources to meet the health needs of these communities. It could also include designating funding to connect students and families with wraparound supports, such as access to food and housing, needed to support their success.

Expand State School Medicaid Programs

Maximizing Medicaid as a funding stream for school health is key to achieving the vision of maintaining sustainable funding for school health. Providing health care in schools is one of the best ways to ensure that children are healthy and ready to learn. In addition, increasing access to school health services is a proven strategy for improving academic outcomes, improving quality of care, and reducing overall health-care costs. Fortunately, there are multiple steps states and school districts can take to fully leverage the potential of school Medicaid programs.

For example, states can take advantage of the 2014 Centers for Medicare and Medicaid Services policy change and allow reimbursement for all students enrolled in Medicaid. This policy change invites states to (1) support school districts in drawing down additional Medicaid funding for school health services and (2) increase access to school health services. As of February 2022, 16 states have leveraged this policy opportunity to expand their school Medicaid program. States that have expanded their programs have seen a significant increase in federal Medicaid revenue generated by the program. This revenue can then be reinvested in education budgets to support ongoing programming, including efforts to support student health and wellness.

In addition, states can ensure the school health providers who are delivering services to students are Medicaid eligible and that school districts can bill Medicaid for the services they deliver. In many states, key school health providers such as school psychologists and school social workers, are not eligible for Medicaid reimbursement. School districts must communicate with the state education and state Medicaid agencies to ensure they understand who is delivering health services to Medicaid-enrolled students so that they can ensure school districts can bill for the services they deliver.

Finally, the Medicaid reimbursement that flows from the state to a school district is often designated as general funding. In other words, school districts are not required to reinvest the funding in school health services; a dollar of reimbursement for school-nursing services is not necessarily a dollar reinvested in school nursing. Additional funding for school districts can be a significant boost for overall school budgets and helps school districts stretch scarce local funding. In addition, this funding can incentivize LEAs to continue providing school health services and even expand access to these services. Some states like Michigan have gone farther, using legislation that encourages or requires school districts to reinvest their reimbursement in school health services. These legislative efforts can be an important step toward increasing a school district's commitment to school health services.

Braid and Blend Funding at the State and Local Levels

Braiding and blending funding to support school health efforts is a highly effective strategy for ensuring sustainable funding for this work. This can include braiding and blending education funding streams, such as ESSA Title funding and IDEA funding, in addition to braiding and blending cross-sector funding streams, such as available funds from education, health care, public health, housing, transportation, and more.

There is also an important opportunity to braid funding streams available through COVID-relief funding. For example, the American Rescue Plan provided $123 billion to K–12 schools, $1 billion for Head Start, $7.66 billion to expand the public-health workforce, and over $1.5 billion for substance-abuse prevention and treatment efforts. All these funds present a tremendous opportunity to support school health. Coordinating across sectors to align goals and determine how funding can be strategically invested in a way that recognizes the critical roles schools play in supporting the health of the population is key to ensuring the full impact of the funding is realized.

Cross-Sector Partnerships in Place

Schools cannot and should not do this work alone. Cross-sector collaboration is necessary to maximize resources at the federal, state, and local levels and ensure alignment across various child-serving agencies and organizations.

For example, increasingly, health-care providers recognize the role that schools can, and do, provide in meeting student health needs. As such, there are emerging opportunities to expand access to health services in school-based settings, including partnerships with a variety of different health-care stakeholders. These types of partnerships already exist in communities across the country in places like Akron, Ohio, between Akron Public Schools (see the Appendix for Chapter 7, online at www.tcpress.com) and hold great potential for bringing additional health-care resources into schools and expanding the workforce to serve students.

Meaningfully Engage Families and Youth

To create healthy school environments that are sustainable, it is critical to ensure families and youth are involved in decision-making around school health efforts and that their perspectives are integrated into the work. This engagement should go beyond occasional classes, volunteering, parent–teacher conferences, or surveys. It means forging a partnership in which families and youth can generate ideas, make decisions, and participate in their school's student health initiatives.

Policymakers can support this type of meaningful engagement by including family and youth engagement as a competitive priority in grant programs, requiring family and youth representation on state and local education advisory councils, and integrating requirements that family and youth perspective is reflected in needs assessments and other education-data collection efforts. In addition, policymakers establish technical assistance programs to support engagement of families and youth in this work by issuing guidance and best-practice protocols on high-quality parent-engagement programs that integrate a focus on health and wellness.

CONCLUSION

To ensure all students and staff have the opportunity to learn and work in a healthy school environment, it is critical to advance changes at the federal, state, and local levels that integrate health and wellness into education policy and practice rather than creating separate policies for school health that only further the silos that currently exist. We must move away from measuring student achievement and school quality solely through academic data and integrate student health-and-wellness data into our efforts to address the opportunity gap. This work is more important than ever, given the light COVID-19 has shed on the health and education disparities students of color and students in low-income communities' face. We must leverage the existing opportunities to achieve a vision of education policy and practice that fully integrates health and wellness and harnesses the critical role health can play in ensuring students thrive.

This includes ensuring health and wellness measures, such as chronic absenteeism and school climate, are integrated into education accountability and improvement systems; implementing staff training and supports that prioritize health; leveraging health data to inform decision-making; ensuring sustainable funding mechanisms are in place to support school health; and catalyzing cross-sector partnerships to support this work. As the examples above highlight, many states and school districts have taken steps toward realizing this vision, but there is more work to be done to supporting the scaling and sustainability of this work.

At the federal level, policymakers must continue to emphasize the intersection of health and education and focus on supporting the needs of the whole child. Action at the federal level is critical to pushing state-education agencies and school districts to look at policies that improve student health, keep children healthy and in school and, in turn, improve their academic success. In addition to upholding core provisions that support student health and wellness under ESSA, it is critical that federal policymakers continue to look for opportunities to integrate health and wellness throughout policies and programs and model this work through their own actions.

For example, there is a need for greater cross-agency collaboration between key agencies that oversee school health and wellness programming, including the U.S. Department of Education, Centers for Disease Control and Prevention, the Substance Abuse and Mental Health Services Administration, and CMS. These agencies must collaborate to align efforts and create joint guidance and resources that support states and school districts in advancing the health and learning connection. All agencies must look for opportunities to explicitly call out how available funds can be used to support school health and integrate a focus on school health into funding opportunities when appropriate.

In addition, federal agencies can play a key role in issuing guidance to support states and school districts in this work. This could include guidance on school-based Medicaid programs, utilizing data outside of academic assessment to understand student needs, and equitable school funding formulas.

At the state and local levels, policymakers can integrate health and wellness measures, such as chronic absence, school climate, and social–emotional learning into accountability and improvement systems. This will help ensure health and wellness are prioritized and that educators understand the health and learning connection. State education agencies can also implement statewide surveys and data-collection efforts to ensure school districts have the data needed to understand student health needs.

State education agencies and school districts can also build cross-sector collaborations with health, public health, housing, transportation agencies and more to support their efforts, reduce duplication of efforts, and maximize resources.

Finally, state education agencies and school districts can integrate health and wellness in school funding formulas, strengthen school Medicaid programs and braid and blend multiple funding streams to support school health programming.

States and school districts across the country are already taking key steps toward this vision, and we must build on their work and the lessons learned to ensure all students and staff have access to school environments that support their current and future success. As policymakers at the federal, state, and local levels develop new education policies and practices and modify existing ones, it is critical that they do so with an eye toward focusing on school health integration within these policies. Achieving this goal will help ensure all students are able to thrive.

NOTES

1. An overview of state-level activity to implement this opportunity is available here: https://healthystudentspromisingfutures.org.
2. Examples of data sites that highlight the social determinants of health and education with localized data include County Health Rankings and Roadmaps and The Opportunity Index.

REFERENCES

Bates, C. R., Bohnert, A. M., & Gerstein, D. E. (2018). Green schoolyards in low-income urban neighborhoods: Natural spaces for positive youth development outcomes. *Frontiers in Psychology, 9*, 805. https://doi.org/10.3389/fpsyg.2018.00805

Centers for Medicare and Medicaid Services. (2014, December 14). *Medicaid payment for services provided without charge (free care)* [Policy guidance SMD# 14-006]. Department of Health & Human Services. https://www.medicaid.gov/sites/default/files/federal-policy-guidance/downloads/smd-medicaid-payment-for-services-provided-without-charge-free-care.pdf

Child and Adolescent Health Measurement Initiative. (n.d.). *National Survey of Children's Health (NSCH) data query, 2016–2017.* Data Resource Center for Child and Adolescent Health, supported by Cooperative Agreement U59MC27866 from the U.S. Department of Health and Human Services, Health Resources and Services Administration's Maternal and Child Health Bureau (HRSA MCHB). http://www.childhealthdata.org

Coleman-Jensen, A., Gregory, C., & Singh, A. (2014). *Household food security in the United States in 2013: Statistical supplement*. United States Department of Agriculture, Economic Research Service.

Division of Population Health, National Center for Chronic Disease Prevention and Health Promotion. (2022). *Whole school, whole community, whole child (WSCC)*. Centers for Disease Control & Prevention, U.S. Depatment of Health & Human Services. https://www.cdc.gov/healthyschools/wscc/index.htm

Dye, B. A., Xianfen, L., & Beltrán-Aguilar, E. D. (2012). *Selected oral health indicators in the United States 2005–2008* (NCHS Data Brief, no. 96). National Center for Health Statistics, Centers for Disease Control and Prevention.

Eisenberg, D., Downs, M., & Golberstein, S. (2009). Stigma and help-seeking for mental health among college students. *Medical Care Research and Review*, 66(5), 522–541

Every Student Succeeds Act, 20 U.S.C. § 6301 (2015). https://www.congress.gov/114/plaws/publ95/PLAW-114publ95.pdf

Grineski, S. E., & Collins, T. W. (2018). Geographic and social disparities in exposure to air neurotoxicants at U.S. public schools. *Environmental Research*, 161, 580–587.

Lindsey, M. A., Sheftall, A. H., Xiao, Y., & Joe, S. (2019). Trends of suicidal behaviors among high school students in the United States: 1991–2017. *Pediatrics*, 144(5), e20191187.

Love, H. E., Schlitt, J., Soleimanpour, S., Panchal, N., & Behr, C. (2019). Twenty years of school-based health care growth and expansion. *Health Affairs*, 38(5), 755–764.

MACPAC. (2018, April). *Medicaid in schools* (Issue brief). https://www.macpac.gov/wp-content/uploads/2018/04/Medicaid-in-Schools.pdf

Millard, M. W., Johnson, P. T., Hilton, A., & Hart, M. (2009). Children with asthma miss more school: fact or fiction? *Chest*, 135(2), 303–306.

National Center for Health Statistics. (2018). *National Health Interview Survey*. Centers for Disease Control and Prevention.

National Survey of Children's Health. (2018). *Number of current or lifelong health conditions, nationwide, age in 3 groups*. United States Census Bureau. https://www.census.gov/programs-surveys/nsch/data/datasets.2018.html

Solomon, B., Katz, E., Steed, H., & Temkin, D. (2018). *Creating policies to support healthy schools: Policymaker, educator, and student perspectives*. Child Trends. https://www.cmhnetwork.org/wp-content/uploads/2018/10/healthyschool stakeholderreport_ChildTrends_October2018.pdf

Sum, A., Khatiwada, I., & McLaughlin, J. (2009). *Joblessness and jailing for high school dropouts and the high cost for taxpayers*. Center for Labor Market Studies, Northeastern University.

Thapa, A., Cohen, J., Guffey, S., & Higgins-D'Alessandro, A. (2013). A review of school climate research. *Review of Educational Research*, 83(3), 357–385.

U.S. Department of Education. (2019). *Chronic absenteeism in the nation's schools*. https://www2.ed.gov/datastory/chronicabsenteeism.html

U.S. Department of Education, Office for Civil Rights. (2019). *2015–16 Civil Rights Data Collection: School climate and safety.* https://www2.ed.gov/about/offices/list/ocr/docs/school-climate-and-safety.pdf

Voight, A. (2013). *The racial school-climate gap.* WestEd.

Willgerodt, M. A, Brock, D. M, & Maughan, E. D. (2018). Public school nursing practice in the United States. *Journal of School Nursing, 34*(3), 232–244.

CHAPTER 8

Air Pollution, Exposure to Contaminants, and Education Policy

Sara Grineski and Timothy Collins

INTRODUCTION

Between 2017 and 2020, Detroit's Marathon Petroleum Company refinery repeatedly exceeded state and federal air-quality rules and regulations. The refinery is located near the Mark Twain School for Scholars where parents are concerned about how the refinery emissions are impacting student learning and health (Burtka, 2021). Across the country in Los Angeles, California, school officials opened the Carson-Gore Academy of Environmental Studies in 2010 on a site contaminated by a leaking underground gas tank after working to remediate it (Salvesen et al., 2010). Despite these efforts, a coalition of environmental groups opposed opening the school, arguing that the remediation was insufficient to prevent soil vapor intrusion into classrooms (Hoag, 2010). In 2021, the Oregon Department of Transportation planned to widen the I-5 freeway, which involves moving it onto school property at Harriet Tubman Middle School, one of the most diverse schools in Portland (Figure 8.1). Even before the expansion, the road already carried 120,000 vehicles per day (Cortright, 2021).

The environmental conditions at the Mark Twain School, Carson-Gore Academy, and Harriet Tubman Middle School are not anomalous (see Figure 8.2). There are 129 public schools within a mile of the 100 highest volume polluters for lead in the United States. All in all, 58% to 80% of the 100 highest volume polluters for six harmful toxins (e.g., lead) have at least one public school within 2 miles (Legot et al., 2010). Schools are also located near highly trafficked roadways. In California, over 700 public schools are located within 150 meters of roads with daily traffic volumes of over 25,000 vehicles (Green et al., 2004). Nationwide, over 30% of U.S. public schools are within 400 meters of a major highway while 10% are within 100 meters (Appatova et al., 2008). Schools are often located in polluted areas due to economic constraints, while environmental quality is rarely a factor in school-siting decisions (Mohai & Kweon, 2020).

Figure 8.1. Aerial view of Harriet Tubman Middle School, the Interstate 5 Freeway, and the proposed area to be taken for freeway expansion in Portland, Oregon.

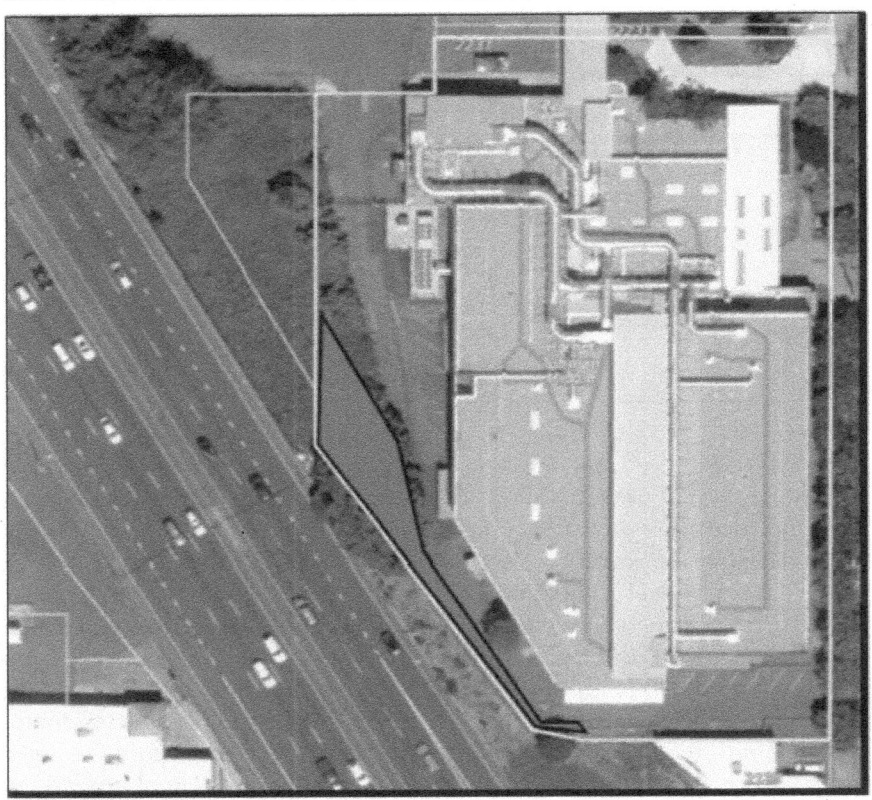

Source: Figure from Cortright (2021).

In this chapter, we start by reviewing academic research on social inequalities in air-pollution exposure at school, evidence linking air pollution to academic achievement, and current environmental policy relevant to school-based air pollution. Then, based on that evidence, we introduce the precautionary principle as a new vision for policy. We apply this principle to inform concrete policy actions at the local, state, and federal levels to conclude the chapter.

ARE THERE SOCIAL INEQUITIES IN AIR-POLLUTION EXPOSURE AT SCHOOL?

Socially disadvantaged students are more likely than those from more privileged backgrounds to attend schools in highly polluted neighborhoods.

Figure 8.2. Salina Elementary School Playground in Dearborn, Michigan

Photo by Nick Hagen, https://planetdetroit.org/2021/03/school-siting-report-marathon-consent-order-address-concerns-about-pollution-in-schools/

The first studies to establish this pattern were conducted in California (USA). In both the Los Angeles Unified School District, California (Pastor et al., 2002; Pastor et al., 2004), and the State of California (Pastor et al., 2006), racial/ethnic minority students, and Hispanic/Latinx students, were overrepresented as attendees of schools with greater health-harming levels of air toxics exposures. An individual-level study of school children in Orange County, Florida (USA), documented how Hispanic/Latinx, and Black children were significantly overrepresented relative to non-Hispanic White children in areas proximate to air pollution sources (Chakraborty & Zandbergen, 2007).

Most recently, we examined air neurotoxicant–exposure at 84,969 U.S. public schools. Metropolitan New York City (US EPA Region 2) is the geographic region most burdened by air neurotoxicant exposures in the United States since one-third of all schools in that region are in the top 10% for ambient neurotoxicant exposure among all schools nationwide. Students attending these "high risk" public schools nationwide are significantly more likely to be eligible for free/reduced price meals, and to be Hispanic/Latinx, Black, or Asian/Pacific Islander. They are significantly less likely to be White. Additionally, *schools serving the youngest students have greater levels of risk than schools serving older students* (Grineski & Collins, 2018). We then examined risks at the school-district level (see Figure 8.3). *School districts with higher proportions of children, children with disabilities, foreign-born*

Figure 8.3. Most Polluted School Districts in the United States in Terms of Carcinogenic Air Toxics

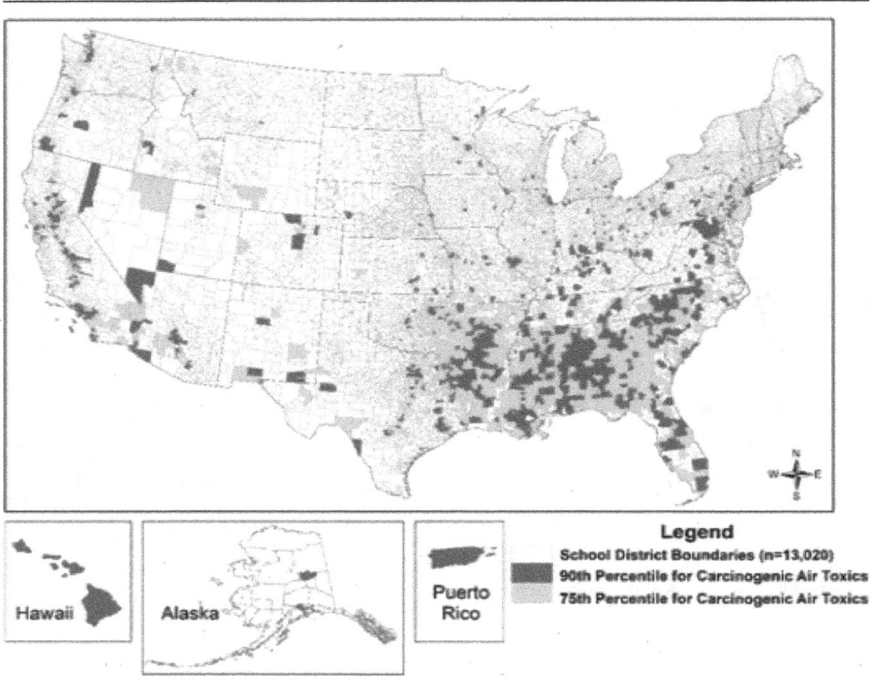

Source: Adapted from Grineski & Collins (2019).

children, and Black children had greater concentrations of cancer-causing air toxics (Grineski & Collins, 2019).

Socially disadvantaged students have also faced increased challenges due to COVID-19. The pandemic has widened existing disparities in academic growth, especially for students of color. It has made learning even more challenging for English Language Learners and disrupted services for students with disabilities (Department of Education, Office for Civil Rights, 2021). Due to the pandemic, school closures and the accompanying loss of skills from remote learning are expected to have longer lasting impacts on children from socioeconomic disadvantaged communities than more affluent ones (Agostinelli et al., 2020). Students facing the most severe COVID-19-related challenges are likely to overlap substantially with those in the group that experiences disproportionate exposures to air pollution, and it is currently well-established that chronic exposure to air pollution exacerbates health challenges from COVID-19 (Fattorini & Regoli, 2020). Particulate matter in the air may facilitate the spread of the SARS-CoV-2 virus and its impact on lung health can increase susceptibility to, and severity of, COVID-19 (Comunian et al., 2020).

IS AIR POLLUTION RELATED TO ACADEMIC ACHIEVEMENT?

While it is well-known that exposures to air pollution cause respiratory ailments and can trigger asthma, air pollution is also associated with low academic performance at school. There are two potential explanations for this, which are not mutually exclusive. First, exposure to air pollution is linked to illness and school absences, which then correlate with students' low performance (Shier et al., 2019). The second explanation relates to changes in the brain. As air pollutants enter the body, they induce neuroinflammation. This contributes to cell loss within the central nervous system, causing cognitive deficits (Brockmeyer & D'Angiulli, 2016). Consequences of this damage are far-reaching. Based on autopsies of otherwise clinically healthy Mexico City youth, for example, Dr. Calderón-Garcidueñas and colleagues (2008) revealed that those exposed to high levels of air pollution had brain structures resembling older adults with early-stage Alzheimer's disease. In a follow-up study of 203 individuals by the same research team, subcortical pre-neurofibrillary tangles (a primary brain marker of Alzheimer's disease) were already present in a highly exposed child under one year of age (Calderón-Garcidueñas et al., 2018).

There is a growing body of research linking air pollution exposures to students' school performance. This research uses statistical analysis to disentangle the effects of air pollution from other factors (e.g., race/ethnicity, socioeconomic status) associated with school-performance metrics. A line of research conducted at the school level indicates that attending schools in more polluted areas measurably worsens children's aggregated standardized academic test scores. This research has been conducted in California (Gaffron & Niemeier, 2015; Pastor et al., 2006; Pastor et al., 2004; Zweig et al., 2009), Louisiana (Legot et al., 2011; London et al., 2015; Lucier et al., 2011; Scharber et al., 2013), Massachusetts (Rosofsky et al., 2014), Michigan (Kweon et al., 2018; Mohai et al., 2011), Utah (Mullen et al., 2020), and Chile (Miller & Vela, 2013).

While there are extant child-level studies of air pollution and cognitive harm (Chiu et al., 2016; Lubczyńska et al., 2017; Raz et al., 2015; Saenen et al., 2016; Sentís et al., 2017), there have been fewer child-level studies of exposure and academic performance, which is our focus in this chapter. We conducted a cross-sectional case study in El Paso and found that higher levels of hazardous air pollutants were associated with lower children's grade point averages (GPAs), based on parental reports of grades (Grineski, Clark-Reyna, & Collins, 2015; Clark-Reyna, Grineski, & Collins, 2015; Clark-Reyna, Grineski, & Collins, 2016).

In a nationally representative sample of U.S. children, high isophorone (i.e., a commonly used solvent and chemical intermediary) levels in the child's zip code during the first year of life were associated with lower math scores in kindergarten among children living in urban areas (Stingone et al.,

2017). In a study examining the effects of pollution in children's birth census tract, New York City students exposed to the highest levels of diesel particulate matter and perchloroethylene had math exam scores that were 6% of a standard deviation lower than children in the lowest quantile. Similar associations between exposure and scores were not found for English performance (Stingone et al., 2016).

In a national sample of U.S. primary school children, annual and cumulative exposure to ozone and $PM_{2.5}$ were significantly associated with lower math test scores (Shier et al., 2019), as was greater pollen exposure (Marcotte, 2017). Asthmatic children were particularly sensitive, scoring 10% lower on math when ozone was high (Marcotte, 2017). Controlling for a comprehensive list of time variant and time invariant covariates, we found statistically significant associations between higher levels of hazardous air-pollutant exposure in kindergarten and lower reading, math, and science scores through the end of 3rd-grade (Grineski, Collins, & Adkins, 2020). These findings require policy action, and the next section reviews policy applicable to school-based pollution.

WHAT IS THE STATUS OF POLICY APPLICABLE TO SCHOOL-BASED AIR POLLUTION?

We focus here on policies applicable to school siting and environmental regulations of criteria air pollutants and chemical pollution.

School Siting. In 2011, the U.S. Environmental Protection Agency published school siting guidelines (U.S. Environmental Protection Agency, 2011), which are still used today. These guidelines were designed to inform voluntary decision-making, since they are not legally enforceable. While we focus on these EPA guidelines here, it is important to note that there are other sets of school-siting guidelines, including those from the World Health Organization (Wargo, 2004) and the Child Proofing Our Communities Campaign (Child Proofing Our Communities Campaign, 2005). The following four principles orient the EPA's guidelines (U.S. Environmental Protection Agency, 2011): (1) safe and healthy school environments are integral components of the education process; (2) the environmental review process should be rigorous, thorough, well documented, and include substantive and ongoing meaningful public involvement; (3) schools should be located in environments that contribute to the livability, sustainability, and public health of neighborhoods and communities; and (4) the school-siting process should consider the environmental health and safety of the entire community, including disadvantaged and underserved populations (Mohai & Kweon, 2020; U.S. Environmental Protection Agency, 2011).

The EPA guidelines recommend that school-siting teams screen potential school sites for environmental risks during a systematic and detailed review process. They offer a series of screening perimeter distances between proposed school sites and environmental hazards, such as air pollution, oil contamination, agricultural pesticides, groundwater contamination, surface-water pollution, safety hazards, noise, odors, Superfund sites, landfills, high-traffic roads, and industrial facilities (U.S. Environmental Protection Agency, 2011). While comprehensive and detailed, these voluntary guidelines have not been widely adopted in the United States yet (Sampson, 2012). The current "system" of school siting in the United States involves regulations at the state-level that are piecemeal and inconsistent. Thirty states have some policies pertaining to school siting in relation to environmental hazards, while 20 states have no policy (Rhode Island Legal Services, 2006). Only 14 states prohibit outright school siting on or near hazards. Of those, five prohibit or severely restrict siting schools on or near hazardous waste sites. Twenty-one states have school-siting policies that suggest school-siting officials should "avoid" siting schools on or near hazards or direct the school district to "consider" those hazards when selecting school sites (pp. 4–5).

Some states provide specific setbacks and procedures for mitigating a broad range of potential environmental threats, including proximity to highways, railroads, airports, and prior land uses. A few states, notably Kentucky, Mississippi, and West Virginia, ban schools from locating near certain hazards (Salvesen et al., 2010). The State of California has adopted the strictest planning norms. Since 2003, California has prohibited the building of "new school sites within 500 feet (166 meters) of the edge of the closest traffic lane of a freeway or busy traffic corridor" (Carrier et al., 2014, p. 67). Other states use broad language that is advisory only. For example, North Carolina urges school districts to avoid locating schools in high-traffic areas (Salvesen et al., 2010).

In addition to existing environmental hazards, schools are threatened by the arrival of new hazards, such as a proximate refinery or the widening of a nearby road. Yet few states have enacted laws preventing new and hazardous uses near schools (Salvesen et al., 2010). This is a gap in state-level school-siting policies that must be addressed through new laws that restrict companies and public-sector institutions from initiating hazardous land use activities near existing schools. One key to promoting environmental health at schools is making policies for harmful air pollutants more stringent.

Air Quality Legislation. The United States has been regulating criteria for air pollutants through the Clean Air Act for decades. These common pollutants (i.e., ground-level ozone, particulate matter, carbon monoxide, lead, sulfur dioxide, and nitrogen dioxide) are called "criteria" pollutants because the U.S. EPA sets National Ambient Air Quality Standards based on scientific criteria. There is growing evidence that these standards are not sufficient to protect human health and well-being (Burnett, 2018; Independent Particulate Matter Review Panel, 2020; Makar et al., 2017; Shi et al., 2015).

In addition, the regulation of chemicals used in industrial and commercial operations is insufficient to protect public health. Commercial production of industrial chemicals skyrocketed after World War II and the first major legislation to regulate chemicals (other than food additives, drugs, and pesticides), Toxic Substances Control Act (TSCA), passed in 1976 (Krimsky, 2017). The TSCA led the U.S. EPA to inventory some 62,000 chemicals in use at the time, which were grandfathered in and assumed safe unless shown otherwise. Between 1976–2013, the United States Government Accountability Office (2013) determined that, under the TSCA, the U.S. EPA had limited/banned just five existing chemicals: fully halogenated chlorofluoroalkanes, polychlorinated biphenyls (PCBs), dioxin, asbestos, and hexavalent chromium. Due to insufficient data and an inadequate chemical-testing approach, the agency had no basis for declaring any other of the tens of thousands of new and potentially harmful chemicals unsafe. This means that countless harmful chemicals have been in circulation for decades. The TSCA was finally revised in 2016 with bipartisan support (Krimsky, 2017) and the U.S. EPA is now mandated to review and make a risk determination for all new chemicals. Without greatly increasing the agency's resources (Applegate, 2008), the EPA will struggle to meet the modest mandate implied in the updated TSCA (Krimsky, 2017). While the current status of environmental health policy in the United States is insufficiently protective, policy improvements are possible.

HOW MIGHT A NEW VISION FOR POLICY IMPROVE ON CURRENT POLICY?

Given the well-documented social disparities in exposures to air pollution, the evidence of linkages between air pollution and academic outcomes, and the limitations in our current regulatory apparatus to protect children, *we articulate a new vision for school environmental policy inspired by the precautionary principle*. The precautionary principle initially emerged in European environmental policies in the late 1970s. By 1980, the PP started to emerge in international law; by 1992, it achieved international prominence and acceptance (Pike et al., 2020). Since 1992, the precautionary principle has been the basis for European environmental law and it is also used to inform environmental health policies (Foster et al., 2000). The UNESCO World Commission on the Ethics of Scientific Knowledge and Technology (COMEST) describes the PP as follows (Pike et al., 2020): When human activities may lead to morally unacceptable harm that is scientifically plausible but uncertain, actions shall be taken to avoid or diminish that harm.

Morally unacceptable harm refers to harm to humans or the environment that is: threatening to human life or health, or serious and effectively irreversible, or inequitable to present or future generations, or imposed without adequate consideration of the human rights of those affected (World Commission on the Ethics of Scientific Knowledge and Technology, 2005).

The precautionary principle has been dissected into the four following dimensions: (1) the threat dimension, (2) the uncertainty dimension, (3) the action dimension, and (4) the command dimension. Based on these dimensions, the PP can be framed through a series of if-clauses: *If* there is (1) a threat, which is (2) uncertain, *then* (3) some kind of action (4) is mandatory. Threat refers to the nature of the imminent harm, particularly its seriousness and irreversibility, while uncertainty indicates our lack of knowledge as to whether and how this threat might materialize (Sandin, 1999). When both the threat and uncertainty meet defined thresholds, an action obligation is triggered to prevent degradation of health or the environment. The command dimension designates the legal status of the action obligation to be taken (Pike et al., 2020).

Application of the precautionary principle to school-based exposures is urgent, due to children's heightened sensitivity to toxicants. Children are especially vulnerable to the health and developmental impacts of environmental exposures, due to their unique biological vulnerabilities, age-related patterns of exposure, and lack of control over their own environmental circumstances (Landrigan et al., 2010). They also spend significant time at school, approximately 6.6 hours per day for 180 days per year for public-school students in the United States (National Center for Education Statistics, 2008), meaning schools are important sites of exposure. There is also evidence that early educational success is associated with later triumphs and vice versa (Case et al., 2005; Dubow et al., 2006; Fergusson et al., 2005). This means that even small negative effects on early achievement associated with pollution exposure may have life-long effects. As per Sandin (1999), "*If* there is (1) a threat (i.e., air pollution), which is (2) uncertain (i.e., many studies show associations, but the exact dose-response curve and mechanisms are not definitively known), *then* (3) some kind of action (i.e., health-protective policy for schools) (4) is mandatory."

WHAT POLICY ACTIONS MUST BE UNDERTAKEN FOR THIS NEW POLICY VISION TO BE REALIZED?

Adoption of the precautionary principle to the environmental health of children at school requires a careful look at school-siting decisions and air quality (as well as other environmental) regulations. We also believe that conceptions of equity from transportation policy (Carrier et al., 2014; Geurs et al., 2009; Thomopolous & Grant-Muller, 2013), which emphasize compensation to those most affected, should also be applied. In what follows, we forward a series of actions that should be integral to this new policy vision.

Multisectoral Involvement in School Siting and Maintenance at the Local Level

First, while school boards and administrators are ultimately responsible for locating new schools and maintaining current schools, the planning process can be made more equitable by involving multiple stakeholders. A review of school-siting policy in all 50 states showed that only eight U.S. states either required or authorized the creation of school-siting advisory committees (Rhode Island Legal Services, 2006). These advisory committees should involve public health and environmental experts as well as local governmental officials and regional planners. Public and environmental health professionals bring a focus on toxic exposures and populations particularly vulnerable to negative health outcomes (Cohen, 2010). There are resources and models in place that can help guide multistakeholder committees to site schools in accordance with EPA recommendations. The Georgia Conservancy is a national leader in educating communities about the EPA school-siting guidelines and offers train-the-trainer curriculum, webinars, and workshops about how to implement the EPA school-siting guidelines since 2011 (Georgia Conservancy, n.d.).

Local governments specifically have a role to play with protective zoning to ensure that already-sited schools are not encroached upon by new hazards. For example, local school boards in North Carolina lack the authority to zone land. This means that even after a school board selects a location safe from environmental hazards, the proximate land can still be zoned for industrial development at some future date. Indiana is one of the few states that refers to future uses locating near existing schools (Salvesen et al., 2010). Planners can bring regional perspectives that help school decision-makers weigh trade-offs between the environmental, cultural, economic, and health implications as they decide to close, open or repair/modify schools (Cohen, 2010; Sampson, 2012). They consider potential exposure to traffic, sidewalks, hazardous facilities, psychological stressors, or other features of the built environment.

In addition, there is also an important role for teachers, parents, and students to collaborate with local officials as they can often enhance the process of identifying risks and proposing solutions (Healthy Schools Network, 2009). In many districts, they have successfully advocated for grants to improve the environment and initiated green-school programming. Their role cannot be underestimated in scoping, siting, environmental assessment, and long-term maintenance of school sites (Sampson, 2012). However, only 12

U.S. states required the sponsors of school projects to solicit public input on school siting using public notices, public meetings, or hearings (Rhode Island Legal Services, 2006), suggesting that public input can be more systematically and broadly utilized.

Building and Maintaining Healthy Schools

Second, once they have selected a site for a new school, school-siting and maintenance teams need to make decisions about building design. These teams can utilize information from several reports to help them make informed and environmentally sound decisions about schools. These include the U.S. EPA's *Not in My Schoolyard* (Rhode Island Legal Services, 2006), the National Research Council's (2006) *Review and Assessment of the Health and Productivity Benefits of Green Schools: An Interim Report*, and the Child Proofing Our Communities Campaign's report, *Creating Safe Learning Zones: The ABC's of Healthy Schools* (Child Proofing Our Communities Campaign & Center for Health, Environment, & Justice, 2005). When considering building materials and energy efficiency, these publications share case studies, offering accessible models of cost-effective, environmentally healthy building design for facility managers and school boards to model (Sampson, 2012). The 2011 U.S. EPA school-siting guidelines also recommend consulting *Creating Healthy Indoor Air Quality (IAQ) in Schools*, *ENERGY STAR for K–12 School Districts*, *Managing Pests in Schools*, and *SunSafety*.

Some states have proactively sought to create healthier learning environments for children. For example, Vermont passed the School Environmental Health Act (Act 125) in May 2000 to improve school indoor-air quality, reduce exposures to hazardous materials, and help schools earn the Envision Certificate of Achievement. Schools earn this certificate through participation in the Envision Program, which provides model environmental-health management plans and helps schools identify, prevent, and solve indoor-air quality issues (Vermont Department of Health, 2021). Over the first 5 years, the certificate was adopted at a lower rate than the target goal (Healthy Schools Network, 2009), but the program persists today.

In 2020, the New York State Department of Health received a grant through the U.S. EPA's Healthy Learning Environment Grants Initiative to implement the Clean, Green, and Healthy Schools Program statewide. The multidisciplinary program provides resources to school employees, students, and parents on best practices to increase knowledge and empower school occupants to improve their school's environmental health. The project will reach all 4,433 schools in the 700+ school districts across New York State, including New York City, the largest school district in the country. The grant is expected to improve environmental conditions in school buildings across New York and support improved health, attendance, and academic performance for approximately 3.2 million school-aged children (U.S. Environmental Protection Agency, 2020).

When it comes to building new schools, Washington State instituted an exemplary program via their High-Performance Public Building Act of 2005. The Act required all Washington state public-school facility projects receiving state funding to achieve at least LEED silver standard or follow the Washington Sustainable Schools Design Protocol. The Washington Sustainable Schools Protocol was developed by a 34-member committee with diverse representation in terms of geographic reach within the state and sector, e.g., architecture firms, engineering firms, governmental representatives, and design firms with varying expertise (i.e., interior, energy efficiency, sustainability) (Cohen, 2010).

Compensation to Schools Affected by Air Pollution at the Local Level

Third, to account for the decades when the precautionary principle was not in place, compensatory measures for schools affected by the highest levels of pollution are needed. To ensure equality in outcomes, these additional resources must be invested. This idea borrows from conceptions of equity used in transportation policies (Carrier et al., 2014; Geurs et al., 2009; Thomopolous & Grant-Muller, 2013;). Specifically, the idea is that those disproportionately affected in health-harming ways by a transportation project should be compensated by those benefiting the most from the project (Thomopolous & Grant-Muller, 2013). In the case of schools, important compensatory measures could involve greenspace, building modifications, and enrichment activities, since there is evidence that those interventions may help protect children from the harmful effects of air pollution exposures. We discuss each in turn.

Increase greenspace. Greater levels of tree canopy cover are associated with boosts in students' academic performance (Sivarajah et al., 2018; Tallis et al., 2018; Wu et al., 2014). Access to greenspace has also been associated with better mental health among lower SES children (Balseviciene et al., 2014), fewer behavioral problems and reduced hyperactivity (Amoly et al., 2014), and better spatial working memory (Flouri et al., 2019). School greenness is particularly beneficial to children's cognitive functioning (Dadvand et al., 2015). Greenspace may provide health benefits through reducing pollution exposure, enabling physiological stress recovery, and enhancing physical activity (Markevych et al., 2017). In one study, associations between greenness around schools and cognitive development were partly mediated by reduction in exposure to air pollution (Dadvand et al., 2015). In addition to greenspace outside of schools, adding indoor plants to classrooms is associated with improved attention spans (Kim et al., 2020).

Given the benefits of greenspace, the Beethoven Street Elementary School, a majority Latinx school in the Los Angeles Independent School District, has a "learning garden." The garden includes plots for planting, fruit trees, composting, benches, and a space for teachers to hold outdoor classes in the garden (Beethoven Street Elementary School, 2021). This garden provides a model for other schools. Moving forward, a Robert Wood Johnson–funded project (initiated in March 2021) will examine the efficacy of green playground renovations on improved health, academic performance, and environmental quality (Evidence for Action, 2021).

School building modifications. School buildings can be modified to improve air quality especially as outdoor air is a key driver of indoor air quality; these modifications can include installing dual painted windows, retrofitting HVAC systems to include air filtration technology, and soundproofing. Replacing old windows with modern windows (e.g., double-glazed a vacuum between the panes) can reduce the intrusion of outdoor air into indoor spaces (Ścibor et al., 2019). Schools can also install air filtration devices in HVAC systems, which improve indoor air quality (Liu et al., 2017) and have been used to reduce particulate matter concentrations in U.S. school contexts (Smythe, 2018). Air filtration has become even more urgent due to COVID-19. In June 2021, Los Angeles Unified School District installed MERV-13 air filters in all classrooms in district schools. The filters will help protect students from COVID-19 as well as outdoor air pollutants, such as those from busy roads or wildfires (Los Angeles Unified School District, 2021). Schools may have a unique opportunity to install air filters to help with COVID-19 and air pollution abatement as American Rescue Plan Elementary and Secondary School Emergency Relief (ESSER) funding money is available for schools to improve ventilation and keep educators, staff, and students safe from COVID-19 (U. S. Department of Education, 2021).

Lastly, numerous studies linked high noise exposure to worsened academic performance (Basner et al., 2017; Clark et al., 2006; Klatte et al., 2013; Klatte et al., 2017; National Academies of Sciences, 2014) and the reduction of noise exposure in school buildings (via the installation of sound insulation) has been associated with improvements in academic performance (National Academies of Sciences, 2014). Plans for the freeway expansion in Portland, mentioned earlier, include two sound walls that will be 22 feet tall and 1,000 feet long (Cortright, 2021).

Invest in enrichment programs. Enriching activities—e.g., yoga, games, art, library, and music during school—can improve children's executive functioning (Diamond & Lee, 2011). It is possible that those activities could protect children's development from harmful effects of air pollution. Animal models suggest that enriching environments can slow neurodegenerative decline (Laviola et al., 2008) and protect against lead (Pb)-induced behavioral deficits (Schneider et al. 2001).

State-Level School-Siting Policy

Fourth, while federal school-siting policy is most desirable, as it would protect all U.S. children equally, we should also pursue new state-level policies in the absence of adequately protective federal policy. For example, California has a mandate to locate no new school sites within 500 feet of the edge of the closest traffic lane of a freeway or busy traffic corridor. Additional policies at the state-level include provisions that prevent new major highways or industrial sites from being built near existing schools (Sampson, 2012). California, New Jersey, North Carolina, New Mexico, Minnesota, and Florida provide models for how to enact state-level school-siting policies (Brown et al., 2012). California has also been singled out as having a comprehensive school-siting policy by Rhode Island Legal Services (2006). Figure 8.4 compares these six states in terms of important school siting criteria.

New Federal Office for School Environmental Health

Fifth, no federal agencies are currently responsible for school environmental health. This creates a policy patchwork that does not protect children equally and contributes to inequities between districts whereby more affluent, Whiter districts provide environmental health amenities that poor districts with higher concentrations of children of color simply cannot (Sampson, 2012). A federal office could help ensure that school environmental health issues are not overlooked in the policy process. This office could be held within the U.S. EPA's Office on Environmental Justice, effectively linking the priorities of school environments and environmental justice.

More Stringent Pollution and Chemical Standards

Sixth, our current pollution and chemical standards are not in line with the current evidence base and must be changed. For example, a panel of esteemed scientists "unequivocally and unanimously concluded that the current $PM_{2.5}$ standards do not adequately protect public health. An annual standard between 10 μg per cubic meter and 8 μg per cubic meter would protect the general public and at-risk groups. However, even at the lower end of the range, risk is not reduced to zero" (Independent Particulate Matter Review Panel, 2020, p. 681). Regarding industrial chemicals, we propose that we consider new industrial chemicals unsafe unless proven otherwise. This would put the onus on the manufacturer to conduct years of research to remove all doubts that a chemical is unsafe, as opposed to the underfunded and understaffed U.S. EPA (Krimsky, 2017). A similar approach is already applied to a degree by the Food and Drug Administration as they regulate pharmaceuticals (Krimsky, 2017), which could serve as a model for industrial chemicals.

Figure 8.4. Comparison of Selected States' School Siting Policy Characteristics

Criteria	Prohibited Sites	Siting Factors	Environmental Evaluation	Remediation	Funding Provisions	Public Participation
Description[1]	State has policy that designates certain types of sites as too dangerous	State has policy guidelines for school siting	State asks local education agencies to make environmental evaluation a priority in school-siting decisions	State has policy that includes additional remediation measures specifically for schools to be built on brownfields	State has funding provisions to allow for stringent school siting policies	State has broadened the school siting conversation beyond local education agencies
California	✓	✓	✓	✓	✓	✓
Florida		✓	✓	✓		
Minnesota		✓	✓			✓
New Jersey	✓		✓	✓	✓	✓
New Mexico	✓		✓			
North Carolina		✓	✓			✓

Adapted from: Brown et al. (2012)

[1] See Fischbach (2011) for a complete description of each school siting criteria.

Improve Current EPA School-Siting Guidelines

Seventh, while the U.S. EPA has school-siting guidelines, we recommend that those guidelines be modified to include exclusion distances. Currently, the guidelines include minimum screening distances (e.g., 1,000 feet from a gas station or 3 miles from a field that is aerially sprayed with pesticides) for most hazards, which then trigger more detailed site review and evaluation (Mohai & Kweon, 2020). These guidelines do not implement exclusion distances that disqualify some sites from hosting schools. While not adopted by the U.S. EPA, their Children's Health Protection Advisory Committee (CHPAC) recommended exclusion distances, which tend to be shorter than screening distances (Fischbach, 2011). For example, CHPAC recommends that no schools be built within 50 feet of a typical gas station, within 300 feet of a large gas station, and within 0.25–2.5 miles of a large agricultural operation employing aerial pesticide spraying (Mohai & Kweon 2020).

The precautionary principle suggests that exclusion zones are needed because harm is likely when children attend school close to hazards. For example, the highest concentrations of traffic pollutants are present within 200 meters of major roads and highways (Brugge et al., 2007). Moreover, children who attend schools located less than 200 meters from a major road are more likely to have reduced lung function and develop asthma (Clark et al., 2010; Gauderman et al., 2007; Jerrett et al., 2008; Salvesen et al., 2010). In addition, the U.S. EPA guidelines need to address cleanup of hazardous sites and address how patterns of racial segregation more consistently should factor into school site selection (Fischbach, 2011).

Make Federal School-Siting Guidelines into Law

Eighth, many argue that environmental health and safety inherently fall under the mission of the U.S. education system to assure quality education and protect children, yet the lack of federal policy on school siting, building, and maintenance do not reflect this charge (Sampson, 2012). Ten years after the release of nonbinding federal guidelines, we have witnessed very limited adoption at the state level. Federal regulation is required to ensure adequate protection for all American school children from environmental hazards. All U.S. states have compulsory education laws that require children to attend public (or accredited private schools) for a specified duration, usually between the ages of 6 and at least 16, for 180 days per year. While attending public school, the health and well-being of these children is the responsibility of the government, which needs to ensure their protection from risks.

At the state level, most states authorize local governments to adopt ordinances to protect school children from moral threats such as liquor stores or adult bookstores (Salvesen et al., 2010); this suggests that a policy framework is in place for the consideration of environmental hazards in school siting, building, and maintenance. The need for federal action on school siting runs parallel to arguments made by education reformers within the Federal Right to Education framework (Robinson, 2019), such that states have failed to close achievement and opportunity gaps, and federal action is needed to ensure that all children have equal educational opportunities. These efforts should include school environmental health, given the linkages between environmental conditions and student outcomes.

REFERENCES

Agostinelli, F., Doepke, M., Sorrenti, G., & Zilibotti, F. (2020). *When the great equalizer shuts down: Schools, peers, and parents in pandemic times* (Working Paper 28264). National Bureau of Economic Research. https://www.nber.org/papers/w28264

Amoly, E., Dadvand, P., Forns, J., López-Vicente, M., Basagaña, X., Julvez, J., Alvarez-Pedrerol, M., Nieuwenhuijsen, M. J., & Sunyer, J. (2014). Green and blue spaces and behavioral development in Barcelona schoolchildren: The BREATHE project. *Environmental Health Perspectives*, 122(12), 1351–1358.

Appatova, A., Ryan, P., LeMasters, G., & Grinshpun, S. (2008). Proximal exposure of public schools and students to major roadways: A nationwide U.S. survey. *Journal of Environmental Planning and Management*, 51(5) 631–646.

Applegate, J. S. (2008). Synthesizing TSCA and REACH: Practical principles for chemical regulation reform. *Ecology Law Quarterly*, 35, 720–779.

Balseviciene, B., Sinkariova, L., Grazuleviciene, R., Andrusaityte, S., Uzdanaviciute, I., Dedele, A., & Nieuwenhuijsen, M. J. (2014). Impact of residential greenness on preschool children's emotional and behavioral problems. *International Journal of Environmental Research and Public Health*, 11(7), 6757–6770.

Basner, M., Clark, C., Hansell, A., Hileman, J. I., Janssen, S., Shepherd, K., & Sparrow, V. (2017). Aviation noise impacts: State of the science. *Noise & Health*, 19(87), 41–50.

Beethoven Street Elementary School. (2021). *Beethoven's learning garden.* https://www.beethovenschool.org/m/pages/index.jsp?uREC_ID=298518&type=d

Brockmeyer, S., & D'Angiulli, A. (2016). How air pollution alters brain development: The role of neuroinflammation. *Translational Neuroscience*, 7(1), 24–30.

Brown, R., Etue, E., Fox, E., Rajaee, M., & Schafrick, N. (2012). *Developing a policy on environmental quality, health, and schools in Michigan* [Masters project]. University of Michigan–Ann Arbor. https://deepblue.lib.umich.edu/handle/2027.42/90938

Brugge, D., Durant, J., & Rioux, C. (2007). Near-highway pollutants in motor vehicle exhaust: A review of epidemiologic evidence of cardiac and pulmonary health risks. *Environmental Health*, 6(23), 1–12.

Burnett, R., Chen, H., Szyszkowicz, M., Fann, N., Hubbell, B., Pope, C. A., Apte, J. S., Brauer, M., Cohen, A., Weichenthal, S., Coggins, J., Di, Q., Brunekreef, B., Frostad, J., Lim, S. S., Kan, H., Walker, D., Thurston, D., Hayes, R. B. . . . & Spadaro, J. V. (2018). Global estimates of mortality associated with long-term exposure to outdoor fine particulate matter. *Proceedings of the National Academy of Sciences of the United States of America, 115*(38), 9592–9597.

Burtka, A. T. 2021. School siting report, Marathon consent order address concerns about pollution in schools. Planet Detroit. https://planetdetroit.org/2021/03/school-siting-report-marathon-consent-order-address-concerns-about-pollution-in-schools/

Calderón-Garcidueñas, L., Gónzalez-Maciel, A., Reynoso-Robles, R., Delgado-Chávez, R., Mukherjee, P. S., Kulesza, R. J., Torres-Jardón, R., Ávila-Ramírez, J., & Villarreal-Ríos, R. (2018). Hallmarks of Alzheimer disease are evolving relentlessly in Metropolitan Mexico City infants, children and young adults. APOE4 carriers have higher suicide risk and higher odds of reaching NFT stage V at ≤40 years of age. *Environmental Research, 164*, 475–487.

Calderón-Garcidueñas, L., Solt, A. C., Henriquez-Roldan, C., Torres-Jardon, R., Nuse, B., Herritt, L., Villarreal-Calderón, R., Osnaya, N., Stone, I., García, R., Brooks, D. M., González-Maciel, A., Reynoso-Robles, R., Delgado-Chávez, R., & Reed, W. (2008). Long-term air pollution exposure is associated with neuroinflammation, an altered innate immune response, disruption of the blood-brain barrier, ultrafine particulate deposition, and accumulation of amyloid beta-42 and alpha-synuclein in children and young adults. *Toxicologic Pathology, 36*(2), 289–310.

Carrier, M., Apparicio, P., Seguin, A-M., & Crouse, D. (2014). Ambient air pollution concentration in Montreal and environmental equity: Are children at risk at school? *Case Studies on Transport Policy, 2*, 61–69.

Case, A., Fertig, A., & Paxson, C. (2005). The lasting impact of childhood health and circumstance. *Journal of Health Economics, 24*(2), 365–389.

Chakraborty, J., & Zandbergen, P. A. (2007). Children at risk: measuring racial/ethnic disparities in potential exposure to air pollution at school and home. *Journal of Epidemiology and Community Health, 61*(12), 1074–1079.

Child Proofing Our Communities Campaign & Center for Health, Environment, & Justice. (2005). *Building safe schools: Invisible threats, visible actions.* http://chej.org/wp-content/uploads/Building-Safe-Schools-Invisible-Threats-Visible-Actions-REP-003.pdf

Chiu, Y. H. M., Hsu, H. H. L., Coull, B. A., Bellinger, D. C., Kloog, I., Schwartz, J., Wright, R. O., & Wright, R. J. (2016). Prenatal particulate air pollution and neurodevelopment in urban children: Examining sensitive windows and sex-specific associations. *Environment International, 87*, 56–65.

Clark-Reyna, S. E., Grineski, S. E., & Collins, T. W. (2015). Residential exposure to air toxics is linked to lower grade point averages among school children in El Paso, Texas, USA. *Population and Environment, 37*, 319–340.

Clark-Reyna, S. E., S. E. Grineski, & T. W. Collins. (2016). Ambient concentrations of metabolic disrupting chemicals and children's academic achievement in El Paso, Texas. *International Journal of Environmental Research and Public Health, 13*, E874.

Clark, C., Martin, R., Van Kempen, E., Tamundo, A., Head, J., Davies, H. W., Haines, M. M., Lopez Barrio, I., Matheson, M., & Stansfeld, S. A. (2006). Exposure-effect relations between aircraft and road traffic noise exposure at school and reading comprehension: The RANCH project. *American Journal of Epidemiology, 163*, 27–37.

Clark, N. A., Demers, P. A., Karr, C. J., Koehoorn, M., Lencar, C., Tamburic, L., & Brauer, M. (2010). Effect of early life exposure to air pollution on development of childhood asthma. *Environmental Health Perspectives, 118*(2), 284–290.

Cohen, A. (2010). Achieving healthy school siting and planning policies: Understanding shared concerns of environmental planners, public health professionals, and educators. *New Solutions: A Journal of Environmental and Occupational Health Policy, 20*(1), 49–72.

Comunian, S., Dongo, D., Milani, C., & Palestini, P. (2020). Air pollution and COVID-19: The role of particulate matter in the spread and increase of COVID-19's morbidity and mortality. *International Journal of Environmental Research and Public Health, 17*(12), 4487.

Cortright, J. (2021, April 13). Taking Tubman: ODOT's plan to build a freeway on school grounds. *City Commentary.* https://cityobservatory.org/taking-tubman-odots-plan-to-build-a-freeway-on-school-grounds/

Dadvand, P., Nieuwenhuijsen, M. J., Esnaola, M., Forns, J., Basagaña, X., Alvarez-Pedrerol, M., Rivas, I., López-Vicente, M., De Castro Pascual, M., Su, J., Jerrett, M., Querol, X., & Sunyer, J. (2015). Green spaces and cognitive development in primary schoolchildren. *Proceedings of the National Academy of Sciences of the United States of America, 11*(26), 7937–7942.

Diamond, A., & Lee, K. (2011). Interventions shown to aid executive function development in children 4 to 12 years old. *Science, 333*(6045) 959–964.

Dubow, E. F., Huesmann, L. R., Boxer, P., Pulkkinen, L., & Kokko, K. (2006). Middle childhood and adolescent contextual and personal predictors of adult educational and occupational outcomes: A mediational model in two countries. *Developmental Psychology, 42*(5), 937–949.

Evidence for Action. (2021). *Impact of schoolyards to playgrounds renovations on academic performance and health of New York City students.* Retrieved 29 September 2021: https://www.evidenceforaction.org/grant/impact-schoolyards-playgrounds-renovations-academic-performance-and-health-new-york-city

Fattorini, D., & Regoli, F. (2020). Role of the chronic air pollution levels in the Covid-19 outbreak risk in Italy. *Environmental Pollution, 24*, 114732.

Fergusson, D. M., Horwood, L. J., & Ridder, E. M. 2005. Show me the child at seven II: Childhood intelligence and later outcomes in adolescence and young adulthood. *Journal of Child Psychology and Psychiatry, 46*(8), 850–858.

Fischbach, S. (2011). *EPA's school siting guidelines: What's missing?* Center for Health, Environment and Justice. https://chej.org/pub-epas-school-siting-guidelines-whats-missing

Flouri, E., Papachristou, E., & Midouhas, E. (2019). The role of neighbourhood greenspace in children's spatial working memory. *British Journal of Educational Psychology, 89*(2), 359–373.

Foster, K. R., Vecchia, P., & Repacholi, M. H. (2000). Science and the Precautionary Principle. *Science, 288*(5468), 979–981.

Gaffron, P., & Niemeier, D. (2015). School locations and traffic emissions—Environmental (in)justice findings using a new screening method. *International Journal of Environmental Research and Public Health, 12*(2), 2009–2025.

Gauderman, W. J., Vora, H., McConnell, R., Berhane, K., Gilliland, F., Thomas, D., Lurmann, F., Avol, E., Kunzli, N., Jerrett, M., & Peters, J. (2007). Effect of exposure to traffic on lung development from 10 to 18 years of age: A cohort study. *Lancet, 369*(956), 571–577.

Georgia Conservancy. (n.d.). School Siting Workshops. https://www.georgiaconservancy.org/schoolsiting/workshops

Geurs, K., Boone, V., & Van Wee, B. (2009). Social impacts of transport: Literature review and the state of the practice of transport appraisal in the Netherlands and the United Kingdom. *Transport Reviews, 29*(1), 69–90.

Green, R. S., Smorodinsky, S., Kim, J. J., McLaughlin, R., & Ostro, B. (2004). Proximity of California public schools to busy roads. *Environmental Health Perspectives, 112*(1), 61–66.

Grineski, S. E., Clark-Reyna, S. E., & Collins, T. W. (2015). School-based exposure to hazardous air pollutants and grade point average: A multi-level study. *Environmental Research, 147*, 164–171.

Grineski, S. E., & Collins, T. W. (2018). Geographic and social disparities in exposure to air neurotoxicants at U.S. public schools. *Environmental Research, 161*, 580–587.

Grineski, S. E., & Collins, T. W. (2019). Lifetime cancer risks from hazardous air pollutants in U.S. public school districts. *Journal of Epidemiological Community Health, 73*, 854–860.

Grineski, S. E., Collins, T. W., & Adkins, D. E. (2020). Exposure to hazardous air pollutants is associated with worse performance in reading, math, and science among U.S. primary school children. *Environmental Research, 181*, 108925.

Healthy Schools Network. (2009). *Sick schools 2009*. http://healthyschools.org/data/files/SICK_SCHOOLS_2009.pdf.

Hoag, C. (2010, September 12). LA environmental school site in toxic soil cleanup. *San Diego Tribune*.

Independent Particulate Matter Review Panel. (2020). The need for a tighter particulate-matter air-quality standard. *New England Journal of Medicine, 383*, 680–683.

Jerrett, M., Shankardass, K., Berhane, K., Gauderman, W. J., Künzli, N., Avol, E., Gilliland, F., Lurmann, F., Molitor, J. N., Molitor, J. T., Thomas, D. C., Peters, J., & McConnell, R. (2008). Traffic-related air pollution and asthma onset in children: A prospective cohort study with individual exposure measurement. *Environmental Health Perspectives, 116*, 1433–1438.

Kim, H., Yeo, I., & Lee, J. (2020). Higher attention capacity after improving indoor air quality by indoor plant placement in elementary school classrooms. *The Horticulture Journal*: 89(3), 319–327.

Klatte, M., Bergström, K., & Lachmann, T.. (2013). Does noise affect learning? A short review on noise effects on cognitive performance in children. *Frontiers in Psychology, 4*. https://doi.org/10.3389/fpsyg.2013.00578

Klatte, M., Spilski, J., Mayerl, J., Möhler, U., Lachmann, T., & Bergström, K. (2017). Effects of aircraft noise on reading and quality of life in primary school children in Germany: Results from the NORAH study. *Environment and Behavior, 49*, 390–424.

Krimsky, S. (2017). The unsteady state and inertia of chemical regulation under the US Toxic Substances Control Act. *PLoS Biology, 5*: e2002404.

Kweon, B., Mohai, P., Lee, S., & Sametshaw, A. M. (2018). Proximity of public schools to major highways and industrial facilities, and students' school performance and health hazards. *Environment and Planning B: Urban Analytics and City Science, 45*(2) 312–329.

Landrigan, P. J., Rauh, V. A., & Galvez, M. P. (2010). Environmental justice and the health of children. *Mount Sinai Journal of Medicine, 77*(2), 178–187.

Laviola, G., Hannan, A. J., Macri, S., Solinas, M., & Jaber, M. (2008). Effects of enriched environment on animal models of neurodegenerative diseases and psychiatric disorders. *Neurobiological Disorders, 31*(2), 159–168.

Legot, C., London, B., & Shandra, J. (2010). Environmental ascription: High-volume polluters, schools, and human capital. *Organization & Environment, 23*(3), 271–290.

Legot, C., London, B., & Shandra, J.. (2011). Proximity to industrial toxins and childhood respiratory, developmental, and neurological diseases: Environmental ascription in East Baton Rouge Parish, Louisiana. *Population and Environment, 33*, 333–346.

Liu, G., Xiao, M., Zhang, X., Gal, C., Chen, X., Liu, L., Pan, S., Wu, J., Tang, L., & Clements-Croome, D. (2017). A review of air filtration technologies for sustainable and healthy building ventilation. *Sustainable Cities and Society, 32*, 375–396.

London, B., Lucier, C., Rosofsky, A., & Scharber, H. (2015). Environmental ascription: Industrial pollution, place, and children's health and learning in the USA. In N. Ansell, N. Klocker, & T. Skelton (Eds.), *Geographies of global issues: Change and threat* (Geographies of children and young people, vol. 8, pp. 347–373). Springer.

Los Angeles Unified School District. (2021, June 9). *Los Angeles Unified launches effort to further improve air quality in schools* [Press release]. https://achieve.lausd.net/site/default.aspx?PageType=3&DomainID=4&ModuleInstanceID=4466&ViewID=6446EE88-D30C-497E-9316-3F8874B3E108&RenderLoc=0&FlexDataID=107018&PageID=1&Comments=true

Lubczyńska, M., Sunyer, J., Tiemeier, H., Porta, D., Kasper-Sonnenberg, M., Jaddoe, V. W., Basagaña, X., Dalmau-Bueno, A., Forastiere, F., Wittsiepe, J., & Hoffmann, B., Nieuwenhuijsen, M., Hoek, G., Hoogh, K., Brunekreef, B., & Guxens, M. (2017). Exposure to elemental composition of outdoor PM2.5 at birth and cognitive and psychomotor function in childhood in four European birth cohorts. *Environment International, 109*, 170–180.

Lucier, C., Rosofsky, A., London, B., Scharber, H., & Shandra, J. (2011). Toxic pollution and school performance scores: Environmental ascription in East Baton Rouge parish, Louisiana. *Organization & Environment, 24*(4), 423–443

Makar, M., Antonelli, J., Di, Q., Cutler, D., Schwartz, J., & Dominici, F. (2017). Estimating the causal effect of fine particulate matter levels on death and hospitalization: Are levels below the safety standards harmful? *Epidemiology, 28*(5), 627–634.

Marcotte, D. E. 2017. Something in the air? Air quality and children's educational outcomes. *Economics of Education Review, 56*, 141–151.

Markevych, I., Schoierer, J., Hartig, T., Chudnovsky, A., Hystad, P., Dzhambov, A. M., de Vries, S., Triguero-Mas, M., Brauer, M., Niewenhuijsen, M. J., Lupp, G.,, Richardson, E. A. Astell-Burt, T., Dimitrova, D., Feng, X., Sadeh, M., Stan, M., Heinrich, J., & Fuertes, E. (2017). Exploring pathways linking greenspace to health: Theoretical and methodological guidance. *Environmental Research, 158*, 301–317.

Miller, S., & Vela, M. 2013. *The effects of air pollution on educational outcomes: Evidence from Chile* [IDB Working Paper No. IDB-WP-468]. Inter-American Development Bank. https://publications.iadb.org/en/publication/11349/effects-air-pollution-educational-outcomes-evidence-chile

Mohai, P., & Kweon, B. (2020). *Michigan school siting guidelines: Taking the environment into account* [Report]. University of Michigan.

Mohai, P., Kweon, B., Lee, S. & Ard, K. (2011). Air pollution around schools is linked to poorer student health and academic performance. *Health Affairs*, 30(5), 852–862.

Mullen, C., Grineski, S., Collins, T. W., & Mendoza, D. (2020). Effects of PM2.5 on third grade students' proficiency in math and English language arts. *International Journal of Environmental Research and Public Health*, 17(18), 6931.

National Academies of Sciences, Engineering, and Medicine. (2014). *Assessing aircraft noise conditions affecting student learning, volume 1: final report*. The National Academies Press. doi.org/10.17226/22433.

National Center for Education Statistics. (2008). Average number of hours in the school day and average number of days in the school year for public schools, by state: 2007–08. https://nces.ed.gov/surveys/sass/tables/sass0708_035_s1s.asp.

Pastor, M., Morello-Frosch, R., & Sadd, J. L. (2006). Breathless: Schools, air toxics, and environmental justice in California. *Policy Studies Journal*, 34: 337–362.

Pastor, M., Sadd, J. L., & Morello-Frosch, R. (2002). Who's minding the kids? Pollution, public schools, and environmental justice in Los Angeles. *Social Science Quarterly*, 83: 263–280.

Pastor, M, Sadd, J. L., & Morello-Frosch, R. (2004). Reading, writing, and toxics: children's health, academic performance, and environmental justice in Los Angeles. *Environment and Planning C*, 22: 271–291.

Pike, H, Khan, F., & Amyotte, P. (2020). Precautionary principle (PP) versus as low as reasonably practicable (ALARP): Which one to use and when. *Process Safety and Environmental Protection*, 237: 158–168.

Raz, R., Roberts, A. L., Lyall, K., Hart, J. E., Just, A. C., Laden, F., & Weisskopf, M. G. (2015). Autism spectrum disorder and particulate matter air pollution before, during, and after pregnancy: a nested case-control analysis within the Nurses' Health Study II cohort. *Environmental Health Perspectives*, 123: 264–270.

Rhode Island Legal Services. (2006). *Not in my schoolyard: Avoiding environmental hazards at school through improve school site selection policies*. New York Lawyers for the Public Interest https://www.nylpi.org/wp-content/uploads/bsk-pdf-manager/49_EJ_-_NOT_IN_MY_SCHOOLYARD_-_IMPROVING_SITE_SELECTION_PROCESS.PDF

Robinson, K. J. (Ed.) (2019). *A federal right to education: Fundamental questions for our democracy*. NYU Press.

Rosofsky, A., Lucier, C. A., London, B., Scharber, H., Borges-Mendez, R., & Shandra, J. (2014). Environmental ascription in Worcester County, MA: toxic pollution and education outcomes. *Local Environment*, 19: 283–299.

Saenen, N. D., Provost, E. B., Viaene, M., K., Vanpoucke, C., Lefebvre, W., Vrijens, K., Roels, H. A., & Nawrot, T. S. (2016). Recent versus chronic exposure to particulate matter air pollution in association with neurobehavioral performance in a panel study of primary schoolchildren. *Environment International*, 95: 112–119.

Salvesen, D., Zambito, P., & McDonnell, D. (2010). *Safe schools: Identifying potential threats to the health and safety of schoolchildren in North Carolina.* Center for Sustainable Community Design, Institute for the Environment, University of North Carolina at Chapel Hill. https://citeseerx.ist.psu.edu/viewdoc/download?doi=10.1.1.368.7811&rep=rep1&type=pdf

Sampson, N. (2012). Environmental justice at school: Understanding research, policy, and practice to improve our children's health. *Journal of School Health*, 82, 246–252.

Sandin, P. (1999). Dimensions of the precautionary principle. *Human and Ecological Risk Assessment: An International Journal*, 5(5), 889–907.

Scharber, H., Lucier, C., London, B., Rosofsky, A., & Shandra, J. (2013). The consequences of exposure to, neurological, and respiratory toxins for school performance: a closer look at environmental ascription in East Baton Rouge, Louisiana. *Population and Environment*, 35: 205–224.

Schneider, J. S., Lee, M. H., Anderson, D. W., Zuck, L., & Lidsky, T. I. (2001). Enriched environment during development is protective against lead-induced neurotoxicity. *Brain Research*, 896: 48–55.

Ścibor, M., Balcerzak, B., Galbarczyk, A., Targosz, N., & Jasienska, G. (2019). Are we safe inside? Indoor air quality in relation to outdoor concentration of PM10 and PM2.5 and to characteristics of homes. *Sustainable Cities and Society*, 48: 101537.

Sentís, A., Sunyer, J., Dalmau-Bueno, A., Andiarena, A., Ballester, F., Cirach, M., Estarlich, M., Fernández-Somoano, A., Ibarluzea, J., Íñiguez, C., & Lertxundi, A.. (2017). Prenatal and postnatal exposure to NO2 and child attentional function at 4–5 years of age. *Environment International*, 1: 170–177.

Shi, L., Zanobetti, A., Kloog, I., Coull, B. A., Koutrakis, P., Melly, S. J., & Schwartz, J. D. (2015). Low-concentration PM2.5 and mortality: estimating acute and chronic effects in a population-based study. *Environmental Health Perspectives*, 124: 46–52.

Shier, V., Nicosia, N., Shih, R., & Datar, A. (2019). Ambient air pollution and children's cognitive outcomes. *Population and Environment*, 40: 347–367.

Sivarajah, S., Smith, S. M., & Thomas, S. C. (2018). Tree cover and species composition effects on academic performance of primary school students. *PLoS One*, 13: doi.org/10.1371/journal.pone.0193254.

Smythe, A. (2018). *Effectiveness of particle air purifiers in improving the air quality in classrooms in three urban public schools in the Northeastern United States* [Masters thesis]. Harvard University. https://dash.harvard.edu/bitstream/handle/1/37945127/SMYTHE-DOCUMENT-2018.pdf?sequence=1

Stingone, J. A., McVeigh, K. H., & Claudio, L. (2016). Association between prenatal exposure to ambient diesel particulate matter and perchloroethylene with children's 3rd grade standardized test scores. *Environmental Research*, 148: 144–153.

Stingone, J. A., Pandey, O.P., Claudio, L., & Pandey, G. (2017). Using machine learning to identify air pollution exposure profiles associated with early cognitive skills among U.S. children. *Environmental Pollution*, 1: 730–740.

Tallis, H., Bratman, G. N., Samhouri, J. F., & Fargione, J. (2018). Are California elementary school test scores more strongly associated with urban trees than poverty? *Frontiers in Psychology*, 9, 2074, https://doi.org/10.3389%2Ffpsyg.2018.02074.

Thomopolous, N., & Grant-Muller, S. (2013). Incorporating equity as part of the wider impacts in transport infrastructure assessment: an application of the SUMINI approach. *Transportation*, 40: 315–345.

U. S. Department of Education. (2021). *Department of Education announces American Rescue Plan funds for all 50 states, Puerto Rico, and the District of Columbia to help schools reopen* [Press release]. https://www.ed.gov/news/press-releases/department-education-announces-american-rescue-plan-funds-all-50-states-puerto-rico-and-district-columbia-help-schools-reopen

U. S. Department of Education, Office for Civil Rights. (2021). *Education in a pandemic: The disparate impacts of COVID-19 on America's students.* https://www2.ed.gov/about/offices/list/ocr/docs/20210608-impacts-of-covid19.pdf

U.S. Environmental Protection Agency. (2011). *School siting guidelines.* https://www.epa.gov/sites/default/files/2015-06/documents/school_siting_guidelines-2.pdf

U. S. Environmental Protection Agency. (2020, October 8). *EPA announces the selection of organizations to receive funding for healthy learning environments* [Press release]. https://www.epa.gov/newsreleases/epa-announces-selection-organizations-receive-funding-healthy-learning-environments

U. S. Government Accountability Office. (2013). Toxic substances: Report to congressional requesters. GAO-13-249 https://www.gao.gov/assets/gao-13-249.pdf

Vermont Department of Health. (2021). *Envision program: Promoting healthy school environments.* https://www.healthvermont.gov/environment/school

Wargo, J.. 2004. *The physical school environment: An essential component of a health-promoting school.* World Health Organization. http://www.who.int/school_youth_health/media/en/physical_sch_environment.pdf.

World Commission on the Ethics of Scientific Knowledge and Technology. (2005). *The Precautionary Principle.* UNESCO. https://unesdoc.unesco.org/ark:/48223/pf0000139578.

World Health Organization. (2021). WHO *global air quality guidelines.* https://apps.who.int/iris/bitstream/handle/10665/345329/9789240034228-eng.pdf?sequence=1&isAllowed=y

Wu, C-D., McNeely, E., Cedeño-Laurent, J. G., Pan, W-C., Adamkiewicz, G., Dominici, F., Lung, S-C. C., Su, H.-J., & Spengler, J. D. (2014). Linking student performance in Massachusetts elementary schools with the "greenness" of school surroundings using remote sensing. *PLoS One*, 9(10), e108548. https://doi.org/10.1371/journal.pone.0108548

Zweig, J., Ham, J., & Avol, E. (2009). Air pollution and academic performance: Evidence from California schools. http://radic8.com.au/wp-content/uploads/2018/03/test-scores-submit-1.pdf

CHAPTER 9

Promoting Equity and Justice Through Integrated Schools and Communities

Jennifer B. Ayscue and Erica Frankenberg

Current and historical racism, manifested in racist education and housing policies, have resulted in racial and socioeconomic segregation across our nation's schools and communities. Since the late 1980s, school segregation has been increasing (Frankenberg et al., 2019). When children and youth learn and develop in schools that are racially and socioeconomically segregated, they have little exposure to and understanding of people from different backgrounds, which is problematic for people of all races. Integrated schools, however, are not only associated with better academic outcomes, but they also improve intergroup relations and have positive long-term life outcomes for students, particularly when structured to provide equal status contact (Linn & Welner, 2007; Mickelson & Nkomo, 2012). Despite their prominence in the lives of children and youth—and although our government has attempted to use education as a solution for many of society's problems—schools alone cannot be held responsible for creating a more equitable and just country. Alongside integrated schools, integrated communities are also essential for providing more equitable and just opportunities for children and youth of all racial and socioeconomic backgrounds.

In this chapter, we describe evidence about the benefits of integrated schools and communities as well as the relationship between residential and school integration. We outline research-based education policies, from the local to the federal level, to facilitate community and school integration as well as provide examples of strategies schools and communities are currently using to promote racial and socioeconomic integration. We conclude with local, regional, state, and federal policy recommendations to promote integration and positive outcomes for students and communities.

INTEGRATION IN SCHOOLS AND COMMUNITIES: WHAT THE RESEARCH SAYS

Through racism, manifested in White people's choices (Turner et al., 2021) and racist policies (Eaton, 2020; Faber, 2021; Rothstein, 2017), such as discriminatory zoning, redlining, and the GI Bill, segregated communities and schools have been constructed across the United States. School segregation by race and income has been intensifying since the peak of desegregation in 1988 (Frankenberg et al., 2019). As of 2016, nearly one out of five schools across the country are intensely segregated, that is, a school that enrolls 90–100% non-White students. The typical Black, Latino, and White student attends a school in which the majority of their peers are from the same racial background.

Trends in residential segregation vary. A recent analysis of residential segregation using the divergence measure of segregation found that racial residential segregation has been intensifying over the last 30 years (Menendian et al., 2021). Earlier research using a different measure of segregation found that residential segregation between Black and White residents has been declining while isolation of Latino and Asian residents has been increasing (Logan & Stults, 2011). Moreover, residential segregation by income has been increasing (Owens, 2016, 2020). Regardless of the measure used or the progress made, school- and neighborhood-segregation remain high (Owens, 2020).

BENEFITS OF RACIALLY INTEGRATED SCHOOLS AND COMMUNITIES

Decades of social science research demonstrate that integrated schools are associated with positive academic, interpersonal, and long-term outcomes while segregated schools are systematically linked with unequal educational opportunities and outcomes. For students of color, desegregated schools are associated with higher levels of academic achievement, lower dropout rates, and higher graduation rates (Balfanz & Legters, 2004; Mickelson et al., 2013; Mickelson et al., 2020; Swanson, 2004). Students who attend desegregated schools have enhanced critical thinking and communication skills as well as cultural competency that is beneficial for entering a racially diverse workplace and society (Siegel-Hawley, 2012). Exposure to students from different backgrounds also results in a reduction in prejudice, decrease in stereotypes, and increase in friendships across groups (Allport, 1954; Pettigrew & Tropp, 2006; Tropp & Prenevost, 2008). In the long term, students who attended a desegregated school have a greater likelihood of living and working in a diverse environment, obtaining a higher status, and better-paying job, and having better health outcomes as well as a lower likelihood of incarceration (Braddock & McPartland, 1999; Johnson, 2011, 2019).

Desegregation—the ending of separation and isolation of different racial and ethnic groups—is a necessary first step; however, it is not sufficient for achieving true integration—fair and equal treatment of members of different racial and ethnic groups within a desegregated environment (Ayscue & Frankenberg, 2016). In desegregated schools that enroll a diverse student body, if integration is not properly facilitated, students of color in diverse schools can experience harm and marginalization, such as placement in less-rigorous courses (Oakes, 2005), underrepresentation in gifted education (Ford et al., 2008; Roda, 2015) and overrepresentation in special education (Losen & Orfield, 2002; Sullivan & Bal, 2013), and exclusionary discipline (Losen & Martinez, 2020).

The research evidence on integrated communities finds that Black and Latino residents in integrated neighborhoods have greater educational attainment, higher incomes, lower poverty rates, lower unemployment rates, and longer life expectancy than their counterparts in segregated neighborhoods (Menendian et al., 2021).

DEMOGRAPHIC CHANGES IN URBAN, SUBURBAN, AND RURAL COMMUNITIES

Demographic changes in urban, suburban, and rural communities are altering the residential makeup of communities and the enrollment in schools. Many urban areas across the country are experiencing gentrification (Ellen & Torrats-Espinosa, 2018). These neighborhoods are experiencing increases in educational levels, housing values, and income; race is also a central feature of gentrification as more affluent people who move into historically low-income communities of color are often White (Ellen & Ding, 2016; Pearman & Swain, 2017). Low-income residents of color may be priced out of their homes; however, residents in these areas tend to be highly mobile so there is mixed evidence about the extent to which displacement is being exacerbated by gentrification (Brummet & Reed, 2019; Dragan et al., 2019).

Gentrification also creates concerns about the loss of community culture and history as well as the marginalization of long-standing residents of color, all of which affect schools. Green et al.'s (2020) typology of gentrifying schools highlights different phases of school changes in gentrifying neighborhoods, including no early changes, followed by loss of enrollment as long-standing students are pushed out of the neighborhood and gentrifiers choose other schools, and finally, various stages of increasing enrollment as gentrifiers enroll in and ultimately predominate the school. Variable patterns and rates of school desegregation can be attributed to gentrifiers not having children, sending their children to charter or private schools, or clustering with other gentrifying families in a few traditional public schools where they can create a critical mass (Kimelberg & Billingham, 2012).

In suburban communities in the largest metros, demographic change has rapidly transformed districts such that the majority of their enrollment is comprised of students of color. These communities have many more students than the central cities of the metros. Further, in some regions of the country where fragmentation is high, residential and school segregation between places and districts, respectively, is high because of sorting by district boundary. In smaller metros, suburban growth and diversification are less extensive, and suburban communities and schools are typically majority White with fewer low-income students and households.

In rural districts, growing diversity is slowly transitioning nearly all-White districts into majority White but somewhat more diverse districts (see Kebede et al., 2021). Rural districts are experiencing a large increase in the percentage of Latinx students, and those with Latinx students are more likely to be growing. Districts with larger shares of Black or American Indian students have especially high levels of student poverty. Moreover, despite some signs of growing diversity, overall, it is unevenly spread across rural districts and does not always lead to increased school-level integration.

CAUSES OF SEGREGATION

In metropolitan communities, invisible district and school-boundary lines are drawn, and sometimes gerrymandered in ways that reinforce segregation (Siegel-Hawley, 2016). Most segregation occurs because students of different racial groups are assigned to different school districts altogether (Monarrez et al., 2019). Choice options, such as magnet, charter, and private schools, disrupt the relationship between residential and school segregation in differing ways. Magnet schools were developed as a tool for voluntary desegregation (Goldring & Smrekar, 2000; Siegel-Hawley & Frankenberg, 2013) while charter schools have not lived up to their potential for creating diversity (Ayscue et al., 2016; Frankenberg et al., 2011; Kahlenberg & Potter, 2014; Ladd et al., 2015; Monarrez et al., 2019).

The relationship between residential and school segregation is reciprocal in that segregated schools influence neighborhood composition and segregated neighborhoods contribute to segregated schools (Frankenberg, 2013; Owens, 2020). *Therefore, instead of trying to address segregation in schools or communities, it would be more beneficial to address segregation in both schools and communities.* A new policy vision for our country should reflect such an approach.

RESEARCH-BASED POLICY VISION FOR INTEGRATION IN SCHOOLS AND COMMUNITIES

This section outlines a new policy vision at the regional, state, and federal level, considering what is known about integration in schools and communities. To promote school integration, all three levels of government could provide funding and technical support for integration efforts. Among other strategies, efforts could include promoting regional approaches, supporting, and strengthening magnet schools, and revising charter regulations and funding so that charters are more integrated. Regarding housing, government entities should support and center racial-justice efforts regarding fair housing and scale up fair share housing requirements. Finally, cross-sector collaboration among education, housing, and transportation is critical.

Regional Policies

A regional approach to integrated schools and cross-sector collaborative efforts are necessary. When possible, school-district consolidation can promote greater integration. When consolidation is not possible, regional approaches such as federated regionalism, regional magnet schools, and interdistrict transfer programs can be used to support integration efforts. Cross-sector collaborative efforts between school and housing communities could include supporting fair housing, shared decision-making about the siting, opening, and closing of public schools and public-housing units, and providing adequate and accessible transportation.

Integrated Schools. The tradition of local control of schooling has, at times, inhibited regional approaches to equity, as did the 1974 *Milliken* decision that overturned a lower court's regional remedy to desegregating Detroit's public schools. The conceptualization of the meaning of "local" differs widely by area of the country. School districts in the South tended to encompass the entire county, contributing to the area having lower Black–White segregation for decades (Ayscue & Orfield, 2014) although a growing trend of district secession may change this (Taylor et al., 2019). Some states like North Carolina encouraged district consolidation while Michigan had more than 500 districts serving fewer than 1.5 million students statewide. Related, Michigan had among the highest levels of segregation for Black students. One approach to achieving district consolidation is passing legislation. Maine, for example, approved a district consolidation law in 2007 that reduced 290 districts to just 80. Changing boundaries can be hard because of the community identity that boundaries carry and how they are often associated with varying opportunities (Weiher, 1991), much less merging two district identities into one. In Memphis, Tennessee, one of the largest and most recent district consolidations lasted for only a year, and six suburban communities had voted to secede to form separate districts before the merged district opened its doors for the academic year (Siegel-Hawley et al., 2018). Most states' laws are silent on whether and how consolidation occurs (Wilson, 2021).

For these reasons, Holme and Finnegan (2018) argue for regional efforts, allowing district boundaries to remain but make them more permeable in terms of resources and students, lessening the stark differences between communities. One example is federated regionalism, which the Transition Planning Commission recommended during the merger of Memphis and Shelby County, but ultimately did not satisfy suburban communities that continued to push for their own districts (Siegel-Hawley et al., 2018). Wilson (2014) has further proposed *equitable* federated regionalism for education, which would help counter the preference for localism in education that results in racial disparities in educational opportunity when coupled with fragmentation in metropolitan areas. Siegel-Hawley's (2016) study of four metros found that more regional districts *when* partnered with student-assignment policies that aimed to desegregate were associated with higher school and residential integration.

Magnet schools that are open to students from multiple districts, such as in San Antonio, Texas, in the Twin Cities region of Minnesota, or the Hartford, Connecticut, region, can provide more integrated experiences than would within-district only options (see Siegel-Hawley & Frankenberg, 2013). In greater Minneapolis, for example, collaborating districts located different levels of a K–12 magnet theme in separate districts to attract students from across the region, including racially changing suburban districts (Gumus-Dawes et al., 2012). Other efforts to encourage movement across boundaries include city–suburban transfer programs, typically one-way (such as Boston's METCO program), but especially promising variations of this model are two-way programs like Hartford's Open Choice that encourage suburban students to choose to attend schools in the city. Such two-way movement of students helps to provide equal status for city and suburban schools as sites of integration.

Interdistrict efforts began in Omaha, Nebraska, after receiving national media backlash from its attempts to create three separate urban districts that would be racially identifiable. Such efforts provided an important impetus for what has now developed, both in terms of innovative regional schooling ideas and in understanding what was necessary to sustain political cooperation for interdistrict schooling initiatives. Having seen the political vulnerabilities of funding allocation for some of the existing city-suburban desegregation efforts, Omaha was pioneering in creating a shared levy to fund its 11-district desegregation collaborative. An analysis found that the levy saved the state of Nebraska money while also increasing the funding that most districts received (Holme et al., 2012). District residents maintained priority in their own district's "focus" schools, which was a particularly strong impediment to attracting students across boundaries. The need to continually bolster education efforts about the benefits of the collaborative's goals and work with districts that were answerable to different political constituencies helped to influence subsequent replication elsewhere.

The growth of interdistrict efforts helps to diversify public schools as students of color constitute higher shares of the enrollment. As public schools take on more regional integration efforts, a by-product of this integration for neighborhoods would be that these schooling programs decoupled the strong link between housing and school location and segregation.

Cross-Sector Collaborative Efforts. Because of the ways in which school-housing patterns reinforce each other—not to mention other domains of social policy that affect schools—research has long suggested that stable and equitable integration should be cross-sector (Frankenberg & Orfield, 2012; Stone, 1989). Examples of implementing the lessons from this research are less widespread, but, for example, research from the Gautreaux housing case found that there were educational benefits for children whose households, with appropriate counseling and support, moved to racially and economically integrated communities (Rosenbaum et al., 2005). Research from the 1990 Moving to Opportunity project was more mixed, partly because Section-8 voucher recipients did not always move to more integrated neighborhoods.

Rusk (2008) has termed housing and education policies as "mutually interdependent," and perhaps especially so when concerning segregation. Yet an array of studies illustrates that there are many political and financial barriers to coordinating policies that might mitigate segregation (DeBray, 2021; Haberle & Tegeler, 2019). A recent example of collaboration at the federal level with implications for regional, interdistrict action is the 2016 "dear colleague" letter and convening by the U.S. Department of Housing and Urban Development, Department of Transportation, and Department of Education. Relying on the new Affirmatively Furthering Fair Housing (AFFH) rule, the federal agencies suggested that the rule "provides an opportunity for cross-agency collaboration and strong community involvement. We urge you to take full advantage of the community participation process of the AFFH rule, so that regional planning promotes economic mobility and equal access to the many benefits provided by affordable housing, great schools, and reliable transportation."

The siting, opening, and closing of both public schools—because of their important roles for communities—and subsidized public housing units, which affect the composition of schools, are critical decisions that have reciprocal effects on communities and integration. Erickson's (2016) work in Nashville shows how siting schools affected neighborhood composition, and court desegregation cases often required consent of parties and the court before schools could be built or major renovations undertaken, recognizing how they could influence segregation. While typically studied in metropolitan districts, Tieken's (2014) study of rural Arkansas also emphasizes the importance of schools in creating community cohesion, given how the closure of a diverse school fragmented the community along racial lines. In urban areas facing declining enrollments because of demographic shifts and increasing movement of students to nondistrict schools like charter or private schools, school closure disproportionately affects Black communities and schools (Tilsley, 2017).

Similarly, Holme et al.'s (2020) analysis of four large counties in Texas illustrates how the placement of site-based subsidized housing was disproportionately clustered in central city districts instead of being more evenly distributed across all districts, including suburban, outlying districts with higher concentrations of more advantaged and White residents. Further, within these districts, attendance-zone boundaries further clustered subsidized housing into some catchment areas. A study in Connecticut had similar findings, namely that at least three-quarters of low-income housing tax credit (LIHTC) units had been built in "low-opportunity areas." Conversely, communities with lower percentages of subsidized housing units also have more restrictive zoning policies, further limiting residential access to these communities. Because municipalities in Connecticut are largely coterminous with school-district boundaries, this also concentrates subsidized housing recipients in areas that likely have racially and/or economically concentrated student enrollments (Open Communities, 2019, as cited in Eaton, 2020).

Transportation has long been another important component of promoting school integration on an equitable basis and is key if desegregation is to decouple the link between school attended and place of residence for students. Bierbaum et al.'s (2021) research suggests the importance of co-ordinating transportation and education across metros to advance equity. Indeed, many children use school-provided or public transportation to attend schools aside from desegregation-related reasons, though politically the framing of desegregation as "forced busing" has caused White opposition to desegregation efforts (Frankenberg & Jacobsen, 2011).[1] Recent research shows that bus transportation for children is particularly important for them to access school choice (Trajkovski et al., 2020), which has important implications for school desegregation efforts since many contemporary desegregation plans are choice based (see also Bell, 2009). Other emerging research has found the importance of bus transportation in improving student attendance, especially among the youngest children and in rural districts (Gottfried et al., 2021), but implementation of the provision of transportation when decentralized in one district provided uneven access for Black and Latino students who were eligible for bus transportation than for White students with similar eligibility (Cordes et al., 2020).

Taken together, these studies suggest the importance of incentivizing collaboration among stakeholders from different sectors. Planning and implementation—much less sustaining—of integrated communities must consider the different arenas and associated policies that affect households' locational decisions. The integral connection of these sectors must be considered when school and community leaders are determining the logistics of where to develop different types of housing and schools as well as when considering plans to close schools, rezone residential areas, or eliminate public transit.

Housing, Schools, and Political Participation in Gentrifying Communities. Gentrification is a powerful force changing many urban communities across the nation. Without proactive and intentional efforts to manage the effects of gentrification, long-standing, low-income residents of color may be displaced from their homes and marginalized from their communities. In such cases, communities may transition through desegregation into disproportionately White communities. Housing policies could be used to prevent displacement and facilitate integration. First, inclusionary zoning policies, which are used in more than 800 communities across the nation, encourage or require developers to set aside a certain percentage, often 10–30%, of units to be rented or sold at below-market prices (Ramakrishnan et al., 2019). Montgomery County, Maryland, implemented one of the nation's first mandatory inclusionary zoning laws in 1973. Also, community preference policies, such as those used in Austin, Portland, San Francisco, and Seattle, provide residents with priority access to newly constructed subsidized housing in their neighborhoods (Goetz, 2018). These policies should consider various aspects of affordable housing location, including proximity to job opportunities and transportation.

In addition to addressing housing, it is essential that gentrifying communities promote true integration by ensuring equitable participation in the political process and creating welcoming public spaces for shared use (Chaskin & Joseph, 2015). Schools are one such public space. Denver Public Schools, located in the second most intensely gentrified city in the country, serves as an example of how one school district has been navigating gentrification to promote greater school integration. In 2017, Denver Public Schools passed a resolution to create the Strengthening Neighborhoods Initiative. A citywide committee provided four overarching recommendations: setting and monitoring targets for increasing integration; providing resources, incentives, and supports for schools to create more integrated environments; collaborating with city agencies and community partners; and expanding community engagement (Denver Public Schools, 2021). Alongside regional policies to promote integrated schools and communities, state-level efforts are also necessary.

State Policies

States have an essential role in facilitating community and school integration, particularly as decentralization of education from the federal level has begun to occur during the last decade. States could provide funding and technical assistance to school districts and regions as they plan and implement integration efforts, incorporate measures of school segregation in state accountability systems, and revise charter regulations to include desegregation requirements. To facilitate more integrated housing, states could adopt affordable housing and fair-share housing laws as well as ensure that residents using federal housing programs have access to highly resourced areas that do not reinforce segregation. In addition to addressing the needs in the education and housing sectors individually, some states offer examples of cross-sector collaborative efforts.

Integrated Schools. To support school districts in achieving integration, states should provide funding and technical assistance to districts as they plan, implement, and evaluate their integration efforts, including magnet schools, interdistrict programs, and student assignment plans. States should also take an active role in ensuring that the construction of new schools and expansion of existing schools or the reorganization of school districts through secession does not exacerbate segregation. States can encourage such efforts by incorporating measures of school segregation into their accountability systems.

In March 2021, a bill was introduced in Massachusetts with two main purposes. First, it would establish data collection on school segregation. The state would publicly report school and district segregation measures and the extent to which students in a school or district have equitable access to advanced courses, gifted and talented programs, early college pathways, and the SAT or ACT. Second, it would establish a school diversity and integration grant program that would allow school districts to develop, implement, and evaluate comprehensive strategies to increase racial diversity.

In New York, the state with the most schools in the country, the Socioeconomic Integration Pilot Program (SIPP) is intended to increase student achievement in the state's Title I priority and focus schools by promoting socioeconomic integration. Districts are eligible to receive a 3-year grant to plan and implement a model, such as a magnet school, that would increase integration. As U.S. Secretary of Education in the Obama Administration, former New York State Education Commissioner John King replicated SIPP at the federal level (described later).

The federal Every Student Succeeds Act allows states to develop their own accountability systems and requires that states include at least one indicator of school quality or student success. States could include a measure of school segregation in their accountability system. Doing so would likely encourage districts and schools to work toward greater desegregation. In 2021, bills were introduced in North Carolina and New York that would require school segregation measures to be incorporated into the states' accountability systems and be added to school report cards. The North Carolina bill proposed assigning a proportionality score to show the extent to which a school's enrollment differs from the county in which the school is located. It also requires reporting on equity in access to gifted programs, advanced courses, and experienced teachers within a school. Finally, it requires measuring access to opportunities and resources, including arts and music classes, psychologists, counselors, and nurses, across schools and subgroups within a district.

In some states, charter schools are authorized at the state level. If charters are to remain part of the educational landscape, including regulations for charters to be desegregated, monitoring enrollments in charters for compliance with diversity targets, and making reauthorization contingent upon adherence to this regulation could help address the more extreme levels of segregation in the charter sector. Furthermore, it is important for states to ensure that charters are not only desegregated themselves but also that they do not contribute to exacerbating segregation in nearby traditional public schools. These guidelines are applicable at the local level as well if charter schools are authorized by local education agencies.

While many states have a charter school office, very few have a similar office for magnet schools. Developing state offices to provide technical assistance, support, and research about magnet schools would be useful for district and regional efforts to plan, implement, and sustain magnet schools.

Integrated Communities. As Megan Gallagher details in Chapter 10, states should provide affordable housing in all communities and school districts (Holme et al., 2020; Siegel-Hawley et al., 2017). States could create more affordable housing outside cities by requiring suburban communities to provide affordable housing. Implementing fair-share housing laws that require all communities to provide a fair proportion of the region's need for affordable housing and eliminating exclusionary zoning would be important steps toward accomplishing this goal (Poverty & Race Research Action Council, 2020). New Jersey's *Mount Laurel* requirement stemming from litigation is perhaps most well-known, although Massachusetts also has a fair share requirement. Montgomery County, Maryland, is another example of a jurisdiction that requires developers to set aside 12.5% of units for moderate-income families and offers nearly 1,000 scattered-site public-housing units across the county for the lowest income families. A study found that this housing policy has enabled lower-income children to attend schools with more affluent peers, with significant positive effects on their achievement (Schwartz, 2010). Montgomery County is also considering a pilot program to provide financial assistance for low-income households as well to reduce the rent burden (Schweitzer, 2021). One way to encourage fair share housing could be through expanding the jurisdiction of local housing authorities to enable them to develop housing units outside of the community in which they are located (Eaton, 2020). States should actively investigate resistance to fair and affordable housing and vigorously enforce antidiscrimination laws.

States should also ensure that residents utilizing federal-housing programs, including LIHTC and the Housing Trust Fund, have access to desegregated, highly resourced areas and do not simply reinforce segregation using these programs (Poverty & Race Research Action Council, 2020). States could provide greater funding for housing vouchers and counseling programs that would assist residents who want to move from segregated to integrated communities (Eaton, 2020). Additionally, Ohio reduces property taxes if landlords in low-poverty neighborhoods rent to Section 8–voucher recipients (Rothstein, 2017). Given the reluctance of landlords to do so, this state-level policy lever could encourage community, and, therefore school, diversity.

Cross-Sector Collaborative Efforts. After the *Sheff* plaintiffs prevailed in their case against the state of Connecticut, which held that the school district lines that segregated students were unconstitutional under the state constitution, the plaintiffs developed a six-pronged plan regarding potential remedies to address segregation. Most of these prongs were aimed at providing stable and thorough integration of students and teachers as well as equitable access to educational opportunities, but one prong also called for the residential integration of the Hartford metro. Recently, Connecticut's General Assembly approved a pilot program to provide eligible families participating in city-suburban school desegregation program housing vouchers to assist Hartford families to relocate to the suburban district where their child attends school. These suggestions build upon earlier analyses by state agencies about the need for cross-sector approaches to combat the ways in which state policies created and should remedy existing segregation of schools and communities. In addition to these state-level policies, the federal government has historically played a central role in facilitating integrated schools and communities.

Federal Policies

At the end of the Obama administration, the federal government was increasingly pursuing a cross-sector, regional agenda to advance educational equity. Many of these efforts, which were largely pursued via executive agencies, were reversed during the Trump administration.

To promote school integration, the federal government could develop a grant program to support integration efforts and reinstate or develop guidance several areas to promote integration. The government could also enhance enforcement of antidiscrimination legislation. Increased funding and support for the Office for Civil Rights (OCR) could aid in facilitating integration. To support integration in communities, the federal government should reinstate a rule to center racial justice efforts with the Fair Housing Act, scale up fair-share housing requirements, and revise Section 8 voucher-funding to further its integrative potential. Finally, cross-sector collaboration at the federal level could include a pilot program that includes housing subsidies and interdistrict school transfers as well as recommit to collaborative efforts among ED, HUD, and DOT.

Integrated Schools. The Biden-Harris administration has committed to addressing systemic racism,[2] and there is Congressional support, particularly in the House. Two pending bills, introduced in the last Congress and again in 2021, are the Strength in Diversity Act and the Equity and Inclusion Enforcement Act (EIEA). The Strength in Diversity Act could be helpful in supporting districts, including consortia of districts, to plan and/or implement voluntary integration efforts. A complementary piece of legislation, EIEA, would enhance the ability to enforce Title VI of the 1964 Civil Rights Act, which prohibits discrimination including by race for any recipient of federal funding. The enforcement of Title VI in the 1960s was a key policy lever used to further desegregation of students and teachers, yet its enforcement has been limited since a 2001 Supreme Court decision.

Additionally, under President Obama, OCR took a broader approach to investigating the myriad ways in which students' civil rights could be violated. In June 2021, in what might be a promising example for other areas, several U.S. Attorneys Offices announced the formation of civil rights teams to focus on policing, housing discrimination, and school segregation (Associated Press, 2021; U.S. Attorney's Office, Eastern District, New York, 2021). Also useful would be a return to the Obama administration's practice of examining district-wide practices when individual students file discrimination complaints. Increased funding for OCR is critical for supporting these efforts (Scott et al., 2020).

To promote integration, the Biden-Harris administration could reinstate or develop guidance in a number of areas: effective and permissible strategies for voluntarily integrating schools, new guidance on how Title I funds can be used for integration, 2014 guidance on disparate impact in school discipline, and 2016 joint guidance from ED, HUD, and DOT on promoting racial and socioeconomic integration. To facilitate cross-sector collaboration, an interagency meeting that includes ED, HUD, and DOT to discuss integration would be another critical step (Scott et al., 2020; The National Coalition on School Diversity, 2021). Alongside guidance, capacity and funding for Equity Assistance Centers should be increased so that such centers can effectively provide meaningful assistance on integration.

The federal government also should support strong civil rights–related research and data collection at ED (Scott et al., 2020; The National Coalition on School Diversity, 2021). Such support could include annual reporting on active desegregation orders and voluntary agreements, publishing data that shows segregation within schools as well as within and across districts, and evaluating MSAP and CSP to determine the programs' impact on segregation.

Integrated Communities. In 2015, HUD announced a regulation to implement the Fair Housing Act's provision to affirmatively further fair housing to assess and take action to "overcome historic patterns of segregation, achieve truly balanced and integrated living patterns, promote fair housing choice, and foster inclusive communities that are free from discrimination" (Affirmatively Furthering Fair Housing, 2015). The rule required that communities would undertake a process to understand where segregation existed by analyzing data, and with community engagement to develop a plan to address this segregation with federal-housing funding. Although the Trump administration suspended implementation of the 2015 rule, in June 2021, HUD published an interim final rule to restore the AFFH regulatory definition. When implementing a new rule, HUD could require or provide incentives to engage in cross-sector collaboration, such as with educational agencies.

Section 8 voucher funding could be increased to provide for more low-income housing, and certain revisions could further its integrative potential. First, there should be greater enforcement of the prohibition against discrimination in accepting Section 8 vouchers. Housing authorities also could be required to give preference to Section 8 recipients who find units in low-poverty, high-opportunity neighborhoods. These housing authorities could then receive additional funding to provide counseling services to support mobility, funding for security deposits that may be required, and additional top-off voucher amounts as needed. These reforms and others could expand choices for families.

Cross-Sector Collaborative Efforts. DeBray-Pelot and Frankenberg (2010) proposed a pilot program that could promote both housing and educational integration by administering housing subsidies on a regional basis that would be combined with interdistrict school transfers, drawing in part on lessons from Gautreaux and Moving to Opportunity. Indeed, as a first step, HUD could offer regionalization and portability of housing vouchers in regions with interdistrict school programs that are focused on desegregation to help integrate eligible families into communities in which their children already attend school. Such efforts could enhance residential and school integration efforts (see also Tegeler et al., 2009).

More broadly, the Biden-Harris administration could reignite cross-sector collaborative efforts among ED, HUD, and DOT that had been announced in 2016 and were aimed at furthering integration. Providing technical expertise and incentives in competitive grants are two such ways to support this work. In addition, it would be important to conduct research to understand opportunities and barriers to share in other communities.

RECOMMENDATIONS FOR MOVING TOWARD INTEGRATED SCHOOLS AND COMMUNITIES

Given the policy vision outlined earlier, we provide recommendations for action at the regional, state, and federal levels. First and foremost, an unwavering commitment to public education is critical for our communities' cohesion and for the health of a multiracial democracy. In all efforts, racial and socioeconomic diversity should be discussed publicly as a positive goal and public education as a public good, in addition to individual benefits for students.

At the regional level, students, educators, representatives from the housing sector, concerned citizens, and representatives of community organizations and local institutions should be organized to share their experiences, assess the current situation in schools and communities, determine needs and assets, and provide direction for the future. As experts about their own experiences, the youth and residents who are most affected by segregation should help shape solutions. At the same time, organizers should be cautious about not overburdening students. Leaders and staff at local institutions should receive training about how to create inclusive environments and facilitate integration. Finally, positive housing and school policies should be developed together to promote and sustain stable integration (Orfield, 2013).

Similarly, at the state and federal levels, policy should be informed by the experiences of those who are impacted by segregation. Efforts should focus on providing funding and technical assistance for local, regional, and statewide efforts to plan, implement, and evaluate collaborative integration efforts in schools and communities.

Schools and communities are interrelated; therefore, a comprehensive and collaborative plan for creating and sustaining integration in both communities and schools is needed. Through the policies presented in this chapter, our country could work toward dismantling some of the racist structures that have inequitably distributed access and opportunities to White students and residents while denying students and residents of color the justice deserved.

NOTES

1. For these reasons, then-HUD secretary George Romney proposed suburban housing integration efforts, believing them to be more palatable than busing to desegregated schools. President Nixon halted this program, and there has only been limited enforcement of the Fair Housing Act.
2. The Biden-Harris administration committed to addressing systemic racism when declaring victory. More recently, in October 2021, the administration issued an executive order to advance educational equity and excellence for Black Americans.

REFERENCES

Affirmatively Furthering Fair Housing, 80 Fed. Reg. 42275 (July 16, 2015).
Allport, G. W. (1954). *The nature of prejudice*. Addison-Wesley.
Associated Press. (2021 July). Feds in Virginia to step up civil rights enforcement. *Richmond Times-Dispatch*. https://richmond.com/news/state-and-regional/feds-in-virginia-to-step-up-civil-rights-enforcement/article_67774213-8c59-5fc7-a12c-7a78d7902ff6.html
Ayscue, J. B., & Frankenberg, E. (2016). Desegregation and integration. In L. H. Meyer (Ed.), *Oxford bibliographies in education*. Oxford University Press. https://doi.org/10.1093/OBO/9780199756810-0139
Ayscue, J. B., & Orfield, G. (2014). School district lines stratify educational opportunity by race and poverty. *Race and Social Problems, 7*(1), 5–20.
Ayscue, J. B., Siegel-Hawley, G., Kucsera, J., & Woodward, B. (2016). School segregation and resegregation in Charlotte and Raleigh, 1989–2010. *Educational Policy, 32*(1), 3–54. doi.org/10.1177/0895904815625287
Balfanz, R., & Legters, N. E. (2004). Locating the dropout crisis: Which high schools produce the nation's dropouts? In G. Orfield (Ed.), *Dropouts in America: Confronting the graduation crisis* (pp. 57–84). Harvard Education Press.
Bell, C. A. (2009). Geography in parental choice. *American Journal of Education, 115*(4), 493–521.
Bierbaum, A. H., Karner, A., & Barajas, J.M. (2021). Toward Mobility Justice, *Journal of the American Planning Association, 87*(2), 197–210.
Braddock, J. H., & McPartland, J. M. (1989). Social-psychological processes that perpetuate racial segregation: The relationship between school and employment desegregation. *Journal of Black Studies, 19*, 267–289.
Brummet, Q., & Reed, D. (2019). *The effects of gentrification on the well-being and opportunity of original resident adults and children* [Working Paper]. Federal Reserve Bank of Philadelphia. https://www.philadelphiafed.org/community-development/housing-and-neighborhoods/the-effects-of-gentrification-on-the-well-being-and-opportunity-of-original-resident
Chaskin, R. J., & Joseph, M. L. (2015). *Integrating the inner city: The promise and perils of mixed-income public housing transformation*. University of Chicago Press.
Cordes, S. A., Rick, C., & Schwartz, A. E. (2020). Do long bus rides drive down academic outcomes? *Educational Evaluation and Policy Analysis*. https://doi.org/10.3102/01623737221092450

DeBray, E. H. (2021). The politics of fair and affordable housing in metropolitan Atlanta: Challenges for educational opportunity. *Berkeley Review of Education*, *10*(2). dx.doi.org/10.5070/B810253852 https://escholarship.org/uc/item/8fc560tb

DeBray-Pelot, E. & Frankenberg, E. (2010). Federal legislation to promote metropolitan approaches to educational and housing opportunity. *Georgetown Journal on Poverty Law and Policy*, *17*(2), 265–286.

Denver Public Schools. (2021). *Strengthening neighborhoods initiative.* https://www.dpsk12.org/neighborhoods/

Dragan, K., Ellen, I. G., & Glied, S. (2019). Does gentrification displace poor children and their families? New evidence from Medicaid data in New York City. *Regional Science and Urban Economics*, *83*. https://doi.org/10.1016/j.regsciurbeco.2019.103481.

Eaton, S. (2020). *A steady habit of segregation: The origins and continuing harm of separate and unequal housing and public schools in metropolitan Hartford, Connecticut.* The NAACP Legal Defense and Educational Fund, The Open Communities Alliance, The Poverty & Race Research Action Council, and the Sillerman Center at Brandeis University.

Ellen, I. G., & Torrats-Espinosa, G.(2018). Gentrification and fair housing: Does gentrification further integration? *Housing Policy Debate*, *29*(5), 835–851. https://doi.org/10.1080/10511482.2018.1524440.

Ellen, I. G., & Ding, L. (2016). Guest editors' introduction: Advancing our understanding of gentrification. *Cityscape*, *18*(3), 3–8.

Erickson, A. (2016). *Making the unequal metropolis: School desegregation and its limits.* The University of Chicago Press.

Faber, J. (2021). *Impact of government programs adopted during The New Deal on residential segregation today.* Institute for Research on Poverty.

Ford, D. Y., Grantham, T. C., & Whiting, G. W. (2008). Culturally and linguistically diverse students in gifted education: Recruitment and retention issues. *Exceptional Children*, *74*(3), 289–306.

Frankenberg, E. (2013). The role of residential segregation in contemporary school segregation. *Education and Urban Society*, *45*(5), 548–570.

Frankenberg, E., Ee, J., Ayscue, J. B., & Orfield, G. (2019). *Harming our common future: America's segregated schools 65 years after Brown.* The Civil Rights Project/Proyecto Derechos Civiles.

Frankenberg, E., & Orfield, G. (Eds.) (2012). *The resegregation of suburban schools: A hidden crisis in American education.* Cambridge, MA: Harvard Education Press.

Frankenberg, E., & Jacobsen, R. (2011). Trends—school integration polls. *Public Opinion Quarterly 75*(4), 788–811.

Frankenberg, E., Siegel-Hawley, G., & Wang, J. (2011). Choice without equity: Charter school segregation. *Education Policy Analysis Archives*, *19*(1), 1–96.

Goetz, E. G. (2018). Criticisms about community preference policies are misguided. *Shelterforce.* https://shelterforce.org/2019/11/14/criticisms-about-community-preference-policies-are-misguided/

Goldring, E., & Smrekar, C. (2000). Magnet schools and the pursuit of racial balance. *Education and Urban Society*, *33*(1), 17–35.

Gottfried, M. A., Ozuna, C. S., & Kirksey, J. J. (2021). Exploring school bus ridership and absenteeism in rural communities. *Early Childhood Research Quarterly*. *56*, 236–47.

Green, T. L., Germain, E., Castro, A. J., Sikes, C. L., Sanchez, J., & Horne, J. (2020). Gentrifying neighborhoods, gentrifying schools? An emerging typology of school changes in a gentrifying urban school district. *Urban Education, 57*(1), 3–31. https://doi.org/10.1177/0042085920974090

Gumus-Dawes, B., Orfield, M., & Luce, T. (2012). East versus west in Minneapolis suburbs. In E. Frankenberg & G. Orfield (Eds.), *The resegregation of suburban schools: A hidden crisis in American education* (pp. 113–138). Harvard Education Press.

Haberle, M., & Tegeler, P. (2019). Coordinated action on housing and school integration: The role of state government. *University of Richmond Law Review, 53*(3), 949–976.

Holme, J. J., Welton, A., & Diem, S. (2012). Pursuing "separate but equal" in suburban San Antonio: A case study of a southern independent school district. In E. Frankenberg & G. Orfield (Eds.), *The Resegregation of Suburban Schools: A Hidden Crisis in American Education* (pp. 45–67). Harvard Education Press.

Holme, J. J., & Finnegan, K. (2018). *Striving in common: A regional equity framework for urban schools*. Harvard Education Press.

Holme, J. J., Frankenberg, E., Sanchez, J., Taylor, K., De La Garza, S., & Kennedy, M. (2020). Subsidized housing and school segregation: Examining the relationship between federally subsidized affordable housing and racial and economic isolation in schools. *Education Policy Analysis Archives, 28*(169). doi.org/10.14507/epaa.28.5290

Johnson, R. C. (2011). *Long-run impacts of school desegregation and school quality on adult attainments* (NBER Working Paper No. 1664). National Bureau of Economic Research. https://doi.org/10.3386/w16664

Johnson, R. C. (2019). *Children of the dream: Why school integration works*. Basic Books.

Kahlenberg, R. D., & Potter, H. (2014). *A smarter charter: Finding what works for charter schools and public education*. Teachers College Press.

Kebede, M., Taylor, K., Maselli, K. A., & Frankenberg, E. (2021). Ethnoracial diversity and segregation in U.S. rural school districts. *Rural Sociology, 86*(3), 494–522.

Kimelberg, S. M., & Billingham, C. M. (2012). Attitudes toward diversity and the school choice process: Middle-class parents in a segregated urban public school district. *Urban Education, 48*, 198–231.

Ladd, H. F., Clotfelter, C. T., & Holbein, J. B. (2015). *The growing segmentation of the charter school sector in North Carolina*. National Center for Analysis of Longitudinal Data in Education Research.

Linn, R., & Welner, K. (2007). *Race-conscious policies for assigning students to schools: Social science research and the Supreme Court cases*. National Academy of Education.

Logan, J. R., & Stults, B. (2011). *The persistence of segregation in the metropolis: New findings from the 2010 Census* (Census Brief prepared for Project US2010). https://www.s4.brown.edu/us2010

Losen, D. J., & Martinez, P. (2020). *Lost opportunities: How disparate school discipline continues to drive differences in the opportunity to learn*. The Center for Civil Rights Remedies at the Civil Rights Project/Proyecto Derechos Civiles and Learning Policy Institute.

Losen, D., & Orfield, G. (Eds.). (2002). *Racial inequity in special education*. Harvard Education Press.

Menendian, S., Gailes, A., & Gambhir, S. (2021). *The roots of structural racism: Twenty-first century racial residential segregation in the United States*. Othering and Belonging Institute.

Mickelson, R. A., Bottia, M. C., & Lambert, R. (2013). Effects of school racial composition on K-12 mathematics outcomes: A metaregression analysis. *Review of Educational Research, 83*, 121–158.

Mickelson, R. A., Bottia, M. C., & Larimore, S. (2020). A metaregression analysis of the effects of school racial and ethnic composition on K–12 reading, language arts, and English outcomes. *Sociology of Race and Ethnicity, 7*(3), 401–419. https://doi.org/10.1177/2332649220942265

Mickelson, R. A., & Nkomo, M. (2012). Integrated schooling, life course outcomes, and social cohesion in multiethnic democratic societies. *Review of Research in Education, 36*(1), 197–238. https://doi.org/10.3102/0091732X11422667

Monarrez, T., Kisida, B., & Chingos, M. (2019). *When is a school segregated? Making sense of segregation 65 years after Brown v. Board of Education*. Urban Institute.

Oakes, J. (2005). *Keeping track: How schools structure inequality* (2nd ed.). Yale University Press.

Orfield, G. (2013). Housing segregation produces unequal schools: Causes and solutions. In P. L. Carter & K. G. Welner (Eds.), *Closing the opportunity gap: What America must do to give every child an even chance* (pp. 40–60). Oxford University Press.

Owens, A. (2016). Inequality in children's contexts: Income segregation of households with and without children. *American Sociological Review, 81*(3), 549–574. doi:10.1177/0003122416642430

Owens, A. (2020). Unequal opportunity: School and neighborhood segregation in the USA. *Race and Social Problems, 12*, 29–41.

Pearman, F. A., & Swain, W. A. (2017). School choice, gentrification, and the variable significance of racial stratification in urban neighborhoods. *Sociology of Education, 90*(3), 213–235.

Pettigrew, T., & Tropp, L. (2006). A meta-analytic test of intergroup contact theory. *Journal of Personality and Social Psychology, 90*(5), 751–783.

Poverty & Race Research Action Council. (2020). *An anti-racist agenda for state and local housing agencies* [Video]. Author. https://www.youtube.com/watch?v=I4KirhmIQoA

Ramakrishnan, K., Treskon, M., & Greene, S. (2019). *Inclusionary zoning: What does the research tell us about the effectiveness of local action?* Urban Institute.

Roda, A. (2015). *Inequality in gifted and talented programs: Parental choices about status, school opportunity, and second-generation segregation*. Palgrave Macmillan.

Rosenbaum, J., DeLuca, S., & Tuck, T. (2005). New capabilities in new places: Low-income Black families in suburbia. In X. Briggs (Ed.)., *The geography of opportunity* (pp. 150–75). Brookings Institution.

Rothstein, R. (2017). *The color of law: A forgotten history of how our government segregated America*. Liveright.

Rusk, D. (2008). Housing policy is school policy. In D. Hamilton & P. Atkins (Eds.), *Urban and regional policies for metropolitan livability* (pp. 204–231). Taylor & Francis.

Schwartz, H. L. (2010). *Housing policy is school policy*. The Century Foundation.

Schweitzer, A. (2021, October 25). Montgomery County to consider sending $800 a month to low-income families for two years. *DCist*. https://dcist.com/story/21/10/25/montgomery-county-800-month-to-low-income-families-for-two-years/.

Scott, J., Siegel-Hawley, G., DeBray, E., Frankenberg, E., & McDermott, K. (2020). *An agenda for restoring civil rights in K-12 federal education policy*. National Education Policy Center.

Siegel-Hawley, G. (2012). *How non-minority students also benefit from racially diverse schools*. The National Coalition on School Diversity.

Siegel-Hawley, G. (2016). *When the fences come down: Twenty-first-century lessons from metropolitan school desegregation*. The University of North Carolina Press.

Siegel-Hawley, G., & Frankenberg, E. (2013). Designing choice: Structuring magnet schools for racial diversity. In G. Orfield & E. Frankenberg (Eds.), *Educational delusions? Why choice can deepen inequality and how to make schools fair* (pp. 107–125). University of California Press.

Siegel-Hawley, G., Kozol, B., Moeser, J., Holden, T., & Shields. T. J. (2017). *Confronting school and housing segregation in the Richmond Region: Can we learn and live together?* University of Richmond, Virginia Commonwealth University.

Siegel-Hawley, G., Diem, S., & Frankenberg, E. (2018). The disintegration of Memphis-Shelby County, Tennessee: School district secession and local control in the 21st century. *American Educational Research Journal*, 55(4), 651–692.

Stone, C. N. (1989). *Regime olitics: Governing Atlanta, 1946–1988*. University Press of Kansas.

Sullivan, A. L., & Bal, A. (2013). Disproportionality in special education: Effects of individual and school variables on disability risk. *Exceptional Children*, 79(4), 475–494.

Swanson, C. B. (2004). Sketching a portrait of public high school graduation: Who graduates? Who doesn't? In G. Orfield (Ed.), *Dropouts in America: Confronting the graduation rate crisis* (pp. 13–40). Harvard Education Press.

Taylor, K., Frankenberg, E., & Siegel-Hawley, G. (2019). Racial segregation in the Southern schools, school districts, and counties where districts have seceded. *AERA Open*, 5(3), 1–16. https://doi.org/10.1177/2332858419860152

Tegeler, P., Eaton, S., & Miller, W. (2009). *Bringing children together: Magnet schools and public housing redevelopment*. Charles Hamilton Houston Institute for Race and Justice and Poverty & Race Research Action Council.

The National Coalition on School Diversity. (2021). *School integration priorities for a Biden/Harris administration*. Author.

Tieken, M. C. (2014). *Why rural schools matter*. The University of North Carolina Press.

Tilsley, A. (2017). *Subtracting schools from communities*. Urban Institute.

Trajkovski, S., Zabel, J., & Schwartz, A. E. (2021). Do school buses make school choice work? *Regional Science and Urban Economics*, 86. https://doi.org/10.1016/j.regsciurbeco.2020.103607

Tropp, L. R., & Prenovost, M. A. (2008). The role of intergroup contact in predicting children's interethnic attitudes: Evidence from meta-analytic and field studies. In S. R. Levy & M. Killen (Eds.), *Intergroup attitudes and relations in childhood through adulthood* (pp. 236–248). Oxford University Press.

Turner, M. A., Chingos, M., & Spievack, N. (2021). *White people's choices perpetuate school and neighborhood segregation. What would it take to change them?* Urban Institute.

U. S. Attorney's Office, Eastern District, New York. (2021, June 18). *Acting United States Attorney Mark J. Lesko announces formation of civil rights team in the Office's civil division* [Press release]. https://www.justice.gov/usao-edny/pr/acting-united-states-attorney-mark-j-lesko-announces-formation-civil-rights-team-office

U. S. Department of Housing, U. S. Department of Education, & U. S. Department of Transportation. (2016). *Dear colleague letter.* https://www.prrac.org/pdf/Joint_Letter_on_Diverse_Schools_and_Communities_AFFH.pdf

Weiher, G. R. (1991). *The fractured metropolis: Political fragmentation and metropolitan segregation.* State University of New York Press.

Wilson, E. (2021). Monopolizing whiteness. *Harvard Law Review, 134*(1), 2382–2448.

Wilson, E. K. (2014). Toward a theory of equitable federated regionalism in public education. *UCLA Law Review, 61,* 1416–1479.

CHAPTER 10

Housing Strategies as Education Policy

Megan Gallagher

INTRODUCTION

Education policies alone are not enough to address structural inequities that affect student performance. A comprehensive education policy agenda must ensure that all students have high-quality, affordable housing that supports educational opportunities. It should include housing policies that prioritize families with children, create conditions for students to thrive, provide more funding for housing, and activate cross-sector collaboration at all levels of government.

This chapter starts with a brief introduction to the housing sector and its key players. Next, it provides an overview of the evidence on the relationship between education and housing conditions in the *housing bundle,* including quality, affordability, stability, location, and the potential for housing to build wealth. Next, the chapter presents a new vision for education policy that ensures affordable housing programs prioritize families with children and create conditions for students to thrive, with examples from the field. The chapter concludes with next steps for achieving educational outcomes through housing policies and programs.

WHAT DO WE MEAN BY HOUSING?

In this chapter, "housing" is the physical place where people live and "housing actors" are the public and private players that are involved in planning, financing, building, regulating, buying and selling, leasing, and managing housing (see Textbox 10.1). Housing actors include individuals like renters, homeowners, and realtors, and they also include institutions like banks and governments. Decisions made by these actors have led to the housing system that we have today. While their influence on the housing market varies, they all affect the availability, quality, price, and location of housing.

> **Box 10.1**
> **Who Are Housing Actors?**
>
> - Banks or other institutions that finance loans for real estate developers and homebuyers.
> - Real estate developers that conceive of new housing developments or rehabilitation projects, orchestrate deals to fund them, and own or sell them.
> - Realtors that help homebuyers and home sellers to find one another and orchestrate the sale of residential property; realtors can also find matches between landlords and renters.
> - Housing authorities that administer federal, state, and local housing programs.
> - Property managers and management companies that are responsible for the day-to-day functioning of rental properties.
> - The Federal government funds and regulates federal housing programs, and federal housing law including the Fair Housing Act of 1968. The federal government also subsidizes homeownership through the federal tax system.
> - State and local governments that allocate federal funding, fund housing programs, regulate housing transactions, and set land use policies.
> - Homeowners that pay mortgages, property taxes, cost of repairs.
> - Renters that pay rent and notify landlord or management about repairs.

Private actors are responsible for most of the nation's housing, and they are subject to federal, state, and local regulations related to discrimination, habitability, and occupancy. Federal, state, and local programs support the creation or operation of publicly or privately owned subsidized rental housing, while federal programs provide most of the subsidies to pay for housing in the private rental market. The most common federal rental programs are public housing, the Housing Choice Voucher Program, project-based Section 8 rental assistance, and the Low-Income Housing Tax Credit. Various organizations administer federal housing programs, including continuums of care for homeless services, municipal housing departments, public housing agencies, state housing finance agencies, and state departments of housing. In addition, a renter facing an affordability crisis could obtain short-term eviction prevention assistance from a city housing or social-service department.

Housing is considered affordable when it costs no more than 30% of a household's income. In 2018, 21 million families were spending more than 30% of their income on housing, and almost 11 million were spending more than 50% (Harvard Joint Center for Housing Studies, 2020). About two-thirds of all households own their home[1] and 62% of children live in homes owned by their families.[2] Homeowners and renters experience housing-cost burden, but homeowners are half as likely as renter households to spend 30% of their income on housing.[3] Public subsidies can reduce rents to improve affordability. Subsidies may be directed to housing developers or rental-property owners in exchange for limiting rents, or to households to enable affordability in the private rental market. Under certain market and policy conditions, nonprofit or for-profit owners may offer affordable rents without a subsidy. While the number of households receiving housing assistance through public housing, the Housing Choice Voucher Program, or project-based Section 8 rental assistance has increased in recent years, their share of the total who need a deep subsidy has dropped to 21% (Kingsley, 2017), leaving most families that need subsidies without them. Housing assistance is not universal, and just one state, Massachusetts, recognizes a right to emergency shelter (Boston Foundation, 2017). In 2021, 1.3 million children were homeless or doubled up with other families (National Center for Homeless Education [NCHE], 2021). For a comprehensive overview of the housing system, see *Advancing Mobility from Poverty: A Toolkit for Housing and Education Partnerships* (Enterprise Community Partners, 2020).

HOW HAS HOUSING CREATED STRUCTURAL INEQUITIES REFLECTED IN EDUCATION OUTCOMES?

Housing policy inequities have established a foundation for inequities in education. Public and private housing actors have played a role in limiting access to housing for Black people and other people of color, thus, translating into disparities in wealth, health, and education (Rothstein, 2017).

Restrictive racial covenants, agreements that developers established and homebuyers agreed to, limited resale to specific racial and ethnic groups. Areas considered to be high risk for mortgage lending were geographically defined or "redlined" by financial institutions, including the Federal Housing Administration (FHA), limiting the ability of people of color to obtain home loans to purchase homes in specific communities. Restrictive covenants and redlining policies limited Black people and other people of color from building wealth through homeownership, and continue to affect their wealth today (Aaronson et al., 2020; Shapiro et al., 2013; Sood et al., 2019). These policies also limited educational opportunity (Lukes & Cleveland, 2021; Ramos, 2001).

Ironically, even programs designed to address housing inequities have contributed to further inequities. From the 1940s until the 1960s, the federal government built public housing but segregated tenants by race and offered better amenities in White developments (Rothstein, 2017). Although it became illegal to discriminate after the Fair Housing Act of 1968, segregationist policies are reflected in the demographics of public housing communities today. The average poverty rate for census tracts that included public-housing units in 2016 was 33%, and 61% of households were non-White (Docter & Galvez, 2020). Similarly, developers using federal tax credits to build affordable housing have perpetuated residential segregation by siting affordable housing in high-poverty, primarily Black communities (Freeman, 2004). Not only are the neighborhoods segregated where subsidies are used, but the schools are too. For example, Low Income Housing Tax Credit–subsidies in California usually site housing near segregated and underperforming schools (Pfeiffer, 2009). Similarly, voucher holders have been limited to private-market rentals in locations with low-performing schools because of the rent limits in the program (Tegeler et al., 2013). Today, state and local residential zoning policies influence where affordable housing can be built, with exclusionary policies limiting affordable housing in areas with high-performing schools (Rothwell, 2012).

HOW DO CURRENT HOUSING CONDITIONS AFFECT EDUCATIONAL OUTCOMES?

Research identifies the following five key characteristics of housing that matter for education:

1. Housing quality
2. Housing affordability
3. Housing stability
4. Neighborhood quality
5. Housing that builds wealth

Together, these characteristics are referred to as the housing bundle. Much of the existing research examines one housing characteristic at a time, even though students and their families experience combinations of housing characteristics. Gallagher and colleagues (2020) summarized the relationship between housing characteristics and education. Below are brief summaries of what we know about the relationship between each housing condition and educational outcomes, and what we know about the housing bundle.

Housing Quality. Housing quality includes the physical conditions of the home and the space it affords its inhabitants.

Housing defects such as lead paint, broken facilities, exposed wiring, holes, mold or mildew, and pests contribute to high rates of elevated blood lead levels, asthma, worse sleep quality, and other negative health outcomes among inhabitants of all ages (Chambers et al., 2016; Howell et al., 2005; Williamson et al., 1997). When children are physically healthy, they are more likely to attend school consistently—a key indicator of educational success—and show improved attentiveness compared with their less-healthy peers (Cunningham & MacDonald, 2012). Low-quality housing has also been tied to lower kindergarten-readiness scores (Coulton et al., 2016). It also takes a toll on children's mental well-being: children living in substandard housing have higher rates of helplessness and worse overall psychological health than their peers (Rollings et al., 2017). When children have limited space to do their homework or otherwise live in close quarters with others, their health and academic performances suffer (Fischer, 2015; Saegert & Evans, 2003). Crowded living conditions have been associated with lower test scores, repeated grades, and decreased graduation rates (Conley, 2001; Fischer, 2015; Goux & Maurin, 2005; Lopoo & London, 2016). (Gallagher et al., 2020, p. 5)

Housing Affordability. Housing affordability is the ability of a household to pay for adequate housing without a significant financial burden.

Housing affordability helps households meet their basic needs, which in turn helps children's mental health and academic performance. When a household spends no more than 30% of its income on rent, it is less likely to be forced into making difficult trade-offs such as having to choose between paying for food, clothing, or medical care and other vital necessities (Newman & Holupka, 2015). Households have more money to spend on their children's basic needs and enrichment activities, and overall familial stress decreases. In addition, housing affordability affects children's academic performance: children in rent-burdened households are held back in school more often and are more likely to have behavioral problems than children in households that are not rent burdened (Aratani et al., 2011). However, rules related to subsidy use and discrimination against households with rental subsidies limit whether and where a household can use its voucher (Cunningham et al., 2018; Su et al., 2020). (Gallagher et al., 2020, p. 4)

As a result, housing programs that subsidize housing for income-eligible families have not consistently offered improved education resources. In one study, participants in units built with federal subsidies were more likely to live near low-performing schools than participants using housing-choice vouchers because subsidized units were built in disinvested communities with struggling schools (Ellen & Horn, 2012).

Housing Stability and Academic Progress. Housing stability is a person's ability to stay in their home if they would like to, without unplanned or unwanted disruptions or moves like foreclosures or evictions.

Residential stability creates a consistent environment for children to learn and grow, reducing the likelihood of chronic absenteeism and toxic stress. Among children, homelessness is associated with an increased likelihood of mental- and physical-health problems, as well as lower passing rates in core academic subjects (Cutuli et al., 2013; Fischer, 2015). Homeless students are also more likely to be chronically absent and to receive disciplinary action than children with stable homes (Ray et al., 2017). Children who are not homeless but experience a high number of residential moves—particularly when the moves are unwanted, such as through formal or informal evictions—also tend to have worse outcomes than their peers who do not experience residential instability, because residential mobility is often tied to school mobility (Cunningham & MacDonald, 2012). Students who change schools frequently have been found to be a year or more behind in reading and math (Cunningham & MacDonald, 2012; Grigg, 2012). Residential stability also creates a sense of belonging among children and their parents, who have better mental-health outcomes than those who experience homelessness or frequent moves (Walton & Cohen 2007). (Gallagher et al., 2020, p. 5)

Neighborhood quality and student learning. The benefits of housing are also linked to its location, which can provide access to safety and resources such as education, transportation, and employment.

When children live in safe neighborhoods with access to resources, they are more likely to experience positive development and growth at home and school. Neighborhood exposure to violence disrupts a child's academic progress (Browning et al., 2008; Harding, 2003). Proximity to homicides has been tied to lower cognitive test scores among young people, and neighborhood violence has been found to account for almost half the association between neighborhood disadvantage and high school graduation (Harding, 2003).

In recent years, studies have found a close association between the neighborhood in which a child grows up and their long-term outcomes, including access to opportunity and economic mobility. A child's neighborhood directly correlates with educational attainment and earnings as an adult (Chetty & Hendren, 2018). In neighborhoods that have faced public and private disinvestment, the neighborhood's marginalization may harm longtime residents through both educational and income opportunity gaps that appear across generations (Sharkey, 2013). Although low-income neighborhoods have been found to have stronger levels of social integration than those that are more affluent, living in a safe and well-resourced neighborhood is a strong indicator of long-term success (Keene et al., 2013). (Gallagher et al., 2020, p. 5)

Housing builds wealth and drives student achievement. Homeownership can provide pathways to educational opportunity, but both structural racism and market conditions can undermine the benefits of homeownership.

Homeownership is beneficial when homeowners can afford to buy, consistently pay mortgage payments, and then benefit from the investment. Ramakrishnan and colleagues (2021) summarize literature that finds that children of homeowners have higher achievement rates but cannot rule out the possibility that other factors drive achievement.

> Wealth from home equity has been shown to positively affect the educational outcomes for the children of homeowners, specifically college attendance and college-degree attainment. Several studies find that increases in home equity increase the likelihood that a child goes to college, with these estimates being even larger for households earning less than $70,000 a year (Cooper & Luengo-Prado, 2015; Lovenheim, 2011). Some literature suggests that the children of homeowners have higher educational achievement and fewer behavioral problems, leading to higher future earnings than children of renters (Haurin et al., 2000). However, other research finds little evidence that homeownership has these beneficial effects on children's cognitive achievement, behavior, and health; rather, these effects may be the product of certain populations being more likely to pursue homeownership (Holupka & Newman 2011). (Ramakrishnan et al., 2021, p. 14)

Housing Can Vary Across All These Dimensions

Researchers often isolate one housing characteristic without understanding how it interacts with other housing characteristics. For example, the effect of living in an unsafe neighborhood for a long period of time may be ambiguous because housing stability has a positive effect and living in an unsafe neighborhood has a negative effect (Browning & Cagney, 2003). Or, housing quality tends to improve as affordability declines (Kingsley, 2017).

Children experience combinations of housing characteristics, but there is limited evidence about how their interconnectedness affects educational outcomes. In one study examining the relative effects of affordability, quality, stability, ownership, and receipt of a subsidy, researchers found that housing quality was the strongest predictor of school performance for adolescents (Coley et al., 2013). Using the same dataset, the researchers also examined neighborhood quality and found differences in reading and math performance for children with different profiles of affordability, housing quality, neighborhood quality, homeownership, and stability (Coley et al., 2014).

How Might a New Vision for Education Policy Take This Evidence Base into Consideration?

A new vision for education policy recognizes that housing is foundational for students. It asserts the importance of the intersecting housing conditions that make up the housing bundle. It aligns the efforts of public- and private-housing actors to improve the quality, stability, affordability, and location of students' housing. But it doesn't stop with physical homes for students. It also ensures that affordable housing programs offer learning environments where students can thrive.

A growing number of models exist for ensuring that affordable housing programs prioritize families with children and create conditions for students to thrive. Over the past 5 years, several models have emerged to demonstrate the potential for housing actors to improve educational opportunity. In the Pacific Northwest, the Bill and Melinda Gates Foundation supported housing and education innovation through grants to housing authorities in King County, Seattle, and Tacoma, Washington, and a community of practice from 2014 to 2019. The Foundation also supported national efforts to inform and support housing and education innovations, in partnership with the Council of Large Public Housing Authorities.[4] Innovations from that effort offer insights for education and housing-authority partnerships (Gallagher, 2015). Starting in 2020, the Ballmer Group has supported the collaboration of Enterprise Community Partners, a national housing organization and the StriveTogether Network, a national education organization, to develop partnerships and improve housing and education outcomes. Ballmer's investment produced Advancing Mobility from Poverty: A Toolkit for Housing and Education Partnerships (Enterprise Community Partners, 2020) and Aligning Housing and Education: Evidence of Promising Practices and Structural Challenges (Gallagher et al., 2020). Other efforts by the Bridges Collaborative and Poverty & Race Research Action Council (PRRAC) connect practitioners and advocates to evidence and other resources to promote racial integration in housing and schools.[5]

Below we explore two models and examples from the field.

Housing subsidies for students. The first model involves a housing subsidy for students who are at high risk of housing instability or homelessness. The subsidy allows them and their families to live in better-quality, more stable, and more affordable homes. Below are four examples from Gallagher and colleagues (2020) research on housing and education partnerships.

Homework Starts with Home in Minnesota aims to reduce family homelessness, student transience, and absenteeism by targeting housing vouchers to unstably housed families with school-age children. Homework Starts with Home combines the benefits of housing, education, and human services agencies at the state level so that local, community-based organizations such as housing and redevelopment agencies can use grants to address housing needs, thereby improving academic outcomes for unstably housed students.

Like Homework Starts with Home, Avenue of Life in Kansas City, Kansas, works with local partners to offer wraparound services for homeless and unstably housed students, with the goal of increasing high school graduation rates and stabilizing families. The effort Impact KCK is designed to support the families of students experiencing homelessness before public benefits are available to them. Navigators employed by Avenue of Life connect families to a robust network of service providers to ensure that immediate needs such as housing, food, and health care are met. Impact Wednesday, a weekly event hosted by Avenue of Life, brings together service providers to meet with families and provide courses on employment, finance, trauma-care parenting, and mental health.

In Tacoma, Washington, homeless and unstably housed community-college students struggle to remain enrolled and make timely progress toward earning a degree. Students facing housing instability may need to take time off, attend part time, or drop out to prioritize basic needs. To address this group's unique housing needs, the Tacoma Housing Authority created the College Housing Assistance Program with Tacoma Community College. Through this partnership, the housing authority provides housing subsidies for 250 formerly homeless or near-homeless students at the community college (and now the University of Washington Tacoma). Graduate Tacoma, a StriveTogether network member, covers move-in expenses for students moving into a new development that the housing authority acquired for this program. The collaboration's higher-education partners provide education navigation services and other supports. An evaluation of the initiative found that students who received housing vouchers had higher grade point averages and were more likely to remain enrolled and make progress toward degree completion after 2 years than their nonassisted peers (Tacoma Housing Authority, 2019).

Young people who are in foster care or have aged out of the system experience high rates of homelessness and housing instability (Dworsky et al., 2012). The Foster Care to College initiative—led by the University of Pennsylvania's Field Center for Children's Policy, Practice, and Research—aims to disrupt this cycle by helping higher-education institutions in Pennsylvania open their doors to young people in or exiting foster care. The Field Center provides technical assistance to higher-education institutions. During these engagements, the Field Center works with schools to identify gaps in their programming and barriers to increasing student support and helps develop strategies for overcoming barriers. As a result, some institutions have created policies that allow students to stay in dorms year-round. Some colleges, such as West Chester University, have established scholarship funds to pay for housing and emergency costs for young people who have aged out of foster care. By supporting the housing needs of students from foster care, Foster Care to College and participating colleges aim to increase this group's college-graduation rates and economic prosperity.

Affordable housing with enhanced educational opportunities. The second model adds supportive and enriching services to housing subsidies to enhance affordable-housing communities. Below are four examples of affordable housing with enhanced educational opportunities from Gallagher and colleagues (2020).

In Boulder, Colorado, the Emergency Family Assistance Association partners with Boulder Housing Partners to provide 3 months of intensive case management to families entering the Bringing School Home initiative, a collaboration between public and nonprofit organizations that brings together high-quality, affordable housing and educational opportunities for the whole family. The Emergency Family Assistance Association administers the Colorado Family Support Assessment when households move in, and they use it to identify, set, and work toward goals related to housing stability, income, or children's educational attainment. After 3 months, families can extend the case management or transition to "lighter-touch" check-ins with Boulder Housing Partners staff members. In this case, the Emergency Family Assistance Association and Boulder Housing Partners case management supports families as they transition to stable housing.

Many housing providers are developing partnerships with after-school programs, school districts, and other service providers to ensure that vulnerable children receive supplemental educational supports. Some housing authorities (and nonprofit and for-profit housing providers) have resident services staff who connect community members with education-related services and bring additional resources on site. Star-C, an Atlanta-based nonprofit organization that partners with private landlords to provide affordable housing and supportive services, has a service coordinator at each property. The coordinator runs an after-school program for children living in the community, and Star-C coordinates with schools to monitor student test scores. The coordinator lives at the property and acts as a resource for residents and a link to health care and other services and benefits.

Other housing providers are providing space for day care and educational and other assistance programs, further integrating services into the housing community. In Ohio, the Akron Metropolitan Housing Authority runs the Early Childhood Initiative, which consists of high-quality early childhood programming and home visiting for residents of housing authority properties. The authority opened the Reach Opportunity Center with U.S. Department of Housing and Urban Development funding in 2014; it houses cradle-to-career educational programming for the community.

In California—and, more recently, several cities across the country—the Housing and Education (HousED) initiative educates and trains housing agencies to develop and implement high-quality educational programming for children in their communities. Nonprofit housing providers such as Mercy Housing, MidPen Housing, and Eden Housing have participated and continue to provide after-school programs with broad educational enrichment opportunities across their sites. HousED encourages housing providers to think critically about program quality and has created tools to help them assess and improve their offerings. Similarly, Star-C educates private landlords on the relationship between stable housing and academic success and offers after-school programming in large apartment communities in Atlanta. Star-C has also hosted workshops on the connections between housing and education and the benefits of the Star-C model for landlords and residents. The next section outlines how evidence and promising models for housing equity can shape local, state, and federal policies.

WHAT ACTIONS MUST BE UNDERTAKEN AT THE LOCAL, STATE, AND FEDERAL LEVEL FOR THIS NEW VISION TO BE REALIZED?

The federal government requires that children attend school, but it doesn't require that children have a home. A comprehensive education strategy demands that all students have high-quality, affordable housing that supports educational opportunity. To achieve this, we must allocate more funding to rental subsidies and activate collaboration between housing and education sectors.

Allocate More Funding for Housing

Since there is not enough affordable housing, federal subsidies are needed to make housing affordable for people with low or no income. Additional funding is needed to achieve the three following goals:

- *To serve more students.* There is not enough housing assistance for those who need it; only 21% of households who qualify for housing subsidies get them (Kingsley, 2017). Of the 16 million unassisted households eligible for housing assistance, about 5.3 million have children.[6] Some housing authorities have been granted authority to offer special programs or preferences for families with children through the Moving to Work (MTW) Demonstration program. For example, Boulder Housing Partners uses MTW flexibility as part of its Bringing School Home initiative to offer housing to eligible families with young children.[7] Less than 40 had MTW authority in 2020 and a mere 40 of the country's 3,000 housing authorities were added to the program in 2021. While MTW authority offers flexibility for housing authorities to target housing assistance (e.g., to families with children), it does not expand the overall amount of housing assistance available. A major investment at the Federal level is needed to expand rental assistance to serve all qualified households.
- *To improve the physical condition of housing.* Too often, affordable housing is not adequately maintained. One estimate suggests over

one-third of all owner- and renter-occupied housing is in need of repair, and many low-income renters in housing with needed repairs live in buildings owned by small "mom and pop" landlords who do not have resources to maintain their properties (Divringi et al., 2019). Some states offer financing for rehabilitation projects to homeowners with lower incomes that will bring their homes up to state or local code.[8] For example, the Maryland Housing Rehabilitation Program offers funds for owner-occupied single-family homes and small rental properties with one to four units to cover costs to address health and safety violations, including lead-based paint violations.[9] The U.S. Department of Agriculture and the U.S. Department of Housing and Urban Development also offer loan and grant programs for home repairs, but many are limited to homeowners that occupy the properties and are not extended to rental properties, where more support is needed. Public housing, home to over 566,000 children nationally, is in dire need of attention.[10] Many public-housing properties were built 50 years ago, and most have not undergone construction in the past 20 years (Docter & Galvez, 2020). Large public-housing authorities, like those in New York City and the District of Columbia, need billions to restore or replace their units (*A Future Without Public Housing?*, 2020). In San Francisco, the HOPE SF initiative is designed to replace four large rundown public-housing developments with mixed-income housing, including replacement units for the original residents.[11] Projects like this can take years to complete and demand elaborate financing schemes that include public and private funding. Federal programs like the Rental Assistance Demonstration (RAD), and to a lesser degree Choice Neighborhoods, provide funding for renovating or redeveloping public housing, but they do not come close to addressing the backlog of needed repairs across the country.[12] Additional resources are needed. The Biden Administration recently announced a plan to increase the supply of rental housing for low- and moderate-income households through legislative and administrative actions.[13]

- *To support moves to more resourced communities.* Families with low wealth are excluded from their preferred neighborhoods and schools. We need to reduce or eliminate the trade-offs between housing and education. One option is to offer larger subsidies that would allow families to access rental properties in more expensive communities with higher performing schools (Dastrup et al., 2019). This strategy is being explored by the U.S. Department of Housing and Urban Development through the Housing Choice Voucher Community Choice Demonstration. The demonstration is funding special vouchers and mobility-related services for nine public housing authorities to support families with children with moves to opportunity areas defined by HUD.[14] The housing authorities will also work with jurisdictions in their regions to implement policies that promote and remove barriers to mobility. This project is motivated by HUD's 1994–1998 Moving to Opportunity (MTO) demonstration, which found that children who moved to higher opportunity neighborhoods before the age of 13 had higher earnings in adulthood than those who moved after the age of 13. It is also informed by housing mobility efforts in Baltimore, Dallas, and Seattle that have improved practitioners' and policymakers' understanding of what it takes to support families in making moves to more resourced communities.[15]

Ensuring that students live in quality, stable, affordable housing is a critical first step. We also need to make sure that affordable housing is enriched with services and supports that students need to thrive. Cross-sector collaborations between housing and education actors are needed.

Activate Housing and Education Sector Collaboration

Despite the importance of housing to children's educational outcomes, education stakeholders don't typically collaborate with housing stakeholders. A lack of coordination to date is partly due to both sectors' complexity and structures; states and school districts have the most direct influence on education policy and practice, while more housing policy and practice is determined at the federal level. Both are spread across different agencies and providers, with no centralized access point.

A comprehensive education strategy requires cross-sector collaboration to tackle challenges that have been discussed in this chapter. Housing and education sector collaboration can take place at the federal, state, or local level. In fact, it can be initiated by public or private actors. Philanthropic partners are currently investing in these collaborations, through technical assistance and direct funding for collaborations. They are supporting programs, policy advocacy, and evaluation frameworks. For more information about starting, sustaining, and scaling up cross-sector collaborations, see *Advancing Mobility from Poverty*, a toolkit for housing and education partnerships published by housing nonprofit Enterprise Community Partners (2020). But these efforts must be sustained and "permanent policy intersections" within government must be established to connect housing and education programs and policy processes (Tegeler & Hilton, 2017). One federal example is the Affirmatively Furthering Fair Housing (AFFH) rule, which was established by HUD in 2015 to support the objectives of the 1968 Fair Housing Act. It requires communities to formally assess fair housing and provides guidance, tools, and data, including data on local schools.[16] In 2016, the secretaries of the U.S. Department of Education, Transportation, and Housing jointly called on local education, transportation, and housing leaders to work together to site schools, create school-assignment strategies, and develop transportation plans that optimize educational opportunity for children from households with low incomes.[17]

Some states are establishing these policy intersections through state-level housing and education policies that supersede exclusionary local residential zoning laws and school policies. Some have established the conditions for regional housing-mobility programs that allow families to use housing subsidies in multiple jurisdictions and incentives for housing developers to site affordable housing in communities with high performing schools (Haberle & Tegeler, 2019). The Homework Starts with Home program discussed above is an example of a sustained state effort that was written into the state budget, and embeds a Minnesota Department of Education staff person in the state-housing finance agency, providing a state-level intersection that can coordinate housing and education efforts at the state and local level. Efforts like this could facilitate and strengthen connections between the systems in other jurisdictions.

CONCLUSION

Educational outcomes are affected by the quality, stability, affordability, and location of students' housing. Many families are forced to compromise on aspects of the housing bundle, trading affordability for quality, and some do not have housing at all. A comprehensive education strategy must ensure that all students have high-quality, affordable housing that supports educational opportunity. We must expand upon existing models that ensure affordable-housing programs prioritize families with children and create conditions for students to thrive, but we need more federal housing subsidies and a commitment to cross-sector collaboration at the state, county, district and city level.

ACKNOWLEDGMENTS

I am grateful to my Urban Institute colleagues Alyse Oneto, Mica O'Brien, and Maya Brennan, who co-authored *Aligning Housing and Education: Evidence of Promising Practices and Structural Challenges* (2020), which was the foundation for the literature summaries and case examples in this chapter. I am also grateful to Keith Fudge, Elizabeth Champion, and Kriti Ramakrishnan, who co-authored *Why Housing Matters for Upward Mobility: Evidence and*

Indicators for Practitioners and Policymakers (2021), from which I drew definitions of housing characteristics and the housing bundle for this chapter. That work was generously funded by Enterprise Community Partners. I also want to thank Jake Joseph for his research assistance.

NOTES

1. U.S. Census Bureau, Current Population Survey/Housing Vacancy Survey, November 2, 2021 (https://www.census.gov/housing/hvs/files/qtr321/hown321.jpg).
2. Population Reference Bureau, analysis of data from the U.S. Census Bureau 2006 through 2019 American Community Survey (https://datacenter.kidscount.org/data/tables/4755-children-living-in-households-that-are-owned#detailed).
3. 2005–2009 American Community Survey (ACS) 5-year estimates, and 2013–2017 ACS 5-year estimates (https://www.federalreserve.gov/econres/notes/feds-notes/housing-affordability-in-the-us-trends-by-geography-tenure-and-household-income-20190927.htm).
4. See Council of Large Public Housing Authorities (https://clpha.org/housing-education).
5. See Bridges Collaborative (https://tcf.org/bridges-collaborative) and Poverty & Race Research Action Council (PRRAC, https://www.prrac.org).
6. Department of Housing and Urban Development (HUD) custom tabulations of the 2019 American Housing Survey; 2018 HUD administrative data; FY2020 McKinney-Vento Permanent Supportive Housing bed counts; 2019–2020 Housing Opportunities for Persons with AIDS grantee performance profiles; and the USDA FY2020 Multi-Family Fair Housing Occupancy Report. (https://www.cbpp.org/research/housing/three-out-of-four-low-income-at-risk-renters-do-not-receive-federal-rental-assistance).
7. Boulder Housing Partners' MTW Plan for 2018 describes their strategy for supporting education by focusing on children under the age of six (https://boulderhousing.org/sites/default/files/page_attachments/2018_mtw_annual_plan_final.pdf).
8. Centers for Disease Control and Prevention resources on home improvement loans and grants (https://www.cdc.gov/policy/hst/hi5/homeimprovement/index.html)
9. Maryland Housing Rehabilitation Program—Single Family (https://dhcd.maryland.gov/Residents/Pages/mhrp-sf/default.aspx).
10. The public housing resident characteristics report (https://pic.hud.gov/pic/RCRPublic/rcrmain.asp) does not include children living in public housing managed by housing authorities with MTW authority (https://hudapps.hud.gov/public/picj2ee/Mtcsrcr?category=rcr_housesize&download=false&count=0).
11. Overview of San Francisco's HOPE SF Program (https://www.hope-sf.org).
12. Policy Basics: Public Housing (https://www.cbpp.org/research/public-housing).
13. For more information about the Housing Supply Action Plan, see "New Biden-Harris Administration Housing Supply Action Plan To Help Close the Housing

Supply Gap in Five Years." (https://www.whitehouse.gov/briefing-room/statements-releases/2022/05/16/president-biden-announces-new-actions-to-ease-the-burden-of-housing-costs).

14. Overview of Community Choice Demonstration (https://www.hud.gov/program_offices/public_indian_housing/programs/hcv/communitychoicedemo, accessed December 5, 2021) and Community Choice Demonstration Opportunity Area map (https://hud.maps.arcgis.com/apps/webappviewer/index.html?id=aa65e712287240bda9b8438a3935854d).

15. For more on the Baltimore, Dallas, and Seattle housing mobility programs see https://housingmatters.urban.org/articles/hud-prepares-new-demonstration-what-do-we-know-about-housing-mobility-and-kids-outcomes.

16. Affirmatively Furthering Fair Housing Rule (https://www.hud.gov/program_offices/fair_housing_equal_opp/affh).

17. 2016 Letter from Secretaries of Education, Transportation, and Housing (https://www2.ed.gov/documents/press-releases/06032016-dear-colleagues-letter.pdf).

REFERENCES

A future without public housing? Examining the Trump administration's efforts to eliminate public housing. Hearing before the Subcommittee on Housing, Community Development, and Insurance of the Committee on Financial Services. U.S. House of Representatives, 116th Congress (2020). https://www.congress.gov/event/116th-congress/house-event/LC65756/text?s=1&r=2

Aaronson, D., Hartley, D., & Mazumder, B. (2020). *The effects of the 1930s HOLC "redlining" maps.* Federal Reserve Bank of Chicago. https://www.chicagofed.org/publications/working-papers/2017/wp2017-12

Aratani, Y., Chau, M., Wright, V. R., & Addy, S. (2011). *Rent burden, housing subsidies and the well-being of children and youth* [Report]. Columbia University, Mailman School of Public Health, National Center for Children in Poverty.

Boston Foundation. (2017). *Massachusetts family homelessness system | City of ideas.* https://www.tbf.org/old-blog/2017/february/massachusetts-family-homelessness-system

Browning, C. R., Burrington, L. A., Leventhal, T., & Brooks-Gunn, J. (2008). Neighborhood structural inequality, collective efficacy, and sexual risk behavior among urban youth. *Journal of Health and Social Behavior, 49*(3), 269–285.

Browning, C. R., & Cagney, K. A. (2003). Moving beyond poverty: Neighborhood structure, social processes, and health. *Journal of Health and Social Behavior, 44*(4), 552–571.

Chambers, E. C., Pichardo, M. S., & Rosenbaum, E. (2016). Sleep and the housing and neighborhood environment of Urban Latino adults living in low-income housing: The AHOME study. *Behavioral Sleep Medicine, 14*(2), 169–184.

Chetty, R., & Hendren, N. (2018). The impacts of neighborhoods on intergenerational mobility I: Childhood exposure effects. *Quarterly Journal of Economics* 133(3), 1,107–162.

Coley, R. L., Kull, M., Leventhal, T., & Lynch, A. D. (2014). Profiles of housing and neighborhood contexts among low-income families: Links with children's well-being. *Cityscape, 16*(1), 37–60. http://www.jstor.org/stable/26326857

Coley R. L., Leventhal, T., Lynch, A. D., & Kull, M. (2013). Relations between housing characteristics and the well-being of low-income children and adolescents. *Developmental Psychology, 49*(9), 1775–1789. https://doi.org/10.1037/a0031033

Conley, D. (2001). A room with a view or a room of one's own? Housing and social stratification. *Sociological Forum, 16*(2), 263–280.

Cooper, D., & Luengo-Prado, M. J. (2018). Household formation over time: Evidence from two cohorts of young adults. *Journal of Housing Economics, 41*, 106–123.

Coulton, C., Fischer, R. L., Garcia-Cobian, F., Kim, R. S.-J., Cho, Y. (2016). *Housing crisis leaves lasting imprint on children in Cleveland* (Policy research brief). MacArthur Foundation. https://www.macfound.org/media/files/hhm_brief_housing_crisis_children_in_cleveland.pdf

Cunningham, M., & MacDonald, G. (2012). *Housing as a platform for improving education outcomes among low-income children*. Urban Institute. https://www.urban.org/research/publication/housing-platform-improving-education-outcomes-among-low-income-children

Cunningham, M., Galvez, M., Aranda, C. L., Santos, R., Wissoker, D., Oneto, A., Pitingolo, R., & Crawford, J. (2018). *A pilot study of landlord acceptance of housing choice vouchers*. U.S. Department of Housing and Urban Development, Office of Policy Development and Research.

Cutuli, J. J., Desjardins, C. D., Herbers, J. E., Long, J. D., Heistad, D., Chan, C.-K., Hinz, E., & Masten, A. S. (2013). Academic achievement trajectories of homeless and highly mobile students: Resilience in the context of chronic and acute risk. *Child Development, 84*(3), 841–857.

Dastrup, S., Finkel, M., & Ellen, I. G. (2019). The effects of small area fair market rents on the neighborhood choices of families with children. *Cityscape, 21*(3), 19–48.

Divringi, E., Wallace, E., Wardrip, K., & Nash, E. (2019). *Measuring and understanding home repair costs: A National typology of households*. Federal Reserve Bank of Philadelphia and PolicyMap.

Docter, B., & Galvez, M. M. (2020). *The future of public housing: Public housing fact sheet*. Urban Institute.

Dworsky, A., Dillman, K.-N., Robin Dion, M., Coffee-Borden, B., & Rosenau, M. (2012). *Housing for youth aging out of foster care: A review of the literature and program typology*. U.S. Department of Housing and Urban Development, Office of Policy Development and Research.

Ellen, I. G., & Horn, K. M. (2012). *Do federally assisted households have access to high performing public schools?* Poverty and Race Research Action Council.

Enterprise Community Partners. (2020). *Advancing mobility from poverty: A toolkit for housing and education partnerships*. https://www.enterprisecommunity.org/resources/advancing-mobility-poverty-10868

Freeman, L. (2004). *Siting affordable housing: Location and neighborhood trends of low-income housing tax credit developments in the 1990s*. Brookings. https://www

.brookings.edu/research/siting-affordable-housing-location-and-neighborhood-trends-of-low-income-housing-tax-credit-developments-in-the-1990s/

Fischer, W. (2015). *Research shows housing vouchers reduce hardship and provide platform for long-term gains among children.* Center on Budget and Policy Priorities.

Gallagher, M. (2015). *Developing housing and education partnerships: Lessons from the field.* Urban Institute.

Gallagher, M., Brennan, M., Oneto, A., & O'Brien, M. (2020). *Aligning housing and education: Evidence of promising practices and structural challenges.* Urban Institute.

Goux, D., & Maurin, E. (2005). The effect of overcrowded housing on children's performance at school. *Journal of Public Economics, 89*(5–6), 797–819.

Grigg, J. (2012). School enrollment changes and student achievement growth: A case study in educational continuity. *Sociology of Education, 85*(4), 388–404.

Haberle, M., & Tegeler, P. (2019). Coordinated action on school and housing integration: The role of state government. *University of Richmond Law Review, 53*, 949–976.

Harding, D. J. (2003). Counterfactual models of neighborhood effects: The effect of neighborhood poverty on dropping out and teenage pregnancy. *American Journal of Sociology, 109*(3), 676–719.

Harvard Joint Center for Housing Studies. (2020). *America's rental housing 2020.* https://www.jchs.harvard.edu/sites/default/files/reports/files/Harvard_JCHS_Americas_Rental_Housing_2020.pdf

Haurin, D. R., Parcel, T., & Haurin, R. J. (2000). *The impact of home ownership on child outcomes* (SSRN Scholarly Paper, ID 218969). Social Science Research Network.

Holupka, C. S., & Newman, S. J. (2011). The housing and neighborhood conditions of America's children: Patterns and trends over four decades. *Housing Policy Debate, 21*(2), 218–245.

Howell, E. M., Harris, L. E., & Popkin, S. J. (2005). The health status of HOPE VI public housing residents. *Journal of Health Care for the Poor and Underserved, 16*(2), 273–285.

Keene, D., Bader, M., & Ailshire, J. (2013). Length of residence and social integration: The contingent effects of neighborhood poverty. *Health and Place, 21*, 171–178.

Kingsley, G. T. (2017). *Trends in housing problems and federal housing assistance.* Urban Institute.

Lopoo, L. M., & London, A. S. (2016). Household crowding during childhood and long-term education outcomes. *Demography, 53*(3), 699–721.

Lovenheim, M. F. (2011). The effect of liquid housing wealth on college enrollment. *Journal of Labor Economics, 29*(4), 741–771.

Lukes, D., & Cleveland, C. (2021). *The lingering legacy of redlining on school funding, diversity, and performance* (EdWorkingPaper: 21-363). https://doi.org/10.26300/qeer-8c25

National Center for Homeless Education. (2021). *Federal data summary school years 2016–17 through 2018–19.* University of North Carolina at Greensboro.

https://nche.ed.gov/wp-content/uploads/2021/04/Federal-Data-Summary-SY-16.17-to-18.19-Final.pdf

Newman, S. J., & Holupka, C. S. (2015). Housing affordability and child well-being. *Housing Policy Debate, 25*(1), 116–151.

Pfeiffer, D. (2009). *The opportunity illusion: Subsidized housing and failing schools in California.* The Civil Rights Project/Proyecto Derechos Civiles, UCLA.

Ramakrishnan, K., Champion, E., Gallagher, M., & Fudge, K. (2021). *Why housing matters for upward mobility: Evidence and indicators for practitioners and policy makers.* Urban Institute.

Ramos, C. (2001). Educational legacy of racially restrictive covenants: Their long-term impact on Mexican Americans. *The Scholar, 4*(1), Article 6. https://commons.stmarytx.edu/thescholar/vol4/iss1/6

Ray, A., Gallo, M., Green, P., Velarde, S., Ibarra, B., Airgood-Obrycki, W., & Kleit, R. G. (2017). *Homelessness and education in Florida: Impacts on children and youth.* University of Florida, Shimberg Center for Housing Studies & Miami Homes for All.

Rollings, K. A., Wells, N. M., Evans, G. W., Bednarz, A., & Yang, Y. (2017). Housing and neighborhood physical quality: Children's mental health and motivation. *Journal of Environmental Psychology, 50*, 17–23.

Rothstein, R. (2017). *The color of law: A forgotten history of how our government segregated America.* Liveright Publishing Corporation.

Rothwell, J. (2012). *Housing costs, zoning, and access to high-scoring schools.* Brookings.

Saegert, S., & Evans, G. W. (2003). Poverty, housing niches, and health in the United States. *Journal of Social Issues, 59*(3), 569–589.

Shapiro, T, Meschede, T., & Osoro, S. (2013). *The roots of the widening racial wealth gap: Explaining the Black–White economic divide* [Research and policy brief]. University of Maryland. drum.lib.umd.edu, doi:10.13016/pvyx-ebny.

Sharkey, P. (2013). *Stuck in place: Urban neighborhoods and the end of progress toward racial equality.* University of Chicago Press.

Sood, A., Speagle, W., & Ehrman-Solberg, K. (2019). *Long shadow of racial discrimination: Evidence from housing covenants of Minneapolis.* https://dx.doi.org/10.2139/ssrn.3468520

Su, Y., Monarrez, T., & Galvez, M. (2020). *Why schools should care about housing voucher discrimination: Technical appendix.* Housing Matters. https://housingmatters.urban.org/sites/default/files/2020-07/Why Schools Should Care about Housing Voucher Discrimination Technical Appendix.pdf

Tacoma Housing Authority. (2019). *College housing assistance program: A summary.* Author.

Tegeler, P., & Hilton, M. (2021). *A shared future: Disrupting the reciprocal relationship between housing and school segregation.* Joint Center for Housing Studies. https://www.jchs.harvard.edu/research-areas/working-papers/shared-future-disrupting-reciprocal-relationship-between-housing-and

Tegeler, P., Haberle, M., & Gayles, E. (2013). Affirmatively furthering fair housing in HUD housing programs: A first term report card. *Journal of Affordable Housing & Community Development Law, 22*(1), 27–60.

Walton, G. M., & Cohen, G. L. (2007). A question of belonging: Race, social fit, and achievement. *Journal of Personality and Social Psychology, 92*(1), 82–96.

Williamson, I. J., Martin, C. J., McGill, G., Monie, R. D. H., & Fennerty, A. G. (1997). Damp housing and asthma: A case-control study. *Thorax, 52*(3), 229–234.

CHAPTER 11

Reimagining School Safety During and After the COVID-19 Pandemic

A Call for Policy Strategies to Address Racial and Social Justice

Heather M. Reynolds and Ron Avi Astor

> We acknowledge the challenges and potential harm inherent in the misuse or inadequate training of law enforcement in schools, particularly for students and communities of color, those with disabilities, and all who experience inequity, racism, or social injustice. The well-being and safety of these individuals and communities must be prioritized in every school. (National Association of School Psychologists, 2020)

A BRIEF HISTORY OF SCHOOL POLICING, SECURITY, AND PUNITIVE DISCIPLINARY POLICIES

School safety practices and policies are at a critical juncture given the intersection of the educational, social, and emotional challenges of the COVID-19 pandemic; calls for racial justice; and tensions between law enforcement and communities of color. This chapter posits that researchers, policymakers, and practitioners need to rethink punitive approaches to school safety to incorporate responses to our nation's COVID-19 pandemic and calls for racial justice.

The United States has a long and negative history related to punitive measures in schools that harms students of color and places them at higher risk of being suspended or expelled, experiencing corporal punishment in school, and entering the juvenile justice system (Coles et al., 2021; Counts et al., 2018; Devlin & Gottfredson, 2018; Thurau & Or, 2019). These outcomes are not surprising given that school security and punitive discipline have been the core of school safety policies and programs in the United States for the last 50 years.

Concern over rising rates of violence and the focus on the War on Drugs in the 1980s and early 1990s resulted in schools rapidly adopting zero-tolerance policies for a wide range of behaviors and infractions in schools (e.g., weapons, drugs, tobacco, alcohol, violence; Hirschfield, 2008). This increase in punitive policies coincided with a dramatic increase in school policing through the creation of the Community Oriented Policing Services (COPS) in Schools program in the U.S. Department of Justice (2021) that provided funding and resources for schools to hire school resource officers (SROs).

Infractions such as possessing small quantities of drugs, making a threat, or carrying something that could be perceived to be a weapon were now frequently handled by school-based police with no consideration for any mitigating or situational circumstances (American Psychological Association Zero Tolerance Task Force, 2008; Hirschfield, 2008). Random locker searches, drug-sniffing dogs, and increases in security technology resulted from the growth of zero-tolerance policies and increased presence of law enforcement in schools (Hirschfield, 2008; Thurau & Or, 2019). Not unexpectedly, these practices and policies in schools resulted in dramatic increases in the suspension, expulsion, and arrest over time for even minor infractions that continue to disproportionately affect students of color and students with disabilities (Astor et al., 2021; U.S. Department of Education, Office for Civil Rights, 2021; Zimmerman & Astor, 2021).

Another factor driving punitive and security-based policies were mass school shootings in the early 1990s that drove a multibillion-dollar school security industry (Hsu, 2018; Schwartz et al., 2016; Tanner-Smith et al., 2018). Fear of mass shootings has affected school safety policies in the United States for decades, even though statistically, schools continue to be one of the safest societal contexts for children (Cornell, 2015; Nekvasil et al., 2015; Wang et al., 2020). Law enforcement and policing-oriented approaches view schools as "soft" targets that need deterrence measures to protect against "intruders" who intend to harm students (Marjory Stoneman Douglas H.S. Public Safety Commission, 2019). A deleterious outcome of pouring large amounts of funding into policing and security (e.g., SROs, metal detectors, search dogs, video surveillance, etc.) is that despite federal or state financial incentives or grants, local districts do not have unlimited funding and change with shifting administrations and priorities.

Recent data show that 14 million students in the United States attend schools with police but no counselor, nurse, psychologist, or social worker (Whitaker et al., 2019). During the pandemic with stimulus funding, these ratios are likely to change in a positive direction for a limited period. However, without permanent funding, the ratio of students to mental-health workers in schools will likely revert to previous levels. In some schools, the work of mental-health and health professionals has been defined as a law enforcement issue, yet with little training and supports for school-based law enforcement entities (Layton & Addo, 2021). The National Association of School Psychologists (NASP, 2020) recommends that the ratio of school psychologists to students not exceed 1 for every 500 students. Only one state currently meets this recommendation, and over 20 states have a ratio of more than 1,500 students per school psychologist (NASP, 2021). There is no national strategy or infrastructure to lower the ratio of students to counselors, social workers, nurses, and other helping professionals to ensure more supports are available to struggling students (e.g., Whitaker et al., 2019).

In addition to diverting resources that could fund better mental-health supports, increases in school security and punitive policies have a strong negative impact on students of color and students with disabilities. More specifically, suspension and expulsion rates, referrals to law enforcement, and punitive discipline rates are disproportionately and consistently higher for students of color and students with disabilities in urban, suburban, and rural communities across the United States, beginning even before students enter kindergarten (U.S. Department of Education, Office for Civil Rights, 2014, 2018, 2021). In fact, in 19 states, corporal punishment is legal in schools, and data show that students of color are more likely to experience corporal punishment than White students, regardless of the racial composition of the school they attend (Gershoff & Font, 2016). We should be asking what our schools need to be welcoming and supportive to all. And more importantly, how can policymakers help support that vision with infrastructure, training, and funding to ensure success and sustainability over time? These questions posed are the focal point of this chapter.

SHIFTING THE FOCUS TO SOCIAL, EMOTIONAL, AND MENTAL HEALTH, AND A POSITIVE SCHOOL CLIMATE

Reenvisioning education and schools across the United States must account for the large bodies of research that schools with strong, caring, culturally supportive, and positive climates can not only address issues of ongoing victimization but also prevent students from being victimized (Astor & Benbenishty, 2019; Astor et al., 2021; Capp & Astor, in press). Little evidence suggests that law-enforcement strategies have prevented school shootings or made schools feel safer for students (Counts et al., 2018; Schwartz et al., 2016; Whitaker et al., 2019). Given the existing evidence, policies need to shift from "hardening" practices to strategies that foster a positive community and civil relationships in schools (Rogers, 2019; Rogers et al., 2017; Rogers & Morrell, 2020). Significant research has highlighted the negative impact that security and law enforcement and punitive approaches can have on school climate, including lowering students' sense of belonging and safety and academic performance (Astor & Benbenishty, 2019; Bracy,

2011). These negative outcomes disproportionately affect students of color and students with disabilities, which can lead to social isolation, disengagement, and dropping out of school (Astor & Benbenishty, 2019; de Brey et al., 2019). Evidence suggests that school safety researchers should promote school policies that reflect a more caring, just, and civil society (Astor et al., 2021; Wray-Lake & Abrams, 2020; Wray-Lake et al., 2020, 2021).

This change requires a shift of funding and support from policing, punishment, and surveillance to long-term investments in holistic prevention and empowerment of schools and communities. Astor et al. (2021) demonstrated that when researchers work with schools to build capacity, infrastructure, and opportunities for all school constituents to have a voice in school safety programming and initiatives, impactful changes can happen and be sustained over time. Given wide local, regional, and state variation in populations, the most effective and appropriate interventions are driven by local school safety assessments, capacity building, integration of academic and social goals, partnerships with community organizations, consideration of the voices of all school stakeholders, and collaborations with universities (Astor & Benbenishty, 2018, 2019; Astor et al., 2021; Reynolds et al., in press).

New School Safety Policies Need to Include Boards of Education and Local District Administrators

School safety research and interventions have become highly politicized. Most school safety policy is nested in the administrators and school boards' local and regional jurisdictions. According to the National School Boards Association (NSBA; 2021), more than 90,000 school-board members in the United States oversee nearly 14,000 districts. School boards, along with local administrators, make critical decisions about some of the programs or policies that come into schools, but often cultural mismatches occur between elected board members and the parents or communities they serve (Samuels, 2020). A survey by the NSBA (2018) noted the mismatch between the characteristics of both elected (88%) and appointed (12%) board of education (BOE) members and the K–12 population in the United States. In 2017, K–12 students were 48% White, 16% Black, and 27% Hispanic or Latino, whereas BOE members were 78% White, 10% Black, and 3% Hispanic or Latino. In addition, BOE members had an average age of 59, were often retired (40%), and 68% of board members did not have children enrolled at the K–12 level (NSBA, 2018).

These demographics provide additional evidence of the need for collaborations and structures that help researchers and local policymakers assess the safety needs of individual districts and recommend data-driven, appropriate, and effective programs and policies that consider the perspectives of all school stakeholders (e.g., Datnow & Park, 2018). For example, a study looking at punitive discipline found that when Black and White school-board members have significant contact, the suspension rates of Black students in that district drop significantly (Hughes et al., 2017).

How do school districts know if safety related programs, personnel, and policies in their schools are effective or problematic? Substantive and well-supported collaborative efforts between districts and school safety researchers need to be first established to ensure data-driven, welcoming school safety programs and policies are implemented and evaluated. Currently, elected officials and local administrators face a plethora of social issues to consider in making programmatic and policy decisions (Samuels, 2020). Culture wars are taking place in local school districts over issues such as racial justice, the role of police in schools, arming teachers, and mandating a culturally appropriate curriculum (e.g., Gabriel & Goldstein, 2021).

The same issues are taking place at the state level. The National Conference of State Legislators (NCSL) indicates that, over the past 4 years, 796 school safety–related bills were proposed that addressed law enforcement, firearms/guns, and School Resource Officers (SRO's). In comparison, only 171 school safety–bills addressed mental health (NCSL, 2022). This again reinforces the disconnect between school and community safety evidence and current policy solutions.

Security and Law Enforcement in the Context of Punitive School Discipline Policies

The arguments to fund security measures in schools are generally based on fear, opinion, and often, political views (Reynolds, 2019; Reynolds & Astor, 2018). It is very important that policies involving firearms be based on empirical data. Most school shootings with mass casualties had armed personnel either on campus at the time of the shooting or there within minutes (Ingraham, 2018), and their presence failed to prevent the shootings or stop the shooter from using weapons on school grounds (e.g., Marjory Stoneman Douglas High School). Similarly, most mass shootings have occurred in schools that had security cameras, security protocols, and electronic monitoring systems (Berman & Meckler, 2018). And finally, most shooters were students or former students who were familiar with the layout of the school rather than a random stranger targeting a school (Ingraham, 2018; Livingston et al., 2019; Paradice, 2017).

More than 20,000 SROs work in schools across the country, which doesn't include the presence of armed security or "guardians" who are not active-duty law enforcement officers (e.g., National Association of School Resource Officers [NASRO], 2021). Federal funding (COPS in Schools and other grants) during the past several decades have encouraged schools to hire active-duty law enforcement to work full time in schools. Research on the effectiveness of SROs is mixed, and no definitive data have indicated that the presence of an SRO deters or lowers casualties in a mass school shooting (Counts et al., 2018; James & McCallion, 2013; Jennings et al., 2011). However, evidence suggests that punitive disciplinary policies and the presence of a law enforcement officer in schools can affect the number of students being suspended or expelled or entering the juvenile justice system or the school-to-prison pipeline, which have had devastating effects on students of color and students with disabilities (Counts et al., 2018; Devlin & Gottfredson, 2018; Ksinan et al., 2019; Okilwa & Robert, 2017).

The presence of law enforcement or security in schools coupled with punitive disciplinary policies (e.g., zero tolerance) creates a particular risk for students of color, in part due to different cultural and historical meanings of the presence of law enforcement. Harsh discipline and security measures have long been directly associated with the school-to-prison pipeline (Coles et al., 2021; Skiba, 2014; U.S. Department of Education, Office for Civil Rights, 2021). Although Black students represent 15% of student enrollment, they represent 29% of students referred to law enforcement and 32% of students subjected to school-related arrest (U.S. Department of Education Office for Civil Rights, 2021). Nearly 14% of Black and 7% of American Indian or Alaska Native students in the United States were suspended from school (one or more times), compared to 3.4% of White students, leading to fewer opportunities for some students to be active and engaged in the school setting (de Brey et al., 2019). Regarding students with disabilities, the rate of school arrests is 3 times that of students without disabilities, and it increases exponentially when police are present on campus (Whitaker et al., 2019). When expulsion rates are analyzed by gender, Black male students make up 8% of K–12 students but 23% of students who are expelled, and four times as many Black female students are arrested at school than White female students (U.S. Department of Education Office for Civil Rights, 2018).

Removing students from schools, especially students of color and students with disabilities, can result in negative perceptions of school and its climate, which can have long-term impacts on students' social and academic progress (de Brey et al., 2019). It is important to note that the removal of students from school through suspension and expulsion does not appear to result in consistent schoolwide or district-wide disciplinary policies. In fact, zero-tolerance practices create a more negative school climate and do not seem to serve as a deterrent for future student's behavior issues (American Psychological Association Zero Tolerance Task Force, 2008; Skiba, 2014). Despite federal and state funding and incentives, most states have very limited guidance and legislation related to SRO training, and 18 states "have no laws on SRO certification, use, or training" (Counts et al., 2018, p. 414). In the aftermath of the tragic shooting in Parkland, Florida, the Marjory Stoneman Douglas H.S. Public Safety Commission (2019) made recommendations focused on security and policing in schools and general support for "hardening" practices. On the other hand, NASRO, the largest training organization for school-based police in the United States, recently released a statement about the importance of "local and collaborative" decision-making that focuses on "weighing the risk of harm" with potential benefits prior to hiring law enforcement to work in schools (NASRO, 2020).

New York State's Every Student Succeeds Act Plan (2018) is an example of how social and emotional learning and climate variables can be prioritized by states. The New York State plan includes strategies and data collection relating to school environments, more specifically, improving school climate and increasing access to social and emotional supports (New York State Education Department, 2018). In 2019, New York State allocated 1.6 million dollars in grant money to 100 select districts to improve climate variables in the form of "Safe and Supportive School" grants (New York State Education Department, 2019). Having the flexibility and support at the state level to examine climate variables and social and emotional wellness of students and teachers as a part of accountability to the federal government, may reduce policing and provide more professional development, teaching, and promotion of welcoming and supportive school environments. Student academic and social development could be enhanced if school safety strategies were integrated into the whole school rather than isolated, standalone programs that may involve fragmented and siloed approaches that are not connected to the school mission or community (Astor et al., 2021).

Focus on the Whole School: Positive Climate, Democracy, Empowerment, and Safety Partnerships With Universities

What do school-safety policies and programs look like if they are data driven, holistic, and based on a whole-child ecological perspective that accounts for district-specific needs and conditions? Evidence-based programs and policies that focus on the whole school community have a significant impact on perceptions of safety in schools (e.g., Blueprints for Healthy Youth Development, 2020; Collaborative for Academic, Social, and Emotional Learning, 2021; Mayer & Jimerson, 2018). Our vision, as we detail in the following sections, involves creating the scaffolding and supports for universities and local policymakers to work collaboratively and focus on the best ways to address each community's unique school- and community-safety needs (e.g., Astor & Benbenishty, 2018, 2019; Astor et al., 2018; James & McCallion, 2013; Tanner-Smith et al., 2018).

Creating a Positive, Supportive, and Welcoming School Climate

A large body of research has demonstrated the positive impact of whole-school and whole-child prevention approaches that focus on developing and maintaining a welcoming and supportive climate and minimizing the removal of students from school (Astor & Benbenishty, 2019). A positive school climate is characterized by respectful student, teacher, and staff relationships; teacher and peer support; clear, fair, and consistent rules and disciplinary policies; support for diversity and inclusion; effective school–home communication; and student engagement and a sense of belongingness in their school and school activities (Astor & Benbenishty, 2018, p. 184). Multiple studies have found that a positive school climate has a strong relationship to reducing levels of overall victimization and the victimization of vulnerable (e.g., at-risk, gang-affiliated, LGBTQ) student groups (Astor et al., 2018; Berkowitz et al., 2017; De Pedro et al., 2018; Klein et al., 2012; Moore et al., 2019; Siegel et al., 2019). Sharing some of the same core principles, social and emotional learning refers to supports and processes that help "children and adults understand and manage emotions, set and achieve positive goals, feel and show empathy for others, establish and maintain positive relationships, and make responsible decisions" (Collaborative for Academic, Social, and Emotional Learning, 2021, para. 1). School safety researchers know that there are promising, data-driven findings indicating that programs that focus on schoolwide or district-wide efforts to improve school climate and promote social and emotional learning can lower levels of victimization in school and increase feelings of safety for all students (e.g., Astor & Benbenishty, 2019; Blueprints for Healthy Youth Development, 2020; Collaborative for Academic, Social, and Emotional Learning, 2021; Mayer & Jimerson, 2018). Strong evidence suggests that efforts to improve school climate or promote social and emotional learning are most impactful when they are schoolwide or district-wide and involve all stakeholders. When these programs are implemented with consistency across a district, all students experience significant improvements in academic and victimization outcomes, along with a reduction in discrepancies in academic achievement and discipline among students of color, students with lower socioeconomic status, and students with disabilities (e.g., Berkowitz et al., 2017).

Restorative-justice techniques and comprehensive threat-assessment teams are also a promising alternative to punitive, zero-tolerance policies when these programs are part of the comprehensive safety plan for a school or district (e.g., Gregory & Evans, 2020; Ispa-Landa, 2017). Restorative-justice practices focus on improving the overall culture and climate of the school through conflict resolution and problem solving; development and nurturing of positive relationships in the school environment; reinforcement of positive communication strategies; encouraging all students to be actively involved in their school; and promoting, teaching, and reinforcing respect for one another (Fronius et al., 2016; Gregory & Evans, 2020; Norris, 2019). Restorative practices, when clearly structured and used schoolwide, can effectively disrupt discrepancies in exclusionary punishment practices based on racial and disability status (Kervick et al., 2019). Another effective alternative to zero-tolerance policies is comprehensive threat assessment (Cornell, Maeng, Burnette, et al., 2018). These teams of trained school professionals use a step-by-step procedure to gather information and assess threats as either transient (not serious or intentional) or substantive (clear intent to carry out the threat). Appropriate interventions and supports are then instituted based on the needs of the student who made the threat and the safety needs of other students (Cornell, Maeng, Burnette, et al., 2018). When threat assessment is implemented on a district-wide basis, multiple studies (e.g., Cornell et al., 2009; Cornell & Bradshaw, 2015; Cornell & Maeng, 2018; Cornell, Maeng, Burnette, et al., 2018) have shown lower suspension rates across all racial and ethnic groups, a more positive school climate, fewer instances of bullying and violence, and increases in teachers feeling safe; one study found a 79% decrease in bullying (Nekvasil et al., 2015).

Addressing Simultaneous Use of Punitive and Restorative Approaches in the Same School or District

Many schools have started to include positive social and emotional learning and climate measures but have not removed preexisting punitive approaches. The simultaneous use of punitive and positive approaches to safety in the same school or district can lead to confusion about student discipline and send inconsistent messages to students about behaviors and consequences. Rather than funding competing programs or policies with conflicting messages, there is a need to develop a unified whole-school approach to safety (Astor et al., 2021; Astor & Benbenishty, 2019; Ispa-Landa, 2017). Although having both approaches is a common practice in schools, in part due to fragmented rather than unified policies and funding opportunities, we do not recommend the coexistence of both punitive and restorative or positive practices in the same school or district. It is critical that school-board members, superintendents, administrators, and teachers have access to research and training, both at the preservice level and through professional development, on the devastating impact exclusionary and punitive disciplinary practices can have on certain groups of students (U.S. Department of Education, Office for Civil Rights, 2018). Adding social and emotional learning or a program focused on improving climate to a school or district while still utilizing policing or punitive discipline does not make sense, is confusing, and is not data driven. Yet many districts opt for both as a form of political compromise without consideration of the mixed message this creates for the entire school community. Collectively, this research points us back to the need for national and state policymakers to work collectively to create structures that support systematic collaborations between local decision-makers and university partners.

Evidence of Grassroots Models and Recommendations for New Approaches to School Safety Policies After the Death of George Floyd

In the immediate aftermath of the killing of George Floyd, several districts (some of the largest in the country) decided to sever or reevaluate ties with local or municipal law enforcement entities in terms of school security. For example, in June 2020, the Minneapolis City School District Board of Education voted unanimously to cut ties with the Minneapolis Police Department. In the confusion of an ongoing pandemic and racial unrest, a data-driven conversation about what "depolicing" means in schools in communities across the country did not happen. This led to a wide range of depolicing measures, like cutting school-based policing (e.g., Oakland, CA; Seattle, WA), delegating decision-making about policing to local districts (e.g., Chicago, IL), reapportioning some or all funds to mental-health or student supports (e.g., Los Angeles, CA; Alexandria, VA), and reconceptualizing the idea of policing to include more training in antiracist practices, de-escalation, and the risk of punitive policies to students of color (e.g., Camera, 2021; Chavez, 2020).

The disentangling of law enforcement from schools after decades of federal support and unclear training protocols is complicated and needs to be done thoughtfully and purposefully. A report from Whitaker et al. (2019) that focused on overspending on law enforcement in schools recommended that "now more than ever, school boards and administrators need guidance to navigate their responsibility to ensure each of their students are safe from discriminatory discipline" (p. 9) and that this is particularly important at the local level. Local policymakers need to be aware of the importance of setting clear training and standards for individuals who may step into security roles in schools who are not police officers and, therefore, may have less training (NASP, 2020). Some cries for racial justice now center on policing not being an appropriate safety approach in every community and the importance of community input in terms of safety plans. For decades, the priority seemed to be providing more funding to get more police officers in schools (COPS in Schools), and the death of George Floyd has resulted in a fundamental shift in the national conversation about police officers in schools.

KEY COMPONENTS OF AN "OPTIMAL" VISION OF SCHOOL SAFETY

The NASP (2017), in collaboration with several other professional organizations, introduced recommendations that would allow districts to create and maintain comprehensive, research-based school safety policies. These recommendations include flexible and sustainable funding streams that allow schools to address their most pressing safety needs, promoting school–community partnerships, multi-tiered support systems, inter- and intra-agency collaborations, and the use of evidence-based standards (NASP,

2017). Partnerships, assessment, and sustainability are critical to the success of any school safety program. From a policy standpoint, funding, flexibility, incentives, and infrastructure to promote collaborations between universities and local decision-makers would make it more viable for districts to use data from a wide range of stakeholders to address their most pressing school-safety needs.

Making Data Central to Local Safety Decisions

When data and research are readily available, administrators and boards of education (BOEs) are more likely to make data-driven decisions when it comes to addressing school-safety needs (e.g., Thompson et al., 2007). This is particularly true if the data appear to be relevant to (or are collected from) individual districts. Studies that have looked at how data, research, or evidence are used in board decision-making reinforce the complexity of how policy-related decisions, particularly for emotionally fraught issues like school safety, are made (Astor et al., 2021; Canada, 2007; Kay & Carruthers, 2017; Thompson et al., 2007; Zlotkin, 1993). Asen et al. (2013) suggested that data can play a critical role in local decision-making through encouraging "productive disagreements that enable continued inquiry and discussion" (p. 59). As previously noted, it is critical to utilize local data from a representative sample of stakeholders to inform decision-making due to the fact that many BOE members do not represent the demographics or experiences of the students for whom they make decisions (NSBA, 2018).

Some factors increase the likelihood that research will drive policy decisions at the local level. A study by Honig and Coburn (2008) provided evidence that links between local school districts and university partners have a positive impact on evidence-based decision-making at the board table. Administrators' "external social capital," including ties with professional organizations and universities, can make social science research and evidence-based practice more accessible for districts. Relationships with external research organizations and entities can also facilitate the link between data and local conditions to ensure relevance (Honig & Coburn, 2008; Kay & Carruthers, 2017). Honig and Coburn (2008) concluded that ties between local districts and external entities (e.g., research foundations or universities) help in getting relevant research to the administration and, ultimately, the board table.

Expansion of University Partnerships

These shifts in perspectives on school safety support the development of a model for partnerships between universities and local district stakeholders to encourage the discussion of data-driven programs and policies on the local level. These partnerships should be integrated into the curriculum of teacher-, social worker-, school psychologist-, principal-, and superintendent-preparation programs in universities. Such partnerships would set up a system for key school personnel to develop an understanding of how to create welcoming, safe, and supportive schools through procedures and structures for collecting and using local data and constituent voices to drive safety policies and procedures in every school. Creating and sustaining infrastructure in preparation programs to encourage local data-driven decisions also would create an opportunity to address issues of school safety in terms of race, gender, disability status, policing and social justice, and punitive safety policies in an academic setting. In addition, this would help university-based preparation programs build capacity to help school professionals understand data-driven, welcoming, and growth-oriented school-safety policies and practices (Astor et al., 2021; Benbenishty & Astor, in press; Reynolds et al., in press). And local decision-makers need to be able to advocate for and have resources and funding available to support a whole-school approach to safety, which is more likely to have an impact and be sustained over time (see e.g., Astor et al., 2021).

It is important to recognize that these university–school and university–district collaborations should be focused on empowerment, local feedback, and local control. If data from a representative sample of stakeholders indicate that adding security is going to address their most pressing issues, these decisions need to be supported and respected, even if we know that national data point to the perils of focusing solely on security. The key is that these partnerships will allow for conversation, deliberation, and exposure to a variety of approaches to making schools safer, which means that all voices are considered, rather than only a few loud voices or interest groups. In addition, a university partnership would include local training opportunities that can focus on best practices, common issues, or barriers to the successful implementation of different school-safety approaches (Astor & Benbenishty, 2018; Astor et al., 2018).

The Importance of Training and Professional Development

It is likely impossible to remove politics from BOEs because many issues that are debated and considered are inherently political, which indicates the importance of training and professional development for local decision-makers regarding data-driven school safety practices and policies (e.g., Asen et al., 2013; Maeroff, 2010; Resnick & Bryant, 2010). In this current era of racial and social justice, it is critical that BOEs (whose members are Whiter and older than most district stakeholders in the United States) receive professional development and education related to best practices for creating safe schools, including (but not limited to) positive school climate, implicit bias, the unique needs of students with disabilities, and antiracism. Professional development for BOE members around issues such as systemic racism is likely to vary, and, in some cases, there may be state laws (e.g., Florida) prohibiting this content being discussed in school settings (Asmelash, 2021). To increase input and diversity of thought it is critical to create support and structures to recruit and retain BOE candidates who are ethnically and culturally representative of the students that they serve (Samuels, 2020). Above all, local data and the perspectives of all school stakeholders are critical for BOEs to make reasoned, evidence-based decisions, and university researchers are well positioned to help local leaders and policymakers compile, analyze, and make sense of both local and national school-safety data.

CONCLUSIONS AND RECOMMENDATIONS: DEMOCRACY, EMPOWERMENT, AND COMMUNITY VOICE

A vast literature indicates what works and what doesn't work in the field of school safety. Drawing from evidence-based programs and policies that have a positive impact on perceptions of safety in schools (e.g., Blueprints for Healthy Youth Development, 2020; Collaborative for Academic, Social, and Emotional Learning, 2021; Mayer & Jimerson, 2018) will help policymakers focus on the best ways to address their community's unique school and community safety needs (e.g., Astor & Benbenishty, 2018, 2019; Astor et al., 2018; James & McCallion, 2013; NASP, 2017; Tanner-Smith et al., 2018). Federal policies and funding that encourage schools to examine strategies for removing zero-tolerance, policing, and punitive policies are vital for a seismic shift to occur in how we approach school safety. It is critical that local stakeholders and decision-makers have the support of university collaborators to collect and analyze their own data and make evidence-based decisions that are appropriate for their district. Decades of research show that any "hardening" of security efforts needs to consider the potential impact on the climate of schools and also the disproportionate impact punitive discipline can have on students of color and students with disabilities in terms of academic success and feelings of connection to school (Astor & Benbenishty, 2019; Counts et al., 2018; Devlin & Gottfredson, 2018).

The COVID-19 pandemic and recent racial-justice movements have made it very apparent that our current approaches to keeping students safe and healthy in schools need major restructuring and reform. We lack mental-health supports in many schools at a time when students need them most (Whitaker et al., 2019). We are punishing and removing students of color from schools at much higher rates than White students, and students with disabilities are three times more likely to receive a punitive punishment than their nondisabled peers (e.g., de Brey et al., 2019). Additionally, there are strong calls from communities across the United States to remove law enforcement from schools immediately, with little planning or data-driven support. With the infusion of federal money into states and schools to help address student achievement losses and mental-health challenges as a result of the COVID-19 pandemic, we have an opportunity for real change (Kelly et al., 2020). This is an opportunity to create sustainable systems and infrastructure that help local districts address their most pressing safety needs through district-wide data-driven strategies that show long-term, positive outcomes for the entire school community (e.g., Datnow & Park, 2018).

Federal and state policymakers need to direct legislation and funding away from school policing to more holistic, supportive, and nonpunitive practices. There are some promising signs, including the Every Student Succeeds Act (ESSA) allowing some flexibility for states to examine school climate and social–emotional variables to help meet the reporting requirements for school quality or student success (Kostyo, Cardichon, & Darling-Hammond, 2018). Although not required, departments of education at the state level can choose to look at school climate and/or SEL through support from the National Center on Safe and Supportive Learning Environments and/or apply for federal-grant opportunities such as the School Climate Transformation Grant (National Center on Safe Supportive Learning Environments, 2022). This is a promising step but the funding for these initiatives is still miniscule when compared to the funding allocated to school-based policing. Incentivizing or requiring all states to evaluate school climate through providing infrastructure and financial support for collaborations between districts and researchers would likely increase the number of districts who include these variables in academic and safety-related discussions.

Years of research show us the value and effectiveness of inclusive and comprehensive safety programs and policies, prevention and investment in data-driven practices, and the creation of welcoming and supportive schools and districts (e.g., Astor & Benbenishty, 2019; Mayer & Jimerson, 2018). Empowering districts to invest in long-term, research-based solutions can begin with national calls to examine punitive disciplinary policies in every district in the United States and considering holistic and empowering models for safety. There are so much data to spark this conversation (e.g., Civil Rights Data Collection, Welcoming Empowerment Monitoring Approach). We now need structures and incentives for bringing decision-makers and researchers together over time for meaningful and goal-oriented interactions. Encouraging discussion and partnerships in the area of school safety is a key component of creating and sustaining holistic, evidence-based, financially viable, relevant, and data-driven school-safety solutions that work for all.

REFERENCES

American Psychological Association Zero Tolerance Task Force. (2008). Are zero tolerance policies effective in the schools? An evidentiary review and recommendations. *American Psychologist*, *63*(9), 852–862.

Asen, R., Gurke, D., Conners, P., Solomon, R., & Gumm, E. (2013). Research evidence and school board deliberations: Lessons from three Wisconsin school districts. *Educational Policy*, 27(1), 33–63.

Asmelash, L. (2021). Florida bans teaching critical race theory in schools. *CNN*. https://www.cnn.com/2021/06/10/us/critical-race-theory-florida-ban-trnd/index.html

Astor, R. A., & Benbenishty, R. (2018). *Mapping and monitoring bullying and violence: Building a safe school climate*. Oxford University Press.

Astor, R. A., & Benbenishty, R. (2019). *Bullying, school violence, and climate in evolving contexts: Culture, organization and time*. Oxford University Press.

Astor, R. A., Benbenishty, R., & Watson, K. R. (2021). A conceptual and large-scale empirical examination of the Welcoming Empowerment Monitoring Approach (WEMA) for school safety and substance use reduction. *Research on Social Work Practice*, 31(5), 454–468.

Astor, R. A., Jacobson, L., Wrabel, S., Benbenishty, R., & Pineda, D. (2018). *Welcoming practices: Creating schools that support students and families in transition*. Oxford University Press.

Benbenishty, R., & Astor, R. A. (in press). School safety and climate in evolving contexts. In C. Franklin, M. Harris, & P. Allen-Meares (Eds.), *The school services sourcebook* (3rd ed., Chapter 26). Oxford University Press.

Berkowitz, R., Moore, H., Astor, R. A., & Benbenishty, R. (2017). A research synthesis of the associations between socioeconomic background, inequality, school climate, and academic achievement. *Review of Educational Research*, 87(2), 425–469.

Berman, M., & Meckler, L. (2018, December 12). Parkland shooting commission describes school security lapses, police missteps. *The Washington Post*. https://www.washingtonpost.com/nation/2018/12/12/parkland-shooting-commission-finds-security-failures-improper-law-enforcement-responses-rampage/

Blueprints for Healthy Youth Development. (2020). *Providing a registry of experimentally proven programs*. https://www.blueprintsprograms.org

Bracy, N. L. (2011). Student perceptions of high-security school environments. *Youth & Society*, 43(1), 365–395.

Camera, L. (2021, May 25). Momentum stalls in fight to remove police from schools. *U.S. News and World Report*. https://www.usnews.com/news/education-news/articles/2021-05-25/momentum-stalls-in-fight-to-remove-police-from-schools

Canada, B. (2007). Gathering intelligence: New board members and administrators must have the right information and know how to use it. *American School Board Journal*, 194, 33–35.

Capp, G., & Astor, R. A. (in press). Improving school climate. In C. Franklin, M. Harris, & P. Allen-Meares (Eds.), *The school services sourcebook* (3rd ed., Chapter 28). Oxford University Press.

Chavez, N. (2020, June 28). A movement to push police out of schools is growing nationwide. Here is why. *CNN*. https://www.cnn.com/2020/06/28/us/police-out-of-schools-movement/index.html

Coles, M., Hicks, D., Portillo, M., Posey, E., Seidman, E., & Shah, K.C. (2021). *Safety beyond policing: Promoting care over criminalization*. Stanford Law School and Stanford Center for Racial Justice. https://www-cdn.law.stanford

.edu/wp-content/uploads/2021/03/Selective-De-Policing-Policy-Lab-report-April-2021.pdf

Collaborative for Academic, Social, and Emotional Learning. (2021). *Fundamentals of SEL*. https://casel.org/fundamentals-of-sel/

Cornell, D. (2015). Our schools are safe: Challenging the misperception that schools are dangerous places. *American Journal of Orthopsychiatry, 85*(3), 217–220.

Cornell, D., & Bradshaw, C. (2015). From a culture of bullying to a climate of support: The evolution of bullying prevention and research. *School Psychology Review, 44*(4), 499–503.

Cornell, D., & Maeng, J. (2018). Statewide implementation of threat assessment in Virginia K–12 schools. *Contemporary School Psychology, 22*, 116–124.

Cornell, D., Maeng, J. L., Burnette, A. G., Jia, Y., Huang, F., Konold, T., Datta, P., Malone, M., & Meyer, P. (2018). Student threat assessment as a standard school safety practice: Results from a statewide implementation study. *School Psychology Quarterly, 33*(2), 213–222.

Cornell, D., Sheras, P., Gregory, A., & Fan, X. (2009). A retrospective study of school safety conditions in high schools using the Virginia threat assessment guidelines versus alternative approaches. *School Psychology Quarterly, 24*(2), 119–129.

Counts, J., Randall, K. Ryan, J., & Katsiyannis, A. (2018). School resource officers in public schools: A national review. *Education and Treatment of Children, 41*(4), 405–430.

Datnow, A., & Park, V. (2018). Opening or closing doors for students? Equity and data use in schools. *Journal of Educational Change, 19*(2), 131–152.

de Brey, C., Musu, L., McFarland, J., Wilkinson-Flicker, S., Diliberti, M., Zhang, A., Branstetter, C., & Wang, X. (2019). *Status and trends in the education of racial and ethnic groups 2018* (NCES 2019-038). National Center for Education Statistics. https://nces.ed.gov/programs/raceindicators/indicator_rda.asp

De Pedro, K. T., Astor, R. A., Gilreath, T. D., Benbenishty, R., & Berkowitz, R. (2018). School climate, deployment, and mental health among students in military-connected schools. *Youth & Society, 50*(1), 93–115.

Devlin, D., & Gottfredson, D. (2018). The roles of police officers in schools: Effects on the recording and reporting of crime. *Youth Violence and Juvenile Justice, 16*(2), 208–223.

Fronius, T., Persson, H., Guckenburg, S., Hurley, N., & Petrosino, A. (2016). *Restorative justice in US schools: A research review*. WestEd Justice & Prevention Training Center.

Gabriel, T., & Goldstein, D. (2021, June 1). Disputing racism's reach, Republicans rattle American schools. *The New York Times*. https://www.nytimes.com/2021/06/01/us/politics/critical-race-theory.html

Gershoff, E. T., & Font, S. A. (2016). Corporal punishment in U.S. public schools: Prevalence, disparities in use, and status in state and federal policy. *Social Policy Report, 30*, 1.

Gregory, A., & Evans, K. R. (2020). *The starts and stumbles of restorative justice in education: Where do we go from here?* National Education Policy Center. http://nepc.colorado.edu/publication/restorative-justice

Hirschfield, P. (2008). Preparing for prison? The criminalization of school discipline in the U.S.A. *Theoretical Criminology, 12*(1), 79–101.

Honig, M., & Coburn, C. (2008). Evidence-based decision making in school district central offices: Toward a policy and research agenda. *Educational Policy, 22*(4), 578–608.

Hsu, T. (2018, March 4). Threat of shootings turns school security into a growth industry. *The New York Times.* https://www.nytimes.com/2018/03/04/business/school-security-industry-surges-after-shoootings.html

Hughes, C., Warren, P. Y., Stewart, E. A., Tomaskovic-Devey, D., & Mears, D. P. (2017). Racial threat, intergroup contact, and school punishment. *Journal of Research in Crime and Delinquency, 54*(5), 583–616.

Ingraham, C. (2018, March 1). For many mass shooters, armed guards aren't a deterrent, they're part of the fantasy. *The Washington Post.* https://www.washingtonpost.com/news/wonk/wp/2018/03/01/for-many-mass-shooters-armed-guards-arent-a-deterrent-theyre-part-of-the-fantasy/

Ispa-Landa, S. (2017). Racial and gender inequality and school discipline: Toward a more comprehensive view of school policy. *Social Currents, 4*(6), 511–517.

James, N., & McCallion, G. (2013). *School resource officers: Law enforcement officers in schools.* Congressional Research Service. https://fas.org/sgp/crs/misc/R43126.pdf

Jennings, W., Khey, D., Maskaly, J., & Donner, C. (2011). Evaluating the relationship between law enforcement and school security measures and violent crime in schools. *Journal of Police Crisis Negotiations, 11*(2), 109–124.

Kay, R., & Carruthers, L. (2017). Examining school board leaders' use of online resources to inform decision-making. *Canadian Journal of Learning and Technology, 43*(1), 1–25.

Kelly, M. S., Astor, R. A., Benbenishty, R., Capp, G., & Watson, K. R. (2020). *Opening schools safely in the COVID-19 era: School social workers' experiences and recommendations.* UCLA Luskin School of Public Affairs, Department of Social Welfare.

Kervick, C. T., Moore, M., Ballysingh, T. A., Raveche Garnett, B., & Smith, L. C. (2019). The emerging promise of restorative practices to reduce discipline disparities affecting youth with disabilities and youth of color: Addressing access and equity. *Harvard Educational Review, 89*(4), 588–610.

Klein, J., Cornell, D., & Konold, T. (2012). Relationships between school climate and student risk behaviors. *School Psychology Quarterly, 27*(3), 154–169.

Kostyo, S., Cardichon, J., & Darling-Hammond, L. (2018). Making ESSA's equity promise real: State strategies to close the opportunity gap. *Learning Policy Institute.* https://learningpolicyinstitute.org/sites/default/files/product-files/ESSA_Equity_Promise_REPORT.pdf

Ksinan, A. J., Vazsonyi, A. T., Ksinan Jiskrova, G., & Peugh, J. L. (2019). National ethnic and racial disparities in disciplinary practices: A contextual analysis in American secondary schools. *Journal of School Psychology, 74,* 106–125.

Layton, D., & Addo, R. (2021). Defunding school resources officers: A new commitment to school safety. *Journal of Policy Practice and Research.* Advance online publication. https://doi.org/10.1007/s42972-021-00042-1

Livingston, M. D., Rossheim, M. E., & Hall, K. S. (2019). A descriptive analysis of school and school shooter characteristics and the severity of school shootings in the United States, 1999–2018. *Journal of Adolescent Health*, 64(6), 797–799.

Maeroff, G. (2010). School boards in America: Flawed, but still significant. *The Phi Delta Kappan*, 91(6), 31–34.

Marjory Stoneman Douglas H.S. Public Safety Commission. (2019). *Initial report submitted to the governor, speaker of the House of Representatives and senate president*. http://www.fdle.state.fl.us/MSDHS/CommissionReport.pdf

Mayer, M., & Jimerson, S. (2018). *School safety and violence prevention: Science, practice, and policy driving change*. American Psychological Association.

Moore, H., Astor, R., & Benbenishty, R. (2019). Substance use off and on school grounds: A California statewide comparison between different groups of homeless students and non-homeless students. *Addictive Behaviors*, 92, 141–147.

National Association of School Psychologists. (2017). *Policy recommendations for implementing the framework for safe and successful schools*. Author.

National Association of School Psychologists. (2020). *NASP joins colleague organizations in clarifying use of SROs in schools*. https://www.nasponline.org/about-school-psychology/media-room/press-releases/nasp-joins-colleague-organizations-in-clarifying-use-of-sros-in-schools

National Association of School Psychologists. (2021). *Shortage of school psychologists*. https://www.nasponline.org/research-and-policy/policy-priorities/critical-policy-issues/shortage-of-school-psychologists

National Association of School Resource Officers. (2020). *NASRO joins other national organizations in call for rigorous training and appropriate use of school resource officers*. https://www.nasro.org/news/2020/08/14/news-releases/nasro-joins-other-national-organizations-in-call-for-rigorous-training-and-appropriate-use-of-school-resource-officers/

National Association of School Resource Officers. (2021). *NASRO mission*. https://www.nasro.org/aboutnasro/our-mission/

National Center on Safe Supportive Learning Environments (2022) *U.S. Department of Education School Climate Surveys (EDSCLS)*. https://www.air.org/centers/national-center-safe-supportive-learning-environments-ncssle

National Conference of State Legislators (2022). *School safety: Overview and legislative tracking*. https://www.ncsl.org/research/education/school-safety.aspx

National School Boards Association. (2018). *Today's school boards and their priorities for tomorrow*. https://cdn-files.nsba.org/s3fs-public/reports/K12_National_Survey.pdf

National School Boards Association. (2021). *About us*. https://www.nsba.org/about-us

Nekvasil, E., Cornell, D., & Huang, F. (2015). Prevalence and offense characteristics of multiple casualty homicides: Are schools at higher risk than other locations? *Psychology of Violence*, 5(3), 235–245.

New York State Education Department (2018). *New York State's final every Student Succeeds Act (ESSA) plan summary*. https://www.p12.nysed.gov/sss/ssae/schoolsafety/school-climate-survey-pilot.html

New York State Education Department (2019). *State Education Department awards $1.6 million in Safe and Supportive Schools Grants*. http://www.nysed.gov/news/2019/state-education-department-awards-16-million-safe-and-supportive-schools-grants

Norris, H. (2019). The impact of restorative approaches on well-being: An evaluation of happiness and engagement in schools. *Conflict Resolution Quarterly*, *36*(3), 221–234.

Okilwa, N. S., & Robert, C. (2017). School discipline disparity: Converging efforts for better student outcomes. *The Urban Review*, *49*(2), 239–262.

Paradice, D. (2017). An analysis of U.S. school shooting data (1840–2015). *Education*, *138*(2), 135–144.

Resnick, M., & Bryant, A. (2010). School boards: Why American education needs them. *Phi Delta Kappan*, *91*(6), 11–14.

Reynolds, H. (2019). Reflections of a board of education member in a time of politicization and intolerance. *Teachers College Record*. https://www.tcrecord.org/Content.asp?ContentId=22976

Reynolds, H., & Astor, R. A. (2018). Life and death school safety choices in search of data and science. *Teachers College Record*. http://www.tcrecord.org/Content.asp?ContentId=22600

Reynolds, H., Astor, R., Watson, K., & Marachi, R. (in press). Current approaches to school safety. In C. Franklin, M. Harris, & P. Allen-Meares (Eds.), *The school services sourcebook* (3rd ed., Chapter 27). Oxford University Press.

Rogers, J. (2019). For school leaders, a time of vigilance and caring. *Educational Leadership*, *77*(2), 22–28.

Rogers, J., Franke, M., Yun, J. E. E., Ishimoto, M., Diera, C., Geller, R. C., Berryman, A., & Brenes, T. (2017). *Teaching and learning in the age of Trump: Increasing stress and hostility in America's high schools*. UCLA IDEA. https://idea.gseis.ucla.edu/publications/teaching-and-learning-in-age-of-trump

Rogers, J., & Morrell, E. (2020). A force to be reckoned with. In M. Orr & J. Rogers (Eds.), *Public engagement for public education: Joining forces to revitalize democracy and equalize schools* (pp. 227–249). Stanford University Press.

Samuels, C. (2020). Why school board diversity matters. *Education Week*, *40*(13), 11–13.

Schwartz, H., Ramchand, R., Barnes-Proby, D., Grant, S., Jackson, B, Leuschner, K., Matsuda, M., & Saunders, J. (2016). *The role of technology in improving K–12 school safety*. RAND Corporation.

Siegel, A., Esqueda, M., Berkowitz, R., Sullivan, K., Astor, R. A., & Benbenishty, R. (2019). Welcoming parents to their child's school: Practices supporting students with diverse needs and backgrounds. *Education and Urban Society*, *51*(6), 756–784.

Skiba, R. J. (2014). The failure of zero tolerance. *Reclaiming Children and Youth*, *22*(4), 27–33.

Tanner-Smith, E, Fisher, B., Addington, L., & Gardella, J. (2018). Adding security but subtracting safety? Exploring use of multiple visible security measures. *American Journal of Criminal Justice*, *43*, 102–119.

Thompson, E., Stainback, G., & Stovall, J. (2007). Survey says: Data to guide policy decisions. *School Administrator*, *64*(1), 27–30.

Thurau, L., & Or, L. (2019). Two billion dollars later: States begin to regulate school resource officers in the nation's schools. *Strategies for Youth*. https://strategiesforyouth.org/sitefiles/wp-content/uploads/2019/10/SFY-Two-Billion-Dollars-Later-Report-Oct2019.pdf

U.S. Department of Education Office for Civil Rights. (2014). *Data shot: School discipline.* https://files.eric.ed.gov/fulltext/ED577231.pdf

U.S. Department of Education Office for Civil Rights. (2018). *2015–2016 civil rights data collection: School climate and safety.* https://www2.ed.gov/about/offices/list/ocr/docs/school-climate-and-safety.pdf

U.S. Department of Education Office for Civil Rights. (2021). *An overview of exclusionary discipline practices in public schools for the 2017–2018 school year.* https://www2.ed.gov/about/offices/list/ocr/docs/crdc-exclusionary-school-discipline.pdf

U.S. Department of Justice. (2021). *Community oriented policing services.* https://cops.usdoj.gov

Wang, K., Chen, Y., Zhang, J., & Oudekerk, B. A. (2020). *Indicators of school crime and safety: 2019* (NCES 2020-063/NCJ 254485). National Center for Education Statistics.

Whitaker, A., Torres-Guillén, S., Morton, M., Jordan, H., Coyle, S., & Mann, A. (2019). *Cops and no counselors: How the lack of school mental health staff is harming students.* American Civil Liberties Union. https://www.aclu.org/sites/default/files/field_document/030419-acluschooldisciplinereport.pdf

Wray-Lake, L., & Abrams, L.S. (2020). Pathways to civic engagement among urban youth of color. *Monographs of the Society for Research in Child Development*, *85*(2), 7–154.

Wray-Lake, L., Arruda, E. H., & Schulenberg, J. E. (2020). Civic development across the transition to adulthood in a national US sample: Variations by race/ethnicity, parent education, and gender. *Developmental Psychology*, *56*(10), 1948–1967.

Wray-Lake, L., Gniewosz, B., Benavides, C., & Wilf, S. (2021). Youth civic engagement: Exploring micro and macro social processes. In A. Kostić & D. Chadee (Eds.), *Positive psychology: An international perspective* (pp. 152–176). John Wiley & Sons.

Zimmerman, M. A., & Astor, R. A. (2021). Racism obstructs the path to school safety and educational equity: The need for an anti-racism focus in school violence prevention. *Journal of School Health*, *91*(6), 443–446.

Zlotkin, J. (1993). Rethinking the school board's role. *Educational Leadership*, *51*(2), 22–25.

CHAPTER 12

Toward Transformative Justice in School Finance

Oscar Jiménez-Castellanos, Danielle Farrie, and David M. Quinn

School finance policies have historically marginalized communities and limited access to resources and opportunity by race, class, culture, and language (Baker, 2016; Carter & Welner, 2013; Darling-Hammond, 2004; Jiménez-Castellanos, 2017). To overcome these past injustices, policymakers must engage in different and difficult conversations about forms of (in)justice and how to reconcile with historical under-investments. This chapter critiques school finance policy through different concepts of (in)justice to make the case for transformative justice in school finance. We articulate that school finance was primarily rooted in racial injustice pre–civil rights and has been rooted in what we call "remedial distributive justice" post-*Serrano*. We argue that school finance policies would be more just and effective if they went beyond a remedial distribution justice approach (coined in this chapter) toward a transformative approach.

It is impossible to accomplish transformational changes in education without rethinking how schools are financed—including costs for personnel, facilities, operations, and curriculum/materials. The allocated resources, and how they are used or misused, help shape the school culture and educational opportunity for students (Jiménez-Castellanos, 2010). Ultimately, these resources help determine student learning and student outcomes (Odden & Picus, 2003). The empirical research clearly shows that the distribution of resources has been historically unequal and inequitable favoring White affluent communities and undermining the plight of low-income, communities of color (Baker, 2016; Jiménez-Castellanos & Garcia, 2017).

SCHOOL FINANCE AS A TOOL FOR RACIAL INJUSTICE

We often pretend the United States operates a color blind, nonracialized meritocracy (Darder, 2015). Yet our school finance system cannot be separated from its systemic racist roots (Green et al., 2020; Jiménez-Castellanos et al., 2021), as explained throughout this book. School funding policies were designed as a tool for injustice to marginalize Black, Indigenous and people of color (BIPOC) and to privilege wealthy White communities (Jiménez-Castellanos et al., 2021). The following four sections will illustrate some of the original pillars (policies) of school-finance injustice.

Funding Public Schools Using Local Property Taxes

The United States is the only nation to fund elementary and secondary education based on local property wealth (Slavin, 1999). The Massachusetts Act of 1647 established that public schools be funded through local property tax, creating inherent inequalities based on the amount of revenue a locality can generate (Coons, Clune & Sugarman, 1970). In addition, this system created an asymmetrical power dynamic between those that owned property (Whites) and those who did not (non-Whites). Whites that owned property naturally would feel that the schools belonged to them and should cater to their children. In these times, very few enslaved Black Americans were able to buy their own freedom and purchase land, and Native people did not subscribe to the concept of "land owning." Funding schools through local property taxes remains a tradition today, albeit not the only source.

Education Is Not a Constitutional Right

The U.S. Constitution does not explicitly mention education nor guarantee any type of education. According to the Constitution Project, 195 out of 203 countries include education in their constitution, including all the countries outperforming the United States on international education performance metrics (www.constituteproject.org). The U.S. Constitution does require that each state have an education provision in its basic laws but does not provide any specific criteria for this provision. The *San Antonio v. Rodriguez* (1973) U.S. Supreme Court case reaffirmed a state's (not federal) obligation to provide an education. This federalism approach allows for 50 different education systems across the United States, largely ignoring the ecology of racial inequity in housing, health, environmental, safety, and many other social policies, as outlined in this book. Not guaranteeing education as a constitutional right, regrettably, has cemented injustice in the educational opportunity afforded to students based on the state and school district in which they reside.

Segregation and Racialized Funding Inequity

The Jim Crow era introduced many state and local racial segregation laws that reaffirmed economic, social, political, and educational racial discrimination (Anderson, 2015). These racist laws were institutionalized in the *Plessy v. Ferguson* U.S. Supreme Court decision of 1896 that legalized "separate but equal" across the United States. This ruling allowed not only southern states but states across the country to enact Jim Crow–type laws such as voter suppression, prohibiting interracial marriage, and segregated public accommodations (Muldoon, 2014). In terms of education, states prohibited racially mixed schools while some withheld funding from nonsegregated schools, and other laws stated that taxes paid by Black Americans go to maintaining African schools (Margo, 1990)—even after the *Brown* decision states (i.e., Texas) passed statutes that no child would be compelled to attend schools that are racially mixed.

Racialized Redlining and Districting

The term "redlining" derives from how the federal government and lenders would literally draw a red line on a map around the neighborhoods (most often in inner cities with predominantly Black Americans), in which they would not invest, based on demographics alone (Rothstein, 2017). Most modern school district boundaries were institutionalized in the mid-1900s, prior to *Mendez* 1946 and *Brown* 1954 desegregation decisions and reflected redlining policies and resulting segregation (Kelly, 2016). Homes in redlined neighborhoods are worth less than half that of the homes in what the government had deemed as "best" (Massey & Denton, 1993). Thus, the revenue generated through property taxes in redlined neighborhoods is significantly less than nonredlined neighborhoods. The more dependent a funding scheme is based on local property wealth, the greater the funding disparities between poor, BIPOC communities and wealthy, White neighborhoods (Rolle & Jiménez-Castellanos, 2014). The civil rights movement ushered in a new era of unparalleled federal and state intervention in schools to combat issues of race and poverty.

CIVIL RIGHTS MOVEMENT AND BEGINNING OF THE SCHOOL FINANCE LITIGATION ERA

Decades after the *Brown v. Board of Education (1954)* victory against *de jure* school segregation, civil rights leaders were still battling the gross inequities in educational opportunity resulting from *de facto* segregation and discriminatory school-funding policies that systematically disadvantaged students of color and those with limited economic power (Orfield & Frankenberg, 2014). Racist housing policies and state school-funding systems that were overly reliant on local property taxes entrenched a system defined by inequality (Jiménez-Castellanos, Kelly, & Carranza, 2021). Addressing the school-funding gaps between property-rich and property-poor communities emerged as a school finance litigation strategy. *Serrano* was the first successful school-finance litigation challenging a state's constitutional obligations.

There have been over 40 states that have faced school finance litigation since (Rebell, 2009).

State courts were the new battleground as civil rights advocates fought to dismantle school finance systems that perpetuated disadvantage and created glaring inequities among districts. The first phase of state finance litigation, ushered in by the *Serrano v. Priest* (1971) case in California, was dominated by cases challenging school funding under states' equal protection clauses (Minorini & Sugarman, 1999). By successfully arguing that California's spending disparities were driven by a reliance on property tax, and, therefore, education opportunity was determined by where one lived, *Serrano* was the first success in a long line of state finance cases using this *fiscal neutrality* standard (Berne & Stiefel, 1999). Post-*Serrano* school finance policy started to reflect Rawlsian principles of distributive justice in its determination of how resources should be allocated across districts and schools.

SCHOOL FINANCE AS A TOOL FOR REMEDIAL DISTRIBUTIVE JUSTICE

According to Rawls's "difference principle," the unequal distribution of some good across members of society can be justified when the unequal distribution benefits the least advantaged more than they would benefit under an equal distribution of that good. In a society in which wealth and privilege confer advantages in access to educational resources and learning opportunities, the difference principle justifies allocating more funding toward the education of students from marginalized or less economically advantaged backgrounds. In a school finance context, this is referred to as "vertical equity," or the appropriately unequal treatment of unequals. This contrasts with "horizontal equity," which does not require more than equal treatment of equals (Berne & Stiefel, 1999).

While this marks a meaningful shift in the goals of school finance policy, we argue that the exclusive focus on distributive justice in school finance limits the ability to create a system of transformative justice. A system of vertical equity in school finance does not attend to the root causes of injustice but rather attempts to remediate, through the institution of schooling, the unequal distribution of benefits and burdens found in society more generally. We term this "remedial distributive" justice. The next sections review how this remedial distributive justice framework in school finance evolved.

Evolution and Limitations of Remedial Distributive Justice in School Finance

Lyndon Johnson's War on Poverty greatly expanded the federal government's role in efforts to reduce poverty through the expansion of social programs. It is important to note that poverty, not race, was selected as the primary area to focus on through federal interventions. The Elementary and Secondary Education Act of 1965 (ESEA) was a major initiative that directed federal funds to states and school districts to improve educational opportunities for low-income students. Under the Title I program within ESEA, the federal government supplements funding in high-poverty districts so these schools can establish programs to compensate for the social and economic disadvantages faced by students raised in low-income communities.

The remedy implicit in subsequent equity-driven school funding litigation is a redistribution of resources to reduce or eliminate spending gaps between wealthy and low-income communities. State legislators responded by adopting equalization plans in which state aid is allocated to supplement property-poor districts' local property taxes (Bosworth, 2001). Equity-focused litigation forced states to focus on the financial consequences of relying on local property taxes for school funding but did not address the ability of districts to provide equal educational opportunity (Odden & Picus, 2003). A next phase of litigation turned instead to states' constitutional obligation to provide citizens a minimum standard of education through adequacy.

Replacing "equity" with "adequacy" allowed the courts to move beyond a relative standard of resource allocation—where district spending is compared to each other—and, instead, focus on an absolute standard—where the central question is: How much funding is required to allow students to meet the state's curricular benchmarks (Clune, 1994)? Adequacy-based claims take the important step of recognizing that true equity cannot be achieved simply with an *equal* distribution of resources, but outcomes of resource allocation also must be taken into consideration. Adequacy-focused litigation often focuses on the diverse needs of the state's student population, with particular attention to the supplementary resources that are necessary to ensure historically marginalized groups, such as students from low-income families, English language learners, and students with disabilities have a meaningful opportunity to achieve the state's educational standards (Jiménez-Castellanos & Topper, 2012; Underwood, 1995).

While Johnson's original explicit goal with the War on Poverty was to use education as a tool to eliminate poverty, this lofty goal was obviously not achieved. ESEA, and its later reauthorizations as the No Child Left Behind Act and the Every Student Succeeds Act, have been decoupled from a wider economic policy agenda, and instead have shifted to a purely remedial focus in which additional, but insufficient, funding is intended to compensate for systemic inequalities that exist among students and schools (Jiménez-Castellanos, 2012; Shores, Lee & Williams, 2021). This remedial approach consists of "solutions" involving academically low-quality programs, inexperienced teachers, and inferior facilities (Jiménez-Castellanos, 2010). Monetary resources alone that are conceived from a remedial perspective have been shown to be insufficient for addressing the root causes of educational injustices.

Policymakers may conceive of the redistribution process as one aimed at compensating for deficiencies of individual classes of students. The rhetoric and data deployed as part of the "racial achievement gap discourse" in such a context obscure the historical and structural sources of educational inequality and reinforce racial stereotypes (Ladson-Billings, 2006; Quinn, 2020). This can contribute to a standard of equity in which certain marginalized groups of students are held to an uncritical, hegemonic standard of "success" in a system that does not necessarily value the strengths and talents they possess.

While these federal education programs have expanded, they do so within a broader society that has failed to truly grapple with inequality, including systemic racism, and instead lays more and more responsibility upon schools to remediate the dysfunction of the greater economic system. A remedial distributive justice approach to school finance takes for granted these inequalities in society broadly, and attempts to use school finance as a tool for providing human capital development opportunities that enable students to compete for the more desirable positions within an economically and socially stratified system. In contrast, a transformative-justice approach would require uprooting the sources of these broader inequalities.

TOWARD TRANSFORMATIVE JUSTICE IN SCHOOL FINANCE

The concept of transformative justice emerges from a critique of restorative justice. Critics have observed that the notion of "restoration" suggests the goal is to return to some prior state of affairs. However, when the prior state of affairs involves systems or structures that produce injustices (such as the instance of injustice that motivated the call for restoration), restoration means reverting to injustice. In contrast, transformative justice requires addressing the conditions that led to the injustice (Coker, 2002; citing Morris, 1994). For example, a transformative-justice approach to a burglary would not only consider the burglary itself but would seek to address the sociopolitical injustices that may have created the context leading to the burglary (Nocella & Anthony, 2011), such as poverty and economic inequality.

A transformative-justice paradigm in school finance requires a fundamental rethinking of how we fund public schools at the federal, state, and district levels to serve the most vulnerable populations. We propose that transformative justice is a combination of structural justice + asset-based distributive justice + dignitary justice + procedural justice. The following sections will briefly describe each component and how they are combined to form transformative justice. While laying out a detailed vision of transformative justice in education funding is beyond the scope of this chapter, we sketch some thoughts on what such a vision would entail.

Structural Justice

Structural injustice has been conceived in various ways in the literature (McKeown, 2021; Young, 1990), but it has generally been understood as injustice that results from the actions of many individuals and institutions acting in their own self-interest but without violating accepted rules or norms. In the context of education, consider the fact that students from higher-income backgrounds tend to have more highly qualified teachers (e.g., Clotfelter et al., 2007). This is not the result of any intentional rule governing the assignment of teachers but rather a result of higher-income school districts being better-funded and more capable of using higher salaries and better working conditions to attract effective teachers.

In the systems perspective on race discrimination (Reskin, 2012), a social subsystem like schooling is understood to be causally interrelated with other social subsystems, such as housing, health care, the labor market, the criminal legal system, and so on. The interconnectedness of these systems means that racial discrimination in any one of them impacts racial disparities in other subsystems (Reskin, 2012). Given the school system's embeddedness in the larger race-discrimination system, the redistribution of school resources alone will be insufficient for providing equal educational opportunity by race.

As argued above, school finance has been a tool for structural racial injustice (Feagin, 2006; Jiménez-Castellanos et al., 2021). A transformative-justice approach would require addressing the broader economic, racial, and political inequalities that give rise to our inequitable school system (Bishop & Noguera, 2019). Moreover, structural justice would require critically interrogating and acknowledging that our school finance system is grounded in coloniality and White supremacy that has historically marginalized Black, Indigenous, Latinx and immigrant people and communities. Structural justice requires embracing an antiracist approach to actively work toward dismantling systems, privileges, and everyday practices that reinforce and normalize the contemporary dimensions of White dominance (Kendi, 2019). Not until we move toward an antiracist school finance system will we be able to achieve the promise of equal educational opportunity for all.

Asset-Based Distributive Justice

Transformative justice requires moving beyond a remedial distributive justice that is narrowly concerned with compensating for both past and present injustices by either equalizing funding or providing modest increases targeted to students and communities who had been historically deprived of adequate educational opportunities.

Crucial to this new vision is replacing a deficit-based model of distributive justice with an asset-based model. In broad terms, this means changing the focus from remedies that compensate for perceived deficits of marginalized groups and communities and instead creating systems that build on and sustain the linguistic and cultural diversity in school communities (Gonzalez, Moll, & Amanti, 2005; Valencia, 1997). Decades of work by education researchers has focused on the pedagogical benefits of an asset-based framework. The field has evolved from Gloria Ladson-Billings's (1995) groundbreaking work on culturally relevant pedagogy to Alim and Paris's (2017) extension to culturally sustaining pedagogy. The foundation of this work is that students' success is dependent on teaching and curriculum that both values students' cultural knowledge and experiences and gives them the tools to critically assess the world around them.

In terms of school finance, this means expanding notions of the "additional" resources that students need to succeed. Instead of programs and services that focus narrowly on students' ability to meet state benchmarks, an asset-based model would focus on programs that build on students' existing talents, explore and deepen their understandings of their own culture through literacy and art, and provide them with the tools they need to critically engage with the social and political systems surrounding them. Developing this curricular framework requires incorporating key concepts of dignitary procedural justice so that diverse stakeholders are included, and their perspectives are valued.

Procedural and Dignitary Justice

Procedural justice pertains to the mechanisms or procedures involved in the exchange or allocation of resources, rights, obligations, rewards, or other things of value (Brighouse et al., 2018, Cook & Hegtvedt, 1983). In contrast to distributive justice, which concerns the fairness of a given outcome distribution, procedural justice concerns the fairness of the process for how that distribution was arrived at. Scholars of procedural justice in policing and the courts have proposed four features of a procedurally just system, which we argue apply to school financing systems. First, stakeholders to school financing decisions must have voice. That is, concerned parties must have a way to express their concerns and participate in the decision-making process. Second, throughout the process, all stakeholders must be treated with dignity and respect. Third, decisions must be made in an unbiased and transparent manner. Fourth, those holding decision-making authority must be trustworthy in their concern for the well-being of affected parties (Quattlebaum et al., 2018). Thus, it is important to democratize who, how, and by what means, policy and practice decisions related to funding and resource allocation are being made. Parents and students should be much more integrated in the decision-making process.

A central feature of procedural justice—the importance of dignity—is sometimes considered as a type of justice in its own right—"dignitary justice" (Darby & Rury, 2018). Dignitary justice requires *status equality,* in which every person is recognized as having equal moral worth (regardless of national origin, religion, race, gender, class, etc.) (Darby & Rury, 2018). In the context of school finance, dignitary justice requires that funding allocations are not determined through oppressive group relations in which some groups are marginalized, exploited, powerless, stigmatized, or culturally imposed upon (Anderson, 2010; Young, 1990). Rather, funding allocations must be determined through relations in which everyone is recognized as moral and social equals. Achieving transformative justice in school finance policy requires a holistic, ecological approach that integrates radical changes to the way state, local, and federal policy are used to distribute revenues and resources to schools.

PROMISING CASE STUDIES: ACROSS ALL LEVELS OF GOVERNMENT

Bishop and Noguera (2019) frame educational equity focusing on systems design, out-of-school factors, practices, and resources to serve a diverse community context of race, class, culture, and language. Borrowing from Bishop and Noguera (2019), Bronfenbrenner (1981) and Jiménez-Castellanos et al. (2010), we suggest an ecological model that includes four embedded levels of systems: 1. Local (school/district) 2. State 3. Federal 4. Time/Space. A major assumption underlying an ecological paradigm is that the different systems within a place and time are interdependent and that all interactions across these systems are bidirectional. It is imperative to address all levels to truly transform school finance—one of the most entrenched and inequitable segments of education.

To be clear, we do not believe or suggest that we have achieved a transformative model yet. However, there are a few promising case studies that have the potential to provide insight into how we might move toward a transformative model. In the following sections, we provide promising case studies at the federal, state, and local levels.

State-Level Promising Case Study: New Mexico

In 2018, a ruling in the consolidated *Yazzie/Martinez v. State of New Mexico* lawsuit found that New Mexico was violating its state constitution by not providing students with the programs and services necessary to prepare them for college and career. The judge explicitly found that the state was failing to comply with state and federal law applying to students of color and English learners. The ruling put the State under court order to comprehensively overhaul the programs and funding necessary to address the overall inadequacy of resources and inequities for Native American students, English learners, students with disabilities and students from low-income families.

New Mexico's legal case was bolstered by a strong advocacy and research effort seeking to provide a new framework to "transform our public schools to embrace the strengths of our students and lay the foundation for learning and success" (Transform Education NM, 2021). Transform Education NM (TENM) developed a platform based on trial evidence and expert reports, and reflecting the knowledge and vision of students, parents, educators, and local experts for what students need to succeed. This platform is centered on student equity and fully embraces a multicultural and multilingual foundation using an asset-based framework to remedy existing inequities. The following are key approaches for what the platform demands:

- An intentional, well-planned, antiracist approach to ensuring equity.
- A just and decent education system that not only responds to the state's unique heritage but honors and works to build upon and leverage the multicultural and multilingual heritage.
- Linguistically responsive curriculum and instructional materials, bilingual education and dual language programs, and teacher preparation to create learning environments that embrace the cultures, languages, and heritages of our students.

The expansive education platform outlined by TENM makes explicit that sufficient funding is required to allow districts and schools to provide the resources and supports called for in their plan. Districts need additional funding to invest in professional development for staff, culturally appropriate curricula and instructional materials, bilingual programs, addressing teacher shortages, health, and social services, and more.

A complementary education platform was developed by the Tribal Education Alliance with a determined focus on how the *Yazzie/Martinez* decision could be leveraged to transform education policy for Native students. The report argues that "one-sided, one-way education policies and practices—whether relating to curriculum, governance, or accountability—must give way to a new balance, a transformational approach to education that enables mutual, reciprocal relations" (Rudiger, 2020, p. 3). This educational platform clearly identifies the harm of an exploitative and inadequate education system imposed upon tribal communities with no intention to understand or cultivate their existing cultural values. In contrast, the Tribal Remedy Framework offers a vision of "significant, systemic transformation to address historical injustices and ensure equitable outcomes" (p. 6). The report includes three strategic solutions:

- Shared responsibility and increased tribal control over the schooling of Native children.
- Community-based education, created by and centered within tribal communities.
- A balanced, culturally, and linguistically relevant education that revitalizes and sustains the strengths of children and their communities.

Unfortunately, these platforms have yet to be adopted into state policy. Despite the 2018 *Yazzie/Martinez* ruling of clear constitutional violations, the state legislature has yet to adapt these platforms into coherent policies that would constitute an acceptable remedy. So, while New Mexico's experience provides a bold example of how successful finance litigation can usher in transformational school finance reforms, New Mexico is still, like so many states, stuck at the remedy phase as the state's leadership fails to rise to the level of urgency demanded and expressed with such clarity by its citizens.

Local-Level Promising Practice: Sanger Unified School District, CA

With the enactment of Local Control Funding Formula (LCFF) in 2013, California completely overhauled its finance system to improve the overall adequacy and equity of school funding in California. The LCFF is a weighted student formula that provides additional resources for students from low-income families, English learners, homeless, and foster youth. The LCFF also provides districts significantly more flexibility in how they spend their funds but does so in exchange for greater accountability. Districts are required to spend certain funds on services for high-need students and must implement Local Control Accountability Plans (LCAP) that define how funds should be spent to achieve district goals. While districts are accountable to the state for implementing plans that reflect the LCFF's priority areas (conditions of learning, student outcomes, and engagement), districts have flexibility in determining how they will use their resources to achieve those goals (California Department of Education, n.d.). This creates a tension between local control and equity goals since local decision-making without equity guidelines often creates inequitable outcomes (Jiménez-Castellanos, Lopez, & Rivera, 2019).

In the following example, we show how one school district has been able to leverage this new flexibility to implement research-tested strategies to improve student outcomes and school culture. While this example may fall short of the transformational change we believe is required, it offers a sense of what is possible under existing finance structures and could be used as a springboard for envisioning and implementing more transformative policies and practices.

Sanger USD is a school district of about 12,000 predominantly low-income, majority Latino students in California's Central Valley. It was recently named one of the Learning Policy Institute's (LPI) "positive outlier" districts for outperforming expectations (Podolsky et al., 2019). LPI's case study of Sanger documented the many ways in which the district built on a successful turnaround record to continue to improve instruction and student support as it transitioned to the Common Core State Standards (CCSS) (Talbert & David, 2019). Many of these strategies include elements that are key to our conception of transformative school finance. For example:

- Challenging traditional power structures by creating a culture of collaboration between administrators and teachers which was crucial for the successful adoption of new policies and programs.
- Invoking procedural justice in the development of Multi-Tiered Systems of Support (MTSS) to reduce suspensions and support academic achievement for English learners, students from low-income families, and students with disabilities. The district created a 25-member committee representing socioeconomically disadvantaged communities, English learners, foster and homeless students, the teacher's union, and certified staff to develop goals and priorities for enhancing social–emotional supports for students.
- A strong commitment to civic-participatory engagement through family literacy nights, educational programs for Spanish-speaking parents, and leading a Community of Caring Task force comprising faith-based organizations, youth organizations, local politicians, and law enforcement.

While districts are dependent on state finance policy to create an adequate and equitable distribution of resources, the local school district often has significant control over how those funds are spent. District policies that prioritize equity and are reflective of community needs and desires can support transformative school finance decision-making that benefits historically marginalized groups. California's LCAP requirements are clearly an attempt to embed these processes within district budgeting practices. However, it must be noted that LCAPs have received a fair amount of criticism, from the difficulty to engage parents in budget conversations to the process being "unwieldy and burdensome" (Koppich et al., 2018). These are the challenging conversations school districts must have with parents and students to authentically engage them in the decision-making process that merges procedural and dignitary justice.

Federal Level Promising Practice: COVID-19 Stimulus Funds

As outlined previously, the federal government has historically played a limited yet important role in school funding in the United States. Under the expansion of federal funding with ESSA and its recent reauthorizations, the federal government does supplement state and local funding with additional resources designated for low-income students, students with disabilities, and English learners. In the context of overall education spending, the total amount of funding is quite small, historically underfunded, and does little to improve the overall adequacy and equity of funding (Baker et al., 2010; Cascio & Reber, 2013).

However, there are two examples of unprecedented federal intervention into school finance that offered the potential for more meaningful change. In response to 2008's Great Recession, the federal government sent $40 billion in American Recovery and Reinvestment Act (ARRA) and State Fiscal Stabilization Funds (SFSF) to states to protect education budgets during the economic crash. Then, in 2020, as states struggled to deal with the economic and logistical challenges of providing public education during the COVID-19 pandemic, Congress authorized over $200 billion in Elementary and Secondary School Emergency Relief Funds (ESSER) (USDOE, 2021).

The differences in how these funds were allocated provide an interesting contrast in how federal money can either contribute to, or help ameliorate, school finance inequities. The SFSF included objectives to (1) restore funding to pre-recession levels, (2) implement prior-enacted increases or equity/adequacy adjustments, and (3) maintain a floor of overall support for K–12 education. However, in practice, many states did not meet these benchmarks, and there was little federal oversight to determine compliance (Sciarra et al., 2010). Moreover, many states appropriated the federal funds so that they eventually faced a fiscal cliff. States essentially created deep holes in their education budgets, filled them with limited and nonrecurring federal funds, then faced drastic cuts to state education aid when those federal funds ran out (Leachman et al., 2017). The resulting state education cuts were often regressive, most negatively affecting high-poverty districts most dependent on state funding.

Congress took a decidedly different tack with ESSER funds. The majority of ESSER funds were allocated to school districts using the Title I formula and, therefore, were progressively distributed relative to student poverty. The largest allocation, under the American Rescue Plan (ARP), has both maintenance of effort and maintenance of equity provisions designed to ensure that the previous backfilling and regressive budget cuts were not repeated. ESSER funds are also more restricted than SFSF, though still quite flexible. Funds can be used for education expenses allowed under existing federal programs and for other specific COVID-related expenses (Griffith, 2021). For example, districts can use the funding to support community schools, innovative bilingual programs, and efforts to diversify the workforce. Notably, the ARP ESSER funds include a requirement that school districts engage the community in decisions about how the funding is spent, though the allowable strategies are often thin and unlikely to result in meaningful collaboration (Makori et al., 2021).

While these federal interventions do not meet our definition of transformative school finance policy, they do at least show a growing commitment, at least temporarily, to prioritize equity in federal education policy. The major drawback with this practice is that in 2 years the funding will need to be spent and no additional funds are scheduled to replace these stimulus funds. With limited power to intervene in how schools are funded, the most recent actions do suggest a willingness for federal policy to more deeply engage with the core concepts of fairness and procedural justice that are necessary for transformative change. The challenge is to sustain this level of investment in education and for districts to receive support in how to use these funds from an asset-based perspective in full concert with the parents and students they serve.

CONCLUSION

The U.S. school finance system was built upon a racist and White supremist foundation that promoted racial injustice (Jiménez-Castellanos et al., 2021; Margo, 1990). Though the last 50 years has seen improvements to the historically overtly racist and classist school finance systems in the United States, in this chapter we outlined the many ways that society's broader injustices remain reflected in states' approaches to school funding. We argue that the remedial distributive framework used in the most recent wave of adequacy-based school finance reforms does not go far enough to engage with notions of justice that are required for transformational change. Despite the proliferation of adequacy litigation, vast disparities in funding among and within states persist and merely a third of states currently allocate funding so that high-poverty districts receive even a small boost in funding over low-poverty districts (Farrie & Sciarra, 2021). There is no shortage of research finding significant disparities in students' access to the resources they need to succeed (Carter & Welner, 2013; Jiménez-Castellanos, 2010).

We offer a new transformational justice paradigm that requires the synthesis of structural justice, asset-based distributive justice, dignitary justice, and procedural justice through an ecological framework that integrates local, state, and federal policy. This approach will require policymakers at all levels to seek meaningful engagement from communities and value the input of diverse stakeholders, redefine success beyond the traditional metrics such as standardized assessments, and integrate culturally relevant curricula. Crucially, this also entails determining and then providing a sufficient level of resources that will allow schools and districts to meet these goals. As our case studies demonstrate, schools and communities already possess much of the knowledge that is needed to radically transform our school systems to meet the diverse and ever-changing needs of students and staff. What is needed now is the political will and financial investment to put these plans into action.

REFERENCES

Alim, H. S., & Paris, D. (Eds.) (2017). *Culturally sustaining pedagogies: Teaching and learning for justice in a changing* . Teachers College Press.

Anderson, E. (2010). *The imperative of integration.* Princeton University Press.

Anderson, J. (2015). A Long shadow: the American pursuit of political justice and education equality. *Educational Researcher, 44*(6), 319–335

Baker, B. D. (2016). School finance & the distribution of equal educational opportunity in the postrecession U.S. *Journal of Social Issues, 72*(4), 629–655

Baker, B. D., Sciarra, D. G., & Farrie, D. (2010). *Is school funding fair? A national report card.* Education Law Center.

Berne R. & Stiefel, L. (1999). Concepts of school finance equity: 1980 to the present, In H. F. Ladd, R. Chalk, & J. S. Hansen (Eds.), *Equity and adequacy in education finance: Issues and Perspectives* (pp. 7–33). National Academies Press.

Bishop, J., & Noguera, P. (2019). The ecology of educational equity: Implications for policy. *Peabody Journal of Education, 94*(2), 122–141.

Bosworth, M. H. (2001). *Courts as catalysts: State supreme courts and public school finance equity.* State University of New York Press.

Brighouse, H, Ladd, H., Loeb, S., & Swift, A. (2018). *Educational goods: Values, evidence, and decision-making.* University of Chicago Press.

Bronfenbrenner, U. (1981). *The ecology of human development experiments by nature and design.* Harvard University Press.

California Department of Education. (n.d.) *LCFF priorities/Whole child resource map.* https://www.cde.ca.gov/eo/in/lcff1sys-resources.asp

Carter, P. L., & Welner, K. G. (2013). *Closing the opportunity gap: What America must do to give every child an even chance.* Oxford University Press.

Cascio, E. U., & Reber, S. (2013). The poverty gap in school spending following the introduction of Title I. *American Economic Review, 103*(3), 423–427.

Clotfelter, C. T., Ladd, H. F., Vigdor, J. L., & Wheeler, J. (2007). *High-poverty schools and the distribution of teachers and principals* (CALDER Working Paper 1). The Urban Institute.

Clune, W. H. (1994). The shift from equity to adequacy in school finance. *Educational Policy, 8*(4), 376–394.

Coker, D. (2002). Transformative justice: Anti-subordination processes in cases of domestic violence. In H. Strang & J. Braithwaite (Eds.), *Restorative justice and family violence* (pp. 128–152). Cambridge University Press.

Constitute Project. (2021). *Free education.* https://www.constituteproject.org/topics?lang=en

Cook, K. S., & Hegtvedt, K. A. (1983). Distributive justice, equity, and equality. *Annual review of sociology, 9*(1), 217–241.

Coons, J. E., Clune, W. H., & Sugarman, S. D. (1970). *Private wealth and public education*. Harvard University Press.

Darby, D., & Rury, J. L. (2018). *The color of mind: Why the origins of the achievement gap matter for justice*. University of Chicago Press.

Darder, A. (2015). *Culture and power in the classroom: Educational foundations for the schooling of bicultural students*. Routledge.

Darling-Hammond, L. (2004). The color line in American education: Race, resources, and student achievement. *Du Bois Review: Social Science Research on Race. 1*(2), 213–246

Farrie, D., & Sciarra, D. G. (2021). *Making the grade 2021: How fair is school funding in your state?* Education Law Center.

Feagin, J. (2006). *Systemic racism: A theory of oppression*. Routledge.

Gonzalez, N., Moll, L., & Amanti, C. (2005). *Funds of knowledge: Theorizing practices in households, communities and classrooms*. Erlbaum.

Green, P., Baker, B., & Oluwole, J. (2020). School finance, race, and reparations. *Washington and Lee Journal of Civil Rights and Social Justice. 27*(2), 483–557.

Griffith, M. (2021). *An unparalleled investment in U.S. public education: Analysis of the American rescue plan act of 2021*. Learning Policy Institute. https://learningpolicyinstitute.org/blog/covid-analysis-american-rescue-plan-act-2021

Jiménez-Castellanos, O. (2010). Relationship between educational resources and school achievement: A mixed method intra-district analysis. *The Urban Review, 42*(4), 351–371.

Jiménez-Castellanos, O. (2012). Revisiting the Coleman report: Deficit ideologies and federal compensatory funding in low- income Latino school communities. *Association of Mexican-American Educators Journal, 6*(2), 48–55.

Jiménez-Castellanos, O. (2017). English language learner education finance scholarship: An introduction to the special issue. *Education Policy Analysis Archives, 25*(14). http://dx.doi.org/10.14507/epaa.25.2943

Jiménez-Castellanos, O., Alfaro, C., & Billings, E. (2010). Beyond the school walls: A critical action research study examining the perils and promise of critical teacher engagement. *International Journal of Critical Pedagogy, 3*(2), 59–81.

Jiménez-Castellanos, O., & Garcia, D. (2017). School expenditures and academic achievement differences between high ELL performing and low ELL performing high schools. *Bilingual Research Journal, 40*(3), 318–330

Jiménez-Castellanos, O., Kelly, M., & Carranza, L. (2021). Pre- and post-serrano: Systemic racism, school funding disparities and Mexican-American communities. *Education Law and Policy Review, 6*(1), 49–72.

Jiménez-Castellanos, O., López, P. D., & Rivera, M. (2019). The politics of K–12 local control funding and accountability for Latinx and ELL students: Lessons learned from California. *Peabody Journal of Education, 94*(2), 115–121.

Jiménez-Castellanos, O., & Topper, A. (2012). The cost of providing an adequate education to English language learners: A review of the literature. *Review of Educational Research, 82*(2), 179–232.

Kelly, M. (2016). Schoolmaster's empire: Race, conquest, and the centralization of common schooling in California, *1848–1879*. *History of Education Quarterly, 445*, 447–448.

Kendi, I. (2019). *How to be an anti-racist*. Random House

Koppich, J. E., Humphrey, D. C., Marsh, J. A., Polikoff, M., & Willis, J. (2018). *The local control funding formula after four years: What do we know? Getting down to facts II*. PACE.

Ladson-Billings, G. (1995). Toward a theory of culturally relevant pedagogy. *American educational research journal, 32*(3), 465–491.

Ladson-Billings, G. (2006). From the achievement gap to the education debt: Understanding achievement in US schools. *Educational researcher, 35*(7), 3–12.

Leachman, M., Masterson, K., & Figueroa, E. (2017). *A punishing decade for school funding*. Center on Budget and Policy Priorities. https://www.cbpp.org/research/state-budget-and-tax/a-punishing-decade-for-school-funding

Makori, A., Dusseault, B., & Pillow, T. (2021). *Analysis: How 100 large urban districts are wrapping family & community input into plans for spending federal emergency school relief funds*. The74. https://www.the74million.org/article/analysis-how-100-large-urban-districts-are-wrapping-family-community-input-into-plans-for-spending-federal-emergency-school-relief-funds/

Margo, R. (1990). *Race and schooling in the South, 1880–1950 an economic history*. University of Chicago Press.

Massey, D., & Denton, N. (1993). *American Apartheid: Segregation and the making of the underclass*. Harvard University Press.

McKeown, M. (2021). Structural injustice. *Philosophy Compass, 16*(7), e12757.

Minorini P. A., & Sugarman, S. D. (1999). School finance litigation in the name of educational equity: Its evolution, impact, and future. In H. F. Ladd, R. Chalk, & J. S. Hansen (Eds.), *Equity and adequacy in education finance: Issues and perspectives*. The National Academies Press.

Muldoon, K. (2014). *The Jim Crow era*. Abdo Publishing.

Nocella, A. J., & Anthony, J. (2011). An overview of the history and theory of transformative justice. *Peace & Conflict Review, 6*(1), 1–10.

Odden, A., & Picus, L. O. (2003). *School finance: A policy perspective* (3rd edition). McGraw-Hill.

Orfield, G., & Frankenberg, E. (2014). Increasingly segregated and unequal schools as courts reverse policy. *Educational administration quarterly, 50*(5), 718–734

Podolsky, A., Darling-Hammond, L., Doss, C., & Reardon, S. (2019). *California's positive outliers: Districts beating the odds*. Learning Policy Institute.

Quattlebaum, M., Meares, T. L., & Tyler, T. (2018). *Principles of procedurally just policing*.The Justice Collaboratory at Yale Law School.https://law.yale.edu/sites/default/files/area/center/justice/principles_of_procedurally_just_policing_report.pdf .

Quinn, D. M. (2020). Experimental effects of "achievement gap" news reporting on viewers' racial stereotypes, inequality explanations, and inequality prioritization. *Educational Researcher, 49*(7), 482–492.

Rebell, M. (2009). *Courts and kids: Pursuing educational equity through the state courts*. University of Chicago Press.

Reskin, B. (2012). The race discrimination system. *Annual Review of Sociology, 38*, 17–35.
Rolle, A., & Jiménez-Castellanos, O. (2014). An efficacy analysis of the Texas school funding formula with particular attention to English language learners. *Journal of Education Finance, 39*(3), 203–221.
Rothstein, R. (2017). *Color of Law: Forgotten history of how our government Segregated America.* Liveright Publishing.
Rudiger, A. (2020). *Pathways to dducation sovereignty: Taking a stand for native children.* The Tribal Alliance, New Mexico. https://nabpi.unm.edu/assets/documents/tea-full-report_12-14-20.pdf
Sciarra, D. G., Farrie, D., & Baker, B. (2010). *Filling budget holes: Evaluating the impact of ARRA fiscal stabilization funds on state funding formulas.* The Campaign for Educational Equity, Teachers College, Columbia University. https://edlawcenter.org/assets/files/pdfs/publications/133_FILLINGBUDGETHOLES.pdf
Shores, K. A., Lee, H., & Williams, E. (2022). *The distribution of school resources in the United States: A comparative analysis across levels of governance, student sub-groups, and educational resources* (EdWorkingPaper No. 21-443). Annenberg Institute at Brown University. https://doi.org/10.26300/58f3-6v39
Slavin, R. (1999). How can funding equity ensure enhanced achievement? *Journal of Education Finance, 24*(4), 519–528
Talbert, J. E., & David, J. L. (2019). *Sanger unified school district: Positive outliers case study.* Learning Policy Institute.
Transform Education NM. (2021, February) *Platform for Transformation.* https://transformeducationnm.org/our-platform/
Underwood, J. K. (1995). School finance adequacy as vertical equity. *University of Michigan Journal of Law Reform, 28*.
U.S. Department of Education, Office of Elementary & Secondary Education. (2021). *Elementary and Secondary School Emergency Relief Fund.* https://oese.ed.gov/offices/education-stabilization-fund/elementary-secondary-school-emergency-relief-fund/
Valencia, R. (1997). *The evolution of deficit thinking: Educational thought and practice.* Routledge.
Young, I. M. (1990). *Justice and the politics of difference.* Princeton University Press.

CHAPTER 13

Youth Wildin' in the (Re)Shaping of Policy
Toward a Critical Model of Racial Justice and Community Accountability

Justin A. Coles, Keisha L. Green, and Jamila Lyiscott

**ADVANCING POLICY *WITH* YOUTH NOT *FOR* YOUTH:
A CRITICAL YOUTH STUDIES PERSPECTIVE**

> The way a society treats its young people is a vital indicator of its quality of life. If U.S. society continues to treat youth—particularly young people of color—as potential criminals and undermines their contributions to social justice, then democracy, freedom, and fairness will only be wishful ideals in times of increasing disparity and despair.
>
> —Ginwright et al., 2005, p. 25

As we think about the ways U.S. society has treated young people of color, particularly in this era of Black Lives Matter where the abundance of incidents of Black youth being harmed by policing has caused protests and calls for reform, we turn our attention to language used by government officials to characterize youth in the aftermath of a high-profile policing incident. In 2015, 25-year-old Freddie Gray, a Black youth, died from spinal cord injuries 7 days after being in the custody of the Baltimore Police Department in Baltimore, Maryland. As depicted in Figure 13.1, in the wake of Gray's death, protests broke out across the nation, with a particularly notable protest occurring on April 27, 2015 (Tkacik, 2018).

Amid the protests (called uprising and riots by some), several local and national government officials, including former Baltimore mayor Stephanie Rawlings-Blake and President Barack Obama (both Black-identifying), referenced the protesters as thugs (All Things Considered, 2015). The fact that Black people, especially Black politicians responsible for shaping policy that

Figure 13.1. Minneapolis Rally and March to Support the People of Baltimore

Source: Photograph by Fibonacci Blue, 2015, Flickr.

directly impacts youth, often self-internalize anti-Blackness and describe Black youth in ways that lessen or deny their humanity demonstrates what is at stake. The endemic nature of racism in U.S. society allows dominant narratives grounded in racism to build the foundation for how we conceptualize policymaking. Often, policymakers may not even realize the ways such racialized logics have infiltrated their decision-making, given how totalizing such ideologies are in the U.S. body politic (Sharpe, 2016). In thinking about the word *thug* and its link to dominant narratives (Adamson, 2016; Smiley & Fakunle, 2016), John McWhorter explained:

> Well, the truth is that thug today is a nominally polite way of using the N-word. Many people suspect it, and they are correct. When somebody talks about thugs ruining a place ... It is a sly way of saying there go those black people ruining things again. (All Things Considered, 2015)

McWhorter's explanation of the term *thug* recalls a photo taken during a protest in Baltimore. In the protest photo, a Black youth is shown from the shoulders down holding a sign that reads "BLACK YOUTH ARE NOT THUGS." The youth holding this sign and the words on the sign function as a counterstory (Solórzano & Yosso, 2002) or a disruption to the dominant narrative (Black youth are thugs) *about* Black youth rather than *with* Black youth during the protests. To explore how racially minoritized youth counterstories can work in tandem with racial justice–informed policymaking, we ask the following questions: How might youth workers invested in new visions of policy be informed by youth of color who have different stories to tell about life and schooling? How might the voices and experiences of youth and their *policy counterstories*—or narratives that refuse the deficit orientations and criminalization of dominant conceptions of policy—help us redefine the way we engage in policy work for racial justice?

In this chapter we advance a new vision for a racial justice grounded in a youth policy orientation, as informed by our individual practices with Black and Brown youth and our collective work as codirectors of a racial justice and youth center. First, we ground our text in critical youth studies to lay out our grounding framework. Next, we discuss youth wilding as an example of how policy has been created to harm minoritized youth. Following the aforementioned, we reclaim youth wilding as a policy counterstory that informs how the three of us have engaged in policy counterstories with youth, embodying a radical departure from harmful policy practices that marginalize youth perspectives. Lastly, we share our Racial Justice Youth Policy Model.

CRITICAL YOUTH STUDIES AND YOUTH POLICY

In our current moment, within this unique timeline of U.S. modernity, our nation (and our world) is characterized by the dynamic ways in which youth, particularly minoritized youth of color, are redefining our cultural practices. From how youth are leading digital platforms of creation like TikTok to the ways they are redefining inclusivity in schools and society by adopting more expansive definitions of community (e.g., along lines of race, sexuality, gender, etc.), youth are continuously creating the world/s they fiercely desire to inhabit. Thus, our goal as three Black scholars and leaders of the Center of Racial Justice and Youth Engaged Research (CRJ) at UMass Amherst is to be oriented to visions of policy that are guided by the lives of youth of color. We are committed to centering the ways youth of color critically challenge oppressive societal structures in overt and covert ways (Player et al., 2020). Thinking back to the youth holding the sign during the Baltimore protests, which functions as a policy counterstory, we believe that the key to unlocking racial justice and disrupting racially harmful schooling processes is to be attuned to what youth have to say and what they do, especially in moments where gross violence is enacted against their psychic and material selves.

Informed by critical youth studies scholars Quijada Cerecer and colleagues (2013), we theoretically ground our new vision of youth policy through the question: How can the lives of youth of color be leveraged in humanizing ways to restructure U.S. schooling? Essentially, how might education policy be more racially just if we conceptualized it through the intricate, everydayness of youth life—*with* youth and not just *for* youth? When we speak of centering youth lived experiences as a pathway to restructuring schooling, we are referring to schooling taking a radical departure from enacting policies that are harmful to racially minoritized students, particularly because of refusing to incorporate or be informed by their conceptions of and relationships to schooling. We conceptualize our new vision of educational policy through theorizing in critical youth studies, given its commitment to move beyond racialized, pathological logics that position youth as mere pawns in society rather than agentive players of change. Through asserting "that young people have the ability to analyze their social context, to collectively engage in critical research, and resist repressive state and ideological institutions" (Akom et al., 2008, p. 2), critical youth studies provide a foundation for our racial justice policy work. In particular, critical youth studies allow us to understand youth as already capable and critical citizens, rather than as individuals striving to become such (Quijada Cerecer et al., 2013). Within critical youth studies, we are theoretically and methodologically guided by Akom and colleagues' (2008) conception of Youthtopias. Youthtopias, which were theorized through a merging of Critical Race Theory (CRT) and Youth Participatory Action Research (YPAR), are organized around the following framings:

- understanding the ways race intersects with other identity markers
- challenging dominant discourses that seek to explain the experiences of racially minoritized youth
- positioning youth experiences as foundational in the coconstruction of educational environments with adults
- developing critical consciousness and being committed to social justice (Akom et al., 2008)

The three broad framings of Youthtopias, and the larger theorizing of critical youth studies, are foundational to how we collectively make sense of racial justice–driven youth policy futures.

In thinking about youth as sites that embody a radical departure from harmful school-based policy structures, it is important to detail why there is an urgent necessity for schools to learn from minoritized youth lifeways. According to Ferguson (2000), radical theories of schooling purport that "educational institutions are organized around and reflect the interests of dominant groups in the society; that the function of school is to reproduce the current inequities of our social, political, and economic system" (Ferguson, 2000, p. 50). Perhaps a central concept of radical theories of schooling is the notion of the hidden curriculum or the ways in which the cultural hegemony of White people in the United States serves as the foundation for how curriculum is designed and developed (Ferguson, 2000). A schooling apparatus that exists within a nation birthed through racialized oppression cannot escape the ways it is a vessel of violence and destruction, especially in the lives of racially minoritized young people. Therefore, what might educational policymakers gain from being informed by youth who, every day, must fight to be counted, to create life in a context where they have been rendered as without life—at least without life worthy of regard or recognition?

YOUTH WILDIN'

Words matter. In the mouths of those with social and political power, words have material ramifications with disproportionate effects on youth of color. Thinking back to how the term *thug* has been weaponized against Black youth (and other youth of color), we now turn our attention to another word: *wilding*. In 1989, when New York Chief of Detectives, Robert Colangelo, told the nation that the infamously named Central Park Five had confessed to "wilding" (Moriearty, 2009), the term took the city and the nation by storm (Welch et al., 2002).

Five Black and Brown teens accused of attacking and murdering a White 28-year-old jogger in Central Park laid at the center of national attention. Even with no evidence, the media spectacle forged narratives of their criminality propelled by language reserved for Black and Brown youth. The counterstories (what the youth had to say about their activities) of the five youths were completely ignored. The word "wilding" appeared across national headlines. With little-to-no understanding of its etymology or colloquial meaning, wilding "became uniquely terrifying in 1989 [because] it played on a pre-existing set of fears regarding race, class, gender, and urbanity" (Mexal, 2013, p. 109). Addressing the racialized misuses of the term, Mexal (2013) argues that the term "wilding" can be traced to early 20th-century Black literature and refers to "a strategic performance of wilderness" that resists false binaries such as "savage and civilized, evolved and primitive, and settled and wild" (p. 102). The term later appeared in hip-hop culture and was playfully used by Northeastern youth in the 1980s and 1990s. Yet the media presented the term with varied interpretations, none of which bothered to regard its actual etymology in Black literature and hip-hop culture. Mexal (2013) tells us,

> Despite the assumption that the word's very existence was due to a mishearing, wilding quickly gained official recognition as a new part of the English language. In 1993, it was added to the Oxford English Dictionary: *wilding, n.: The action or practice by a gang of youths of going on a protracted and violent rampage in a street, park, or other public place, attacking or mugging people at random along the way.* (p. 107)

Such language and narratives used to guide public discourse about youth of color (without input from youth of color) have direct ramifications in their everyday lives. For instance, in the wake of the Central Park Jogger case and larger discourses regarding the rise of the super predator, a majority of U.S. states "passed laws that made it easier to punish children as young as 13 as adults and, in some cases, sentence them to life without the possibility of parole" (Hinton, 2019). Around the same time, state-sanctioned schooling practices including, but not limited to, punitive zero-tolerance policies and truancy laws, mirrored the national fears conjured up by the fictional narratives used to imprison the five innocent teen boys. In the late 1980s to early 1990s came the introduction of zero-tolerance policies (Skiba, 2014), an outgrowth of broken windows theory as adopted by law enforcement, which rained down on New York City's Black and Brown schools.

Reclaiming Youth Wildin' as a Policy Counterstory

> In its proper historical, racial, and cultural context, the word wilding contains an important, and long overlooked, critique of the hegemony of white, "civilized" liberal selfhood and the social construction of wilderness.
>
> —Mexal, 2013, p.102

We reclaim the word *wilding* (referred to in this chapter as *wildin'*) to highlight racially minoritized young people's performance of wilderness (Mexal, 2013) as resistance and disruption against racialized discourses and policies designed without their input. In this chapter, we offer our reclamation of wildin' as an embodiment of our theorization of a policy counterstory. To enact wildin' in a youth-policy sense is to advance a different story that runs counter to dominant narratives of policy that work to shape youth life without youth input. Thus, to engage in wildin' as a policy aim is to insert one's voice into the fabric of traditional policy discourse to (re)structure and shape justice-driven educational futures. Through this lens of policy counterstorying, we insist on youth culture, voice, activism, and leadership as central to new conceptions of education policy, both in terms of goals and process.

Several examples of youth wildin' in the reshaping of policy futures across the nation and the history of our youth work, respectively, inform our new vision for youth policy and grounds our frameworks as directors of the CRJ at UMass Amherst. The Youth Board on Boston (YOB), facilitated through the Boston Student Advisory Council (BSAC), organizes as a collective to shift policy around school discipline, budget-cuts, student rights, and many other relevant issues (Edward W. Hazen Foundation, 2016). The board is composed mostly of youth of color who resist old, hierarchical models of policy that seek to control individual behavior and suppress youth agency in predominantly Black and Brown school districts. Instead, they insert their voices (as a mechanism for tangible action/change) to design policies that challenge systemic racism. The work of the YOB includes dismantling the school-to-prison pipeline and restorative justice practices to amplify students' rights for alternative supports.

In another example, on January 14, 2022, Chicago Public Schools' Radical Youth Alliance joined thousands of youths across the country in a national walk-out in a stance against COVID-19 in-person school conditions (Alfonseca, 2022) amidst a surge in the Omicron variant of the virus (Elamroussi, 2021). Rather than embrace the insertion of their voices as an attempt to be heard in any policy decisions affecting their material lives, the media and politicians alike dismissed the actions as an opportunity to cut classes. Still, in their commitment to restructuring more just and equitable classroom environments, especially in under-resourced schools within communities of color, the group of Black and Brown youth that make up Radical Youth Alliance created a list of demands. The demands were sent directly to Chicago Mayor Lori Lightfoot, CEO of Chicago Public Schools Pedro Martinez, and Chicago Department of Public Health Commissioner Allison Arwady, requiring both apologies and a radical shift in policies enforced to mandate in-person schooling.

While we highlighted the YOB and the Radical Youth Alliance to demonstrate policy counterstories, we must make it clear that youth across the nation and the world enact policy counterstories in more subtle ways, as well. For instance, several policies work to limit the presence of technology in urban schools. Yet the world was able to see the graphic video of Sharaka at Spring Valley High because Niya Kenney, a Black girl youth, decided to leverage technology (Sorkin, 2015) to document a policy counterstory: One where Black youth are not creators of violence, but in fact victims of wanton and rampant school violence. Additionally, during the Detroit Sickouts, several students walked out of classes in solidarity with teachers and to advocate for their own schooling conditions, by completely abandoning the school building as a site of safety and wellness (Kozlowski, 2016). The policy counterstory examples we have discussed in this section, and countless other instances of youth of color engaging in radical departures from harmful enactments of policy, directly inform our advancement of a new vision of youth policy.

GROUNDING OUR VISIONS OF YOUTH-INFORMED POLICY (COUNTERSTORIES): A TRIPARTITE POSITIONING

To theorize our model of a new vision for youth-informed policy, through a lens of wildin', we explore the lines of youth-centered research and praxis that have shaped our scholar-activism, respectively. In our brief synthesis of

Double-Dutch Methodology, Black Storywork, and *Liberation Literacies Pedagogy,* we outline how our ongoing work has been grounded in youth of color ways of knowing, needs, and interests. We leverage our scholarship to detail how our own youth-engaged research has worked as policy counterstories through a lens of youth wildin'. We see our three framings as pathways to the myriad ways policy counterstories can take shape in the lives of youth, but not as the only ways such counterstories can and should be developed.

Double-Dutch Methodology

As a once young Black girl child—both hyper visible and invisible—Keisha strives to disrupt the ways adult documentation of and decisions about youth are narrow and ill-informed, at best. The vibrancy of youth multiliteracies and the powerfully instructive nature of young peoples' ways of being and knowing in this world have always been at the core of her engagement in and outside of the academy. From her work as a teaching artist to an associate professor, Keisha's goal has been to leverage resources and maximize opportunities for youth voice and participation. Double-dutch methodology (DDM) (Green, 2014; Green, 2020) is a way of (re)conceptualizing participant observation or an "alternative" way of thinking about qualitative research with youth, or *youth processing.*

DDM is an invitation to a range of methodological strategies that is humanizing, participatory, reflexive, and grounded in Black feminist theory—lived experiences as knowledge. It is necessarily embodied, asset-based, and requires pausing to name and make meaning from our multiple intersecting identities, social locations, and positionalities in relationship to our work with youth. DDM emphasizes the embodied nature of facilitating policy counterstories. Through DDM, youth policy can be conceptualized as a set of practices or protocols for youth work, youth leadership, or knowledge development that is to be fluid, participatory, grounded in cultural/heritage practices and strengths-based, textured, contextual, inviting lived/living experiences. In this way, youth are learning together, collaboratively, teaching one another, peer mentoring, older youth members becoming youth leaders. DDM also suggests ways youth might map their own identities and think critically about the systems, structures, policies, and practices that contribute to their material realities. Youth have knowledges overlooked, dismissed, ignored; DDM suggests otherwise.

Black Storywork

As a Black man who identifies as a descendant of those enslaved in U.S. chattel slavery, Justin's orientation to policy is grounded in a lens of resistance/resilience (Akinyela, 2003), characterized by the ways he sees policy as needing to acknowledge the agentive nature of those it is designed to serve.

Wildin' as a disruptive interference into the ways Black youth lifeways, as articulated by them, are excluded from policy development is central to policy counterstories. Justin's research and teaching with youth (see Coles, 2021) is centered on how they make sense of the world around them; he invites them into spaces of criticality to name and challenge structures that negatively impact their lives (*youth criticality and sensemaking*). A major way he has worked with Black youth regarding how they can advance policy has been through the cultivation of the oral stories they tell and that we *need* to hear, which he has conceptualized as Black Storywork (Coles, 2020; Coles, in press). Black Storywork, which is rooted in the Black oral tradition, is an educational method and practice that is wholly about capturing how Black youth are critical of their societal and academic experiences, guided by their sensemaking of the world through their unique social lens/es. Centered on collective dialogue, a tapestry of youth storytelling, Black Storywork creates the time and environs necessary for Black youth to tell the (counter) stories of how various schooling structures and processes advance their overall wellness and academic success or how they cause harm and hinder that success.

Liberation Literacies Pedagogy

The language of Black America is unique, beautiful, nuanced, and often contested. Within this cultural milieu, one where Black language practices have been continuously disregarded as inferior to standardized Eurocentric language practices, Jamila works with youth around the reclamation of their authentic voices in policy change. Liberation Literacies Pedagogy (LLP) posits that since language is ideologically, historically, and politically saturated (Alim & Smitherman, 2012), attempts to disconnect Black and Brown youth from the languages of their communities through schooling are grounded in the racialized colonial logics. This linguistic marginalization reifies racialized hierarchies in school and ignores the genius that youth of color bring with them into learning spaces. Jamila has worked with youth of color to (re)turn to the linguistic and cultural practices from their cultures to affirm their identities, resist the marginalization of their voices, and engage in social action toward decolonial curricular and policy changes. Framed by five "paradigm principles" (Lyiscott, 2018), Awareness, Agency, Action, "Achievement," and Alteration, LLP creates avenues for policy counterstories as youth of color draw on their rich linguistic repertoires to *author* policy change in ways that are grounded in their *youth voices and being*.

Pathways to Policy Counterstories

Through linking DDM, Black Storywork, and LLP, we tease out the ways each offering is attentive to youth processing, youth criticality and sensemaking, and youth being and voice, which are core components to our youth-informed policy model. Given that we situate our chapter in response to the ways policy is done on youth and not with youth, we position our approaches to youth-based research as potential policy counterstories due to the explicit and unapologetic focus on youth ways of knowing. What equitable educational policy futures might be created if we ground our visions through collective work with youth of color?

A RACIAL JUSTICE YOUTH POLICY MODEL: AN OFFERING

Central to what we are forwarding as our vision of youth policy are three core elements: youth processing, youth criticality and sensemaking, and youth being and voice. Why are these central to a new vision of policy (from our work) and at this time? As we described earlier in this chapter, it has been well documented that youth are typically excluded or marginalized in public policy deliberation and decision-making processes, even in policy decisions that primarily impact young people (Sheth & Salisbury, 2022). Our highlighted examples of youth organizing demonstrate policy counterstorying or, said another way, illustrate how young people bring necessary perspectives, knowledge, and expertise regarding how to think about and address enduring problems that have sustained and exacerbated social inequities. In this section, we describe and offer a new vision for youth policy, specifically a racial justice youth policy model, by exemplifying how we enact a new vision for youth policy within our CRJ work.

CRJ as a Racial Justice Youth Policy Model Case Study

As a racial justice youth policy model case study, the CRJ is an example of a disruption in institutional hierarchies. At the CRJ, we position youth at the center across all our research and programming areas, particularly in the field of social-science research. Youth-engaged research challenges our traditional conceptions of who is allowed to be knowledge producers, researchers, and policymakers. At CRJ, we understand that, historically, policies and practices that impact youth of color schooling experiences are theorized and implemented by people who have never stepped foot in their communities. Scholarship on youth oppression reveals that the social construction of age continues to position youth as inferior to adults in problematic ways (DeJong & Love, 2015). CRJ is grounded in the ways of being, needs, and epistemologies of youth of color. Our policy model is answerable to youth of color (Player et al., 2021). CRJ is informed by a critical youth studies and critical pedagogy perspective that refuses a banking model of education (Freire, 2000) and, instead, positions youth in an inquiry stance to codiscover and cocreate their world through youth policy alongside education practitioners, educational researchers, and community members.

As CRJ codirectors, we intentionally established a community-engaged research center for critical, transdisciplinary, multimodal, participatory, and humanizing youth-centered research. We create space, possibilities, and opportunities for youth processing, youth criticality and sensemaking, as well as youth being and voice throughout our five areas of influence: Racial Equity, Critical Teacher Education, Youth Leadership, Fugitivity and Abolitionism, *and* Community Engagement. Youth leadership is integrated across our five youth-informed commitments as an effective approach to (or new vision for) racial justice youth policy. In Figure 13.2, we share our model that visualizes the relationship between our core youth-informed principles (stemming from our respective research agendas) as they intersect with CRJs areas of influence.

Toward Racial Justice and Community Accountability in Education: Areas of Influence

In our racial justice youth policy model (informed by our respective research areas: double-dutch methodology, Black storywork, and liberation literacies pedagogy), we—spotlighting the following set of guiding principles—create space for youth processing, youth criticality and sensemaking, and youth voice and being across the following five areas of influence.

1. **Racial equity:** Mapping diasporic identities and youth solidarities to interrogate and collaboratively/collectively dismantle systems of oppression that impact our communities, while also engaging in freedom dreaming and world-building practices.
2. **Critical teacher education:** Youth-informed theorizations of teaching and learning.

Figure 13.2. Racial Justice Youth Policy Model

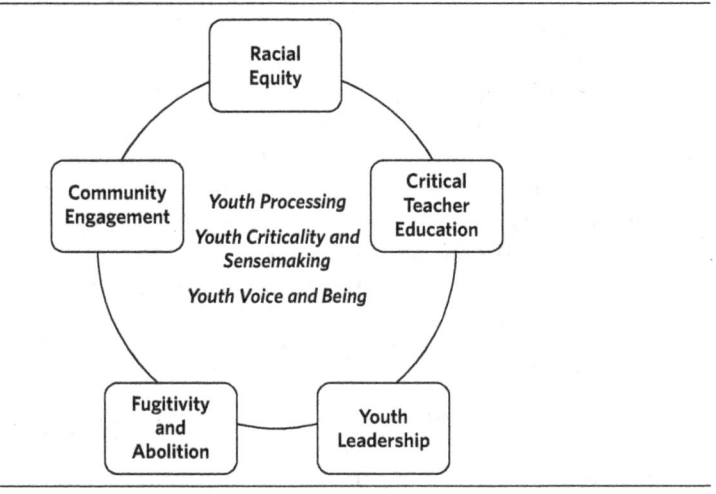

3. **Youth leadership:** Centering the interests and needs of youth of color.
4. **Fugitivity and abolition:** Youth agency and collective action.
5. **Community-engaged:** Drawing from the indigenous knowledge/s of youth of color and their communities to better understand social issues.

For example, in the context of *youth leadership*, CRJ work is participatory and collaborative, centering the interests and needs of youth of color. Our second commitment, *community-engaged*, draws from the knowledges of youth of color and their communities to better understand social issues embracing multimodal forms of engagement. Regarding our third space, *fugitivity and abolition*, youth are cultivating their voices and agency toward collective action, as well as amplifying youth literacies and youth culture. Our fourth area of influence, *critical teacher education*, positions youth as teacher educators and curriculum designers leading professional development, and (re)shaping school (discipline) policies and practices that define youth of color experiences in education. The fifth and important thread throughout the other four areas is *racial equity* where youth are equipped with skills to interrogate and dismantle systems of oppression that impact our communities, while also engaging the freedom dreaming and world-building practices that have held our people for generations.

Each of our five areas of influence will necessarily include youth (processing, criticality, sense making, voice, and being). In other words, each of our five community-engaged research and programmatic areas have youth as team members collaborating on naming the purpose, goals, and research agendas. In the next section, we discuss how our Youth Board functions as our main site for cultivating and sustaining youth policy counterstories.

Walking the Talk: CRJ Youth Board

The CRJ Youth Board (YB) is setting in motion our visions and recommendations around what youth processing, youth criticality and sense making, as well as youth voice and being look like in action. Our goal, through the CRJYB is to position youth as leaders at the table helping to inform and shape policies related to education, including racial justice and equity in schools, training of teachers, curriculum-design practices, and assessment. This youth work is grounded in racial justice (as so much of old youth policy adversely affects youth of color, Black youth, in particular) and takes the form of building collective communities among youth of color based on principles of care, solidarity, participatory and democratic learning, youth-led inquiry, and political education. CRJYB team members are identified through a humanizing application process that involves an informal interview and requires youth to have the support of at least one adult ally or mentor. During their first year, YB youth participants receive a stipend and engage in a series of youth leadership development activities that cultivate their skills and knowledge in critical social inquiry, racial literacies, youth-led research, and participatory advocacy. Year 1 culminates in a youth-led teach-in for local educators and community members. Additionally, you are awarded a certificate of completion. YB youth participants have the option of continuing for a second year as YB fellows continuing to develop their youth leadership skills through three YB tracks or paid internships:

1. *The Youth-Centered Curriculum and Teaching Internship*: Within this internship, youth will work closely with current and future teachers, as well as with school administrators and teacher education faculty to center racial equity in school curriculum and teaching practices, as part of the College of Education Secondary Teacher Education Program.
2. *The Youth-Centered Racial Healing Internship*: Within this internship, youth will work with UMass graduate students and faculty of color to lead a racial healing project contributing to the work of the UMass Equity and Inclusion Office.
3. *The Youth-Centered Education Assessment Justice Internship:* Within this internship, youth will serve as youth advisors for an antiracist educational assessment program, Center for Measurement Justice.

Each of the three tracks is an opportunity for youth leadership to (re)shape institutional policies and practices. Our YB youth participants are connecting and cultivating community with BIPOC youth from other cities and towns across our region; leading in racial-justice work at UMass and in their own school, city, and town communities; taking part in spaces of healing and joy—all by collectively building awareness and action toward racial equity and justice through the creation of a youth board that centers: BIPOC youth voices, cocreation, visioning, and support within their communities as well as the UMASS community. We prioritize reflection and joy around identities and cultures of color and amplify these identities in our communities. We are integrating this board into the visioning and work of all the CRJ's teams, centering youth perspectives, power, and action throughout. In this way, the CRJ Youth Board is a framework for a new vision of a critical youth policy model of racial justice and community accountability.

IMPLICATIONS FOR LOCAL, STATE, AND FEDERAL EDUCATION POLICY

In thinking across local, state, and federal levels of policy, the core organizing ideal of this model is that policy designed to benefit youth of color is historically as crucial for equitable policy advancement. That is, whether designing policy at the local, state, or federal level, inventory must be taken for those deemed with leading policy changes to speak from their experience/s with youth of color in rich and meaningful ways to be clear, the United States is a nation structured through racism, so we are not claiming that our model would have categorically eliminated anti-Black carceral logics, but we do offer that they would have lessened the effects of such logics. All too often, policy is shaped by numbers and big data sources to serve as the driving force for decision-making, which lacks a familiarity with the nuances of youth life. Our policy model prompts a commitment by policymakers to attune themselves to the racism (as it intersects with other interlocking systems of oppression) that youth of color face daily in schools and society. The uniqueness of such a prompting is that it requires policymakers to be in community with youth or at least to be informed by actors who are in community with youth.

Local Implications

Given the intimate community building that needs to take place for youth policy counterstories to be heard and centered in policymaking, we see the local level of policy deliberations as extremely significant for how a racial justice policy model might be implemented. For example, at the local level of education, educational leaders (e.g., superintendents and school board members), politicians, and community leaders are directly responsible for the policies that are created and implemented in schools and classrooms. More than milling through data that documents what youth have experienced and how they have been impacted by previous policy initiatives, we posit that true youth-based racial-justice policy must incorporate youth (via youth processing, youth criticality and sensemaking, and youth voice and being) into the decision-making process. Our CRJ youth board is a direct model for how local educational actors can carve out a space for youth participation in policy decisions. We invite local actors to think creatively and intentionally about how to incorporate youth participation in public policy, as it should not be a performative display of inclusion, which would be antithetical to the meaning of the racial justice youth policy model. While creating a youth (policy) board would be ideal, educational leaders, for example, can also create youth positions on school boards and/or youth advisory councils.

State Implications

When considering state educational policy, we recall to mind policies dealing with testing and standards, funding structures, school performance reviews, charters, and teacher training and certification. We also consider the role of policy in housing, environmental justice, and public safety and how these operate within the ecology of schooling. In our current socio-political climate, it is imperative that we also acknowledge the ways states can ban books and the teaching of content discussing matters of oppression (e.g., Critical Race Theory bans and the Don't Say Gay Bill). Since states play a significant role in education policy, youth involvement at the state or municipal level is key. Because states generally have more direct power, influence, and regulation over resources for youth and their communities, particularly being "key guarantors of equal educational opportunity in the U.S. federal system" (McDermott, 2009, p. 749), youth participation in public policy is paramount as state-level decisions are made affecting their lives.

Several states have adopted the practice of constituting youth commissions to serve in an advisory capacity to the mayor, city council, municipal agencies, or state lawmakers. For example, in our region, Holyoke, Massachusetts, formed a Youth Task Force composed of several youth-led and youth-serving nonprofit or community-based organizations of which the Youth Commission is one. Holyoke Youth Commission, Baltimore Youth Commission, or the Sacramento Youth Commission are just a few of the many state youth commissions across the United States. These kinds of youth commissions are opportunities for young people to amplify their voices, build on their lived experience as knowledge, and take initiative to organize around policy issues that concern them, and is also a context where youth have a "seat at the table" and are part of policy proceedings of public agencies and are working within intergenerational partnerships. Not all these youth commissions, however, feature youth as voting members. To make real on evidence-based reports on the effectiveness of youth participation in the public sphere, local and state governments should be sure to incorporate youth in every facet of the process, including the drafting of and voting on legislation and public (youth) policy. As more and more youth are protesting school closures, school shootings, and police brutality and walking out to demand stronger COVID-19 protocols, access to equitable education, and racial justice, we can no longer give lip service to youth representation. Rather, real opportunities for youth participation in consequential decision-making processes must be provided related to the (re)shaping of youth policies.

Federal Implications

Historically, there is a precedent for youth being at the forefront of social movements and the fight for civil and human rights at the national or federal level. The civil rights movement and the Black Lives Matter movement are, perhaps, among the most prominent examples of nationwide coalitions of youth leadership and coordinated activism for policy changes. The landmark 1954 case *Brown v. Board of Education* and the pivotal 1965 Civil Rights Act continue to have an impact on youth futures, as we experience school resegregation and increased surveillance and criminalization of Black, Brown, and queer youth-of-color. Currently, what is typical at the federal level is the legislating of youth lives without youth participation; White House commissions on youth studies without youth input; market-based school reforms as seen in large sweeping policies including No Child Left Behind Act, Race to the Top, or the more recent Elementary and Secondary Education Act often have direct racial-justice implications, particularly for youth of color (U.S. Department of Education, Office of Elementary and Secondary Education[1]). We understand federal policies to be situated in a racialized terrain. Considering the legacies of landmark supreme-court cases like *Brown v. Board*, our policy model helps us think through racial justice in the wake of desegregation and resegregation.

Additionally, we note that there is a shifting trend toward inclusion of youth in spaces like Interagency Working Group on Youth Programs (IWGYP), a large body of federal departments and agencies that "was formed in 2008 to improve outcomes for young people by promoting collaboration among federal, state, tribal, and local organizations." The American Institute for Research "supports IWGYP by engaging youth in meaningful roles and productive adult-youth partnerships." Similarly, there are bipartisan efforts to address youth labor, juvenile justice reform, and resources for the health and well-being of children. Still though, according to a Congressional report "Vulnerable Youth: Background and Policies,"[2] "the federal government has not adopted a single overarching federal policy or legislative vehicle that addresses the challenges at-risk youth experience in adolescence or while making the transition to adulthood. Rather, federal youth policy today has evolved from multiple programs established in the early 20th century and expanded through War on Poverty and Great Society initiatives. These programs, concentrated in six areas—workforce development, education, juvenile justice and delinquency prevention, social services, public health, and national and community service—provide vulnerable youth with opportunities to develop skills that will assist them in adulthood." However, developing opportunities *with* youth and not just *for* youth at the federal level creates avenues for substantially engaging a demographic that has coordinated nation-wide protests for federal change in gun laws, climate justice, and the global pandemic, all over the last 5 years. With youth making up nearly 42 million people in the U.S. population (Office of Population Affairs, n.d.), their perspectives on these major federal issues are pertinent for the future of policy.

A common concern in centering youth-of-color voices across local, state, and federal levels is the temptation for youth to be included either symbolically or in ways that tokenize their identities (Tuck & Yang, 2011). Further, when youth of color *are* called upon to shape policy futures, they are too often tasked with centering trauma and pain narratives to underscore the urgency of social change (Tuck, 2009). Our racial justice youth policy model calls for meaningfully engaging the local knowledges of youth of color in ways that move away from symbolic or surface gestures. It also calls for state and federal bodies to create legislative pathways that address significant challenges in the lives of youth of color in ways that do not replicate damage-centered (Tuck, 2009) policies such as the War on Drugs, for example, but that rely on the power of youth processing, youth criticality, and youth voice to design social futures that build capacity for their agency and success.

CONCLUSION

In this chapter, we wrestled with two questions: How might youth leaders invested in new visions of policy be informed by youth of color who have different stories to tell about life and schooling? How might the voices and experiences of youth and their *policy counterstories* (or narratives that refuse the deficit orientations and criminalization of dominant conceptions of policy) help us redefine the way we engage in policy work for racial justice? We explored the state of youth organizing and its role in youth-led policy change as a remedy to push for changes shaped by those who are impacted directly by policies, youth, and families themselves. Our analysis of two youth organizing examples, naming our individual youth-informed research areas, and highlighting our center as a model for racial justice youth policy work provides insights on the intersectional nature of the *Our Children Can't Wait* chapters, recognizing that the lives and identities of young people are systemic across social issues including education, health care, housing, transportation, and the environment. Growth of youth of color and examples of organizing efforts across the country in urban and rural communities will inform new ideas for building and sustaining social, economic, and political power for young people broadly and young people of color specifically.

We benefit from honestly examining the ways we currently work with youth—inviting feedback from youth and other trusted critical scholar colleagues and by being uncomfortable and okay with dislocating ourselves (i.e., adults) from perceived locations of power or authority. White supremacy, patriarchy, and adultism, under which we have been socialized and conditioned or that shape old youth policy, undermine the promise and possibility of youth-policy futures. Even among our best social-justice and equitable intentions, we (adults) have blind spots. So, what is youth policy at this moment? In future moments? This moment requires attending to and taking seriously the many ways youth are challenging oppressive institutions and structures, shifting policy landscapes guided by their own life experiences, and demanding that these policy counterstories and new visions for a racial justice world be (re)centered as a matter of youth-of color-survival and thriving at local, state, and federal levels.

NOTES

1. More information about NCLB, Race to the Top, and ESEA can be found at https://oese.ed.gov/offices/office-of-formula-grants/the-elementary-and-secondary-education-act-the-no-child-left-behind-act-of-2001/
2. More information about this report can be found at https://www.google.com/url?q=https://crsreports.congress.gov/product/pdf/RL/RL33975&sa=D&source=docs&ust=1654115641633075&usg=AOvVaw29gU-gr20cPG2tJRv2d81v

REFERENCES

Adamson, B. (2016). Thugs, crooks, and rebellious negroes: Racist and racialized media coverage of Michael Brown and the Ferguson demonstrations. *Harvard Journal on Racial & Ethnic Justice, 32*, 189–278.

Akinyela, M. M. (2003). Battling the serpent: Nat Turner, Africanized Christianity, and a Black ethos. *Journal of Black Studies, 33*(3), 255–280.

Akom, A. A., Cammarota, J., & Ginwright, S. (2008). Youthtopias: Towards a new paradigm of critical youth studies. *Youth Media Reporter, 2*(4), 1–30.

Alfonseca, K. (2022, January 14). Students walk out over COVID-19 in-person learning conditions in schools. ABC News. https://abcnews.go.com/US/students-walk-covid-19-person-learning-conditions-schools/story?id=82265171

Alim, H. S., & Smitherman, G. (2012). *Articulate while Black: Barack Obama, language, and race in the US.* Oxford University Press.

All Things Considered. (2015, April 30). The racially charged meaning behind the word "thug." NPR. https://www.npr.org/2015/04/30/403362626/the-racially-charged-meaning-behind-the-word-thug

Coles, J. A. (2021). Black desire: Black-centric youthtopias as critical race educational praxis. *International Journal of Qualitative Studies in Education*, 1–22. https://doi.org/10.1080/09518398.2021.1888163

Coles, J. A. (2020). A BlackCrit re/imagining of urban schooling social education through Black youth enactments of Black storywork. *Urban Education.* https://doi.org/10.1177/0042085920908919

Coles, J. A. (in press). Beyond silence: Disrupting antiblackness through Blackcrit ethnography and Black youth voice. In S. May & B. Caldas (Eds.), *Critical ethnography, bi/Multilingualism, race(ism) and education*. Multilingual Matters.

DeJong, K., & Love, B. J. (2015) Youth oppression as a technology of Colonialism: Conceptual frameworks and possibilities for social justice education praxis. *Equity & Excellence in Education, 48*(3), 489–508

Edward W. Hazen Foundation. (2016). *Youth build USA for youth on Board (YOB).* http://hazenfoundation.org/youth-build-usa-for-youth-on-board-yob-2/

Elamroussi, A. (2021 December 31). *Omicron surge is "unlike anything we've ever seen," expert says*. CNN. Retrieved from https://www.cnn.com/2021/12/30/health/us-coronavirus-thursday/index.html

Ferguson, A. (2000). *Bad boys: Public schools in the making of black masculinity*. The University of Michigan Press.

Freire, P. (2000). *Pedagogy of the oppressed* (30th anniversary ed.). Continuum.

Ginwright, S., Cammarota, J., & Noguera, P. (2005). Youth, social justice, and communities: Toward a theory of urban youth policy. *Social Justice, 32*(3), 24–40.

Green, K. (2020) Radical imagination and "otherwise possibilities" in qualitative research. *International Journal of Qualitative Studies in Education, 33*(1), 115–127.

Green, K. (2014). Doing double dutch methodology: Playing with the practice of participant observer. In D. Paris & M. T. Winn (Eds.), *Humanizing research: Decolonizing qualitative inquiry with youth and communities* (pp. 147–160). Sage Publications.

Hinton, E. (2019, June 2). How the "Central Park Five" changed the history of American law. *The Atlantic*. https://www.theatlantic.com/entertainment/archive/2019/06/when-they-see-us-shows-cases-impact-us-policy/590779/

Kozlowski, K. (2016, January 25). Cass Tech students walk out to support teachers. *The Detroit News*. https://www.detroitnews.com/story/news/local/detroit-city/2016/01/25/detroit-teachers-protest/79298360/

Lyiscott, J. (2018). *Why English class is silencing students of color* [Video]. TEDxTheBenjaminSchool. https://www.ted.com/talks/jamila_lyiscott_why_english_class_is_silencing_students_of_color

McDermott, K. A. (2009). The expansion of state policy research. In G. Sykes, B. Schneider, & D. N. Plank (Eds.), *Handbook of education policy research* (pp. 749–766). Routledge.

Mexal, S. J. (2013). The roots of "wilding": Black literary naturalism, the language of wilderness, and hip hop in the Central Park jogger rape. *African American Review, 46*(1), 101–115.

Moriearty, P. L. (2009). Framing justice: Media, bias, and legal decision-making. *Maryland Law Review, 69*(4), 849–909.

Office of Population Affairs. (n.d.). *America's diverse adolescents*. Retrieved at https://opa.hhs.gov/adolescent-health/adolescent-health-facts/americas-diverse-adolescents

Player, G. D., Coles, J. A., & Ybarra, M. G. (2020). Enacting educational fugitivity with youth of color. *The High School Journal, 103*(3), 140–156.

Quijada Cerecer, D. A., Cahill, C., & Bradley, M. (2013). Toward a critical youth policy praxis: Critical youth studies and participatory action research. *Theory Into Practice, 52*(3), 216–223.

Sharpe, C. (2016). *In the wake: On blackness and being*. Duke University Press.

Sheth, M. J., & Salisbury, J. D. (2022). "School's a lie": Toward critical race intersectional pedagogy for youth intellectual activism in policy partnerships. *Educational Policy, 36*(1), 100–141.

Skiba, R. J. (2014). The failure of zero tolerance. *Reclaiming Children and Youth, 22*(4), 27–33.

Smiley, C., & Fakunle, D. (2016). From "brute" to "thug": The demonization and criminalization of unarmed Black male victims in America. *Journal of Human Behavior in the Social Environment, 26*(3–4), 350–366.

Solórzano, D. G., & Yosso, T. J. (2002). A critical race counterstory of race, racism, and affirmative action. *Equity & Excellence in Education, 35*(2), 155–168.

Sorkin, A. D. (2015, October 30). What Niya Kenney saw. *The New Yorker.* https://www.newyorker.com/news/amy-davidson/what-niya-kenny-saw

Tkacik, C. (2018). Remembering the Baltimore riots after Freddie Gray's death, 3 years later. *The Baltimore Sun.* https://www.baltimoresun.com/maryland/baltimore-city/bs-md-ci-riots-three-years-later-20180426-story.html

Tuck, E., & Yang, K. (2011). Youth resistance revisited: New theories of youth negotiations of educational injustices. *International Journal of Qualitative Studies in Education, 24*(5), 521–530.

Tuck, E. (2009). Suspending damage: A letter to communities. *Harvard Educational Review,*79(3),409–427.https://doi.org/10.17763/haer.79.3.n0016675661t3n15

Welch, M., Price, E. A., & Yankey, N. (2002). Moral panic over youth violence: Wilding and the manufacture of menace in the media. *Youth & Society, 34*(1), 3–30.

CHAPTER 14

Youth Incarceration and Education Policy

Angela James

INTRODUCTION

Several years ago, one of my siblings started talking to me about a student in their 1st-grade classroom. She described the student, who I will refer to here as "Malcolm," as having a rather remarkable temper and an equally remarkable talent with verbal expression. By the end of the school year, my sister had gifted him with a little notebook which he began carrying everywhere. In it, he wrote poetry and detailed his thoughts and feelings, as well as humorous observations that he sometimes shared with her. I am not sure if Malcolm was ever again technically in my sister's class, but she maintained a communication with him, and he frequently shared his writing with her throughout his elementary-school career. Malcolm kept journaling and generally kept a notebook with him during that time. My sister would shake her head as she recalled one of the numerous times Malcolm was sent to the principal's office because of a fight sparked by that little notebook. Marcus had a difficult home life. Sometimes Malcolm showed up to school hungry, and he was often teased by the other kids about the shabbiness of his clothes. Malcolm's family was poor, his mother was largely absent, and he lived in a tough neighborhood. Although deeply loved by his dad with whom he lived, Malcolm was often left unsupervised with his siblings, as his dad worked multiple jobs to make ends meet. At some point in middle school, Malcolm began to get in real trouble. Although he no longer attended my sister's school, he would sometimes visit when he had been suspended or expelled from whatever school he was attending. One day I received a weeping call from my sister. She had learned from Malcolm's father that Malcolm had been arrested and was locked up.

For most readers of this chapter, there are few surprises in Malcolm's story. It is hardly remarkable to read of an emotionally volatile, Black boy from a high-poverty community getting "caught up" in the juvenile justice system. Certainly, Malcolm has all the "risks" that research tells us are associated with youth involved in the juvenile justice system. Perhaps because Malcolm is more than a set of demographic characteristics, his experience animates my interest in education policy impacting justice-involved youth. Malcolm was an incredibly smart and charming child. My sporadic interactions with him between ages 7 and 14 were such that I hoped one day to write a heartwarming "against all odds" story about him and my sister. I wish there was a happy ending to this story, and that the care of one dedicated teacher was all that was needed. However, right now the story of my sister's brilliant but troubled little poet is bleak in a way that, for me at least, illuminates the costs of the last several decades of educational policy with its reliance on exclusionary discipline and zero tolerance.

After Malcolm left elementary school where his teachers knew the "whole child" in terms of both his difficulties and his talents, Malcolm went on to middle school, where his struggles deepened considerably. Malcolm missed a lot of schooling during his middle and high school years. While I do not know the details of his educational experiences while in camp, I know that they were academically disruptive and that he had considerable difficulty finding a school to enroll in upon release. Ultimately, Malcolm did not obtain a high school diploma and is now incarcerated in an adult prison. In my view, Malcolm's story suggests the terrible cost of zero-tolerance and exclusionary discipline in schools; the nexus between problems in public schools; and the challenges facing educators in juvenile justice contexts as the accrued educational debts demand a reckoning. A diligent and caring teacher is not sufficient; we need to ensure that such teachers are supported (and fostered) by local, state, and federal educational policies aligned toward ensuring that youth like Malcolm receive transformative educational experiences, capable of helping place them on track for successful adulthood.

CHAPTER OVERVIEW

This chapter provides an overview of the magnitude and demographic characteristics of justice-involved youth with a special focus on California in the pages that follow. It offers an account of the social circumstances underlying both the decades-long increases and more recent declines in the numbers of youth housed in juvenile-justice facilities. Of critical concern to educators is the way educational policies undergirding the so-called "school-to-prison" pipeline relate simultaneously to systemic inequities within school systems, as well as to the alarming educational neglect of students in state custody. Following this descriptive overview, the chapter identifies key aspects of more successful approaches to grappling with the educational challenges of justice-involved youth. Specifically, the highly touted Missouri Model is summarized along with specific evidence-based strategies for improving literacy and learning outcomes for justice-involved youth (Mendel, 2010). The chapter closes with implementation concerns derived from research fieldwork done in California facilities, along with key recommendations for action at the federal, state, and local levels to enact educational policy that supports the full educational and human potential of young people under public charge.

THE JUVENILE JUSTICE LANDSCAPE IN THE UNITED STATES

All young people deserve a chance to overcome their difficulties and to reach their full potential, including my sister's former student, as well as the young writers, mathematicians, and scientists that currently sit in juvenile-justice facilities throughout the nation.

The United States has a uniquely harsh, punitive approach to youth behavior, having the highest rate of youth incarceration in the world. In 2019, over 43,000 young people were in some form of carceral facility (Sawyer, 2019). Juvenile detention began over 100 years ago with the "progressive" aim of educating and teaching life skills to children, rather than incarcerating them with adults. The logic of underpinning a separate juvenile system with a unique response to youth "delinquency" was that criminality was a survival mechanism produced by a social environment bereft of healthy influences (Bell, 2015; Champion, 1998). Deindustrialization and the War on Drugs brought about dramatic policy changes. This period of the early 1980s through 1990s led to dramatic increases in the number of juveniles arrested and sentenced to detainment (Abrams, 2013; Shook & Sarri, 2008; Skiba, 2013). These changes are in concert with shifts in the logic guiding the juvenile justice system, namely that young people are no longer construed as different and more amenable to rehabilitation than adults (Abrams, 2013). Increases in the number of incarcerated youths happened alongside an increased policy focus on punishment, as opposed to rehabilitation of troubled youth both inside and outside of schools. The link between academic struggles and incarceration is so strong that many have quipped that planning for the construction of new carceral facilities could use the numbers of struggling 3rd- and 4th-graders as a predictor of future space requirements (Hudson, 2012).

The juvenile justice system in the United States comes with a hefty price tag. Currently, confinement of youth has an estimated average cost of $588 daily per person (Justice Policy Institute, 2020). This means that, nationally, over 25 million dollars *per day* is spent incarcerating youth.[1] This staggering amount only accounts for direct costs incurred in the context of incarceration, and does not account for either the multitude of direct or the indirect costs incurred by youth, families, and communities. Currently, the ideological pendulum has begun to swing back toward the focus on treatment and rehabilitation of youth held in secure facilities. Those charged with creating educational policy must seize this opportunity of public reckoning with juvenile-justice systems to develop a new vision of educational practice students currently held in carceral settings, as well as for the larger numbers of students whose demographic and social characteristics put them "at-risk."

All children deserve an education that helps them develop the core skills and competencies necessary to fully participate in their communities as adults. In California, the state's constitution asserts education as a fundamental right essential to preserving the rights and liberties of all. The foundational documents of all 50 states of the union contain some version of this assertion, and it is the basis by which each state assumes responsibility for public education (Aragon, 2016). In California, the state constitution references and affirms both the U.S. Constitution and the Bill of Rights, by explicitly extending this right to all students.

The challenge of meeting the mandate of equal educational opportunity for the 4,131 youth detained in various California facilities has not been met. Far too many young people in the state of California, and throughout the nation, share the fate of Malcolm, whose story was given at the opening of this chapter. Many students in juvenile-justice facilities, are either Black or Brown (Suitts et al., 2014); they are male, more often than they are female (Suitts et al., 2014); and are disproportionately challenged with disabilities (Development Services Group, 2019; Bullis & Yovanoff, 2005; Burrell & Warboys, 2000). Sadly, most will not have a rehabilitative experience in juvenile-justice facilities; instead, most will leave without the academic and social–emotional competencies that would help them to avoid reoffending and to fully engage as productive citizens (Shook & Sarri, 2008).

Evidence suggests that most states have not come close to meeting their educational obligations to incarcerated youth. Surveys of Juvenile justice facilities reveal the lack of foundational classes like Algebra 1 that are required for high school graduation, and that 1 in 5 juvenile facilities have either fewer school days, and/or much lower number of hours per week than public schools in their state (Korman et al., 2019). Key legal cases brought in local, state, and federal courts further suggest the lacuna between where the system of educating court-involved youth is and where it needs to be. A case brought in Connecticut in the 1990s charged that the education being provided to wards of the state was inadequate, instruction time was insufficient, the needs of disabled children were being ignored, and there was insufficient space to accommodate a meaningful instruction program. In California, settlement of a 2010 class-action suit involving a young person who had been awarded a diploma from a juvenile justice facility without being able to read or write revealed that students in the facility were systematically denied appropriate instruction, or even allowed the required minimum time in school (*Casey A., et al. v. Robles*, 2010).

Racial and other social disparities in academic outcomes in public school systems across the nation are magnified in the juvenile justice system. Punitive and exclusionary school practices, along with policing practices targeting specific communities for intensive surveillance, combine to result in young people from those communities having disproportionate presence inside carceral contexts (Armour & Hammond, 2009). In addition to racial disproportionality, youth in juvenile-justice facilities are far more likely to have a disability that qualifies them for special-education services, and to have a personal history of maltreatment or neglect (Bullis & Yovanoff, 2005; Grisso, 2004; Quinn et al., 2005). Although these youth have arguably the greatest need for educational services and social support, they often receive the least. However, sustained community and legal advocacy have served to highlight the obligations of state and local agencies, and to ensure that detained youth receive an education in full compliance with state and federal mandates.

Population Changes and Continuities: Characteristics of Detained Youth

In the last 2 decades, the number of youths detained in residential facilities has declined rather dramatically, after a similarly dramatic rise throughout the 1980s–1990s (Abrams, 2013). As noted in Figure 14.1, these declines reflect declines in arrests, and to a certain extent, declines in crime.[2]

The declines in the number of youths detained in carceral settings are remarkable. As shown in Figure 14.1, the early 2000s brought dramatic shifts, with steady declines thereafter in the numbers of youth in judicially

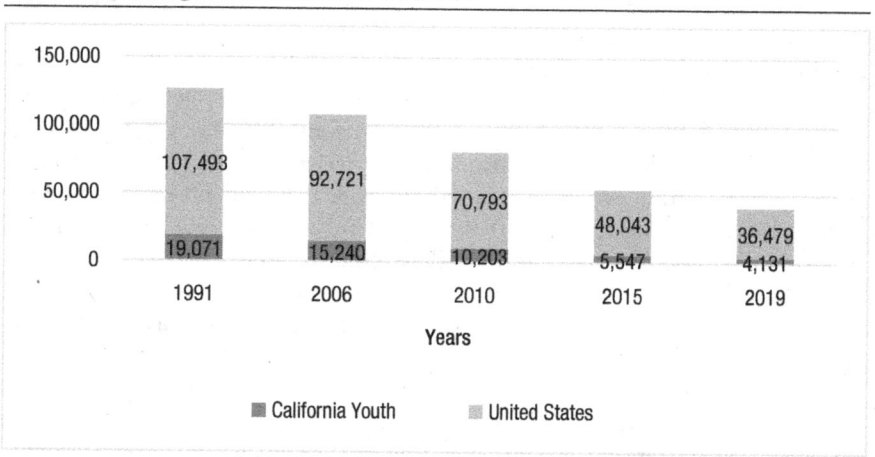

Figure 14.1. Changes in Residential Placement

Source: Sickmund, M., Sladky, T.J., Puzzanchera, C., & Kang, W. (2021). *Easy access to the census of juveniles in residential placement.* https://www.ojjdp.gov/ojstatbb/ezacjrp/

Figure 14.2. Detained Youth: Most Serious Offense 2019

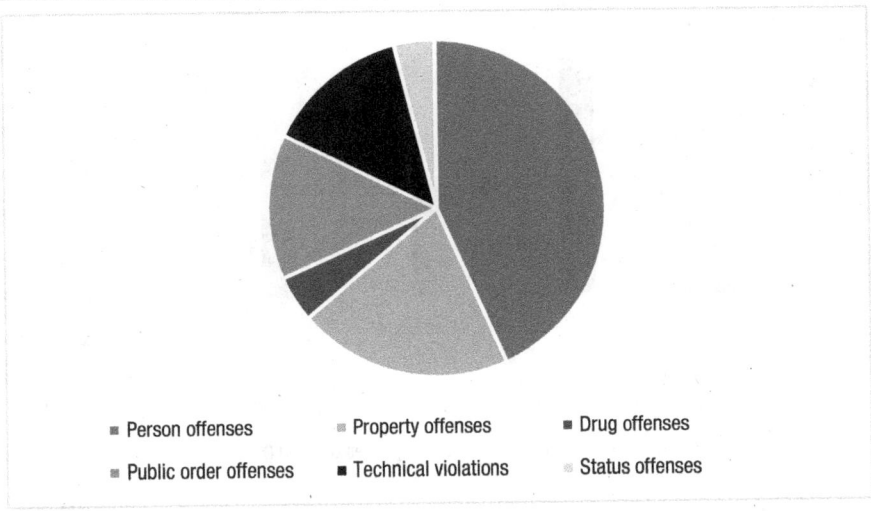

Source: Sickmund, M., Sladky, T.J., Puzzanchera, C., & Kang, W. (2021). *Easy access to the census of juveniles in residential placement.* https://www.ojjdp.gov/ojstatbb/ezacjrp/"

mandated residential placement facilities. As illustrated by Figure 14.2, most offenses for which young people are removed from their families and communities are nonviolent offenses. In fact, well over half of the most serious offenses of record for detained youth involved property offenses, technical violations, public order, status offenses, or drug offenses. While 43% of the most serious offenses are categorized as "person offenses" involving violence, that category is inclusive of threats, as well as incidents of violence.

Figures 14.3–14.5 display race/ethnic and gender characteristics of the children being detained in juvenile-justice facilities. As these charts reveal, the demographic characteristics of incarcerated youth have been historically constant in both California and in the nation; Black children, Latinx children, and Indigenous (AI) children are dramatically overrepresented relative to their demographic numbers in the general population of young people, and boys are dramatically more prevalent relative to girls. This remains as true in 2019 as it was in 1999. It is worth noting that gender disparities are greatest among Black children and least among Indigenous (AI) children.

The magnitude of decline is largest for Black boys and girls, a fact that is frankly illustrative of the degree to which they had been targeted for arrest/detainment from the mid-1980s onward (Alexander, 2012). During that time, academics, media, and politicians colluded to fill the public sphere with menacing images and descriptions of Black and Brown

Figure 14.3. Juvenile Justice Rates in the United States by Race/Ethnicity

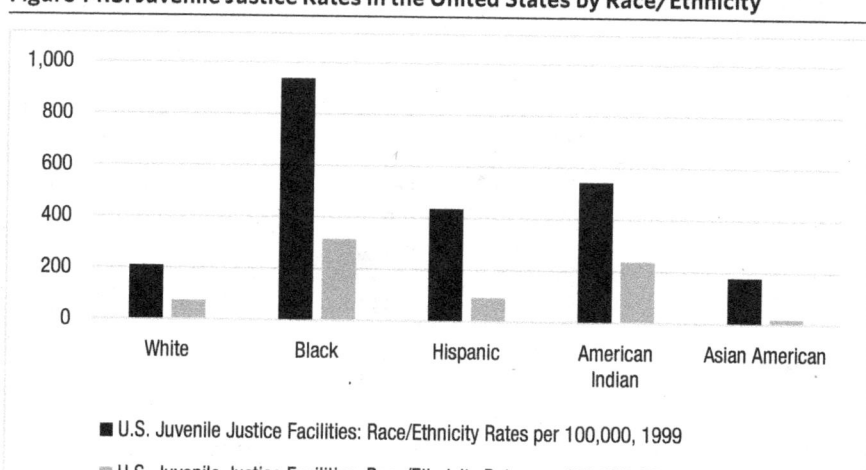

Source: Sickmund, M., Sladky, T.J., Puzzanchera, C., & Kang, W. (2021). *Easy access to the census of juveniles in residential placement.* https://www.ojjdp.gov/ojstatbb/ezacjrp/

Figure 14.4. California Juvenile Justice Facilities: Rates by Race 1999 and 2019

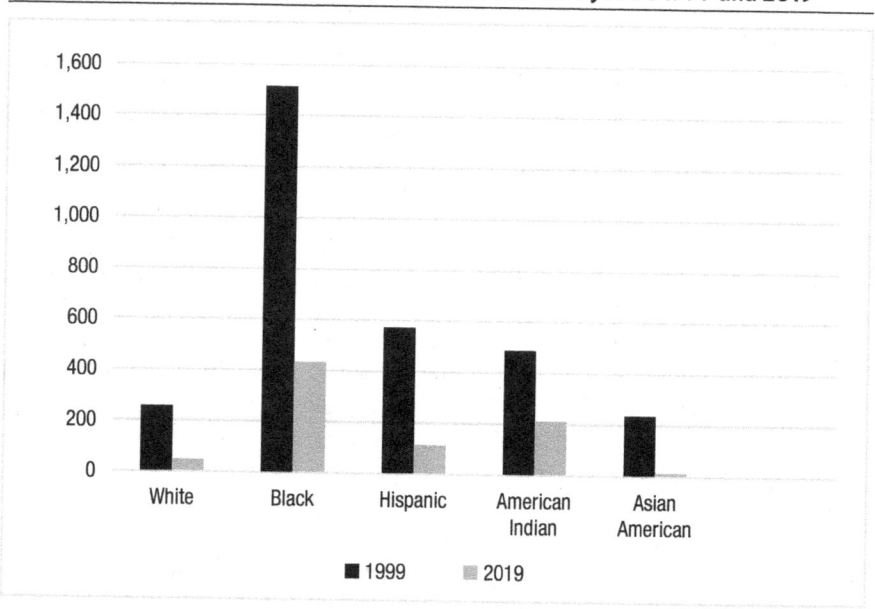

Source: Sickmund, M., Sladky, T.J., Puzzanchera, C., & Kang, W. (2021). *Easy access to the census of juveniles in residential placement.* https://www.ojjdp.gov/ojstatbb/ezacjrp/

Figure 14.5. Juvenile Justice Facilities by Race and Gender, 2019

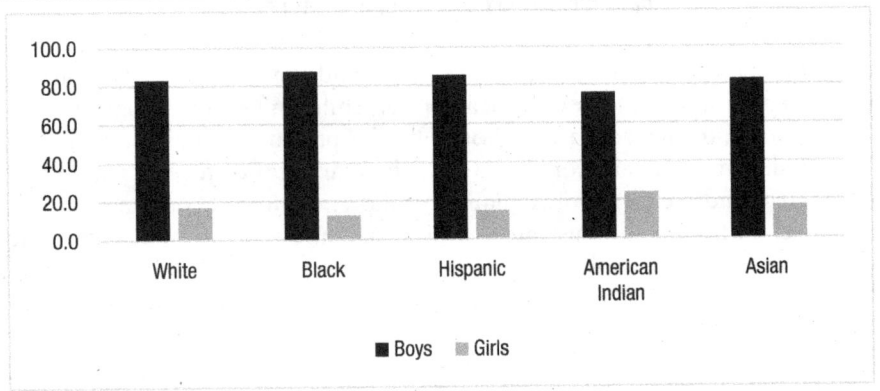

Source: Sickmund, M., Sladky, T.J., Puzzanchera, C., & Kang, W. (2021). *Easy Access to the Census of Juveniles in Residential Placement.* Available: https://www.ojjdp.gov/ojstatbb/ezacjrp/

youth as "super predators," unworthy and impervious to care (Bogert & Hancock, 2020).

The behavior of youth and adults in urban areas across the nation were hyper-criminalized, meaning that everyday behaviors and even styles of dress made them subject to punishment and criminal sanction (Alexander, 2012). For example, dressing a certain way, wearing colors, or being in the company of people defined as "gang members" could legitimately provoke scrutiny, arrest, and if found to be engaged in criminal activity, longer and more harsh sentences. Recent declines in the overall numbers of youth detained in secure facilities, it must be noted, have not been accompanied by declines in racial/ethnic disparities (Sickmund et al., 2021).

Juvenile-justice facilities contain a dramatically disproportionate number of youth with disabilities. Studies indicate that half of all justice-involved youth have some form of learning disability, and that the vast majority of youth in secured correctional facilities have at least one type of mental-health diagnosis (Bullis & Yovanoff, 2005; Cruise & Ford, 2011; Quinn et al., 2005; Lansing et al., 2014). The presence of youth with special-educational needs in juvenile-justice settings are anywhere from three to five times the percentage of public-school children with that designation (Meisel et al., 1998). The prevalence of students with disabilities in juvenile-justice settings is so high that several researchers have noted that incarceration appears to be the default education policy for providing services to such students (Nelson et al., 2010; Quinn et al., 2005). The next section reviews existing educational policy in these areas.

EDUCATIONAL POLICIES FOR INCARCERATED YOUTH AND FOR STUDENTS WITH DISABILITIES

In 2014, the U.S. Department of Education and the Department of Justice released a joint statement, that incarcerated children deserve a high-quality education, and that education should be the priority in their detainment. The guidance document confirmed that the mandates of federal legislation (i.e., IDEA and NCLB) apply equally to children in juvenile justice settings.[3] However, although administrators, legislators, and advocates all agree that this legislation must apply to students in carceral facilities, education policy has *not* provided sufficient guidance as to *how* such mandates are to be implemented or monitored.

For example, IDEA gives extensive mandates to ensure that all young people with disabilities receive individualized education services. However, implementation in carceral settings vary widely, and there is no nationwide accountability mechanism. Children in the juvenile justice system are often left unidentified, and when they are identified, often receive inadequate services (Mendel, 2010; Sedlak & Bruce, 2010). In schools across the nation, children who screen positive for having a disability must have an Individualized Education Plan (IEP) developed in consultation with parents/guardians no more than 30 days after diagnosis. Primary barriers to policy implementation of these policies in juvenile-justice facilities are the carceral design of such facilities and lack of coordinated youth development plans among agencies. In most juvenile justice settings, *if* a prior diagnosis and IEP was developed for the youth in the public school, there may be a considerable lag in communication of that diagnosis to court schools. Further, novel identification for youth lacking previous diagnosis may be delayed or may never occur at all, as the average stay in juvenile-justice facilities is about 30 days (Sickmund, 2017). Beyond communication and identification, educators and staff in juvenile-justice settings often have insufficient training. Nationwide shortages of special-education teachers are particularly acute in juvenile-justice settings (Development Services Group, 2019; U.S. Department of Education, 2016).

In 2015, Federal legislative amendments were made to Title 1 part D. of the Every Student Succeeds Act (ESSA), the reauthorized version of No Child Left Behind (NCLB). ESSA specifically requires states to provide assurances of "timely re-enrollment," credit transfer, and availability of traditional educational programs. While these changes certainly represent important federal support for meaningful educational service delivery to children in correctional settings, they do not address the key aspects of the policy to ensure the rights to quality education for students detained in juvenile justice settings.

In addition to critical concerns regarding the need for prompt identification of disabilities and learning deficits and the need for individualized accountability mechanisms, policy must provide guidance and support to ensure that research-driven educational programs are delivered by highly trained staff, as well as to ensure the availability of such staff. Oversight bodies for schools in juvenile-justice settings must also develop systems that support accountability and utilization of the IEP in juvenile-justice settings. All these concerns, it must be recognized, are made more complex by the transitory nature of youth in such facilities. Unlike most traditional school contexts where the calendar of the school year provides a suitable overarching context for planning and auditing, justice-involved students show up at various points in the school year, and their sentences are often relatively short. *For this reason, it is imperative to explicitly develop policies to ensure that youth in juvenile-justice facilities with special education needs are identified at intake, and that IEPs are developed and appropriately followed.*

In recent decades, states across the country have launched reforms in juvenile-justice systems intended to reduce the numbers of so-called "delinquent" youth, as well as recidivism (Nelson et al., 2010; Suitt et al., 2014). Educational success, it is believed, has the greatest potential for transforming the trajectory of the lives of troubled youth through its impact on career and economic opportunities, as well as the impact of education on self-concept and efficacy of young people. Students in juvenile justice contexts have generally received inadequate education prior to their detainment and are among those with the greatest need for intensive educational support (Leone & Weinberg, 2012). Delivering impactful educational services in such contexts would involve strong planning and coordination with numerous other agencies, including law enforcement/probation. What in other schooling contexts might be considered purely pedagogical considerations can only be accomplished in concert with agencies, like law enforcement, that have very different priorities and bases of expertise. The next section highlights this and other key challenges that education policymakers must address.

KEY CHALLENGES

A new vision for educational delivery for justice-involved youth must begin with full recognition of the significant unique challenges, along with a commitment to creating a truly transformative educational system.

Accountability. Among the most critical challenges facing those seeking to create transformative education in juvenile-justice contexts is ensuring accountability. While the reporting mandates of ESSA ostensibly include court schools, the schedule and indicators developed for other education contexts are not well suited to the vastly different circumstances of court schools. Among the most important considerations is the transitory nature of student's time in various types of juvenile justice facilities, which vary dramatically in length. For example, the average time a youth spends in juvenile halls, where youth stay before their case is adjudicated, is typically anywhere from a few weeks to a year. Student's time spent in "camps," or post-adjudication, secured facilities range from a few months to several years, depending on the severity of offense as well as a range of other issues. Youth assignment, and, therefore, time spent, in each type of facility begins and ends according to highly individualized circumstances, and not according to an academic or any other annual schedule. Accordingly, federal accountability guidelines created for the public schools that most young people attend are not well suited for assessing student progress in juvenile-justice settings, nor for producing accountability measures necessary to secure ongoing improvement of schools in juvenile-justice contexts.

Staffing. Another significant challenge is staffing. Issues of recruitment and retention of well-prepared teaching staff, which are critical concerns facing public schools nationwide, are even more dramatic in court schools (Billingsley, 2004). Estimates suggest that annually 20% of teachers in urban areas leave their jobs, and this problem is acute in subfields of special-education and juvenile justice (Houchins et al., 2004; Rosenow, 2005). Juvenile-justice facilities report extremely high rates of teacher turnover and teacher shortages, with upward of 50% classes staffed by substitute teachers at any given time. Substitute teachers receive little professional development to support their work in juvenile-justice contexts. In this manner, chronic staff shortages negatively impact the implementation of reforms to improve educational delivery in juvenile-justice settings.

Declining Juvenile Incarceration Numbers. As numbers of youth in residential juvenile-justice facilities decline due to shifts in public appetite for harsh punishment, it becomes more difficult, using traditional methods of educational funding, to offer the same range of academic opportunities. When funding for educational services is tied to ADA (Average Daily Attendance), it is difficult to offer a full range of courses. This is as true for court schools, as well as rural schools, and schools in rapidly gentrifying areas of large urban districts. Technology may be used to facilitate court schools in providing students access to a broader range of course offerings, as well as help teachers (including long-term substitute teachers) to engage in ongoing professional-development opportunities.

Multiagency Collaboration. At minimum, court schools require significant coordination between judicial systems (usually probation departments), and systems of education. Most court schools engage with a range of state agencies relating to the health and well-being of children. In the move away from punishment, multiagency involvement must go beyond coordination, to collaboration. In practice, this is often difficult to achieve. Funding and differences in ideological orientation are often barriers to the kind of ongoing deep communication and collaboration necessary to achieve desired outcomes for youth.

The challenges I have highlighted are certainly not exhaustive, however, they each suggest that meaningful improvements in educational outcomes for system-involved youth cannot be achieved with a piecemeal approach to reform. The next section of this chapter highlights model programs that have been developed in response to the challenges of educating youth in juvenile-justice contexts.

JUVENILE-JUSTICE MODELS: POSSIBILITIES AND CAUTIONS

In the last decade, state systems with positive, treatment-based approaches to juvenile justice have drawn considerable attention (Barton & Butts, 2008; Mears et al., 2010; Mendel, 2010; McKinny, 2019). These programs were developed in recognition of the mental-health needs of young people in juvenile-justice facilities, as well as the plethora of research demonstrating the greater efficacy of therapeutic programming, relative to traditional approaches emphasizing control and coercion (Lipsey, 2009; McKinny, 2019). The Missouri Model has been held a gold standard of this approach. Missouri employs a "whole-system" approach, with intensive ongoing counseling and support for youth that comprise the center around which all other services, including educational services, are delivered. Educational programming occurs in the same small cottages with 10–12 youth. This small group of young people live and receive most of their therapeutic and educational services together. Each of the youth have individualized treatment plans (ITP), and if they have been classified as having a disability, they will also have individualized educational plans (IEP) and will receive individual services from time to time. However, in general, there is very little time spent alone. The Missouri approach has been successful in reducing recidivism, reducing in-custody suicides, and in improving educational achievements (Mendel, 2010; Burdick et al., 2011).

In Los Angeles County, influenced by Missouri and other states enacting similar reforms, policymakers have sought to build an "LA Model" for juvenile justice that focuses on building a "culture of care" and moving away from the culture of "control" that has been predominant in its youth camps and halls (Korman & Dierkhising, 2016). Although envisioned as a "therapeutic model," the Los Angeles County Probation Department is the lead agency delivering services with a great deal of emphasis on education and "skill-building." As a key part of the agency collaboration, The Los Angeles County Office of Education developed Road to Success Academies (RTSA), which utilizes project-based learning and social–emotional learning to develop and deliver educational services. Project-based learning, as a teaching method, seeks to engage students in more personally meaningful, interdisciplinary projects that, it is believed, will result in deeper content knowledge, critical thinking, and other necessary skills. RTSA curriculum themes were developed by engaging stakeholders at each school site to address California state standards, as well as the academic and mental-health needs of the student population. Implementation of the LA Model and the RTSA model have been challenged by many of the issues highlighted in this chapter. While the LA model is inspired by the therapeutic focus implemented in Missouri, it is unclear how that focus can be adequately designed or implemented with the county's probation department as the lead agency. These two examples, along with the issues raised in this chapter, frame the following recommendations.

KEY RECOMMENDATIONS: FEDERAL, STATE, LOCAL

Ultimately, students in justice contexts are entitled to the full range of educational options available, including credit recovery; GED prep; academic coursework; career and technical education; as well as post-secondary coursework opportunities. Education must be at the center of efforts to re-envision and reform juvenile justice, and effective educational services must be trauma informed, and attend to the mental-health needs of youth in juvenile-justice settings. Whereas, in most juvenile-justice facilities across the country, public safety concerns as expressed by probation/policing agencies generally predominate, available research suggests the high educational and social costs of that approach (Aizer & Doyle, 2015; Gagnon et al., 2012). Successful reforms have been systemic and have prioritized focus on the ongoing evaluation of emotional/mental health and educational needs of youth.

The following recommendations reflect an assessment of what changes in policy needs to occur to create transformative educational systems in juvenile justice contexts.

Federal-Level Actions. It is important to begin a consideration of potentially impactful federal policy by restating that all the civil rights of students in traditional schools apply to students being educated in juvenile-justice settings. Secondly, it is also important to note the role of federal policy in creating the circumstances we are now attempting to transform (Weisburst, 2019).

In terms of explicit and public policymaking in this area, recent amendments in law under ESSA, as well as guidance issued jointly by the U.S. Department of Justice and the U.S. Department of Education, are steps in the right direction. However, to ensure intended impact, federal policy guidelines must support decarceration of youth at least as generously as it supported increased arrests of youth and policing in schools. The following are proposed critical changes at the federal level:

- There should be federal mandates to conduct regular student assessments to improve instruction and learning for youth in longer-

term juvenile-justice settings. Although juvenile-justice educational systems are not explicitly exempt from federal reporting mandates, in practice, the requirement is subverted by the conditions attendant to youth incarceration. Additionally, most youth are remanded for short stays of less than 2–3 months. Yearly reporting mandates do not currently provide information regarding the specific educational impact of various types of detention, nor any information that would help guide ongoing demands for educational improvement in juvenile-justice settings.
- Federal agencies can also play a significant role by funding the development of assessment tools, and accountability systems appropriate for the unique context of youth detention. Currently, most systems use assessment tools created for regular public schools. While this might seem to offer the ability to easily compare academic outcomes of juvenile justice-involved youth with their peers, the circumstances of youth detainment make the comparison patently ineffective and unfair.
- Funding the Special Education Mandates of IDEA in all public schools. Although current policy suggests federal funding of 40%, estimates are that current federal funding makes up just 16%. Perhaps unsurprisingly, it is reported that only 22 states and one territory are currently meeting their general educational obligations to disabled students.

State-Level Actions. As noted earlier in the chapter, the right to public education is enshrined in most state constitutions. Juvenile-justice facilities must be held accountable for maintaining educational standards that are aligned with their state's educational requirements. Currently, state legislatures across the country have begun developing reforms to reduce the numbers of youth referrals to law enforcement and student arrests. In addition to continuing taking steps to dramatically reduce the number of children in secured facilities, the following are recommendations for actions that state legislators and policymakers can take to improve educational services for youth in juvenile-justice settings:

- States must mandate that curriculum is aligned with state-education standards, and that youth in justice facilities allocate a similar amount of time to schooling.
- States must also ensure that data sharing between state agencies occurs promptly, and that youth get academic credit for coursework completed in juvenile-justice facilities.
- Demand regular accountability reporting of court schools. Reports should be aggregated at the county level to balance privacy concerns with the need for accountability.

- Create oversight mechanisms that specify supportive measures and closer review for counties with problematic academic outcomes.

Local-Level Actions. Policymakers must support partnerships between local school districts, community service providers, and area businesses to provide the full range of academic services necessary to engage students in juvenile-justice settings. Local policymakers are critical to ensuring that the community's resources are fully leveraged to support the successful transition of our most vulnerable students back into community settings. Strategies used should include:

- Creative use of technology to ensure that youth in juvenile-justice facilities have access to a full range of academic and training opportunities.
- Working in partnership with the state and local universities to address teacher recruitment and professional development to ensure full and faithful implementation of educational innovations and reforms.
- Local agencies must ensure that educational services in juvenile-justice facilities are in full compliance with federal law so that students with disabilities are identified and have an IEP that supports them in meeting academic and behavior goals.
- Local educational agencies charged with the education of youth in juvenile-justice facilities must continuously and effectively audit programs to support the use of high-impact, evidence-based educational practices.
- When local education agencies are responsible for juvenile-justice education, they should establish formal processes for annual review of aggregate student data and develop systems of sanctions and support for facilities with poor record keeping and excessive missing data.

CONCLUSION

This chapter's review of the social characteristics of justice-involved youth suggests that they are almost exclusively poor and socially disadvantaged youth who have been underserved by educational systems well before their incarceration. Accordingly, our collective vision for integrated education policy in this area must start with clear educational values for justice-involved youth, as well as for all youth in similar circumstances.

Educational policymakers, administrators, and educators working with at-risk and justice-involved youth start with the understanding not only that their work must not only address past educational harm/deficits, but that they must endeavor to ensure that the educational setting itself does not inflict additional harm on students. By that, I mean that zero-tolerance policies are antithetical to the delivery of quality education. Such policies have not only proven themselves to be ineffective in reducing the likelihood of youth crime, but they also do further harm by significantly interrupting educational delivery. Many of the policy suggestions made in this chapter can be extended to the schools from which system-engaged youth originate. Both as a way of preventing youth detention in such facilities and ensuring the successful reintegration of youth upon release.

Educators in juvenile-justice facilities, like those in the impoverished communities from which their students originate, are challenged to teach children who have experienced a great deal of trauma, and may be experiencing a range of poverty-related life challenges. Educators in both settings need ongoing training and support in *how* to coordinate education practices with professionals from other social-service agencies to ensure that educational needs of children in detention are fully met.

Educational innovations that support learning and student engagement should become the foci, around which all other agencies operate. Meaning that priority must be given to implementation of pedagogy over concerns of the apparatus of juvenile justice (public safety concerns, court appointments, and other agency's involvement).

My vision for transformative educational experiences for system-involved youth is framed by the regret that the compassionate educational delivery that my sister's student received in elementary school did not persist through his middle and high school. Instead, he was subjected to punitive and exclusionary approaches that put him in the pipeline to juvenile justice facilities and ultimately prison. My vision therefore is that we have the courage to imagine transformative educational experiences for all children, including but not limited to those in carceral settings.

NOTES

1. Using the national average daily number of youths confined multiplied by estimated average daily cost for confinement.

2. It should be noted that dramatic numbers of the prior 2 decades were not linearly related to increased reports of victimization or crime.

3. Most recently affirmed and guaranteed in 2004 clarification of the Individuals with Disability Education ACT (IDEA).

REFERENCES

Abrams, L. S. (2013) Juvenile justice at a crossroads: Science, evidence, and twenty-first century reform. *Social Service Review*, 87(4), 725–752.

Aizer, A., & Doyle, J. J., Jr. (2015). Juvenile incarceration, human capital, and future crime: Evidence from randomly assigned judges. *The Quarterly Journal of Economics, 130*(2), 759–803.

Alexander, M. (2012). *The new Jim Crow: Mass incarceration in the age of colorblindness* (rev. ed). New Press.

Aragon, S. (2016). *State and federal policy: Incarcerated youth*. Education Commission of the States.

Armour, J., & Hammond, S. (2009). *Minority youth in the juvenile justice system: Disproportionate minority confinement* [Report]. National Conference of State Legislatures.

Barton, W. H., & Butts, J. A. (2008). *Building on strength: Positive youth development in juvenile justice programs*. Chapin Hall Center for Children at the University of Chicago. http://www.yapinc.org/Portals/0/Documents/Resources/Chapin%20Hall%20Report-YAP%20Mention.pdf.

Bell, J. (2015). *Repairing the breach: A brief history of youth of color in the justice system*. https://www.burnsinstitute.org/wp-content/uploads/2015/09/Repairing-the-Breach_BI.pdf

Billingsley, B. S. (2004). Special education teacher retention and attrition: A critical analysis of the research literature. *The Journal of Special Education, 38*(1), 39–55. https://doi.org/10.1177/00224669040380010401

Bogert, C., & Hancock, L. (2020). *Superpredator: The media myth that demonized a generation of Black Youth*. The Marshall Project. https://www.themarshallproject.org/2020/11/20/superpredator-the-media-myth-that-demonized-a-generation-of-black-youth).

Bullis, M. & Yovanoff, P. (2005). More alike than different? Comparison of formerly incarcerated youth with and without disabilities. *Journal of Child and Family Studies, 14*(1), 127–139.

Burdick, K., Feierman, J., & McInerney, M. (2011). Creating positive consequences: Improving education outcomes for youth adjudicated delinquent. *Duke Forum for Law & Social Change, 3*(1), 5–28.

Burrell, S., & Warboys, L. (2000). *Special education and the juvenile justice system*. U.S. Department of Justice, Office of Justice Programs, Office of Juvenile Justice and Delinquency Prevention.

Casey A., et al. v Robles, et al. No. 2:2010cv00192 - Document 98 (C.D. Cal. 2011)

Champion, D. J. (1998). *The juvenile justice system: Delinquency, processing, and the law*. Prentice Hall.

Cruise, K .R., & Ford, J.D. (2011). Trauma exposure and PTSD in justice-involved youth. *Child Youth Care Forum, 40,* 337–343. https://doi.org/10.1007/s10566-011-9149-3

Development Services Group, Inc. (2019). *Education for youth under formal supervision of the juvenile justice system. Literature review*. DC: Office of Juvenile Justice and Delinquency Prevention. https://www.ojjdp.gov/mpg/litreviews/Education-for-Youth-in-the-Juvenile-Justice-System.pdf.

Gagnon, J. C., Houchins, D. E., & Murphy, K. M. (2012). Current juvenile corrections professional development practices and future directions. *Teacher Education and Special Education, 35*(4), 333–344.

Grisso, T. (2004). *Double jeopardy: Adolescent offenders with mental disorders*. University of Chicago Press.

Houchins, D. E., Shippen, M. E., & Cattret, J. (2004). The retention and attrition of juvenile justice teachers. *Education and Treatment of Children*, 27(4), 374–393.

Hudson, J. (2012, July 2). An urban myth that should be true. *The Atlantic*. https://www.theatlantic.com/business/archive/2012/07/an-urban-myth-that-should-be-true/259329/

Justice Policy Institute (2020). *Sticker shock: The cost of youth incarceration*. https://justicepolicy.org/wp-content/uploads/2022/02/Sticker_Shock_2020.pdf

Korman, H., & Dierkhising, C. B. (2016). *A culture of care for all: Envisioning the LA model*. Children's Defense Fund.

Korman, H., Hailley T. N., Marchitello, M., & Brand, A. (2019). *Patterns and trends in educational opportunities for students in juvenile justice schools* [Slide presentation]. Bellwether Education. https://bellwethereducation.org/publication/patterns-and-trends-educational-opportunity-students-juvenile-justice-schools-updates.

Lansing, A. E., Washburn, J. J., Abram, K. M., Thomas, U. C., Welty, L. J., & Teplin, L. A. (2014). Cognitive and academic functioning of juvenile detainees: Implications for correctional populations and public health. *Journal of Correctional Health Care*, 20(1), 18–30. https://doi.org/10.1177/1078345813505450

Leone, P., & Weinberg, L. (2012). Addressing the unmet educational needs of children and youth in the juvenile justice and child welfare systems. Center for Juvenile Justice Reform, Georgetown University Public Policy Institute. http://cjjr.georgetown.edu/pdfs/ed/edpaper2012.pdf.

Lipsey, M. W. (2009). The primary factors that characterize effective interventions with juvenile offenders: A meta-analytic overview. *Victims & Offenders*, 4(2), 124–147. https://doi.org/10.1080/15564880802612573

McKinney, H. (2019). *CYPM in brief: Research supports model's effectiveness in improving outcomes for youth*. Center for Juvenile Justice Reform, Georgetown University McCourt School of Public Policy.

Mears, D. P., Shollenberger, T. L., Willison, J. B., Owens, C. E., & Butts, J. A. (2010). Practitioner views of priorities, policies, and practices in juvenile justice. *Crime and Delinquency*, 56(4), 535–563. https://doi.org/10.1177%2F0011128708324664

Meisel, S., Henderson, K., Cohen, M., & Leone, P. (1998). *Collaborate to educate: Special education in juvenile correctional facilities. Building collaboration between education and treatment for at-risk and delinquent youth*. National Juvenile Detention Association, Eastern Kentucky University. http://www.edjj.org/Publications/list/meisel_henderso n_cohen_leone-1998.html

Mendel, R.A. (2010). *The Missouri model: Reinventing the practice of rehabilitating youthful offenders*. The Annie E. Casey Foundation. https://www.aecf.org/resources/the-missouri-model/

Nelson, C. M., Jolivette, K., Leone, P. E., & Mathur, S. R. (2010). Meeting the needs of at-risk and adjudicated youth with behavioral challenges: The promise of juvenile justice. *Behavioral Disorders*, 36(1), 70–80. https://doi.org/10.1177/019874291003600108

Quinn, M. M., Rutherford, R. B., Leone, P. E., Osher, D. M., & Poirier, J. M. (2005). Youth with disabilities in juvenile corrections: A national survey. *Exceptional Children*, 71, 339–345.

Rosenow, D. (2005). Stress, burnout, and self-esteem among educators. *Journal of Educational Research*, 4, 87–90.

Sawyer, W. (2019). *Youth confinement: The whole pie 2019*. Prison Policy Initiative.

Sedlak, A. J., & Bruce, C. (2010). *Findings from the survey of youth residential placement facilities*. https://www.ojp.gov/pdffiles1/ojjdp/227730.pdf

Shook, J. J., & Sarri, R. C. (2008). Trends in the commitment of juvenile offenders to adult prisons: Toward an increased willingness to treat juveniles as adults? *Wayne Law Review, 54*(4), 1725–1765.

Sickmund, M. (2017). National council of juvenile and family court judges passes a set of practice reform resolutions. *Juvenile and Family Court Journal, 68*(4), 43–47. https://doi.org/10.1111/jfcj.12102

Sickmund, M., Sladky, T. J., Puzzanchera, C., & Kang, W. (2021). *Easy access to the Census of Juveniles in Residential Placement*. https://www.ojjdp.gov/ojstatbb/ezacjrp/

Skiba, R. J. (2013). Reaching a critical juncture for our kids: The need to reassess school-justice practices. *Family Court Review, 51*(3), 380–387.

Suitts, S., Dunn, K., & Sabre, N. (2014). *Just learning: The imperative to transform juvenile justice systems into effective educational systems*. Southern Education Foundation.

U.S. Department of Education, Office for Civil Rights. (2016). *Protecting the civil rights of students in the juvenile justice system*. https://www2.ed.gov/about/offices/list/ocr/docs/2013-14-juvenile-justice.pdf

Weisburst, E. (2019). Patrolling public schools: The impact of funding for school police on student discipline and long-term education outcomes. *Journal of Policy Analysis and Management, 38*(2), 338–365.

CHAPTER 15

Students Experiencing Homelessness
A National Crisis

Matthew H. Morton, Earl J. Edwards, and Melissa Kull

STUDENT HOMELESSNESS AS A CENTRAL EDUCATION POLICY ISSUE

In the past 30 years, student homelessness has become a growing concern marked by alarming disparities. Advocacy organizations once described students experiencing homelessness in the United States as the "invisible million." Unfortunately, that description now falls short of reality. According to official statistics reported by the U.S. Department of Education (ED), 1,387,573 students in pre-kindergarten through 12th grade enrolled in public school districts experienced homelessness during school year (SY) 2018–19 (National Center for Homeless Education [NCHE], 2021). As a frame of reference, the number of identified students who experience homelessness in a year exceeds the entire populations of Boston and Nashville combined. This statistic reflects an 8% decrease from the previous school year, which set a record high,[1] but these data show a general trend of increasing reports of student homelessness over the last decade.

The trauma of student homelessness is pervasive and unequally distributed among the population. Although the official ED data have not included breakdowns by race, ethnicity, sexual orientation, or gender identity, survey data on student homelessness illuminate stark disproportionalities. Independent survey studies consistently find Black, Indigenous, and Latinx students disproportionately face the trauma of homelessness (Morton et al., 2018a; Morton et al., 2019; SchoolHouse Connection, 2021b). They also find youth identifying as lesbian, gay, bisexual, transgender, or queer (LGBTQ) to experience homelessness at two to three times the rates of their heterosexual and cisgender peers (Morton et al., 2018b; SchoolHouse Connection, 2021b). Youth of color who also identified as LGBTQ faced especially high rates of homelessness due to compounding risks associated with both structural racism and LGBTQ discrimination

(Morton et al., 2018b). Put simply, we cannot seriously advance education equity without prioritizing housing justice as a requisite and promoting the educational and social policies that contribute to preventing and ending youth homelessness.

Policy actions and investments in tackling student homelessness are critical to improving educational outcomes and equity among our nation's historically disenfranchised communities. The data reinforce that students' experiences of homelessness and related adversities present enormous obstacles for their ability to engage and excel in school. A study in Michigan found that 40% of students experiencing homelessness were chronically absent in school year (SY) 2016–17, a rate 2.5 times the statewide average (Erb-Downward & Watt, 2018). Research has demonstrated detrimental effects of homelessness on students' math and reading achievement (Obradovic et al., 2009; Pavlakis et al., 2017). Longitudinal studies of public-school students in Minnesota found that homelessness and high residential mobility were associated with lower math and reading achievement even compared to similar low-income but stably housed peers, and that the achievement gap widened as students got older (Cutuli et al., 2013; Obradovic et al., 2009). Recent national statistics similarly show that students experiencing homelessness score lower than a broader group of students classified as economically disadvantaged by eight to nine percentage points (NCHE 2021). As students experiencing homelessness get older, widening achievement gaps and high levels of chronic absenteeism escalate to high rates of school dropout (Galvez & Luna, 2014).

Not only is the fight against homelessness critical to our nation's educational mission, but school systems can also play central roles in that fight if adequately resourced, supported, and incentivized through policy. Schools have more interaction with youth and families than any other public institution. As such, they are often best positioned to identify youth and families experiencing homelessness, connect them with immediate resources, and help them secure long-term support for mitigating homelessness. No other single public institution has the potential to make as broad of an impact on youth and family homelessness in this since, and this fact is greatly underappreciated.

As alarming as the numbers are, it can be easy to lose sight of the human toll of homelessness on students. The experience of homelessness means so much more to a student than not having a stable place to sleep. It pervades every aspect of their day-to-day life, in and outside of the classroom. For most students experiencing homelessness, the stress of their current instability adds to complex trauma that they may have endured for years, if not throughout their lives. Beyond educational implications, research has demonstrated associations between youth homelessness and a myriad of adverse social and health outcomes, such as mental-health difficulties, substance use, sexual exploitation, exposure to violence and bullying, suicidal ideation and attempts, and early death (Auerswald et al., 2016; Perlman et al., 2014; SchoolHouse Connection, 2021b). In turn, these adversities present substantial barriers for young people's development during a key developmental period that can affect their life trajectories.

This chapter provides an overview of the current policy landscape on student homelessness followed by fleshing out three areas of policy action that stand to strengthen our national position in the struggle to end it. They involve improving identification and data, strengthening schools as a hub for wraparound and equitable support, and moving "upstream" into homelessness prevention. These are not quick fixes—they are systemic changes requiring cross-systems collaboration and leaning into the hard work of racial equity and housing justice—but they are doable and essential. Ultimately, we argue that a better system of care and support for preventing and ending student homelessness constitutes a central educational policy issue. *Put differently, the evidence underscores that we cannot reach parity in educational outcomes without ending youth homelessness.*

THE CURRENT POLICY LANDSCAPE

Federal Policies. The McKinney-Vento Homelessness Assistance Act (MVA), established in 1987 and recently reauthorized under the Every Student Succeeds Act (ESSA), is the most comprehensive federal legislation designed to support the academic achievement of students impacted by homelessness (National Center for Homeless Education, 2021). The policy defines student homelessness as students who, "due to a lack of a fixed, regular, and adequate nighttime residence," live in shelters; motels or hotels; outside, in cars, or other places not meant for human habitation; or in doubled-up situations with relatives or friends due to loss of housing or economic hardship (42 U.S. Code § 11434a(2)(A)).

The education definition of homelessness distinguishes itself from the definition used by the Department of Housing and Urban Development (HUD) for the purpose of counting homelessness and delivering homelessness services. The key distinction in the MVA definition is its inclusion of children from families who temporarily live with relatives or other adults—also known as "doubled up." The inclusion of children doubling up is critical because this population represents over 70% of the children identified as experiencing homelessness in schools, as shown in the section above. Further, children and families who are doubled up have the least amount of access to homeless services through HUD-funded agencies.

MVA mandates that once the school district identifies students as experiencing homelessness, schools are legally responsible for ensuring that their housing conditions do not interfere with their ability to access a quality education comparable to that of their stably housed peers (42 U.S. Code

§ 11431; ESSA Pub. L. No. 114-95. Stat. 2131). MVA attempts to stabilize the educational experience of students experiencing homelessness by ensuring they have the right to stay at their school of origin and have accessible transportation to and from school and school-related activities (Miller, 2011).

While MVA has improved student enrollment and identification practices of students experiencing homelessness (Miller, 2011), the policy is underfunded and over-reliant on individual district homelessness liaisons (Bishop et al., 2021; Havlik et al., 2020). In SY 2018–2019, only 67% of students experiencing homelessness graduated high school on time. In other words, over 49,000 students were identified by their school district as students experiencing homelessness and lacked sufficient support to attain a high school diploma within 4 years (National Center for Homeless Education, 2021). When schools—and the government that funds them—do not provide the necessary academic and social–emotional support to help youth impacted by homelessness graduate, our educational system not only fails to fulfill its mission to ensure that "every student succeeds," but it also sets the conditions for youth leaving the K–12 education system to experience homelessness thereafter. But policy obstacles exist for identifying students that have been the focus of new federal efforts.

A bill recently introduced by Senators Dianne Feinstein (D-Calif.) and Rob Portman (R-Ohio), the Homeless Children and Youth Act (HCYA), would amend the definition of homelessness used by the Department of Housing and Urban Development (HUD) to verify eligibility for federal homeless assistance programs. Currently, different federal agencies and programs deploy different definitions of homelessness to determine eligibility for housing resources and other supports and services. HUD's definition used to allocate housing resources is more restrictive than ED's, for example excluding doubled up or couch surfing young people and families except for certain circumstances (e.g., in cases of exploitation or fleeing violence). The discrepancy in federal agencies' definitions of homelessness has resulted in just 1 out of 10 homeless children being recognized as eligible for federal homeless programs. The HCYA would standardize definitions across the government to ensure young people living in motels and staying with people have better access to resources and to facilitate cross-program collaboration. Advocates who oppose the legislation underscore that expanding the definition does not address the broader issue of too few resources for too many people who need them. They are right, too. As this chapter argues, centering homelessness as a central education policy issue means transcending a scarcity mindset in the world's richest country and dramatically increasing the prioritization of and investment in housing resources, social and economic supports, and youth and family services to prevent and address homelessness for everyone who needs them.

The 2021 American Rescue Plan (ARP) includes nearly $50 billion in housing and homelessness resources, with approximately $800 million to support schools in identifying and supporting students experiencing homelessness. However, challenges around housing for young people did not start or mend with the pandemic. We need enduring policy commitment to housing and support resources for preventing and ending homelessness that continue until homelessness is truly rare, brief, and nonrecurring, as the federal strategic plan on homelessness states as its goal.

New funding from ARP also provides valuable opportunities for schools to be adequately funded to support students experiencing homelessness in the wake of the COVID-19 pandemic (SchoolHouse Connection, 2021a). Through this landmark legislation, the federal government has allocated $123 billion for K–12 education; in addition to providing support directly to schools, the ARP makes various resources available in communities to which MVA liaisons can facilitate connections among students experiencing homelessness. The plan includes $5 billion for emergency housing-choice vouchers and $21.5 billion for rental assistance. It also includes $40 billion for institutions of higher education to prevent experiences of material hardship, including housing instability and homelessness. Together, these resources can help young people who experienced homelessness during the pandemic to secure safe and stable housing that permits them to advance their educational pursuits.

State Policies. Some states and localities have also taken important policy steps where federal policy to support and protect students experiencing or at-risk for homelessness have been lacking. For example, in Illinois, state law (HB 261, 2017) permits school districts to provide rental or mortgage assistance, and other financial assistance, to students experiencing or at-risk for homelessness. Also, in the vein of increasing resources for these students, Washington has dedicated funding for a state grant program to connect students experiencing homelessness to stable housing in the student's school district (SB 5324, 2019). Some states have sought to address barriers that unaccompanied minors face to accessing support and advancing in school. Indiana (SB 464, 2019), for instance, allows unaccompanied youth experiencing homelessness age 16 and older to take the high-school equivalency exam without parental consent at no cost.

In addition to addressing gaps in MVA for K–12 students experiencing homelessness, some states have also expanded their student homelessness policies to support post-secondary students. States like California, Illinois, Louisiana, Maryland, and Tennessee have passed laws requiring designated student homelessness liaisons at these institutions—although the roles of and resources behind these liaisons can vary significantly. These state efforts point toward the types of supports that are needed more robustly and consistently at the federal level and provide the opportunity for evaluation and learning to inform better federal policy in the future.

IMPROVE IDENTIFICATION AND DATA

Few policy actions are more important to systemic efforts to support students experiencing homelessness than those that seek to improve identification and data. So long as so many students' experiences of homelessness remain invisible, we lack that insight and ability to meet the full scale of the challenge. Therefore, recent ARP investments, the Education for Homeless Children and Youths (EHCY) program authorized under the McKinney-Vento Homeless Assistance Act, and so many school districts have included a significant emphasis on identification.

The hidden sleeping arrangement of so many students experiencing homelessness contributes to the issue's hiddenness. Figure 15.1 presents the percentage breakdown of accompanied and unaccompanied homeless students' primary nighttime residences. For both groups, doubled-up situations comprised most homeless students' primary nighttime sleeping arrangements, but unaccompanied youth relied even more on double-up sleeping arrangements, and considerably less on hotel or motel arrangements. With the vast majority of homelessness experiences occurring outside of shelters, student homelessness is far more likely to go unknown without deliberate strategies and investments to understand young people's housing situations.

Although alarming, official statistics indubitably fail to capture the full extent of the challenge. For some students or their families, a sense of fear or shame inhibits their disclosure of homelessness experiences to school personnel or through housing questionnaires that many schools include in their annual enrollment packets. A survey of 158 18- to 24-year-olds who experienced homelessness during their middle and/or high school years found that 67% were uncomfortable talking with people at their school about

Figure 15.1. Percentages of Accompanied and Unaccompanied Homeless Youth by Primary Nighttime Residence in School Year 2018–19

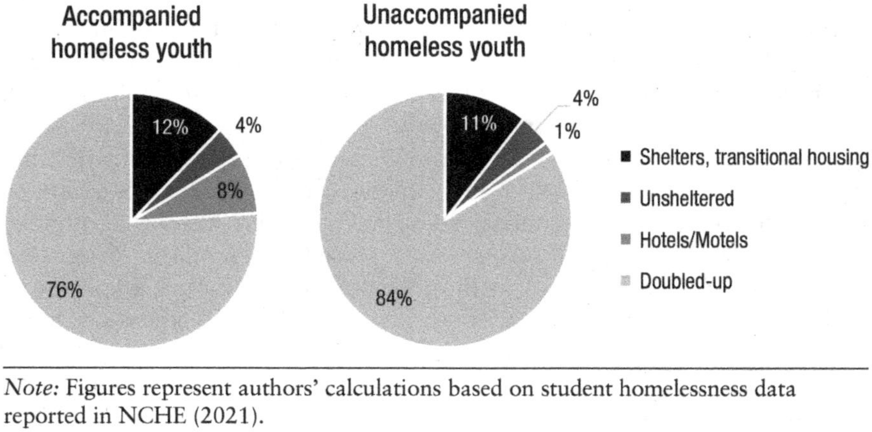

Accompanied homeless youth: 12% Shelters/transitional housing, 4% Unsheltered, 8% Hotels/Motels, 76% Doubled-up

Unaccompanied homeless youth: 11% Shelters/transitional housing, 4% Unsheltered, 1% Hotels/Motels, 84% Doubled-up

Note: Figures represent authors' calculations based on student homelessness data reported in NCHE (2021).

their housing situation and related challenges (Ingram et al., 2017). Indeed, national and local surveys point to under-identification of students experiencing homelessness.

In light of these identification issues, policy strategies to support credible and replicable representative surveys and universal screening for homelessness have the potential to shed a much better light on the scale and scope of the challenge. To gauge how officially reported student homelessness statistics compare to estimates derived from representative surveys, it helps to convert the ED counts to prevalence percentages and compare those percentages to prevalence estimates from survey studies. According to the National Center for Education Statistics (2020), 50.7 million students attended public elementary, middle, and high schools across the United States in fall 2020; 15.4 million public school students attended grades 9 to 12. Official ED statistics cited in Figure 15.1 suggest that about 2.7% of public-elementary and secondary-school students experienced homelessness in 2018–19. The 379,027 students in grades 9 through 12 experiencing homelessness comprised approximately 2.5% of public high school enrollees. The federal data report (NCHE, 2021a) does not disaggregate unaccompanied youth numbers, but even if we assume all 124,555 unaccompanied youth in SY 2018–19 were high school students, that would constitute approximately 0.8% of public high school students in the nation.

The Youth Risk Behavior Survey (YRBS) offers the closest basis for comparison of students officially identified as experiencing homelessness to a representative sample survey. The Centers for Disease Control and Prevention (CDC) first developed the YRBS in 1990 to assess the health risk behaviors of youth in the United States, and it is administered to representative samples of students in high schools across the country every 2 years. The survey includes both standard items and optional items, including two optional questions about homelessness. In 2019, 27 states included the optional homelessness questions in their YRBS questionnaires. SchoolHouse Connection's (2021) analysis of YRBS data from these 27 states found that 5.8% of high school students experienced homelessness in SY 2018–19, more than twice the rate of students identified by school districts and reported in ED's official statistics. Notably, the 2021 YRBS standard questionnaire, for the first time, included one question about homelessness, which will strengthen national estimates in the future.

A separate analysis of YRBS from just three regions also reported disaggregated estimates of unaccompanied homelessness and found prevalence rates ranging from 2.2% to 2.9% (Cutuli et al., 2015). These rates exceed two to three times the rates of unaccompanied youth homelessness indicated by official ED statistics based on identification in schools. Similarly, Voices of Youth Count (VoYC), a recent national study of youth and young-adult homelessness found that about 4.3% of households with 13- to 17-year-olds experiencing at least one night of homelessness during a 12-month period

(Morton et al., 2018a). Comparing findings from both YRBS and VoYC representative surveys reported by schools reveals clear cause for concern: Educational systems are significantly under-identifying students experiencing homelessness. The homelessness experiences of students in doubled-up and unaccompanied situations are especially hidden to school districts and undercounted in official statistics. These discrepancies underscore both the value of representative sample surveys to produce more accurate prevalence and incidence estimates of student homelessness, and the importance of increased investments and improved methods and training for school-based identification of student homelessness.

As we consider the following opportunities to improve identification and data, it is imperative for future educational policy to incentivize and fund interrelated activities. First, representative self-report survey data—like we obtain from some school districts through YRBS on student homelessness, characteristics, and other outcomes—should be collected across all our nation's school districts on a regularized basis (e.g., every 2 years), so that we have a fuller understanding of the student homelessness prevalence, incidence, and correlates. The YRBS's homelessness module and the VoYC national survey provide examples to build on, and policy actions can enable their scale up, replication over time, and infrastructure for data analysis and policy translation. Notably, the 2021 YRBS Standard Questionnaire includes, for the first time, a question on students' housing situation during the past 30 days. However, the Standard Questionnaire asked of all students will not include the (currently optional) item that captures whether a young person experiences unaccompanied homelessness. Additionally, the advantage of also investing in the replication of a national survey like the VoYC survey that is not conducted in schools is that it would capture homelessness experiences among young people who do not attend school regularly or who have dropped out; these young people are at particularly high risk for homelessness.

Second, policy should invest in the refinement of universal screening of student homelessness and its risk factors. This can include efforts that an increasing number of school districts across the country are taking on, including housing situation questions in annual school enrollment packages. For example, the New York State Education Department requires that all school districts use a housing questionnaire as the first page of the enrollment packet for all newly enrolling students and anytime they report a change of address. Pinellas County Schools in Florida have also integrated this practice over several years. Going a step further, policy investments can include efforts to develop and strengthen universal screening surveys on experiences of and risk factors for student homelessness, and school dropout that are currently under development and evaluation with the Upstream Project prevention model (introduced later in this chapter).

Finally, policy actions can increase training and support to all school personnel—administration, teachers, cafeteria staff, maintenance workers, librarians, coaches, bus drivers, and so forth—to identify signs and risk factors of homelessness and connect students with the appropriate supports. Los Angeles County's Long Beach Unified School District (LBUSD), for instance, has recently expanded its training on student homelessness identification and support from school site administrators to include school-based staff, such as school bus drivers, enrollment clerks, teachers, school counselors and psychologists, and nutrition food services staff.

STRENGTHEN SCHOOLS AS A HUB FOR WRAPAROUND AND EQUITABLE SUPPORTS

As important as improved identification of and data on student homelessness are, these efforts will lead to better outcomes if accompanied by improvements in the supports and services to which identified young people and their families can be connected to. Schools are not just institutions of learning. For some children and youth, outside of family, school is the primary, if not the sole source of social, emotional, and material support; schools provide access to quality meals, predictable routines, and nurturing relationships with school staff and peers. No population of students needs such comprehensive support from schools more than students experiencing homelessness. Further, by meeting the needs of students experiencing homelessness, schools could be better positioned to promote their achievement and graduation objectives. Figure 15.2 highlights findings regarding in-school critical supports for students from Ingram et al. (2017) finding that physical, material, and emotional support were highlighted as essential needs that were not adequately met by their schools.

Establishing Wraparound Services

Edwards (2019), in a qualitative study of youth who formerly experienced homelessness, revealed that while young people were able to obtain the necessary support to graduate high school, they accessed such support primarily through informal networks that they created, not via school. Formerly homeless youth primarily received motivational, social, emotional, and tangible support from different sources, including family members, peers, caring school faculty and staff, and adults in community-based organizations. Ultimately, the collective impact of individuals, institutions, and organizations play a critical role in providing support to housing insecure youth in Edwards (2019). However, the onus is often on each individual youth and family to find and piece the services together. When identifying

Figure 15.2. Critical Supports Students Reported Needing to Stay in and Succeed in School

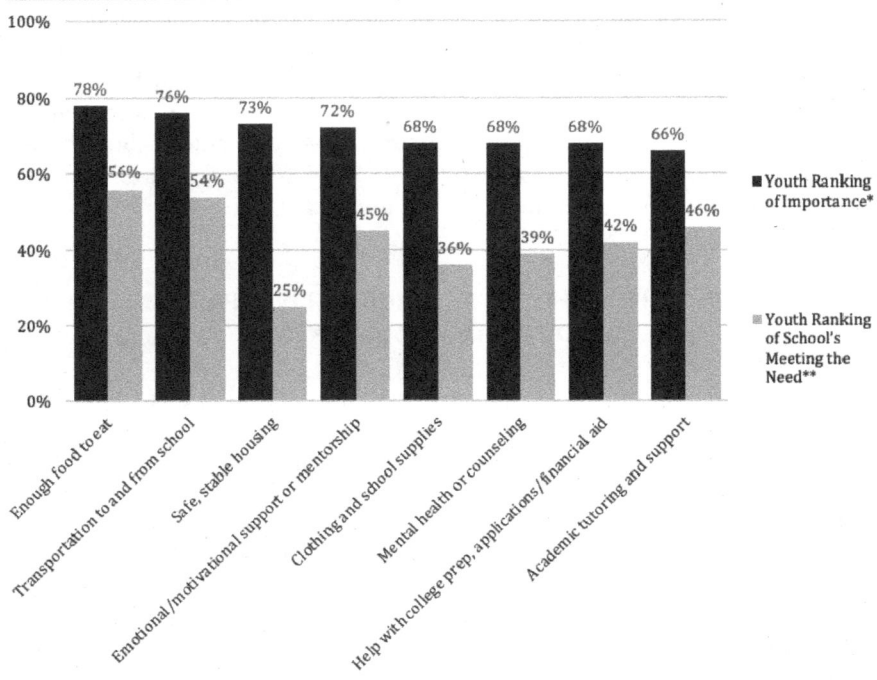

Note. Survey Data Responses from Ingram et al., 2017.

*Survey Question: How important is this in helping homeless students stay in and succeed in school? The percentage column represents the number of students who ranked the need between 8–10, 10 = very important, 0 = much less important.

**Survey Question: How good a job did your school do for you in this area when you were homeless? The percentage column represents the number of students who ranked the need between 7–10 ratings on a zero-to-10 scale, 10 = very good job, 0 = falling far short.

critical partnerships for supporting students experiencing homelessness, our education policies must look beyond the homeless liaison to find and construct a network of support for youth and families facing housing insecurity. Similarly, educators and policymakers need to be critical of the institutions that schools currently rely on for support and the ways that they criminalize students experiencing homelessness.

Divesting from Criminalizing Youth

Most schools have not yet become hubs for wraparound services, but they are often where students are arrested and investigated. Currently, schools are over-reliant on law enforcement and child-welfare agencies to address issues related to homelessness and poverty. Schools' strong connections to criminalizing agencies become a barrier to supporting students experiencing homelessness. While the fear of child protective services or law enforcement may prevent any student from disclosing their homeless status, Black youth are disproportionately targeted by these institutions and, thus, more vulnerable to their effects.

Education policymakers, teachers, and administrators cannot dictate the policies and practices of Child Protective Services (CPS), but they can mitigate its negative impact on students experiencing homelessness. For example, school personnel make up 21% of all CPS maltreatment reports (Child Welfare Information Gateway, 2020). Establishing clear norms and policies stipulating that poverty and homelessness are not acceptable reasons to call CPS can help limit the amount of unsubstantiated CPS reports. Such policies are particularly important for supporting Black youth and families as Black children are disproportionately represented in CPS. When students experience challenges, school leaders must ensure that their schools provide services for helping our most vulnerable young people rather than relying on institutions that investigate them.

To meet the needs of students experiencing homelessness, school leaders and policymakers must work to braid funding and services together that provide wraparound supports. Our current practice of misusing law enforcement and child protective services as a social support prevents students experiencing homelessness from seeking help, causing our most vulnerable children to stay in the shadows, and disproportionately traumatizing students of color, particularly Black students.

MOVING "UPSTREAM" TO PREVENTION

Across the country, homelessness systems are triaging individuals and families during housing crises and connecting them with crisis services or housing resources (e.g., shelters and rental assistance, respectively). These resources typically become available to individuals "downstream"—young people and families frequently can only access or be prioritized for safe and stable housing resources after they have experienced myriad traumas that have a pernicious effect on their health and well-being. Instead of waiting for individuals and families to endure extended periods of homelessness, communities have begun to identify the potential of cross-sector policy solutions and systems changes that better meet the needs of families further upstream—before they reach a point of crisis. Setting up systems for prevention is essential to helping young people and families avoid unnecessary traumatic events, while simultaneously positioning homelessness systems to appropriately distribute resources to youth and families with the most urgent needs.

Place-Based Opportunities to Move Upstream for Youth Homelessness Prevention

Schools and communities clearly need more innovative, equity-focused solutions that leverage school-based infrastructure to connect with young people and their families before they become homeless. One policy solution that centers youth equity, prioritizes ending youth homelessness, and builds community infrastructure to meet these aims is the Youth Homelessness Demonstration Program (YHDP). YHDP is a program funded by the Department of Housing and Urban Development (HUD) to strengthen local capacity to reduce the number of youths experiencing homelessness (NCHE, 2021b). Related objectives include building national momentum towards the cause of ending youth homelessness, promoting equitable delivery of homeless services that lead to equitable outcomes for youths, establishing a community-wide collective impact model for systemic change, and expanding the capacity of local organizations to meet the needs of youths experiencing homelessness, among others.

The first round of YHDP funding was disbursed to 10 communities in 2016, and since then HUD has supported more than 75 communities to become better equipped to meet the needs of youth experiencing homelessness. In the most recent round of awards, HUD selected 33 communities to receive $145 million dollars in funding supporting youth-homelessness prevention. Each community is required to develop a Coordinated Community Plan (CCP) that outlines a strategy toward ending youth homelessness that incorporates inputs from youth, youth-serving community-based organization representatives, local and state government representatives, other community stakeholders, and technical-assistance providers.

The Promise Neighborhoods are another community-based approach focused more specifically on building community capacity to support the educational attainment efforts of residents provides funding and support through a public-private partnership that includes braided funding from individuals, corporations, philanthropies, and public resources from HUD and other federal agencies. The aim of the Promise Neighborhoods is to center a community's entire educational pipeline—from early learning to college and career training—and strengthen cross-sector relationships while building local capacity in other community supports that enable youth to achieve educational success, such as housing and health care.

School-Based Approaches for Homelessness Prevention and Early Intervention

As noted previously in this chapter, understanding which youths are at risk for homelessness is the critical challenge in preventing youth homelessness. Universally screening students offers one way to address this challenge, and systematic universal screening has deep roots in the education sector.

Response to Intervention (RTI) is a model that schools have been using for decades to help identify students at risk of academic difficulties and learning disabilities (Fletcher & Vaughn, 2009). RTI involves three components: universal screening of students for academic and behavioral problems, monitoring of student progress, and connecting students with supports of varying intensity that align with their needs. Public health models of disease prevention have been influential in developing and applying RTI models, later referred to as multi-tiered system of support models (MTSS; Center on Multi-Tiered System of Supports, n.d.).

These models, in essence, apply prevention strategies at three levels: universal, targeted, and intensive. A widely used example is the Positive Behavioral Intervention and Supports (PBIS), an evidence-based MTSS model for preventing problem behaviors in schools (Center on PBIS, n.d.). PBIS is not a homelessness prevention model, but it provides an example of how a MTSS approach can work in broad terms. With PBIS, at the universal level (Tier 1), schools set expectations and establish a general climate conducive to student well-being and success. Among students for whom the universal supports are not sufficient to meet their needs (Tier 2), schools involve students in targeted prevention activities, including group-based social and emotional skills workshops. For the small population of students for whom Tier 1 and Tier 2 do not fully meet the need (Tier 3), the school provides individualized and intensive behavioral services and wraparound support.

In 2014, Sulkowski and Michael highlighted the potential for schools to adopt a MTSS framework to support youth experiencing homelessness, particularly regarding mental-health needs. Although no screening tools currently exist to identify youth at risk of homelessness, the authors suggest that MVA liaisons and school support staff can work together to identify students experiencing or at risk of homelessness and connect them with appropriate resources. Recent research has shown that implementation of MTSS models that incorporate services and supports for student mental health are associated with improved academic achievement, increased attendance, and better behavioral outcomes (Kase et al., 2017).

These studies highlight the possibilities of applying universal school-based screening to identify students at risk of homelessness, but there are two vital important concerns to keep in mind. First, no studies of which we are aware have taken a population approach to screen an entire student body for risk of homelessness. The extant literature on student and family self-identifying as homeless lead us to believe that universal screening is essential for reducing the stigma and related consequences associated with disclosing experiences of homelessness (Edwards, 2020; Ingram et al., 2017). Second, there are no reliable screening tools for identifying youth at risk of homelessness in school-based settings. Any screening tools used to identify students at risk of homelessness need be rigorously tested with diverse groups of students and concluded to be valid and reliable for Black, Indigenous, Latinx, and other youth.

One new model that incorporates student screening, integrated service delivery, and leverages school staff capacity is called the Upstream Project. The Upstream Project is a pioneering, place-based intervention that uses a multi-tiered system of support framework to identify, triage, and refer students who report being homeless or at risk for homelessness or school dropout. This program was originally developed and implemented in Australia and called the Geelong Project, where it was associated with a 40% reduction in youth entering the local homelessness system and a 20% reduction in student dropout (Mackenzie, 2018). This model is currently being adapted, implemented, and evaluated by Chapin Hall at the University of Chicago and its local partners in three school districts in the United States.

The Upstream Project contains four core components: (1) community collaboration, which involves incorporating the voices of students, families, and stakeholders to inform program design and implementation; (2) early identification, which uses a universal screening survey to annually assess students' risks for homelessness and school dropout; (3) flexible practice framework, which ensures that the CBO partner is providing strength-based and culturally responsive programming to students and their families; and (4) longitudinal outcomes measurement, which includes monitoring implementation and using data to inform decision-making. The Upstream model strives to ensure that youth experiencing or at risk of homelessness, particularly those holding marginalized identities, have equitable access to services and resources that allow them to achieve their educational and career goals, and ultimately avoid any future experiences of homelessness.

There remain challenges to implementing programs like the Upstream Project, including program funding, partner relationship building and trust, and the capacity of school and CBO staff and the availability of community resources. Communities could overcome these types of challenges through policy solutions like YHDP or Promise Neighborhoods, which infuse communities with resources, leading to enhanced infrastructure and the time and opportunity to build connections between partners and systems. Still, building cross-sector partnerships between schools and systems that address youth homelessness, including housing, physical and behavioral health, social services, and others, requires tremendous time and effort of all partners to accomplish the goal of preventing and ending youth homelessness.

CONCLUSION

This chapter summarizes research and data revealing the widespread challenge of homelessness among students enrolled in our public schools, the significant barriers for both young people's educational success and well-being associated with student homelessness, and the deep racial disparities in student homelessness experiences. As such, we underscore ending student homelessness as a central education policy issue and racial justice issue. This chapter elevates several ways forward for school systems and policymakers, including the following recommendations:

- Increase investments in more replicable and reliable local and national estimates of student homelessness prevalence and characteristics, including in primary, secondary, and postsecondary education. We cannot end student homelessness in the dark.
- Increase resources and training for MVA liaisons in schools and for community-based affordable housing and wraparound services to which school liaisons can connect students and their families. Policymakers need to see these investments as central to the educational mission.
- Dismantle racist policies and systems that exacerbate racialized student homelessness disparities, such as disproportionate school discipline or reporting the families of Black, Indigenous, and Latinx students to CPS. Replace them with policies and systems of housing, financial, and social supports created with and for students and families most likely to experience homelessness.
- Move "upstream" through investing in the development and evaluation of adapted MTSS models for preventing student homelessness. Like the Upstream Project example shared in this chapter, MTSS models can identify student risk factors for homelessness and school disengagement early through universal screening or early warning indicators and deliver systems of care and support appropriate to the level of need of students and their families. The only way to avoid the traumas and educational disruptions associated with homelessness is to prevent it from occurring in the first place.

Student homelessness is a solvable problem. Yet to solve this problem, our educational systems and policies need to acknowledge homelessness as a fundamental barrier to the mission of education in our society. The U.S. Department of Education's mission is to "promote student achievement and preparation for global competitiveness by fostering educational excellence and ensuring equal access." For all our students to have equal opportunity to excel in school and ultimately contribute to society, we must ensure their continuous safe and stable housing and access to support for education whenever homelessness occurs.

NOTE

1. The U.S. Interagency Council on Homelessness (2020) attributed a school year (SY) 2017–18 spike in student homelessness partly to major hurricanes that displaced large numbers of Texans that year. The student homelessness count in Texas increased from 111,177 in SY 2016–17 to 231,305 in SY 2017–18 and came back down to 114,055 in SY 2018–19 (NCHE, 2021a).

REFERENCES

Auerswald, C. L., Lin, J. S., & Parriott, A. (2016). Six-year mortality in a street-recruited cohort of homeless youth in San Francisco, California. *PeerJ, 4*, e1909.

Bishop, J., Gonzalez, L. C., & Rivera, E. (2021). America's inescapable crisis: Student homelessness. *Phi Delta Kappan, 102*(7), 42–46. https://doi.org/10.1177/00317217211007338

Center on Multi-Tiered System of Supports. (n.d.). *Essential components.* https://mtss4success.org/essential-components.

Center on PBIS. (n.d.). Getting started. https://www.pbis.org/pbis/getting-started.

Child Welfare Information Gateway. (2020). *Child maltreatment 2018: Summary of key findings.* U.S. Department of Health and Human Services, Administration for Children and Families, Children's Bureau. https://www.childwelfare.gov/pubPDFs/canstats.pdf

Cutuli, J. J., Desjardins, C. D., Herbers, J. E., Long, J. D., Heistad, D., Chan, C. K., . . . & Masten, A. S. (2013). Academic achievement trajectories of homeless and highly mobile students: Resilience in the context of chronic and acute risk. *Child Development, 84*(3), 841–857.

Cutuli, J. J., Steinway, C., Perlman, S., Herbers, J. E., Eyrich-Garg, K. M., & Willard, J. (2015). Youth homelessness: Prevalence and associations with weight in three regions. *Health & Social Work, 40*(4), 316–324.

Edwards, E. J. (2019). Hidden success: Learning from the counternarratives of high school graduates impacted by student homelessness. *Urban Education.* https://doi.org/10.1177/0042085919877928

Edwards, E. J. (2020). Young, Black, successful, and homeless: Examining the unique academic challenges of Black students who experienced homelessness. *Journal of Children and Poverty, 26*(2), 125–149.

Erb-Downward, J., & Watt, P. (2018). *Missing school, missing a home: The link between chronic absenteeism, economic instability and homelessness in Michigan.* Poverty Solutions, University of Michigan.

Fletcher, J. M., & Vaughn, S. (2009). Response to Intervention: Preventing and remediating academic difficulties. *Child Development Perspectives, 3*(1), 30–37. https://doi.org/10.1111/j.1750-8606.2008.00072.x

Galvez, M., & Luna, J. (2014). *Homelessness and housing instability: The impact on education outcomes.* Urban Institute.

Havlik, S. A., Schultheis, K., Schneider, K., & Neason, E. (2020). Local Liaisons: Roles, Challenges, and Training in Serving Children and Youth Experiencing

Homelessness. *Urban Education, 55*(8–9), 1172–1202. https://doi.org/10.1177/0042085916668954

Ingram, E. S., Bridgeland, J. M., Reed, B., & Atwell, M. (2017). *Hidden in plain sight: Homeless students in america's public schools*. Civic Enterprises. Retrieved from https://eric.ed.gov/?id=ED572753

Kase, C., Hoover, S., Boyd, G., West, K. D., Dubenitz, J., Trivedi, P. A., Peterson, Hilary J., & Stein, B. D. (2017). Educational outcomes associated with school behavioral health interventions: A review of the literature. *Journal of School Health, 87*(7), 554–562.

Mackenzie, D. (2018). *The interim report: The Geelong project 2016–2017*. https://www.grllen.com.au/static/uploads/files/tgp-interim-report-2018-final-wfbsibseebhq.pdf.

Miller, P. M. (2011). A critical analysis of the research on student homelessness. *Review of Educational Research, 81*(3), 308–337. https://doi.org/10.3102/0034654311415120

Morton, M. H., Chávez, R., & Moore, K. (2019). Prevalence and correlates of homelessness among American Indian and Alaska native youth. *The Journal of Primary Prevention, 40*(6), 643–660.

Morton, M. H., Dworsky, A., Matjasko, J. L., Curry, S. R., Schlueter, D., Chávez, R., & Farrell, A. F. (2018a). Prevalence and correlates of youth homelessness in the United States. *Journal of Adolescent Health, 62*(1), 14–21.

Morton, M. H., Samuels, G. M., Dworsky, A., & Patel, S. (2018b). *Missed opportunities: LGBTQ youth homelessness in America*. Chapin Hall at the University of Chicago.

National Center for Homeless Education. (2021). *Federal data summary school years 2016–17 through 2018–19*. University of North Carolina at Greensboro.

National Center for Education Statistics, U.S. Department of Education. (2020). *Back to school statistics*. https://nces.ed.gov/fastfacts/display.asp?id=372.

National Center for Homeless Education. (2021a). *Federal data summary: School years 2016–17 through 2018–19: Education for homeless children and youth*. https://nche.ed.gov/wp-content/uploads/2021/04/Federal-Data-Summary-SY-16.17-to-18.19-Final.pdf

National Center for Homeless Education. (2021b). *Incorporating education into coordinated community responses to youth and young adult homelessness: Lessons from the youth homelessness demonstration program*. https://nche.ed.gov/wp-content/uploads/2021/03/yhdp-round3-summary-profile.pdf

Obradovic, J., Long, J. D., Cutuli, J. J., Chan, C. K., Hinz, E., Heistad, D., & Masten, A. S. (2009). Academic achievement of homeless and highly mobile children in an urban school district: Longitudinal evidence on risk, growth, and resilience. *Development and psychopathology, 21*(2), 493.

Pavlakis, A. E., Goff, P., & Miller, P. M. (2017). Contextualizing the impacts of homelessness on academic growth. *Teachers College Record, 119*(10), 1–23.

Perlman, S., Willard, J., Herbers, J. E., Cutuli, J. J., & Eyrich Garg, K. M. (2014). Youth homelessness: Prevalence and mental health correlates. *Journal of the Society for Social Work and Research, 5*(3), 361–377.

SchoolHouse Connection. (2021a). *Student homelessness: Lessons from the Youth Risk Behavior Survey (YRBS)*. https://schoolhouseconnection.org/student-homelessness-lessons-from-the-youth-risk-behavior-survey-yrbs/

SchoolHouse Connection. (2021b). *Summary of American Rescue Plan (COVID-19 Package) Provisions on education, early care, housing, and homelessness.* https://schoolhouseconnection.org/congress-passes-the-american-rescue-act-plan-funding-for-homeless-children-and-youth-included/

Sulkowski, M. L., & Michael, K. (2014). Meeting the mental health needs of homeless students in schools: A Multi-Tiered System of Support framework. *Children and Youth Services Review, 44,* 145–151. https://doi.org/10.1016/j.childyouth.2014.06.014

U.S. Interagency Council on Homelessness. (2020). *Expanding the toolbox: The whole-of-government response to homelessness.* https://www.usich.gov/resources/uploads/asset_library/USICH-Expanding-the-Toolbox.pdf.

CHAPTER 16

Bringing the Vision Together
How to Reach the Policies We Need

Joseph P. Bishop

Each chapter in *Our Children Can't Wait* has deepened our understanding of the historical and political landscape that has shaped policies and education outcomes across America. We have drawn linkages to the emerging sciences on how students learn and develop, reinforcing the urgency for a far-reaching policy agenda that centers race, embodying whole-family and whole-community policies. The authors have also highlighted strategies at the local, state, and federal levels that present new possibilities for how social policies can be developed, implemented, and supported by key stakeholders, especially young people themselves. In many instances, the authors have pointed to the pandemic as an illuminating moment for our country when business-as-usual politics and policymaking are insufficient. COVID has made it clear that the neat and tidy ways in which policies are often developed, separating issues, people, and policies into separate buckets is inadequate for addressing racial and economic inequities that date back to the origins of our country.

This chapter aims to expand upon existing ideas for policy processes. It seeks to show how new and iterative policy cycles can achieve racial justice for communities that have been overlooked or not served well in public policy, proposing a new framework for application. We are trying to reach "the how" of a reinvented idea of what education policy is and, thus, cannot be limited to the analysis in this chapter. The social sciences are still uncovering the complexity, fluidity, and nuances associated with public policy that aims to bridge issues, budgets, and priorities as a path towards justice. However, key tools in this chapter can help inform a guide for making the monumental jump from "what we need" to "how we get there." The chapter is organized into three sections: (1) a summary of research on more integrated, intersectional approaches to policy; (2) a new model for policymaking that can be applied to interrelated issue areas; and (3) a conclusion with next steps for readers wishing to move on the ideas of this book.

THE PROMISE OF MORE-INTEGRATED, INTERSECTIONAL APPROACHES TO PUBLIC POLICY

There has been growing interest in intersectional policy approaches that address "the way specific acts and policies address the inequalities experienced by various social groups" (Bishwakarma, Hunt & Zajicek, 2007) and to avoid the pitfalls of one-size-fits-all policy approaches that can be ineffective (Parken & Young, 2007). *Social groups* as a broad term includes social identities such as race, class, gender, ability, geography, and age as the focal point of policy (Hankivsky & Cormier, 2011), acknowledging that no identities are monolithic or unitary in nature (African American Policy Forum, 2009; Parken & Young, 2007). Scholars have raised the significance of policies that point to the relationship and interdependence of people, laws, and institutions in crafting solutions intended to address historic inequities (Hankivsky & Cormier, 2011) and multiple layers of inequality (Parken & Young, 2007, 2008).

These examples and theories can be tied back to the story of Sean, a young man I referenced in Chapter 1 who I met at a drop-in center after his long bus ride. Sean was visiting a nonprofit that serves youth experiencing homelessness to provide access to services, food, and support. As a young man, Sean had been in and out of school systems, and was moving to different locations to sleep every night based on where he felt safe to sleep in Los Angeles. His story describes the relationship between education, housing, transportation, city, county, and community-based partners and how they interact with him. Sean's description of "feeling like I was passing through" the schools present a public-policy direction not only for the school system but also for interdependent entities that have served him as a resident of Los Angeles. This leaves readers with a number of questions. For example, what could have partners done differently in-school and out-of-school in Sean's "ecosystem" to make him feel valued, a sense of agency, and cared for? What type of collaboration currently occurs between education, housing, transportation, and community-based organizations? Grounding an appropriate social response to Sean from more of an ecological, collaborative approach that takes his lived experience into consideration is why more integrated strategies working across people, systems, and sectors has clearly been lacking in his experiences (Bishop & Noguera, 2019).

Looking ahead toward solutions and more racially responsive systems for young people like Sean that are closely aligned are the focal points of this book. We've examined a host of issues, including health, housing, racially integrated communities, community safety, and how they can better support youth like Sean experiencing homelessness and other structural challenges. Yet few of these efforts begin as a policy idea and in some instances, policies can get in the way of partnerships that prioritize the education, health, and care of young people of color (Smith et al., 2021). So how can policies and policy processes be an instrument for justice and change? This next section expands upon a working model for a policy process (Parken & Young, 2007) based on the ideas of intersectionality and more integrated, community-driven policy solutions. The model is also grounded in the ideas and promise of codesign for public policy (Blomkamp, 2018).

New Policy Process Framework

This description of Figure 16.1 captures the book's core values and the central tenets of a new way of constructing, implementing, and learning from policy as a nonlinear, fluid process. These steps reflect a dynamic process that views policies as powerful instruments for accomplishing justice and beginning to address the gap between policy intent and impact, common in different social contexts (Qian & Walker, 2011). The framework acknowledges that policies are only effective when there is fidelity in implementation and that policies inherently are not solutions to addressing inequities. Rather, they are often a starting point, not a ceiling for possibilities.

Listen. The significance of listening to students and families and those closest to issues that affect them is gaining prominence as essential to informing policy goals (Krumer-Nevo, 2005). Keisha L. Green, Justin Coles, and Jamila Lyiscott described new strategies and examples in their chapter for making young people central to policy processes, a key perspective too often overlooked. Asking youth and families about their lived experience is a valuable source of knowledge. Doing so can also help lawmakers make

Figure 16.1. Justice-Centered Policy Process

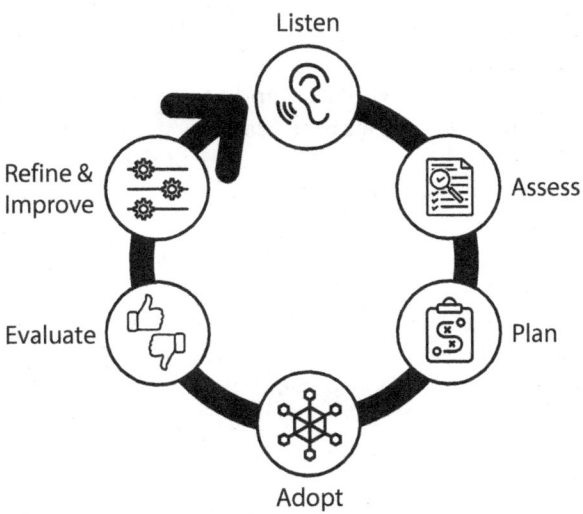

sense of patterns across issues and social identities to help generate potential policy solutions. Research makes clear that listening to community members as authentic partners in the policy process and seeking their expertise can be generative and bridge the intent and impact gap for policy (Diez et al., 2018).

For example, a new policy centered on health access to bring more community-based health centers to schools could be ineffective for working families who may struggle to get to school sites during normal school hours while working multiple jobs. Asking families how they can best be served and supported, instead of telling them about a new policy, can begin to shorten the intent and impact gap (Diez et al., 2018). Communities of color who are sometimes the target of policies, if not valued as partners in policy development, or not even aware of strategies, will never reap the benefits of good intent to advance racial justice (Goldin & Kasnabis, 2021). These points all underscore the significance of why reaching out and listening to community members needs as partners and experts is such an integral part of any policy process.

Assess. Lawmakers and policy decision-makers can benefit from examining existing data at the local, regional, state, or national level that may explain the relationship between issues like health access and education outcomes to inform the development of appropriate policies. For example, our research team at UCLA found a strong relationship between education, health access, and air quality for K–12 Black students in Los Angeles County (Johnson et al., 2021). We discovered that the same school districts serving a majority Black students with comparatively lower school attendance, achievement scores, and college readiness rates in the county also were experiencing stark environmental, economic, and health inequities in their neighborhoods. In response to our research, we recommend race and place-based strategies to improve local, state, and federal-level conditions. County officials are now pursuing some of these recommendations based on our study. Often, lawmakers and community leaders do not have this type of racialized and geographic data to shape their policy agenda. However, if they do and if laws can be better informed by more precision data points, based on data collected from interviews and multiple social variables (Ghani, 2018), lawmakers can be more effective in developing strategic, targeted policy solutions.

Plan. Building upon codesign for public policy principles (Blomkamp, 2018; see Table 16.1), joint-policy planning and development between community members and those serving in traditional policymaker roles reinforces the ideas of the previous two components of a justice-centered policy process that starts with *listening* to "enabling or empowering people affected by a policy issues to actively contribute to developing a solution for it" (Blomkamp, 2018, p. 732) and *assessing* the current landscape or close examination of a problem from multiple vantage points.

Table 16.1. Blomkamp (2018) Key Components of Co-Design for Policy

Process	Iterative stages of design thinking, oriented toward innovation
Principles	People are creative; people are experts in their own lives; policy should be designed by people with relevant lived experience
Practical Tools	Creative and tangible methods for telling, enacting, and making

As part of a rigorous planning process, developing policies requires taking stock of introduced legislation, existing policies, and implementation hurdles to avoid duplicating efforts or to determine whether there is a need for new policies or better guidance and implementation of current priorities. This can be a labor-intensive endeavor. According to the National Conference of State Legislatures, more than 109,000 pieces of legislation are introduced each year (NCSL, 2017) and state houses and the 116th Congress introduced 12,000 bills over a period of 2 years (Gov Track, 2022). Familiarity with policies that have been adopted already that align with a broader vision of education policy outlined in this book and better understanding the impact of those efforts can help to discern what is still needed to accomplish a justice-centered agenda.

Returning to the earlier themes of this book around the historical and political landscape that has shaped policy in the United States, it is essential to prioritize what policies are based on existing evidence (*listen and assess*) and consider what may be achievable based on existing resources and the political terrain. Doing so requires an analysis of perspectives on organizations and constituents supporting policies, especially race-centered approaches, potential opponents, and champions. Analysis should include community members who have shaped policy and other lawmakers. In today's hyper-politicized context, prioritizing short-term and long-term policy priorities to determine what can get support today and what may be feasible as a long-term goal is worth consideration to limit resistance. Not everything can be accomplished in a legislative session, cycle, or even political terms, especially the agenda outlined in this book to address systemic racism through social policies.

Adopt. The process of policy adoption and policy implementation is the primary focus of the tenet of "adopt" as part of a justice-centered policy framework. Social-science research has historically focused on early policy development like agenda setting, policy formation, and decision-making with little focus on the execution of policy until more recently (Howlett, 2019; Jones, 1984). To establish new ways of thinking around policy implementation, I propose that, instead, we should be moving toward ways to build capacity, aid, and connect an ecosystem of partners (Bishop & Noguera, 2019; Bronfenbrenner, 1986) as they move toward operationalizing the equity-centered ideas of policy. This is different from other policy implementation work that often looks at the effectiveness of individual actors, organizations, and governance to determine which policies have been successfully implemented (O'Toole, 2000).

Encouraging important connections between community members, service providers, school districts, and county governments can help implementation foster what Honig and Hatch (2004) calls "boundary spanners." Boundary spanners are essential to a policy vision outlined in this book for experts who can operate in nontraditional roles to bring about more collaborative social policies. Codesigned, collaborative policies call for new roles and relationships among schools, community agencies, city and state governments, and other public bureaucracies to improve learning, health, and the lives of all young people, especially young people of color. However, there is a need for more models that can help cross-sector collaboratives function in unprecedented ways that center on young people, models that we've begun to uncover within specific issues and chapters. New cross-cutting efforts are desired if "moat approaches" or isolated efforts as referenced in Chapter 1 are not only problematic for policy development but also for adoption and implementation. Bridging the intent and impact gap (Diez et al., 2018) requires greater capacity in policy development and especially in implementation to meet local needs.

Evaluate. Determining the impact of a policy and having multiple proof points or variables to do so is a critical part of any policy process. This is especially true for a process that mirrors many of the issues included across each chapter to gauge the impact of policies with a racial analysis. However, evaluation serves a much greater role in the policy process than one might realize. It presents a unique opportunity to reflect on where in the policy process, ideas, intent, and implementation have fallen short or where new and unexpected findings have taken shape. Lemire et al. (p. 48, 2020) describes its value. "Evaluation is a particular type of policy analysis that uses systematic data collection and analysis to determine the worth—often the formative or summative effectiveness—of a program or policy. Formative evaluation considers program processes, and summative evaluation examines a program or policy's ultimate outcomes and impacts."

In a political context, often the default response is, "Did a policy work or not?" "Should it be funded again?" "What do we have to show for it?" While these questions are worthy, they often oversimplify the very nature of policies and the purpose of evaluation as a critical form of knowledge to shape policy processes. For one, policies are not implemented in a vacuum and, two, local context can profoundly affect the success of a law. Lemire et al.'s (2020) evaluation framework (Figure 16.2) pushes us to think about the inherent values, methods, and use of policies to advance a particular cause or multiple causes. The authors organize evaluation as a source of knowledge into three categories: the *methods* by which evidence about social programs and policies are derived (the types of evidence called for), the *valuing* of the merit and worth of social policies and programs (the standards and criteria used), and

Bringing the Vision Together: How to Reach the Policies We Need 275

Figure 16.2. Recent Trends on the Evaluation Tree (Lemire et al., 2020)

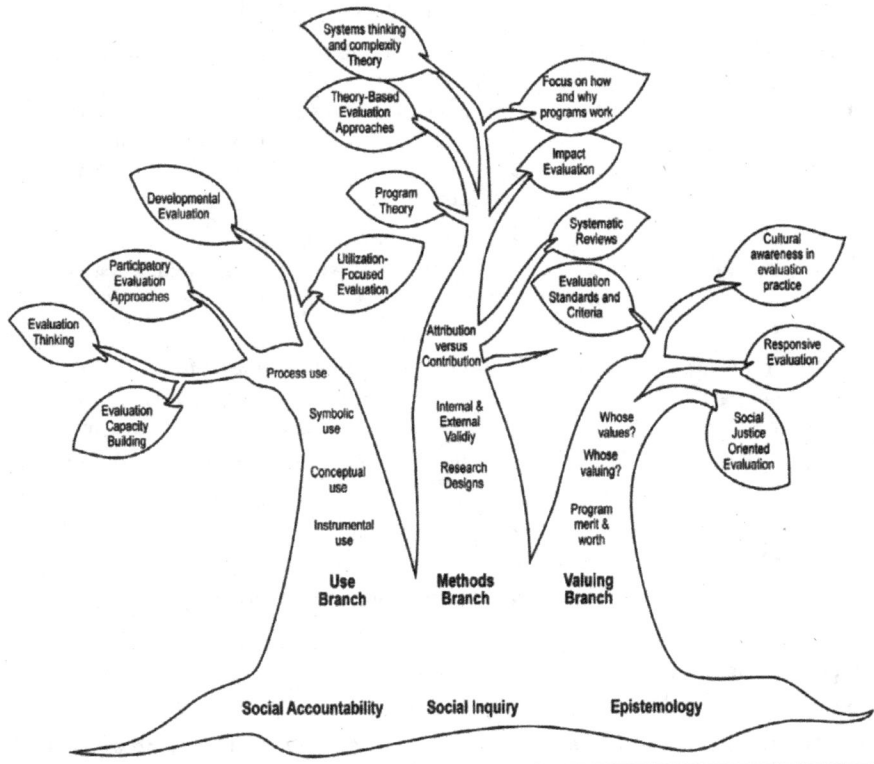

the potential *use* (or misuse) of these judgments as reflective of and responsive to policy and program decision-making.

Tied to many of the themes of this book, Table 16.2 outlines questions that could be asked as key drivers as part of a racial equity–centered evaluation strategy to inform the effectiveness of policy and future related efforts related to such policies. Questions and examples correspond to Figure 16.2, Lemire et al.'s (2020) framework. Each chapter and example could utilize this schema to dissect whether policy intent is indeed meeting local needs.

This is a more comprehensive way of thinking about evaluation compared to standard evaluations that consider input, process, and outcome indicators, like program-evaluation data points that gauge the effectiveness of a particular policy like the Centers for Disease Control Approach to Evaluation Program Performance & Evaluation Office (Centers for Disease Control, 2021; see Figure 16.3).

Evaluation is still an often-underutilized form of analysis to better understand the promise or potential pitfalls of a policy. Even more broadly, meaningful data (e.g., policy design, implementation, progress toward goals) and

Table 16.2. Applying Our Children Can't Wait Policy Themes to Lemire et al., (2020): Recent Trends on the Evaluation Tree

Social Policy Example	Branches of Evaluation	Question To Inform Evaluation Method
Healthy Chicago Public Schools (Chapter 7)	Methods Branch	What strategies are being used to implement Healthy CPS to help streamline health and wellness initiatives already taking place at school? (e.g. including physical activity, nutritious foods, school-based health services, health education)
Vermont School Environmental Health Act (Chapter 8)	Valuing Branch	Is the legislation helping schools identify, prevent, and solve indoor air quality issues as a central equity value for education in the state?
COVID Education Relief Dollars (Chapter 12)	Use Branch	Are districts utilizing **federal funds** to support equity goals that align to allow use of funds including community schools, innovative bilingual programs, and efforts to diversify the workforce?

Figure 16.3. Centers for Disease Control Approach to Evaluation

Summary: Indicators can relate to any part of the program or policy and its logic model or program description. Here are three big and most common categories of indicators.

Input Indicators: Measures the contributions necessary to enable the program or policy to be implemented (e.g., funding, staff, key partners, infrastructure).

Process Indicators: Measures the programs or policies activities and outputs (direct products/deliverables of the activities). Together, measures of activities and outputs indicate whether the program is being implemented as planned. Many people use output indicators as their process indicators; that is, the production of strong outputs is the sign that the program's activities have been implemented correctly. Others may collect measures of the activities and separate output measures of the products/deliverables produced by those activities. Regardless of how you slice the process indicators, if they show the activities are not being implemented with fidelity, then the program risks not being able to achieve the intended outcomes.

Outcome Indicators: Measures whether the program or policy is achieving the expected effects/changes in the short, intermediate, and long term. Some programs or policies refer to their longest-term/most distal outcome indicators as impact indicators. Because outcome indicators measure the changes that occur over time, indicators should be measured at least at baseline (before the program/project begins) and at the end of the project. Long-term outcomes are often difficult to measure and attribute to a single program. However, that does not mean a program or policy should not try to determine how it is contributing to the health impact of interest (e.g., decrease in morbidity related to a particular health issue).

strong evidence could play a much larger role in policy processes (Pearson & Smith, 2020). Often, however, politics and political forces outlined at various points in this book trump good evidence or use of research in policymaking (Kraft & Furlong, 2019). This is especially true when policy aims to address race-based and more structural social inequities (McIlwain & Caliendo, 2020).

Refine and improve. The final tenet of "refine and improve" as part of a justice-centered policy process provides the opportunity to enhance not only policy implementation but also future policy development that seeks to dismantle systemic racism. This work and the chapter themes in this book are complex enough that no one policy or institution can own a silver bullet for progress. Rather, like a layered cake, policies must have multiple strands of work happening simultaneously (Parken & Young, 2007). The quick-fix mindset that often dominates public policy requires a major shift in thinking (Hankivsky & Cormier, 2011) over many legislative cycles, political terms, and even generations. The common thread in the domains of a justice-centered policy process remains a desire to refine, improve, and persist toward justice during the entire policy process for codesigned policy (Blomkamp, 2018; Hankivsky & Cormier, 2011).

Intersectional policy geared toward equity, improvement, and learning includes a policy process that is (1) inherently an iterative interplay requiring constant refinement involving many decision-makers and sectors (e.g. organizers, community-based organizations, interest groups, lawmakers, agencies); (2) a process of reflection and prioritizing how laws can further equity goals; (3) defined by efforts that aim to integrate policies that consider how institutions and lived experiences influence the lives of young people; (4) informed by multiple decision points and indicators of success as described in the previous description of *evaluate*.

Summary

Establishing clarity in policy goals (*assess*) to advance a justice agenda based on the expertise of a variety of key stakeholders, including students, families, and caregivers of color (*listen*) who are often most affected by policies, and using strategic systems and monitoring for successful implementation (*adopt*) and monitoring (*evaluate*) as part of a robust policy process (*refine and improve*) was the focus of this final chapter. These components are never static or linear but essential to a justice-centered policy process (Figure 16.1). Building in time for reflection, data-driven decision-making and ways to integrate efforts becomes especially necessary knowing that policy efforts to address past harms and make strategic investments in communities of color have been met with resistance. Collective action and a multistrand approach (Parken & Young, 2007, 2008) tackling issues of education, health, environmental justice, community safety, funding, housing, and segregation simultaneously increases the likelihood of a policy working in one space even if it may face too much opposition in one arena.

CONCLUSION

This book should give readers a heartened feeling that a new type of justice agenda does exist that bridges issues, ideas, and people in ways that we've never seen before or even imagined until now. The impossible should become the imperative. An education policy playbook that looks both within and outside the school walls for solutions that begin to dismantle the entrenched forces of systemic racism in our country has never deserved greater attention or focus.

Our children can't wait for the urgent policies needed now in cities, school boards, state legislatures, and congress to help the country bounce back from a pandemic that has profoundly impacted millions of young people and families across the country. Our children can't wait for a shared conviction from lawmakers and voters alike to acknowledge our past wrongs and to push forward an affirmative plan for transforming our current trajectory by race, ethnicity, economics, gender, and generation. As Milbrey McLaughlin wisely noted, governments cannot mandate what matters most (1991, p. 7). But we can say what does matter to us as a country through our policies. That redemptive journey starts with making an unapologetic commitment to our young people, especially youth like Sean. Our children can't wait.

REFERENCES

African American Policy Forum. (2009). *A primer on intersectionality.* Columbia University Press

Bishop, J. P., & Noguera, P. A. (2019). The ecology of educational equity: Implications for policy. *Peabody Journal of Education, 94*(2), 122–141.

Bishwakarma, R., Hunt, V., & Zajicek, A. (2007). Intersectionality and informed policy. *Copy in possession of the authors.*

Blomkamp, E. (2018). The promise of co-design for public policy. *Australian Journal of Public Administration, 77*(4), 729–743.

Bronfenbrenner, U. (1986). Ecology of the family as a context for human development: Research perspectives. *Developmental Psychology, 22*(6), 723–742. doi: 10.1037/0012-1649.22.6.723

Centers for Disease Control. (2021). *Indicators: CDC approach to evaluation.* Program Performance and Evaluation Office (PPEO). https://www.cdc.gov/evaluation/indicators/index.htm

Díez, J., Gullón, P., Sandín Vázquez, M., Álvarez, B., Martín, M. D. P., Urtasun, M., & Franco, M. (2018). A community-driven approach to generate urban policy recommendations for obesity prevention. *International Journal of Environmental Research and Public Health, 15*(4), 635.

Ghani, R. (2018, June). Data science for social good and public policy: examples, opportunities, and challenges. In *SIGIR '18: The 41st International ACM SIGIR Conference on Research & Development in Information Retrieval*. Association for Computing Machinery. https://doi.org/10.1145/3209978.3210231

Goldin, S., & Khasnabis, D. (2021, December). In the pursuit of justice: Moving past color-evasive efforts. *The Educational Forum, 86*, (1), pp. 1–4.

GovTrack (2022). *Bills: Statistics and historical comparison*. https://www.govtrack.us/congress/bills/statistics

Hankivsky, O., & Cormier, R. (2011). Intersectionality and public policy: Some lessons from existing models. *Political Research Quarterly, 64*(1), 217–229.

Honig, M. I., & Hatch, T. C. (2004). Crafting coherence: How schools strategically manage multiple, external demands. *Educational Researcher, 33*(8), 16–30. doi:10.3102/0013189X033008016

Howlett, M. (2019). Moving policy implementation theory forward: A multiple streams/critical juncture approach. *Public Policy and Administration, 34*(4), 405–430.

Johnson, S. L., Jr., Bishop, J. P., Howard, T. C., James, A., Rivera, E., & Noguera, P. A. (2021). *Beyond the schoolhouse, digging deeper: COVID-19 & reopening schools for Black students in Los Angeles*. Center for the Transformation of Schools, School of Education & Information Studies, University of California, Los Angeles.

Jones, C. O. (1984). *An introduction to the study of public policy*. Brooks/Cole.

Kraft, M. E., & Furlong, S. R. (2019). *Public policy: Politics, analysis, and alternatives*. CQ Press.

Krumer-Nevo, M. (2005). Listening to "life knowledge": A new research direction in poverty studies. *International Journal of Social Welfare, 14*(2), 99–106.

Lemire, S., Peck, L. R., & Porowski, A. (2020). The growth of the evaluation tree in the policy analysis forest: Recent developments in evaluation. *Policy studies journal, 48*, S47–S70.

McIlwain, C. D., & Caliendo, S. M. (2020). Race, politics, and public policy. In *The Routledge Companion to Race and Ethnicity* (pp. 42–50). Routledge.

McLaughlin, M. (1991). The Rand change agent study: Ten years later. In A. R. Odden (Ed.), *Education policy implementation* (pp. 143–156). State University of New York Press.

National Conference of State Legislatures. (2017). Limiting bill introductions: Legislative brief. https://www.ncsl.org/research/about-state-legislatures/limiting-bill-introductions.aspx

O'Toole, L. J., Jr. (2000). Research on policy implementation: Assessment and prospects. *Journal of Public Administration Research and Theory, 10*(2), 263–288.

Parken, A., & Young, H. (2007). *Integrating the promotion of equality and human rights for all*. Unpublished report for Welsh Assembly Government and Equality and Human Rights Commission.

Parken, A., & Young, H. (2008). *Facilitating cross-strand working*. Unpublished report for the Welsh Assembly Government.

Pearson, M., & Smith, K. E. (2020). What does it mean to "use evidence"? Applying a broader understanding to inform the design of strategies to enable the use of evidence. *Evidence & Policy, 16*(1), 3.

Qian, H., & Walker, A. (2011). The "gap" between policy intent and policy effect: An exploration of the interpretations of school principals in China. In T. Huang and A. W. Wiseman (Eds.), *The impact and transformation of education policy in China* (pp. 187–208). Emerald.

Smith, E. P., Yunes, M. A. M., & Fradkin, C. (2021). From prevention and intervention research to promotion of positive youth development: Implications for global research, policy and practice with ethnically diverse youth. In *Handbook of positive youth development* (pp. 549–566). Springer.

About the Contributors

Ron Avi Astor, MSW, PhD, is the Crump Professor in the UCLA Luskin School of Public Affairs, department of Social Welfare with a joint appointment in the School of Education. His work focuses on the socio-ecological influences of the society, family, community, school and culture on different forms of school violence. Astor's studies have informed school safety policies across the globe. Findings from these studies have been published in more than 200 scholarly manuscripts.

Jennifer B. Ayscue, PhD, is an assistant professor in the Department of Educational Leadership, Policy, and Human Development at North Carolina State University. Her research focuses on desegregation and integration in K–12 schools and federal education policy.

Joseph Bishop, PhD, is the executive director and co-founder of the Center for the Transformation of Schools in UCLA's School of Education & Information Studies. His research explores the role of policy in our society, specifically its impact on historically marginalized communities in education settings.

Channa Mae Cook, PhD, is the executive director of District & School Support at Sacramento County Office of Education. Her background spans teaching and leading in both small charter schools and large districts as well as conducting research on science of learning and development, whole child practice and policy, and deeper learning.

Justin A. Coles, PhD, is an assistant professor of social justice education at University of Massachusetts, Amherst in the Department of Student Development. At UMass Amherst, Dr. Coles also serves as the director of arts, culture, and political engagement at the Center of Racial Justice and Youth Engaged Research (CRJ). Dr. Coles serves as coeditor of the academic journal *Equity & Excellence and Education*.

Timothy Collins, PhD, is a professor in the Department of Geography and the Environmental & Sustainability Studies Program at the University of Utah, where he codirects the Center for Natural and Technological Hazards. His research focuses on environmental justice, health disparities, and social vulnerability to environmental hazards and disasters.

Linda Darling-Hammond, EdD, is president and CEO of the Learning Policy Institute and professor of education, emeritus, at Stanford University. Her work, which connects issues of education policy and practice, focuses on teaching quality, school and system design, and educational equity. Among her more than 600 publications is the award-winning book, *The Flat World and Education: How America's Commitment to Equity Will Determine our Future*.

Rochelle Davis is the founder of Healthy Schools Campaign and served as its president and CEO for over 20 years. Rochelle has extensive knowledge and experience in developing cross-sector partnerships to address system level change to support healthy schools, as well as policy development and advocacy at the local, state, and federal levels.

Sonya Douglass, EdD, is professor of education leadership at Teachers College, Columbia University, and director of the Black Education Research Collective. Her research focuses on education leadership, policy, and politics.

Earl J. Edwards, PhD, is an assistant professor at the Boston College Lynch School of Education and Human Development. His research interests include racial equity and the impacts of structural racism across public institutions and education equity and access in urban schools. His current research focuses on how American public schools can better support youth experiencing homelessness.

Danielle Farrie, PhD, is research director at Education Law Center (ELC), the nation's legal defense fund for public education rights. Her research on school finance and other equity-focused educational issues supports ELC's policy, advocacy, and litigation efforts.

Arnold F. Fege is the president of Public Advocacy for Kids, a Washington, DC–based organization that focuses on federal and national public education and child advocacy policy at the intersection of research and practice, and raising the voices of minority and low-income parents and students. Fege brings over 40 years of public and nonprofit experience as a teacher, principal, director of desegregation, staff assistant to Senator Robert F. Kennedy, Associated Press Vietnam war reporter, governmental relations director for the National PTA, and director of advocacy for the Public Education Network to issues of equity, diversity, inclusion, power, and voice.

Erica Frankenberg, EdD, is professor of education and demography and director of the Center for Education and Civil Rights at Pennsylvania State University. Her research interests focus on racial desegregation and inequality in PK–12 schools, and the connections between school segregation and other federal, state, and metropolitan policies.

Megan Gallagher is a principal research associate at The Urban Institute. Her research focuses on how schools, housing, and community programs affect the lives of low-income children and families. Ms. Gallagher researches and evaluates housing and education collaborations designed to boost educational outcomes. She also conducts training and technical assistance for U.S. Department of Education Promise Neighborhoods grantees.

Keisha L. Green, PhD, University of Massachusetts, Amherst is an associate professor of teacher education and curriculum studies at UMass Amherst College of Education, where she is the cofounder and codirector of the Center of Racial Justice and Youth Engaged Research and co-editor of Equity & Excellence in Education. Her research interests are in humanizing qualitative research methods, English Education, youth literacy practices, and critical pedagogy.

Sara Grineski, PhD, is a professor in the Department of Sociology and the Environmental & Sustainability Studies Program at the University of Utah. She codirects the Center for Natural & Technological Hazards and serves as the director of undergraduate studies in sociology. Her research focuses on environmental justice and children's health and development.

Tyrone C. Howard, PhD, is the Pritzker Family Endowed Chair and professor of education in the School of Education Studies at UCLA. He was elected president-elect of the American Educational Research Association in 2022. His research focuses on educational equity and access for students in urban schools.

John H. Jackson, EdD, is president and CEO of the Schott Foundation for Public Education, a public foundation focused on resourcing racial and education justice organizations and campaigns. He is a former lecturer of race, gender, and public policy at the Georgetown Public Policy Institute and a senior policy advisor in the Office for Civil Rights at the U.S. Department of Education.

Angela James, PhD, is a sociologist and demographer dedicated to educational equity and improvement. She is currently research director at the Center for the Transformation of Schools in the School of Education and Information Sciences at UCLA.

Oscar Jiménez-Castellanos, PhD, is director of P–12 research at The Education Trust in DC. He completed this chapter as a visiting scholar at the University of Southern California's Rossier School of Education. Jiménez-Castellanos has published extensively in education finance equity policy among other education equity issues.

Melissa Kull, PhD, is a senior researcher at Chapin Hall at the University of Chicago. Her research aims to improve screening for risks for homelessness, strengthen community-based supports for children and youth facing housing instability, and to enhance school–community partnerships to prevent homelessness.

Anna Kushner is a PhD student in education policy at Teachers College, Columbia University. Their research interests include the politics of race, diversity, and equity in K–12 education and the role of community and student voice in education decision-making.

Bruce Lesley is president of First Focus on Children, a research and policy-development organization focused on improvements to public policy for children and families. He worked on Capitol Hill for a dozen years and has previous experience working at state and county levels of government and for a public hospital on policy development with an emphasis on child and family policy related to health care, social services, education, early childhood, and immigration policy.

Jamila Lyiscott, PhD, University of Massachusetts, Amherst is an associate professor of social justice education. There, she is the founding codirector of the Center of Racial Justice and Youth Engaged Research, and the co-editor-in-chief of the journal *Equity & Excellence in Education*. Her community-engaged research examines the liberatory capacity of literacies in the lives of youth of color, racial healing, youth-led research, and the capacity of African Diasporic culture to transgress white coloniality.

Alexandra Mays, was most recently the senior national program director at Healthy Schools Campaign. Her work focuses on changing policies and systems at the federal, state, and local levels to advance school health and wellness. Her recent efforts include working with states and school districts across the country to strengthen their school Medicaid programs and building partnerships between school districts and health care systems to meet student health needs.

Matthew Morton, PhD, is a research fellow at Chapin Hall at the University of Chicago, co-leading the youth homelessness agenda. Morton has expertise in youth development, youth homelessness, evaluation of complex interventions, and evidence-based practice.

David M. Quinn, EdD, is an associate professor at the University of Southern California's Rossier School of Education. His research, which focuses on ending educational inequity, has examined topics such as seasonal learning patterns, teachers' racial biases, and the effects of "achievement gap" discourses.

Heather M. Reynolds, PhD, SUNY Empire State College, is a full professor of teacher education in the School for Graduate Studies where she works as a teacher and researcher focused on creating safe, engaging, and welcoming school/classroom environments.

Index

Aarøe, L., 34
Aaronson, D., 156
Abram, K. M., 239
Abrams, L. S., 177, 234, 236
Absenteeism, 99, 252
Accountability. *See also* Standardized testing; education delivery and, 241–242; indicators of success and, 96–97; public health and, 99–100; school finances, 204–205
Achievement gap, 46–47, 113–114
Adamkiewicz, G., 120
Adamson, B., 213
Addington, L., 175, 180, 186
Addo, R., 176
Addy, S., 158
Adelman, H. S., 68
Adequacy of funding, 198, 202–207
Adequate yearly progress (AYP), 46–47
Adkins, D. E., 114
Adopting, in policy process, 273–274
Affirmatively Furthering Fair Housing (AFFH), 139, 146, 166–167, 169n16
African American Policy Forum, 270
Agostinelli, F., 112
Ahmed, S., 51
Ailshire, J., 159
Air quality. *See* Environmental issues
Airgood-Obrycki, W., 159
Aizer, A., 31, 244
Akar, H., 62
Akinyela, M. M., 219
Akom, A. A., 215
Alexander, M., 89, 237, 239
Alfaro, C., 202
Alfonseca, K., 218
Alim, H. S., 201, 220
All Things Considered, 212–213
Allen, D., 41
Allen, G. B., 33
Allensworth, E., 64
Allport, G. W., 134
Altamirano, R. P., 63
Álvarez, B., 272, 274

Alvarez-Pedrerol, M., 120
Amanti, C., 201
American Academy of Adolescent Psychiatry, 58
American Academy of Pediatrics, 58
American Counseling Association, 81
American Family Act, 35
American Psychological Association Zero Tolerance Task Force, 175, 179
American Recovery and Reinvestment Act (ARRA), 20, 206
American Rescue Plan (ARP), 20, 24, 26, 97, 103, 121, 206, 255–256
American Viewpoint, 29
Amoly, E., 120
Amyotte, P., 116–117
Ancess, J., 67
Anderson, D. W., 121
Anderson, E., 202
Anderson, G. L., 41, 43–44
Anderson, J., 195
Andiarena, A., 113
Andree, A., 62
Andrusaityte, S., 120
Annie E. Casey Foundation, 8
Anthony, J., 199
Antonelli, J., 116
Apparicio, P., 115, 117, 120
Appatova, A., 109
Apple, M. W., 44
Applegate, J. S., 116
Apte, J. S., 116
Aragon, S., 234
Aranda, C. L., 158
Arasteh, K., 7
Aratani, Y., 158
Ard, K., 113
Arizona Education Association, 34
Armour, J., 236
Arruda, E. H., 177
Asen, R., 184–185
Asmelash, L., 186
Assessing, in policy process, 272
Asset-based distributive justice, 200–201, 207–208

Associated Press, 145
Asthma, 94, 114, 124
Astor, R. A., 175–178, 180–182, 184–187
Atwell, M., 257, 259, 260, 263
Auerswald, C. L., 253
Avenue of Life, 161–162
Ávila-Ramírez, J., 113
Avol, E., 113, 124
Ayscue, J. B., 133–137

Bader, M., 159
Badges of inferiority, 46–47
Baker, B. D., 24, 194, 206
Bal, A., 135
Balcerzak, B., 121
Balfanz, R., 134
Ballester, F., 113
Ballmer Group, 161
Ballysingh, T. A., 181
Balseviciene, B., 120
Banks, J. A., 80
Barajas, J., 140
Barmer, A., 6–7
Barnes-Proby, D., 175–176
Barron, B., 67–68
Barton, W. H., 243
Basagaña, X., 113, 120
Basner, M., 121
Bassett, P., 80
Bates, C. R., 94
Bear, G., 66
Bednarz, A., 158
Beechum, N. O., 64
Beethoven Street Elementary School, 121
Behr, C., 95
Bell, C. A., 140
Bell, D., 46–47, 50
Bell, J., 234
Bell, J. M., 50
Bellinger, D. C., 113
Beltrán-Aguilar, E. D., 94
Benavides, C., 177
Benbenishty, R., 175–177, 180–182, 184–187
Berg, J., 59, 61
Bergström, K., 121
Berhane, K., 124
Berkowitz, R., 181
Berliner, D. C., 7
Berman, M., 178
Berrey, E., 50
Berryman, A., 176
Biden, Joe, 145, 147, 148n2
Bierbaum, A. H., 140
Bill and Melinda Gates Foundation, 161
Billingham, C. M., 136
Billings, E., 202

Billingsley, B. S., 242
Binning, K. R., 50
BIPOC communities; CRJYB participants from, 223–224; justice-centered policy process and, 270–278; school funding and, 195–196; structural racism and, 88; youth voices, centering of, 227–228
Bishop, J. P., 7–8, 47–48, 76–78, 80, 200, 202, 254, 270, 272–273
Bishwakarma, R., 270
Black, D. W., 13, 23
Black Education Research Collective, 51
Black storywork, 219–220
Blanc, E., 35
Blatchford, P., 80
Blomkamp, E., 271–272, 277
Bloom, H. S., 62
Blueprints for Healthy Youth Development, 180–181, 186
Blumenfeld, P. C., 67
Boards of Education (BOEs); safety decisions/policies and, 177–178, 184; training for, 185–186
Bogert, C., 239
Bohnert, A. M., 94
Bolton, N., 62
Book banning, 17, 42
Boone, V., 117, 120
Borges-Mendez, R., 113
Bosso, D., 34
Boston Foundation, 156
Bosworth, M. H., 198
Bottia, M. C., 134
Bouffard, M. B., 65
Boulder Housing Partners (Colorado), 163, 168n7
"Boundary spanners," 274
Boxer, P., 117
Boyd, G., 263
Bracy, N. L., 176–177
Braddock, J. H., 135
Bradley, M., 214–215
Bradshaw, C., 182
Brain development, 59–61
Brand, A., 235
Brand, S., 62
Bransford, J. D., 67
Branstetter, C., 177, 179, 186
Bratman, G. N., 120
Brauer, M., 116, 120, 124
Brenes, T., 176
Brennan, M., 47, 157–159, 161, 163
Bridgeland, J. M., 257, 259, 260, 263
Bridges Collaborative, 53n3, 161, 168n5
Bringing School Home initiative, 163
Brock, D., 95
Brockmeyer, S., 113

Index

Bronfenbrenner, U., 202, 273
Brooks, D. M., 113
Brooks-Gunn, J., 159
Brown, Henry Billings, 49
Brown, P., 80
Brown, R., 122–123
Brown, X., 32
Brown v. Board of Education, 14, 18, 43, 45, 49–50, 195–196, 226–227
Browning, C. R., 159–160
Brownstein, R., 31
Bruce, C., 240
Bruehl, E. Y., 33
Brugge, D., 124
Brummet, Q., 135
Brunekreef, B., 113, 116
Bryant, A., 185
Bryk, A., 63
Buffardi, L. E., 50
Bullis, M., 235–236, 239
Bullock Mann, F., 6–7
Bullying, 182, 253
Burdick, K., 243
Bureau of Labor Statistics, 8
Burnett, R., 116
Burnette, A. G., 182
Burns, A., 62
Burns, D., 62
Burrell, K., 235
Burrington, L. A., 159
Burtka, A. T., 109
Burton, J., 26
Bush, George W., 42
Butts, J. A., 243

Cabral, L., 52, 80
Cagney, K. A., 160
Cahill, C., 214–215
Calderón-Garciduenas, L., 113
Caliendo, S. M., 277
California Department of Education, 204
Camargo Gonzalez, L., 8
Camera, L., 183
Cammarota, J., 212, 215
Canada, B., 184
Cantor, P., 59, 61
Capp, G., 176, 187
Card, D., 50
Cardichon, J., 187
CARES Act, 20
Carranza, L., 194–196, 200, 207
Carrier, M., 115, 117, 120
Carruthers, L., 184
Carter, P. L., 194, 207
Cascio, E. U., 206
Case, A., 117

Casey A., et al. v. Robles, 235
Castro, A. J., 135
Cattret, J., 242
Cedeño-Laurent, J. G., 120
Center for Racial Justice and Youth Engaged Research (CRJ), 214, 221–224
Center for the Transformation of Schools, 78
Center on Multi-Tiered System of Supports, 263
Center on PBIS, 263
Centers for Disease Control and Prevention (CDC), 19, 82, 95–96, 257, 275–276
Centers for Medicare and Medicaid Services (CMS), 98, 102
Chakraborty, J., 111
Chambers, E. C., 158
Champion, D. J., 234
Champion, E., 160
Chan, C. K., 159, 252
Charter schools, 16
Chaskin, R. J., 141
Chau, M., 158
Chavez, N., 183
Chávez, R., 113, 251, 258
Chen, H., 116
Chen, X., 121
Chen, Y., 175
Chetty, R., 159
Child and Adolescent Health Measurement Initiative, 94
Child Proofing Our Communities Campaign, 114, 119
Child Protective Services (CPS), 261, 265
Child Tax Credit (CTC), 26–27, 35
Child Welfare Information Gateway, 261
Children's Hospital Association, 58
Children's rights, 25–31
Chingos, M., 134, 136
Chiu, Y. H. M., 113
Cho, Y., 158
Chudnovsky, A., 120
Chzhen, Y., 24
Cipriano, C., 59
Cirach, M., 113
Civil Rights Act of 1964, 14, 45, 145
Civil rights movement, 196–197
Clark, C., 121
Clark, N. A., 124
Clark-Reyna, S. E., 113
Claudio, L., 113–114
Clawson, K., 66
Clean Air Act, 115
Clements-Croome, D., 121
Cleveland, C., 156
Clotfelter, C. T., 136, 200
Clune, W. H., 195, 198
Coburn, C., 184

Codesign for public policy, 271–273, 277
Coffee-Borden, B., 162
Coggins, J., 116
Cohen, A., 116, 118, 120
Cohen, G. L., 159
Cohen, J., 99
Cohen, M., 239
Cohn-Vargas, B., 61
Coker, D., 199
Coleman-Jensen, A., 94
Coleman Report, 45–46
Coles, J. A., 214, 220–221
Coles, M., 174, 179
Coley, R. L., 160
Collaborative for Academic, Social, and Emotional Learning (CASEL), 65, 180–181, 186
College Housing Assistance Program (Tacoma, WA), 162
Collins, T. W., 94, 111–114
Collyer, S., 26
Colorado Family Support Assessment, 163
Commager, H. S., 12
Commission to Eliminate Child Abuse and Neglect Fatalities, 27
Committee for a Responsible Federal Budget, 30–31
Community(ies). *See also* Community voice; of color. *See* BIPOC communities; housing and, 1, 159; integration and, 143–144, 146; racial justice youth policy model and, 222–223; resources for, 1, 165–166; sense of, 61–64
Community-based organization (CBO), 259, 264
Community Choice Demonstration, 165–166, 169n14
Community Oriented Policing Services (COPS) in Schools, 175, 179, 183
Community Schools model, 83–84
Community voice, 17; school safety and, 186–187
Comprehensive threat-assessment teams, 181–182
Comunian, S., 112
Conley, D., 158
Conners, P., 184–185
Constitute Project, 195
Cook, J., 50
Cook, K. S., 201
Cook-Harvey, C. M., 19, 47, 62, 68, 71n1
Coons, J. E., 195
Cooper, D., 160
Cordes, S. A., 141
Cormier, R., 270, 277
Cornell, D., 175, 181–182
Cortright, J., 109, 121
Costin, V., 32
Coull, B. A., 113, 116
Coulton, C., 158
Council of Large Public Housing Authorities, 161
Counterstories. *See* Policy counterstories

Counts, J., 174, 176, 179, 186
COVID-19, 6–8, 14–16, 92; education policy and, 51–52, 269; impact on overall health, 23–24; income/racial inequality and, 8, 15, 51–52, 112; mental health and, 7, 23, 58, 80–81; public funding and, 24, 81, 103; school safety practices and, 174, 186–187; systemic racism and, 78–81; unemployment and, 8; UNICEF report on, 23–24; whole child policy and, 58–59
COVID-19 stimulus funds, 206–207
Coyle, S., 175–176, 179, 183, 186
Crawford, J., 158
Creating Healthy Indoor Air Quality in Schools (EPA report), 119
Creating Safer Learning Zones (Child Proofing Our Communities Campaign), 119
Cremin, L., 12
Criminal offenses, 237
Criminalization of youth, 260–261
Critical policy analysis, 43–44
Critical Race Theory (CRT), 17. *See also* Equity; education policy and, 42, 51, 53n1; systemic racism and, 79–80; youthtopias and, 215
Critical supports, 259–260
Critical teacher education, 222–223
Critical youth studies, 214–216
Cronkite News, 34
Cross-sector partnerships, 104–105; environmental issues and, 118–119; housing and, 160–161; integration and, 139–141, 144, 146–147
Crouse, D., 115, 117, 120
Crowley, D. M., 65
Cui, J., 6
Cultural competence, 63–64
Culture wars, 27
Cunningham, M., 158–159
Curran, M. A., 26
Currie, J., 25
Curry, S. R., 251, 258
Cutler, D., 116
Cutuli, J. J., 7, 159, 252, 257

Dadvand, P., 120
Dailey, A. C., 28
D'Alessandro, A., 99
Dalmau-Bueno, A., 113
Dalton, L., 80
Dalton, S., 67
Daly, H., 24
D'Angiulli, A., 113
Darby, D., 202
Darder, A., 194
Darling-Hammond, L., 19, 47, 50, 62–63, 67–68, 71n1, 80, 187, 194, 205
Darville, S., 42
Dastrup, S., 165

Datar, A., 113–114
Datnow, A., 177, 187
Datta, P., 182
David, J. L., 205
Davidson, H., 26
Davis, A., 66
de Brey, C., 177, 179, 186
De Castro Pascual, M., 120
De La Garza, S., 140, 143
De Pedro, K. T., 181
de Vries, S., 120
DeBray, E. H., 139, 145–146
DeBray-Pelot, E., 146
DeCandia, C. J., 68
Decision-making, 101, 184
Dedele, A., 120
Dee, T. S., 50
DeJong, K., 221
DeLeon, P., 30
Delgado, R., 53n1
Delgado-Chávez, R., 113
"Delinquent" youth, response to, 234
DeLuca, S., 139
Demers, P. A., 124
Democracy, school safety and, 180, 186–187
Denton, N., 196
Denver Public Schools, 141
DeParle, J., 23
Depolicing measures, 183
Desegregation, 135
Desjardins, C. D., 159, 252
Development Services Group, Inc, 235, 240
Devlin, D., 174, 179, 186
Di, Q., 116
Diamond, A., 121
DiAngelo, R., 12–13, 77
Diem, S., 43, 138
Diera, C., 176
Dierkhising, C. B., 243
Díez, J., 272, 274
Dignitary justice, 202, 207–208
Diliberti, M., 177, 179, 186
Dilig, R., 6–7
Dillman, K.-N., 162
Dimitrova, D., 120
Ding, L., 135
Disability, students with, 239–241
Discipline policy. *See also* Punitive disciplinary policies; suspensions and, 85–87, 179; systemic racism and, 84–88; whole child policy and, 65–66
Distance learning, 15–16, 58–59, 112
Distributive justice, 194, 197–201, 207
Districting, racialized, 196
Diversity, 15. *See also* Integration; education policy and, 50–51; neoliberalism and, 44

Divringi, E., 165
Dixon, E., 82
Dixson, A. D., 76
Docter, B., 157, 165
Doepke, M., 112
Dominici, F., 116, 120
Dongo, D., 112
Donner, C., 179
Donovan, M. S., 67
Dorn, E., 16, 52
Doss, C., 205
Double-Dutch methodology (DDM), 219
Doucet, F., 51
Downs, M., 94
Doyle, J. J., 244
Doyle, W., 66
Dragan, K., 135
Du Bois, W. E. B., 50
Dubenitz, J., 263
Dubow, E. F., 117
Duncan, G., 25
Dunn, K., 235, 241
Durant, J., 124
Durlak, J. A., 65
Dusseault, B., 207
Dweck, C. S., 67
Dworsky, A., 162, 251–252, 258
Dye, B. A., 94
Dymnicki, A. B., 65
Dzhambov, A. M., 120

Early Childhood Initiative (Akron, OH), 163
Eaton, S., 134, 140, 144, 147
Economic Growth and Tax Relief Reconciliation Act (EGTRRA), 20
Economic issues. *See* Food insecurity; Housing; Income inequality; Unemployment
Edgerton, A. K., 80
Education for Homeless Children and Youths (EHCY) program, 256
Education policy. *See also specific policy initiatives*; achievement gap and, 46–47; codesign/collaborative. *See* Codesign for public policy; COVID-19 and, 51–52, 269; CRT and, 42, 51, 53n1; discipline policy and. *See* Discipline policy; diversity and, 50–51; equity and, 51–53; housing and. *See* Housing; integrated/intersectional approaches to, 270–278; learning loss and, 16, 52; public health and, 95–98; racial inequality and, 41–53; segregation and, 49–51; standardized testing and, 46–48; suspensions and, 85–87; systemic racism and, 76–89; whole child. *See* Whole child policy
Edward W. Hazen Foundation, 217
Edwards, E. J., 259, 263

Ee, J., 133–134
Ehinger, Alicia, 34
Ehrman-Solberg, K., 156
Eisenberg, D., 94
Elamroussi, A., 218
Elementary and Secondary Education Act (ESEA), 13–14, 45–46, 198, 227, 229n1
Elementary and Secondary Emergency Education Relief (ESSER) Fund, 97–98, 121, 206–207
Ellen, I. G., 135, 158, 165
Elliot, A., 77
Ellison, B. S., 43
Emancipation Proclamation, 14
Emergency Family Assistance Association, 163
Empowerment, school safety and, 180, 186–187
Engzell, P., 52
Enrichment programs, 97, 121
Enterprise Community Partners, 156, 161, 166
Environment of schools. *See also* Positive school climate; "identity safe," 61–64; public health and, 99–100; school design and, 119–121; teacher and, 70–71
Environmental issues, 1, 7, 94, 109–125; academic achievement and, 113–114; cross-sector partnerships and, 118–119; greenspace and, 120–121; income/racial inequality and, 110–112; precautionary principle and, 116–117; public funding and, 119–121; public policy and, 115–125; school design/siting and, 114–125; standards and, 122–123
Environmental Protection Agency (EPA), 114–116, 118–120, 122, 124
Equal Employment Opportunity Act, 50
Equality of Educational Opportunity (Coleman Report), 45–46
Equity, 41–53. *See also* Adequacy of funding; Critical Race Theory (CRT); Racial inequality; AYP and, 46–47; critical policy analysis and, 43–44; education policy and, 51–53; integration and, 133–147, 148n1–148n2; mental health and, 48; NCLB and, 46–48; politics of, 41–43; public funding and, 48; school safety and, 48; segregation and, 45–46; standardized testing and, 46–48; systemic racism and, 42, 51–52
Equity and Excellence Commission, 25, 102
Equity and Inclusion Enforcement Act, 145
Erb-Downward, J., 252
Erickson, A., 139
Esnaola, M., 120
Esqueda, M., 181
Estarlich, M., 113
Estrada, P., 67
Etue, E., 122–123
Evaluation, in policy process, 274–277; CDC approach to, 275–276; indicators for, 276
Evaluation Tree, 275–276

Evans, G. W., 158
Evans, K. R., 181
Every Student Succeeds Act (ESSA), 93, 95–97, 103, 105, 143, 187, 206, 240–241, 244, 253–254
Evidence for Action, 121
Eyrich-Garg, K. M., 257

Faber, J., 134
Factory model for schools, 17–18
Fair Housing Act, 145–146, 148n1, 155, 157
Fakunle, D., 213
Family engagement; housing and, 163; public health and, 104; whole child policy and, 63
Fan, X., 182
Fann, N., 116
Fargione, J., 120
Farrell, A. F., 251, 258
Farrie, D., 206–207
Farrington, C. A., 64, 66
Fattorini, D., 112
Feagin, J., 200
Federal Housing Administration (FHA), 156
Federal policy/policymakers; juvenile-justice action recommendations, 244–245; racial justice youth policy model and, 225–228; school funding practices (case study), 206–207; student homelessness, 253–255
The Federalist, 42
Feierman, J., 243
Feldman, S., 26, 32
Felner, R. D., 62
Feng, X., 120
Fennerty, A. G., 158
Ferguson, A., 215
Fergusson, D. M., 117
Fernández-Somoano, A., 113
Fertig, A., 117
Field Center for Children's Policy, 162
Figueroa, E., 206
Finkel, M., 165
Finnegan, K., 138
First Focus on Children, 24–25, 29
Fiscal neutrality standard, 197
Fischbach, S., 124
Fischer, R. L., 158
Fischer, W., 158–159
Fisher, B., 175, 180, 186
Fletcher, J. M., 263
Flook, L., 68
Flouri, E., 120
Floyd, George, 79, 183
Foad, C., 32
Font, S. A., 176
Fontana, D., 19
Food insecurity; COVID-19 and, 16; public health and, 94

Index

For-profit education, 16
Forastiere, F., 113
Ford, D. Y., 135
Ford, J., 239
Forns, J., 120
Foster, K. R., 116
Foster Care to College initiative, 162
Fourteenth Amendment, 12, 49
Fox, E., 122–123
Fradkin, C., 271
Franco, M., 272, 274
Franke, M., 176
Frankenberg, E., 133–140, 143, 145–146, 196
Freeman, L., 157
Freeman, M., 29–30
Freire, P., 221
Frey, A., 52
Frey, W. H., 31–32
Friedlaender, D., 62, 67
Fronius, T., 66, 181
Frostad, J., 116
Fudge, K., 160
Fuertes, E., 120
Fugitive Slave Act, 14
Fugivity and abolition, racial justice youth policy model and, 222–223
Funding. *See* School finance
Furlong, S. R., 277

Gabriel, T., 178
Gaffron, P., 113
Gagnon, J. C., 244
Gailes, A., 135
Gal, C., 121
Galbarczyk, A., 121
Gallagher, M., 47, 157–161, 163
Gallo, M., 159
Galvez, M. M., 157–158, 165, 252
Galvez, M. P., 117
Gambhir, S., 135
Garcia, D., 194
García, R., 113
Garcia-Cobian, F., 158
Gardella, J., 175, 180, 186
Garnett, F. G., 50
Gauderman, W. J., 124
Gautreaux housing case, 139, 146
Gay, G., 64
Gayles, E., 157
Geelong Project (Australia), 264
Geller, R. C., 176
Gentrification, 135–136, 141–142
Georgia Conservancy, 118
Gerewitz, J., 66
Germain, E., 135
Gershoff, E. T., 176

Gerstein, D. E., 94
Geurs, K., 117, 120
Ghani, R., 272
Gibbons, A., 42
Gilliland, F., 124
Gilreath, T. D., 181
Ginwright, S., 84, 212, 215
Givens, J., 76
Glied, S., 135
Glover, C. P., 80
Gniewosz, B., 177
Goetz, E. G., 141
Goff, P., 252
Golberstein, S., 94
Goldin, S., 272
Goldring, E., 136
Goldstein, D., 178
Gonzalez, L. C., 254
Gonzalez, N., 201
González-Maciel, A., 113
Goodman, M. L., 23
Gottfredson, D., 174, 179, 186
Gottfried, M. A., 140
Goux, D., 158
Government Accountability Office, 116
GovTrack, 273
Grant, S., 175–176
Grant-Muller, S., 117, 120
Grantham, T. C., 135
Gray, Freddie, 212–213
Grazuleviciene, R., 120
Green, K., 219
Green, P., 159, 194
Green, R. S., 109
Green, T. L., 135
Greenberg, E., 50
Greenberg, M. T., 65
Greene, S., 141
Greenspace, 120–121
Gregory, A., 66, 181–182
Gregory, C., 94
Grewal, E. T., 50
Griffith, M., 81, 206
Grigg, J., 159
Grimke, F., 12
Grineski, S. E., 94, 111–114
Grinshpun, S., 109
Grisso, T., 236
Gromada, A., 24
Grosland, T. J., 46–47
Grutter v. Bollinger, 15
Guckenburg, S., 66, 181
Guffey, S., 99
Gullón, P., 272, 274
Gumm, E., 184–185
Gumus-Dawes, B., 138

Gurke, D., 184–185
Gutierrez, K., 63
Guxens, M., 113

Haberle, M., 139, 157, 167
Haddock, G., 32
Hahn, H., 24
Hall, K. S., 178
Ham, J., 113
Hamedani, M. G., 62
Hammond, S., 236
Hammond, Z., 61
Hancock, B., 16
Hancock, L., 239
Hankivsky, O., 270, 277
Hannan, A. J., 121
Hansell, A., 121
Harding, D. J., 159
Harkin, J., 26
Haro, B. N., 79
Harris, Kamala, 145, 147, 148n2
Harris, L. E., 158
Harris III, F., 85
Hart, J. E., 113
Hart, M., 94
Hartig, T., 120
Hartley, D., 156
Hartmann, D., 50
Harvard Joint Center for Housing Studies, 156
Harvey, D., 44
Hatch, T. C., 274
Hate crimes, 44
Haurin, D. R., 160
Haurin, R. J., 160
Havlik, S. A., 254
Hayes, R., 116
Head Start, 103
Health concerns. *See* Public health
Healthy Learning Environment Grants, 119–120
Healthy Schools Network, 118–119
Heckman, J. J., 25
Hegtvedt, K. A., 201
Heim, D., 66
Hein, S., 6–7
Heinrich, J., 120
Heistad, D., 159, 252
Helping professionals, 176
Henderson, A. T., 63
Henderson, K., 239
Hendren, N., 159
Henriquez-Roldan, C., 113
Herbers, J. E., 159, 252, 257
Herink, J., 34
Hernández, L. E., 42
Herritt, L., 113
Hess, F. M., 5

Hestres, L. E., 34
Hetherington, M. J., 33
Hicks, D., 174, 179
High-Performance Public Building Act (Washington State), 120
Hileman, J. I., 121
Hilton, A., 94
Hilton, M., 166
Hinton, E., 217
Hinz, E., 159, 252
Hirschfield, P., 175
Hoag, C., 109
Hoek, G., 113
Hoffmann, B., 113
Holbein, J. B., 136
Holden, T., 143
Holme, J. J., 138, 140, 143
Holupka, C. S., 157–158, 160
Homeless Children and Youth Act (HCYA), 254
Homelessness. *See* Student homelessness
Homeownership, 159–160
Homework Starts at Home, 161, 167
Honig, M. I., 184, 274
Hoogh, K., 113
Hoover, S., 263
HOPE SF (San Francisco, CA), 165
Horn, K. M., 158
Horne, J., 135
Horsford, S. D., 41, 43–47, 50, 52, 80
Horwood, L. J., 117
Houchins, D. E., 242, 244
Housing, 1, 5–6, 154–167; affordability of, 158, 161–164; agencies/stakeholders, 154–156, 161, 166; community and, 159; COVID-19 and, 14, 16; cross-sector partnerships and, 160–161; defined, 154–156; fair housing laws and, 14; family engagement and, 163; gentrification and, 135–136, 141–142; income inequality and, 156–158, 161–164; integration and, 137–147, 148n1; Moving to Opportunity project and, 139, 146, 166; public, 137, 139, 144, 155–157, 161, 165; public funding and, 140, 154–167; public health and, 157–158; quality of, 157–158, 164–165; racial inequality and, 156–157; school safety and, 159; segregation and, 7; stability of, 158–159
Housing and Education (HousED) initiative (California), 163
Housing bundle, 154, 157–160, 167
Housing Choice Voucher Program, 155–156, 165–166
Housing mobility programs, 166, 169n15
Housing Supply Action Plan, 165, 168n13
Howard, T. C., 76–77, 85, 272
Howell, E. M., 158
Howlett, M., 273

Hoynes, H. W., 24, 31
Hsu, H. H. L., 113
Hsu, T., 175
Huang, F., 175, 182
Hubbell, B., 116
Huddy, L., 26, 32, 34
Hudson, J., 234
Huesmann, L. R., 117
Hughes, C., 178
Humphrey, D. C., 205
Hunt, V., 270
Huntington, C., 29
Hurley, N., 66, 181
Hussar, B., 6
Hyler, M. E., 63
Hyper-criminalization, of urban youth, 237, 239
Hystad, P., 120

Ibarluzea, J., 113
Ibarra, B., 159
"Identity safe" school environment, 61–64
Immigration, 14
In-school suspension, 85–86
Incarcerated youth; characteristics of, 236–239, 247n2; cost of detention, 234, 247n1; criminal offenses of, 237; education delivery challenges, 241–243; educational policies for, 240–241
Inclusion, 15
Income inequality, 1–5; air quality and, 110–112; as barrier to success, 31–34; COVID-19 and, 8, 112; housing and, 156–158, 161–164; public funding and, 34–35; statistics on, 26–27; whole child policy and, 61
Independent Particulate Matter Review Panel, 116, 122
Indicators; input/outcome, in policy evaluation, 276; of success, 96–97
Individualized Education Plans/Programs (IEPs), 98, 240–241, 243, 246
Individualized Family Services Plan (IFSP), 98
Individualized Treatment Plans (ITP), 243
Individuals with Disability Education Act (IDEA), 240, 247n3
Inferiority, badges of, 46–47
Ingraham, C., 178
Ingram, E. S., 257, 259, 260, 263
Ingram, H., 30
Íñiguez, C., 113
Integrated approaches to education policy, 270–278
Integration, 133–148, 148n1–148n2. *See also* Diversity; Segregation; benefits of, 134–135; community and, 143–144, 146; cross-sector partnerships and, 139–141, 144, 146–147; demographic changes and, 135–136; gentrification and, 135–136, 141–142; housing and, 137–147, 148n1; public policy and, 137–147, 148n1–148n2; research on, 134; transportation and, 140–141
Interagency Working Group on Youth Programs (IWGYP), 227
Intersectional approaches to education policy, 270–278
Iosifyan, M., 32
Iqtadar, S., 43
Irwin, V., 7
Isaacs, J. B., 24
Ishimoto, M., 176
Ispa-Landa, S., 181–182

Jaber, M., 121
Jackson, C. K., 25
Jacobs, J., 52, 80
Jacobsen, R., 140
Jacobson, L., 180–181, 185–186
Jaddoe, V. W., 113
James, A., 76, 272
James, N., 179–180, 186
Janssen, S., 121
Jasienska, G., 121
Jefferson, Thomas, 12
Jennings, W., 179
Jerrett, M., 120, 124
Jia, Y., 182
Jim Crow laws, 13–14, 42, 49, 195–196
Jiménez-Castellanos, O., 194–196, 198, 200, 202, 204, 207
Jimerson, S., 180–181, 186–187
Job Creation and Worker Assistance Act (JCWAA), 20
Joe, S., 94
Johnson, A., 8
Johnson, D. W., 64
Johnson, H. B., 7
Johnson, P. T., 94
Johnson, R. C., 50, 135
Johnson, R. E., 78
Johnson, S., 76–77
Johnson, S. L., 272
Johnson, S. L., Jr, 76
Jolivette, K., 239, 241
Jones, C. O., 273
Jones, D. J., 65
Jones, S., 82
Jones, S. M., 65
Jordan, H., 175–176, 179, 183, 186
Joseph, M. L., 141
Journell, W., 81
Julvez, J., 120
Just, A. C., 113
Justice-centered policy process, 270–278; evaluation in. *See* Evaluation, in policy process

Justice-involved youth; characteristics of, 236–239. *See also* Incarcerated youth; education delivery challenges, 241–243; example case, 232–233
Justice Policy Institute, 234
Juvenile justice facilities; detainee characteristics, 236–239; education delivery/policy in, 241–243; educators in, 247
Juvenile justice system, 233–236; models, 243–246; reforms in, 241

Kahlenberg, R. D., 136
Kalogrides, D., 50
Kan, H., 116
Kang, W., 236–239
Kapnick, I., 28
Karner, A., 140
Karr, C. J., 124
Karremans, J. C., 32
Kase, C., 263
Kasper-Sonnenberg, M., 113
Katsiyannis, A., 174, 176, 179, 186
Katz, E., 92, 101
Kay, R., 184
Kebede, M., 136
Keene, D., 159
Kelly, M., 194–196, 200, 207
Kelly, M. S., 187
Kendi, I., 200
Kendziora, K., 65, 68
Kennedy, M., 140, 143
Kervick, C. T., 181
Kettering Foundation, 13
Keyes, T. S., 64
Khan, F., 116–117
Khasnabis, D., 272
Khatiwada, I., 94
Khey, D., 179
Kidman, R., 23
Kidron, Y., 68
Kim, H., 120
Kim, J. J., 109
Kim, R. S.-J., 158
Kimelberg, S. M., 136
King, John, 142
King, Martin Luther, Jr., 1, 21
King, S. M., 25
Kingsley, G. T., 156, 160, 164
Kirksey, J. J., 140
Kisida, B., 136
Klatte, M., 121
Klein, J., 181
Kleit, R. G., 159
Kloog, I., 113, 116
Koehoorn, M., 124
Kokko, K., 117
Konold, T., 181–182

Koomen, H. M., 61
Koppich, J. E., 205
Korman, H., 235, 243
Kostyo, S., 187
Koutrakis, P., 116
Kozlowski, K., 218
Kozol, B., 143
Kozol, J., 77
Kraft, M. E., 277
Krause, E., 19
Krems, J. A., 32
Krimsky, S., 116, 122
Krumer-Nevo, M., 271
Ksinan, A. J., 179
Ksinan Jiskrova, G., 179
Kucsera, J., 136
Kuhfeld, M., 8
Kulesza, R. J., 113
Kull, M., 160
Künzli, N., 124
Kweon, B., 109, 113–114, 124

"LA Model," 243
Labaree, D. F., 44
Lachmann, T., 121
Ladd, H. F., 136, 200–201
Laden, F., 113
Ladson-Billings, G., 199, 201
Lake Research Partners, 35
Lambert, R., 134
Landrigan, P. J., 117
Lansing, A. E., 239
Larimore, S., 134
Larkin, D. T., 66
Lassetter, B., 32–33
Lauderback, E., 24
Laviola, G., 121
Law enforcement. *See* Police/Policing
Layton, D., 176
Le Menestrel, S., 25
Leachman, M., 206
Learning disability, 239
Learning loss, 16, 52
Lee, H., 198
Lee, J., 120
Lee, K., 121
Lee, M. H., 121
Lee, S., 113
Lefebvre, W., 113
Legot, C., 109, 113
Legters, N. E., 134
LeMasters, G., 109
Lemire, S., 274–276
Lencar, C., 124
Leone, P. E., 236, 239, 241
LePage, P., 62

Lertxundi, A., 113
Lesley, B., 24, 28, 31, 35
Lesley, B. A., 24
Lester, D., 52, 80
Leuschner, K., 175–176
Leventhal, T., 159–160
Levinson, B. A., 43
Levy, A. R., 66
Lewis, R., 65
Lewis-Charp, H., 62
Lewis-McCoy, R. L., 78
LGBTQ students, 15, 181, 251
Liberation Literacies Pedagogy (LLP), 220
Lidsky, T. I., 121
Lim, S. S., 116
Lin, J. S., 253
Lindsey, M. A., 94
Linn, R., 133
Lipman, P., 44
Lipsey, M. W., 243
Listening, in policy process, 271–272
Liu, G., 121
Liu, J., 8
Liu, L., 121
Livingston, M. D., 178
Lleras-Muney, A., 31
Local Control Accountability Plans (LCAP), 204–205
Local Control Funding Formula (LCFF), 204
Local policy/policymakers; juvenile-justice action recommendations, 246; racial justice youth policy model and, 225; school safety and, 177–178, 184; school-siting policy, 118–119
Loeb, S., 201
Logan, J. R., 134
London, A. S., 158
London, B., 109, 113
Long, J. D., 159, 252
López, P. D., 204
López-Vicente, M., 120
Lopoo, L. M., 158
Los Angeles Unified School District, 121
Losen, D. J., 84–85, 135
Lou, C., 24
Love, B. J., 221
Love, H. E., 95
Lovenheim, M. F., 160
Loving Cities Index, 5, 16–17, 19
Low-Income Housing Tax Credit (LIHTC), 140, 144, 155, 157
Lown, P., 26, 32
Lubczyńska, M., 113
Luce, T., 138
Lucier, C. A., 113
Luengo-Prado, M. J., 160
Lukes, D., 156

Luna, J., 252
Lupp, G., 120
Lurmann, F., 124
Lyall, K., 113
Lyiscott, J., 220
Lynch, A. D., 160
Lynch, L., 29
Lynn, M., 76

MacDonald, G., 158–159
Mackenzie, D., 264
Mackevicius, C., 25
Mackintosh, B. B., 25
MACPAC, 98
Macri, S., 121
MacWilliams, M. C., 33
Maeng, J. L., 182
Maeroff, G., 185
Magnet schools, 136, 142
Maier, A., 80
Maio, G. R., 32
Major, B., 64
Makar, M., 116
Makori, A., 207
Malone, M., 182
Manchin, Joe, 26
Mann, A., 175–176, 179, 183, 186
Mann, H., 41
Mapp, K. L., 63
Marachi, R., 177, 185
Marchitello, M., 235
Marcotte, D. E., 114
Marginalization, of children, 31–34
Margo, R., 196, 207
Marjory Stoneman Douglas H.S. Public Safety Commission, 175, 179
Markevych, I., 120
Marsh, J. A., 205
Marshall, Thurgood, 11
Martin, C. J., 158
Martín, M. D. P., 272, 274
Martinez, A. B., 28
Martinez, P., 84–85, 135
Maryland Housing Rehabilitation Program, 165, 168n9
Maselli, K. A., 136
Maskaly, J., 179
Mason, L., 34
Massey, D., 196
Masten, A. S., 159, 252
Masterson, K., 206
Mathews, D., 13
Mathur, S. R., 239, 241
Matjasko, J. L., 251, 258
Matsuda, M., 175–176
Maughan, E. D., 95

Maurin, E., 158
Mayer, G. R., 65–66
Mayer, M., 180–181, 186–187
Mayerl, J., 121
Mazumder, B., 156
McCallion, G., 179–180, 186
McConnell, R., 124
McCoy-Roth, M., 25
McCrory, C., 34–35
McDermott, K. A., 145–146, 226
McDonnell, D., 109, 115, 118, 124
McFarland, J., 177, 179, 186
McGhee, C., 52, 80
McGill, G., 158
McIlwain, C. D., 277
McInerney, M., 243
McKeown, M., 200
McKinney, H., 243
McKinney-Vento Homelessness Act (MVA), 253–256, 265
McLaughlin, J., 94
McLaughlin, M., 278
McLaughlin, R., 109
McNeely, E., 120
McPartland, J. M., 135
McVeigh, K. H., 114
McWhorter, John, 213
Meares, T. L., 201
Mears, D. P., 178, 243
Meckler, L., 178
Medicaid, 98, 102–103
Mehta, J., 46
Meisel, S., 239
Melly, S. J., 116
Melnick, H., 80
Mendel, R., 240, 243
Mendez decision, 196
Mendoza, D., 113
Menendian, S., 135
Mental health, 16, 19, 94; Community Schools model and, 83–84; COVID-19 and, 7, 23, 58, 80–81; diagnosis, incarcerated youth and, 239; school safety and, 175–177; standardized testing and, 48; systemic racism and, 78–84
Mental Health Association of NY, 82
Mergendoller, J., 67
Meschede, T., 156
Mexal, S. J., 216–217
Meyer, J. L., 59
Meyer, P., 182
Michael, K., 263
Mickelson, R. A., 133–134
Midouhas, E., 120
Milani, C., 112
Millard, M. W., 94
Miller, A., 33

Miller, P. M., 252, 254
Miller, S., 113
Miller, W., 147
Milliken, M., 62
Milliken v. Bradley, 11, 137
Milner, H., 76–77, 80
Minoritized youth; achievement gaps and, 43, 46; learning opportunities for, 78; policymaking and, 214; restructuring of schooling and, 215–216; wilding and, 217. *See also* Youth wilding/wildin'
Minow, M., 45
Miranda, J., 82
Missouri Model, 233, 243
Mistral, Gabriela, 35
"Moat approach" to public policy, 6–7, 274
Moeser, J., 143
Mohai, P., 109, 113–114, 124
Möhler, U., 121
Molitor, J. N., 124
Molitor, J. T., 124
Moll, L., 201
Monarrez, T., 136, 158
Monie, R. D. H., 158
Moody, C. D., 45
Moore, H., 181
Moore, K., 251
Moore, M., 181
Moore, W. L., 50
The Moral Status of Children (Freeman), 29
Morales, C., 28
Morel, D., 17
Morello-Frosch, R., 111, 113
Moriearty, P. L., 216
Morley, C., 26
Morrell, E., 176
Morris, E. W., 84
Morris, J. E., 45
Morton, M., 175–176, 179, 183, 186
Morton, M. H., 251–252, 258
Motivation, 66–67
Mount Laurel requirements (New Jersey), 143
Mousin, C. A., 26
Moving to Opportunity, 139, 146, 166
Moving to Work (MTW) Demonstration program, 164, 168n10
Mueller, C. M., 67
Mukherjee, P. S., 113
Muldoon, K., 196
Mullen, C., 113
Multi-tiered system of supports (MTSS), 68, 70, 263–266
Multiagency collaboration, 242
Murphey, D., 25
Murphy, K. M., 244
Musu, L., 177, 179, 186
Myles, A., 29, 33

Index

Nagaoka, J., 64
Nagel, S. S., 43
Nance, J. P., 87
Nash, E., 165
Nash, K. T., 80
Nation at Risk: . . . (National Commission on Excellence in Education), 46
National Academies of Sciences, Engineering, and Medicine, 121
National Ambient Air Quality Standards, 115–116
National Association of School Psychologists, 174, 176, 183–184
National Association of School Resource Officers (NASRO), 178–180
National Center for Education Statistics (NCES), 117, 257
National Center for Health Statistics (NCHS), 94
National Center for Homeless Education (NCHE), 8, 156, 251–252, 254, 256–257, 262, 266n1
National Center on Safe Supportive Learning Environments, 187
National Coalition on School Diversity, 146
National Commission on Excellence in Education, 46
National Conference of State Legislatures (NCSL), 178, 273
National Research Council, 119
National School Boards Association, 177, 184
National Survey of Children's Health, 92
National Survey on Drug Use and Health, 82
Naturalization Act, 12
Nawrot, T. S., 113
Nazaryan, A., 50
Neason, E., 254
Neel, R., 32–33
Neighborhoods. *See* Community; Promise Neighborhoods
Nekvasil, E., 175, 182
Nelson, C. M., 239, 241
Neoliberalism, 44
Neuberg, S. L., 32
New York State Education Department, 180
New York Times, 42, 53n2
Newkirk, V. R., 25
Newman, S. J., 157–158, 160
Nicosia, N., 113–114
Niemeier, D., 113
Nieuwenhuijsen, M. J., 113, 120
Nixon, Richard, 148n1
Nkomo, M., 133
No Child Left Behind (NCLB), 6, 46–48, 93, 227, 229n1
Nocella, A. J., 199
Noguera, P. A., 5, 7, 47–48, 62, 67, 76–78, 200, 202, 212, 270, 272–273
Norris, H., 181

Not in My Schoolyard (EPA report), 119
Nuse, B., 113

Oakes, J., 135
Obama, Barack, 42, 142, 144–145
Oberle, E., 65
Obesity, 94
Obradovic, J., 252
O'Brien, M., 47, 157–159, 161, 163
O'Connor, Sandra Day, 15
Odden, A., 194, 198
Office of Population Affairs, 227
Okilwa, N. S., 179
Oluwole, J., 194
Oneto, A. D., 47, 157–159, 161, 163
Oort, F. J., 61
Or, L., 174–175
Oral health, 94
Orfield, G., 133–135, 137, 139, 147, 196
Orfield, M., 138
Organization for Economic Cooperation and Development (OECD), 15, 24–25
Ort, S. W., 67
Osher, D. M., 59, 61, 63, 65–66, 68, 236, 239
Osher, T. W., 63
Osnaya, N., 113
Osoro, S., 156
Ostro, B., 109
O'Toole, L. J., 274
Oudekerk, B. A., 175
Our Kids: . . . (Putnam), 29
Owens, A., 134, 136
Owens, C. E., 243
Ozuna, C. S., 140

Palestini, P., 112
Pan, S., 121
Panchal, N., 95
Pandey, G., 113
Pandey, O., 113
Papachristou, E., 120
Paradice, D., 178
Parcel, T., 160
"Parent bubble," 31–32, 35
Parental rights, 27
Paris, D., 201
Park, V., 177, 187
Parken, A., 270–271, 277
Parker, S., 7
Parks, S., 52, 80
Parolin, Z., 26
Parriott, A., 253
Pastor, M., 31, 111, 113
Patel, S., 251–252
Pavlakis, A. E., 252
Paxson, C., 117

Pearman, F. A., 135
Pearson, M., 277
Peck, L. R., 274–276
Pedrerol, M., 120
Peleg, N., 28
Penner, E. K., 50
Pennington, C. R., 66
Perlman, S., 253, 257
Perry, A. M., 19
Perry, B. L., 84
Persson, H., 66, 181
Peters, J., 124
Petrosino, A., 66, 181
Pettigrew, T., 134
Peugh, J. L., 179
Pew Research Center, 2
Pfeiffer, D., 157
Phillips, R. L., 78
Pichardo, M. S., 158
Pick, C. M., 32
Picus, L. O., 194, 198
Pierce, C. M., 33
Pineda, D., 180–181, 185–186
Pirlott, A. G., 32
Pitingolo, R., 158
Planning, in policy process, 272–273
Plaut, V. C., 50
Player, G. D., 214, 221
Plessy v. Ferguson, 49, 195
Podolsky, A., 205
Poirier, J. M., 236, 239
Police/Policing, in schools, 174–177. *See also* School Resource Officers (SROs); COPS program, 175, 179, 183; critical policy analysis and, 44; depolicing measures and, 183; punitive school disciplinary policies and, 178–180
Policy counterstories, 218–221; youth wilding/ wildin' as, 214, 217–218
Polikoff, M., 205
Politics; as barrier to success, 25–31; of equity, 41–43; policy evaluation and, 274–277
Polson, B., 80
Pope, C. A., 116
Popkin, S. J., 158
Porowski, A., 274–276
Porta, D., 113
Portillo, M., 174, 179
Portuba, J. M., 31–32
Posey, E., 174, 179
Positive Behavioral Interventions and Supports (PBIS), 87, 263
Positive school climate; creating, 180–181, 187; school safety and, 176–177, 180
Potter, H., 136
Poverty. *See* Income inequality

Poverty & Race Research Action Council (PRRAC), 143–144, 161
Powell, John, 6
Precautionary principle (PP), 116–117
Prenovost, M. A., 134
Price, E. A., 216
Pringle, B., viii
Private education, 16
Procedural justice, 201–202, 207–208
Professional development, for BOE members, 185–186
Promise Neighborhoods, 166, 262
Property taxes, 195
Protests, 212–214
Provost, E. B., 113
Public funding, 24–26, 30–31. *See also specific initiatives, e.g.* Title IV-A funding; adequate. *See* Adequacy of funding; building and, 13; COVID-19 and, 24, 81, 103, 206–207; environmental issues and, 119–121; housing and, 140, 154–167; income inequality and, 34–35; integration and, 137–147, 148n1–148n2; public health and, 97–98, 101–103; for schools, 195–196. *See also* School finance; standardized testing and, 48; systemic racism and, 79
Public health, 1, 92–106. *See also* Environmental issues; Mental health; absenteeism and, 99, 252; access to, 6–7; accountability and, 99–100; asthma and, 94; COVID-19 and. *See* COVID-19; cross-sector partnerships and, 104–105; decision-making and, 101; education policy and, 95–98; environment of schools and, 99–100; family engagement and, 104; food insecurity and, 94; housing and, 157–158; impact of, 93–95; obesity and, 94; oral health and, 94; public funding and, 97–98, 101–103; staff support and, 94–95, 100–101; systemic racism and, 78–80; WSCC model, 95–96, 180
Public housing, 137, 139, 144, 155–157, 161, 165
Public Partnership for Wellbeing, 78
Public policy. *See also* Education policy; Politics; *specific policy initiatives*; barriers to success and, 25–31, 34–35; codesign for, 271–273, 277; COVID-19 and, 16; critical policy analysis and, 43–44; environmental issues and, 115–125; integration and, 137–147, 148n1–148n2; "moat approach" to, 6–7; school siting and, 124–125; systemic racism and, 76–89; whole child. *See* Whole child policy
Pulkkinen, L., 117
Punitive disciplinary policies, 174–176; restorative approaches and, simultaneous use of, 182; security and policing in context of, 178–180
Puro, P., 67

Putnam, R. D., 24, 29
Puzzanchera, C., 236–239

Qadir, F., 52, 80
Qian, H., 271
Quattlebaum, M., 201
Querol, X., 120
Quijada Cerecer, D. A., 214–215
Quinn, B., 62
Quinn, D. M., 199
Quinn, M. M., 236, 239
Quirk, A., 82

Race to the Top (RTTT), 6, 227, 229n1
Racial equity/justice; school finance and, 194–196; in youth justice policy model, 221–224, 227–228
Racial inequality, 1–5, 11–21. *See also* Jim Crow laws; Segregation; Slavery; AYP and, 46–47; as barrier to success, 31–32; COVID-19 and, 8, 15, 51–52; critical policy analysis and, 43–44; diversity and, 15; education policy and, 41–53; environmental issues and, 110–112; equity and, 41–53; housing and, 156–157; inclusion and, 15; in juvenile justice system, 236–239; mental health and, 48; NCLB and, 46–48; population statistics and, 12–13; public funding and, 48; school safety and, 48; SROs and, 79; standardized testing and, 46–48; structural racism and, 14–16, 88; suspensions and, 85–87; three-fifths compromise and, 12; whole child policy and, 61
Racism, 213; school finance and, 207; structural, 14–16, 88; systemic. *See* Systemic racism
Radical Youth Alliance, 218
Raffaele Mendez, L. M., 66
Raisman, A., 29
Rajaee, M., 122–123
Ramakrishnan, K., 141, 160
Ramchand, R., 175–176
Ramos, C., 156
Ramos-Beban, N., 63
Randall, K., 174, 176, 179, 186
Rapa, E., 80
Rauh, V. A., 117
Raveche Garnett, B., 181
Ray, A., 159
Ray, R., 42
Raz, R., 113
Reardon, S. F., 50, 205
Rebell, M., 197
Reber, S., 206
Recidivism, 241
Reconstruction, 13, 15
Red for Ed, 34–35

Redlining, 196
Reed, B., 257, 259, 260, 263
Reed, D., 135
Reed, W., 113
Rees, G., 24
Reeves, R. V., 19
Refining/Improving, in policy process, 277
Regoli, F., 112
Remedial distributive justice, 194, 197–199, 207
Remote learning, 15–16, 58–59, 112
Rental Assistance Demonstration, 165
Repacholi, M. H., 116
Resegregation, 227
Reskin, B., 200
Resnick, M., 185
Response to Intervention (RTI), 263
Restorative justice, 66, 181–182; punitive school discipline policy and, simultaneous use of, 182
Review and Assessment of the Health and Productivity Benefits of Green Schools (National Research Council), 119
Reville, S. P., 16
Reynolds, H., 177–178, 185
Reynoso-Robles, R., 113
Rhode Island Legal Services, 115, 118–119
Richardson, E. A. Astell-Burt, 120
Richeson, J. A., 32
Rick, C., 141
Ridder, E. M., 117
Rioux, C., 124
Rivas, I., 120
Rivera, E., 8, 76, 254, 272
Rivera, M., 204
Road to Success Academies, 243–244
Robert, C., 179
Roberts, A., 6–7
Roberts, A. L., 113
Robin Dion, M., 162
Robinson, K. J., 125
Rochman, A., 34
Roda, A., 51, 135
Roderick, M., 64
Roels, H. A., 113
Rogers, J., 176
Rogoff, B., 63
Rolfe, A., 26
Rolle, A., 196
Rollings, K. A., 158
Romney, George, 148n1
Rooks, N., 13
Roorda, D. L., 61
Rose, T., 59, 61
Rosenau, M., 162
Rosenbaum, E., 158
Rosenbaum, J., 139

Rosenbury, L. A., 28
Rosenow, D., 242
Rosofsky, A., 113
Ross, P., 62
Rossheim, M. E., 178
Rothstein, J., 50
Rothstein, R., 134, 144, 156–157, 196
Rothwell, J., 157
Rucker, J. M., 32
Rudiger, A., 203
Ruiz, M., 42–43
Rury, J. L., 202
Rusk, D., 139
Rutherford, R. B., 236, 239
Ruzek, E., 8
Ryan, J., 174, 176, 179, 186
Ryan, P., 109

Sabre, N., 235, 241
Sadd, J. L., 111, 113
Sadeh, M., 120
Saegert, S., 158
Saenen, N. D., 113
"Safe and Supportive School" grants, 180
Salisbury, J. D., 221
Salvesen, D., 109, 115, 118, 124
Sametshaw, A. M., 113
Samhouri, J. F., 120
Sampson, N., 115, 118–119, 122, 124
Samuels, C., 178, 186
Samuels, G. M., 251–252
Sanchez, J., 135, 140, 143
Sanchez-Burks, J., 50
Sanctuary cities, 14
Sandin, P., 117
Sandín Vázquez, M., 272, 274
Sandler, G., 34–35
Sanger Unified School District (California), 204–205
Santos, R., 158
Sarakatsannis, J., 52
Sarri, R. C., 234–235
Sartakatsannis, J., 16
SAT scores, 46
Saunders, J., 175–176
Sawyer, W., 234
Schachner, A., 80
Schaeffer, K., 8
Schafrick, N., 122–123
Schanzenbach, D. W., 24, 31
Scharber, H., 113
Schellinger, K. B., 65
Schlitt, J., 95
Schlueter, D., 251, 258
Schmader, T., 64
Schneider, A., 30

Schneider, B., 63
Schneider, J. S., 121
Schneider, K., 254
Schoierer, J., 120
School climate. *See* Positive school climate
School design, 119–121
School Environmental Health Act (Vermont), 119
School finance; adequacy and, 198, 202–207; case studies, 202–207; historical background, 194, 207; litigation and, 196–197; local property taxes and, 195–196; racial injustice and, 194–196; remedial distributive justice and, 197–199; transformative justice in, 199–202
School personnel; education delivery and, 242; homelessness identification training, 258–259; recruitment/retention and, 71; student-teacher ratios and, 81; support for, 70–71, 94–95, 100–101
School psychologists, 176
School Resource Officers (SROs), 79, 175, 178–179
School safety, 1; contexts and policies, 178–180; critical policy analysis and, 44; depolicing measures and, 183; historical overview, 174–176; housing and, 159; new policies for, 177–178; "optimal" vision of, 183–186; standardized testing and, 48; university partnerships and, 180, 184–185
School siting, 114–120, 122–125
School-to-prison pipeline, 218, 233
SchoolHouse Connection, 251, 253, 255, 257
Schott Foundation for Public Education, 5, 16–17, 19
Schulenberg, J. E., 177
Schultheis, K., 254
Schwartz, A., 140
Schwartz, A. E., 141
Schwartz, H., 144, 175–176
Schwartz, J. D., 113, 116
Schweitzer, A., 144
Sciarra, D. G., 206–207
Ścibor, M., 121
Scoggins, J., 31
Scott, E., 29
Scott, J. T., 41–44, 145–146
Scott, R., 27
Security. *See* School safety
Sedlak, A. J., 240
Segregation, 1, 42, 136. *See also* Integration; Racial inequality; critical policy analysis and, 44; desegregation and, 135; education policy and, 49–51; equity and, 45–46; housing and, 7; resegregation and, 227; school funding inequity and, 195–196; Seidman, E., 174, 179
Seitsinger, A. M., 62
Self-report survey data (student homelessness), 258
Seltzer & Co., 34
Sensoy, Ö., 77

Sentís, A., 113
Separate-but-equal schooling, 45, 49–50
Serena, K., 28
Sergiovanni, T. J., 66
Serrano v. Priest, 196–197
Services/supports, for homeless students, 259–260
1776 Commission, 42
Sexual abuse, 29
Shah, K., 174, 179
Shandra, J., 109, 113
Shankardass, K., 124
Sharkey, P., 159
Sharpe, C., 213
Sheff case, 144
Sheftall, A. H., 94
Shepherd, K., 121
Sheras, P., 182
Sheth, M. J., 221
Shi, L., 116
Shier, V., 113–114
Shih, R., 113–114
Shippen, M. E., 242
Shollenberger, T. L., 243
Shook, J. J., 234–235
Shope, L., 34
Shores, K., 198
Sickmund, M., 236–240
Siegel, A., 181
Siegel, B., 27
Siegel-Hawley, G., 134, 136–138, 143, 145–146
Sikes, C. L., 135
Singh, A., 94
Sinkariova, L., 120
Sivarajah, S., 120
1619 Project, 42, 53n2
Skiba, R. J., 179, 217, 234
Sladky, T. J., 236–239
Slavery, 12–14, 42
Slavin, R., 195
Sleeping arrangements, 256, 258
Smiley, C., 213
Smith, A. E., 33
Smith, E. P., 271
Smith, K. E., 277
Smith, L. C., 181
Smith, M., 6
Smith, P. A., 52, 80
Smith, S. M., 120
Smitherman, G., 220
Smorodinsky, S., 109
Smrekar, C., 136
Smythe, A., 121
Sng, O., 32
Social disparity, in juvenile justice system, 236
Social-emotional learning (SEL), 58–61, 65–66, 160, 176–177, 187

Social-identity threat, 63–64
Socioeconomic Integration Pilot Program (SIPP), 142
Soland, J., 8
Soleimanpour, S., 95
Solinas, M., 121
Solomon, B., 92, 101
Solomon, R., 184–185
Solórzano, D. G., 213
Solt, A. C., 113
Sood, A., 156
Sorkin, A. D., 218
Sorrenti, G., 112
Southern Education Foundation, 8
Spadaro, J. V., 116
Sparrow, V., 121
Speagle, W., 156
Special education needs, 239
Spengler, J. D., 120
Spievack, N., 134
Spilski, J., 121
Spilt, J. L., 61
Sprague, J., 66
Spring, J., 77
Staff. *See* School personnel
Stafford, L., 26
Stainback, G., 184
Stan, M., 120
Standardized testing, 16; AYP and, 46–47; equity and, 46–48; mental health and, 48; NCLB and, 46–48; public funding and, 48; SAT scores and, 46; school safety and, 48
Star-C program (Atlanta), 163–164
State Fiscal Stabilization Funds (SFSF), 206
State policy/policymakers; juvenile-justice action recommendations, 245–246; racial justice youth policy model and, 225–226; school funding practices (case study), 204–205; school-siting policy, 122–123; student homelessness, 255
Status equality, dignitary justice and, 202
Steed, H., 92, 101
Steele, C. M., 64
Steele, D. M., 61
Stefancic, J., 53n1
Stein, A., 80
Stein, B. D., 263
Steinway, C., 257
Stereotype threat, 64
Steurle, C. E., 24
Stevens, John Paul, 28
Stewart, E. A., 178
Steyer, L., 59, 61
Stiefel, L., 196–197
Stingone, J. A., 113–114
Stolberg, G., 7
Stone, C. N., 139
Stone, I., 113

Stovall, J., 184
Strambler, M. J., 59
Strength in Diversity Act, 145
Strengthening Neighborhoods Initiative (Denver), 141–142
Structural justice, 200, 207–208
Structural racism, 14–16, 88
Student behavior, 64–66
Student homelessness; adverse outcomes, 252–253; critical supports ranking, 259–260; current policies on, 253–255; definitions, 253–254; demographics, 251–252; identifying extent of, 251, 256–259, 266n1; prevalence, 257–258; prevention measures, 262–264; recommendations, 265–266; school support for, 259–261
Student Support and Academic Enrichment Grants program, 97
Students with disabilities, 239–241
Stults, B., 134
Su, H.-J., 120
Su, J., 120
Su, Y., 158
Subsidies. *See* Public funding
Sugarman, S. D., 195–196
Suitts, S., 235, 241
Sulkowski, M. L., 263
Sullivan, A. L., 135
Sullivan, K., 181
Sum, A., 94
Sunyer, J., 113, 120
Suspensions, 85–87
Sutton, M., 43
Swain, W. A., 135
Swanson, C. B., 134
Swift, A., 201
Systemic racism, 11, 14–15, 20; COVID-19 and, 78–81; CRT and, 79–80; discipline policy and, 84–88; education policy and, 76–89; equity and, 42, 51–52; mental health and, 78–84; public funding and, 79; public health and, 78–80; public policy and, 76–89; SROs and, 79; student-teacher ratios and, 81; suspensions and, 85–87
Szyszkowicz, M., 116

Tacoma Housing Authority, 162
Tajfel, H., 63
Talbert, J. E., 205
Tallis, H., 120
Tamburic, L., 124
Tang, L., 82, 121
Tarasawa, B., 8
Targosz, N., 121
Taylor, K., 136–137, 140, 143

Taylor, L., 68
Taylor, R. D., 65
Taylor, S., 32
Tegeler, P., 139, 147, 157, 166–167
Temkin, D., 92, 101
Temporary Assistance for Needy Families (TANF), 26
Teplin, L. A., 239
Thapa, A., 99
Tharp, R. G., 67
Theron, L., 23
Thomas, D., 124
Thomas, D. C., 124
Thomas, S. C., 120
Thomas, U. C., 239
Thomopolous, N., 117, 120
Thompson, E., 184
Thorne, S. R., 32
Threat-assessment teams, 181–182
Three-fifths compromise, 12
"Thug." use of term, 212–213
Thurau, L., 174–175
Thurston, D., 116
Tieken, M. C., 140
Tiemeier, H., 113
Tillman, L. C., 45
Tilsley, A., 140
Title I funding, 97, 142, 145, 198, 206, 240
Title IV-A funding, 97
Title VI funding, 145
Tkacik, C., 212
Todres, J., 25–26
Tomaskovic-Devey, D., 178
Topper, A., 198
Torrats-Espinosa, G., 135
Torres-Guillén, S., 175–176, 179, 183, 186
Torres-Jardón, R., 113
Touloukian, C., 52, 80
Townsend, B., 65
Toxic Substances Control Act, 116
Trajkovski, S., 140
Transform Education NM, 203
Transformative justice, 199–202
Transition Planning Commission, 138
Transportation, 7, 140–141
Treglia, D., 7
Treskon, M., 141
Treuhaft, S., 31
Triguero-Mas, M., 120
Trivedi, P. E., 264
Tropp, L. R., 134
Troxel v. Granville, 27–28
Trump, Donald, 24, 41–42, 146
Tubman, Harriet, 14
Tuck, E., 51, 227–228
Tuck, T., 139

Turnaround for Children, 66
Turner, E. O., 51
Turner, J. C., 63
Turner, M. A., 134
Tyler, T., 201

UN Convention on the Rights of the Child, 26
Underwood, J. K., 198
Unemployment, 8
UNESCO World Commission on the Ethics of Scientific Knowledge and Technology, 116–117
UNICEF; on COVID-19, 23–24; on public funding, 24
Universal screening (student homelessness), 258
University partnerships, 180, 184–185
Unterman, R., 62
Unzueta, M. M., 50
Upstream Project, 258, 264–265
Urban youth, hyper-criminalization of, 237, 239
Urtasun, M., 272, 274
U.S. Attorney's Office, Eastern District, New York, 145
U.S. Constitution; education and, 195; Fourteenth Amendment, 12, 49
U.S. Department of Education, 99–100, 121, 139, 145–147, 167, 240; Office for Civil Rights, 112, 145, 175–176, 179, 182
U.S. Department of Health & Human Services, 7
U.S. Department of Housing and Urban Development (HUD), 139, 145–147, 148n1, 163, 166–167, 168n6; homelessness definition/eligibility, 253–254; YHDP funding from, 262
U.S. Department of Justice, 175
U.S. Department of Transportation, 139, 145, 147, 167
U.S. Environmental Protection Agency., 114–115, 120
U.S. House of Representatives, 165
U.S. Interagency Council on Homelessness, 266n1
U.S. Supreme Court Decisions. *See also specific cases/decisions*; on children's rights, 27, 36n1; on Title VI, 145
Uzdanaviciute, I., 120

Valencia, R., 201
Van Wee, B., 117, 120
Vanpoucke, C., 113
Vaughn, S., 263
Vazsonyi, A. T., 179
Vecchia, P., 116
Vela, M., 113
Velarde, S., 159
Verhagen, M., 52
Vermont Department of Health, 119
Viaene, M., 113

Vigdor, J. L., 200
Villarreal-Calderón, R., 113
Villarreal-Ríos, R., 113
Viruleg, E., 16, 52
Voices of Youth Count (VoYC), 257–258
Voight, A., 100
Volmert, A., 34
Volokh, E., 28
Vora, H., 124
Voting Rights Act, 14
Vouchers, 16
Vrijens, K., 113
"Vulnerable Youth: . . ." (Congressional report), 227, 229n2

Walker, A., 271
Walker, D., 116
Wallace, E., 165
Walton, G. M., 67, 159
Wang, J., 136
Wang, K., 6–7, 175
Wang, X., 7, 177, 179, 186
War on Drugs, 175, 228, 234
War on Poverty, 13, 198
Warboys, L., 235
Wardrip, K., 165
Wargo, J., 114
Warikoo, N. K., 51
Warren, P. Y., 178
Washburn, J. J., 239
Washington Sustainable Schools Design Protocol, 120
Watson, K. R., 175–177, 180, 182, 184–185, 187
Watt, P., 252
Wechsler, M., 80
Weichenthal, S., 116
Weiher, G. R., 137
Weiler, J., 33
Weinberg, L., 241
Weisburst, E., 244
Weissberg, R. P., 65, 68
Weisskopf, M. G., 113
Welch, M., 216
Wells, A. S., 51
Wells, K., 82
Wells, N. M., 158
Welner, K. G., 133, 194, 207
Welton, A., 138
Welty, L. J., 239
West, K. D., 264
Wheeler, J., 200
Where Do We Go From Here: . . . (M. L. King, Jr.), 21
Whitaker, A., 175–176, 179, 183, 186
Whiting, G. W., 135

Whole child policy, 18–21, 58–71; brain development and, 59–61; COVID-19 and, 58–59; cultural competence and, 63–64; discipline policy and, 65–66; distance learning and, 58–59; family engagement and, 63; income/racial inequality and, 61; motivation and, 66–67; MTSS and, 68, 70; recommendations for, 69–71; SEL and, 58–61, 65–66; sense of community and, 61–64; student behavior and, 64–66
Whole School, Whole Community, Whole Child (WSCC) model, 95–96, 180
"Whole-system approach," to juvenile justice, 243
Wilding. See Youth wilding/wildin'
Wilf, S., 177
Wilkinson-Flicker, S., 177, 179, 186
Willard, J., 253, 257
Willgerodt, M., 95
Williams, E., 198
Williams, J. S., 12
Williams, K. E. G., 32
Williamson, I. J., 158
Willis, J., 205
Willison, J. B., 243
Wilson, E. K., 138
Wilson, J., 28
Winstead, T., 43
Wise, A., 42
Wissoker, D., 158
Wittsiepe, J., 113
Wolf, L. J., 32
Wolf, S. H., 78
Wong, E. C., 82
Wood, J. L., 85
Woodward, B., 136
World Health Organization, 114
Wrabel, S., 180–181, 185–186
Wraparound services, 260
Wray-Lake, L., 177
Wright, R. J., 113
Wright, R. O., 113
Wright, V. R., 158
Wronski, J., 26, 32
Wu, J., 121

Xianfen, L., 94
Xiao, M., 121
Xiao, Y., 94

Yale Center for Emotional Intelligence, 58
Yamaguchi, L. A., 67
Yang, K. W., 51, 227
Yang, Y., 158
Yankey, N., 216
Yazziel/Martinez v. State of New Mexico, 202–204
Ybarra, M. G., 214, 221
Yeager, D. S., 67
Yeo, I., 120
Yoon, E.-S., 50
York, C., 7
Yosso, T. J., 213
Young, H., 270–271, 277
Young, I. M., 200, 202
Young, M. D., 43
Youth counterstories. *See* Policy counterstories
Youth criticality/sensemaking, 220
Youth Homelessness Demonstration Program (YHDP), 262, 265
Youth leadership, 222–223
Youth on Board (YOB), 217–218
Youth Participatory Action Research (YPAR), 215
Youth policy; narratives informing, 213–214, 220–221. *See also* Policy counterstories; Youth wilding/wildin'; racial justice model, 221–224; youth studies and, 214–216
Youth processing, 219
Youth Risk Behavior Survey (YRBS), 257–258
Youth studies, 214–216
Youth wilding/wildin'; historical background, 216–217; as policy counterstory, 214, 217–218
Youthtopias, 215
Yovanoff, P., 235–236, 239
Yun, J. E. E., 176
Yunes, M. A. M., 271

Zabel, J., 140
Zadrozny, B., 28
Zajicek, A., 270
Zambito, P., 109, 115, 118, 124
Zandbergen, P. A., 111
Zanobetti, A., 116
Zeballos-Roig, J., 27
Zero tolerance, APA Task Force, 175, 179
Zhang, A., 177, 179, 186
Zhang, J., 6–7, 175
Zhang, X., 121
Zheng, X., 62
Zieher, A. K., 59
Zilibotti, F., 112
Zimmerman, M. A., 175
Zlotkin, J., 184
Zuck, L., 121
Zweig, J., 113